Rationality in the Social Sciences

Helmut Staubmann • Victor Lidz
Editors

Rationality in the Social Sciences

The Schumpeter-Parsons Seminar 1939-40 and Current Perspectives

Springer

Editors
Helmut Staubmann
University of Innsbruck
Innsbruck, Austria

Victor Lidz
Drexel University College of Medicine
Chesterbrook, Pennsylvania, USA

ISBN 978-3-319-62376-4 ISBN 978-3-319-62377-1 (eBook)
DOI 10.1007/978-3-319-62377-1

Library of Congress Control Number: 2017958034

Printed on acid-free paper

This Springer imprint is published by Springer Nature
The registered company is Springer International Publishing AG
The registered company address is: Gewerbestrasse 11, 6330 Cham, Switzerland

Acknowledgements

The manuscripts of Part I and Part III herein are published through the courtesy of the Harvard University Archives, Talcott Parsons Papers.

We want to thank Ruth Grathoff and Walter M. Sprondel for permission to publish the letter exchange in Part III between Richard Grathoff, Walter M. Sprondel and Talcott Parsons.

This publication is supported by the Anniversary Fund of the Österreichische Nationalbank, Projekt Nr. 15236, The Unpublished Legacy of Talcott Parsons.

Contents

Editors' Introduction: The Harvard Rationality Seminar

Helmut Staubmann and Victor Lidz

The Harvard Rationality Seminar

In the academic year of 1939–1940, an unusual interdisciplinary seminar on the general topic of Rationality was conducted by a number of faculty members and advanced graduate students at Harvard University. Of particular interest throughout was the question of how rationality should fit into the basic premises and categories of intellectually disciplined thought about human conduct, especially in the social sciences—economics, sociology, political science, anthropology, psychology, and psychiatry. Of note, many of the participants were figures already distinguished in their respective disciplines or who, we now know, had distinguished careers in their futures.

The present volume is organized about the seminar. The first section presents documentary materials from presentations to and discussions in the seminar—all that remain, we believe—or essays that some participants later published based on their seminar presentations. The seminar materials were collected by Helmut Staubmann in 2013/2014 during a sabbatical in Cambridge, Massachusetts, where he was able to retrieve them from the Harvard University Archives, predominantly from the Talcott Parsons Papers. The second section consists of contemporary essays by a variety of social scientists who reflect either on the major essays themselves or on aspects of the topic of rationality in relation to human social action. In a briefer third section, we present correspondence pertaining to the

H. Staubmann (✉)
Department of Sociology, University of Innsbruck, Innsbruck, Austria
e-mail: Helmut.Staubmann@uibk.ac.at

V. Lidz
Department of Psychiatry, Drexel University College of Medicine, Philadelphia, PA, USA
e-mail: lidzvic@gmail.com

H. Staubmann, V. Lidz (eds.), *Rationality in the Social Sciences*,
DOI 10.1007/978-3-319-62377-1_1

seminar, including plans to publish papers from it and later reflections about its importance.

Joseph A. Schumpeter and Talcott Parsons

Joseph A. Schumpeter and Talcott Parsons were the two main figures who proposed, convened, and organized the seminar or discussion group. Both were ideally qualified as scholars familiar with developments in sociology and in economics concerning the place of rationality. Both had focused their interests on the theoretical and conceptual foundations of the socio-economic disciplines in very comprehensive terms.

Talcott Parsons was among the first social scientists, after Max Weber, to think comprehensively and intensively about techniques for constructing frames of reference for the interdisciplinary study of human action or conduct. In *The Structure of Social Action*, published in late 1937, he had explored the conceptual schemes that key sociologists and economists of a previous generation had utilized. He argued that, although the several figures on whom he focused had written in basically different intellectual traditions, they had settled upon—he wrote of their having "converged" upon—equivalent sets of core concepts. He then demonstrated that these ideas, when probed, proved to derive from basically the same methodological and conceptual assumptions. Parsons called this procedure of identifying and then relying upon agreed-upon formulations the method of convergence, and he proposed that the essential areas of conceptual agreement could, and should, be used as an initial formulation of a general frame of reference for sociology. He maintained that the very fact that a common frame of reference had emerged from disparate and in some respects conflicting intellectual traditions spoke to its fundamental validity and essential nature. Later, in several stages, he explored further convergences through probing and technical analyses of the conceptual schemes of a wide range of additional figures, including a number of his contemporaries, thereby expanding the scope and increasing the precision of his frame of reference.

Throughout his lifetime, Parsons held that works written in the field of economics were essential to include in a general theory of action. Looking back to the early years of his work during a series of discussions he had with faculty and students at Brown University in 1973, he remembered: "I decided I would make a study of Marshall to try to tease out his sociological ideas. I wrote what turned out to be two papers, which I submitted to Taussig, who was then editor of the *Quarterly Journal of Economics*, and he kindly accepted them for publication. That was the real starting point of *The Structure of Social Action*, because I had a kind of a fulcrum in Marshall for systematizing the comparison between Marshall, English economics, the background in utilitarianism, and so on, with Durkheim, Pareto, and Weber. That was the main jumping-off place of that book and a very decisive one for me. That's something that has stayed with me" (Parsons 2006 in Moss and Savchenko2006).

We may note that Parsons had arrived at Harvard having studied, at the University of Heidelberg, the conception of modern capitalism in late nineteenth and early twentieth century German historical economics and had written his doctoral dissertation on that topic, emphasizing especially the contributions of Max Weber. Although he had some sponsorship for his scholarly interests in German historical economics from the important senior figure of F. W. Taussig, he had been astute enough to see that the predominant interest in the Economics Department, especially among its rising young faculty and graduate students, had been with the mathematical neo-classical economics built on the heritage of Marshall. It was on the basis of this perception that he had made the critical study of Marshall's work emphasized in the quotation above.

One of Parsons' influential encounters with economists in his early years at Harvard was with his senior colleague, Joseph A. Schumpeter. Schumpeter had come to Harvard around the same time (1927) that Parsons joined the faculty. But while Parsons was a comparatively lowly Instructor in Economics, Schumpeter was an internationally prominent Austrian economist, well known in the United States for his early work on economic development. Parsons mentioned several times his encounters with Schumpeter and how important they were for his own theoretical development.[1] In a "short account" of his intellectual development he wrote: "In the first year I was at Harvard Joseph Schumpeter was there as a visiting professor. I sat in on his course on General Economics, and it was here that I first began to get a clear conception of what a theoretical system was" (Parsons 1959: 6).

Schumpeter later dealt with Parsons' *oeuvre* at an early stage: he was one of the original reviewers of *The Structure of Social Action* for the Harvard Committee on Research in the Social Sciences (see Schumpeter 1991b). He thus knew the schema of social action as Parsons formulated it, emphasizing the concepts of ends, means, norms, conditions, and effort, as the outcome of his convergence analysis. Schumpeter was also to address broad issues of the institutional makeup of modern societies in later works, such as *Capitalism, Socialism and Democracy*. He clearly perceived the tension between Parsons' basic concepts and the conceptual frameworks of the economics of that time. It seems likely that he proposed the seminar in order to probe Parsons' understanding that the rationality, including that of buyers and sellers of economic goods and services, is not inherent to social actors, but derives from specific complexes of values and norms.

In *The Structure of Social Action*, Parsons had in two incisive chapters summarized the central emphasis of Weber's comparative studies of religious ethics on the different "directions" that rationality takes in different civilizations—for example, Confucian China, Hindu India, classical antiquity, and the modern West (Parsons1937, Chaps. XIV and XV). In another chapter, he had underscored Emile Durkheim's emphasis in *The Division of Labor in Society* on the law of contract as essential to the stabilization of market exchanges within which actors can make

[1]For a comprehensive overview on the personal and intellectual relationship between Schumpeter and Parsons and their collaboration on the rationality seminar, respectively, see Swedberg (2006, 2015).

rational transactions (Parsons1937, Chap. VIII). In other sections of the volume, he noted Pareto's analysis of the various social conditions needed to support logical action and Marshall's emphasis on how the wants of actors are adjusted to social activities. Thus, his convergence analysis placed the matter of rational social action in a theoretically contested status quite different from most economic theory.

Rationality as a Key Concept in the Social Sciences

Rationality was in 1939 and remains today one of the fundamental theoretical and empirical issues in all of the social sciences. Since the early attempts to approach human action in modern scientific terms, the question of rationality has stood at the center of conceptual frameworks and methodological premises. In the words of Alfred Schütz, in his essay included in this volume, "The term 'rationality,' or at least the concept it envisages, has, within the framework of social science, the specific role of a 'key concept'."

The consensus that rationality is of key importance for the social sciences, however, is complemented by sharp disagreement on its actual meaning. The disagreement encompasses the part of rationality in conceptualizing the motivation of action, in theories of the basic components of processes of action, and in establishing the essential instruments of social scientific inquiry, as in Joseph A. Schumpeter's emphasis, in his essay in this volume, on the rationality of the observer. All three of these problem areas associated with the whole "problem of rationality" have received different solutions in different schools of thought, triggering disputes that have accompanied the development of the social sciences from early beginnings up to today. Moreover, the disputes remain unresolved.

The turn from the nineteenth to the twentieth century saw the emergence of classic attempts at unifying socio-economic knowledge into coherent disciplinary perspectives and general theories. The resulting definitions of basic concepts and methodological ideas, with important variations, now comprise the canon of social scientific theories. Although the canonical bodies of work—in sociology, Max Weber's, Emile Durkheim's, and Georg Simmel's, for example—were largely coherent within themselves, the divergences among them on fundamental choice points in theory construction established the basis for the multi-paradigmatic situation we find today. In each of the classic formulations, the concept of rationality played a key part, but in different forms, different meanings, and different theoretical statuses in the analysis of economy and society.

A number of scholars in the next generation, that following the foundational period of modern social scientific thought, attempted to resolve the conceptual divergences and obvious contradictions in their—and our—theoretical inheritance. The works included in the first section of this volume were written in that spirit and represent milestones in that endeavor. We believe that essays in the second section also address the same undertaking of conceptual resolution, although it will be apparent that, together, they also show the continuing multi-paradigmatic character of the contemporary social sciences, especially in sociology.

The Joint Faculty Seminar on Rationality in the Social Sciences

An important event in the cooperation between the two colleagues, Schumpeter and Parsons, was the joint seminar. The initiative for it obviously came from Schumpeter.[2] The idea of the "Seminar on Rationality in the Social Sciences" was first of all to have a forum for discussion with advanced students to enable them to develop their own views on the issues, according to their respective areas of expertise. Schumpeter's talk was on rationality as it figures in economic theory. Parsons' talk, though quite compact, addressed rationality in social action more generally. In addition, the plan was to invite presentations from some other prominent social scientists. In the eventuality, the most important of them was Alfred Schütz, the follower of Edmund Husserl and the founder of phenomenological sociology.

As noted above, the papers, discussion materials, and letters presented in the first and third sections of this volume are from *The Talcott ParsonsPapers* at the Harvard University Archives. The contribution of Schütz is reproduced here in its finally published version (Schütz 1964). Some of the papers were not intended by their authors to be published in the form presented at the rationality seminar (especially the discussion protocols), but we include them here to provide a fuller understanding of the seminar discussions.

Let's start with an overview of the events of the seminar insofar as they can be reconstructed from the archival materials. The available documents confirm ten sessions during the academic year 1939/1940, as outlined in the following timetable:

Friday October 27 and Monday November 13: Joseph A. Schumpeter
Monday November 27 and Monday December 11: Talcott Parsons[3]
Monday February 12 and Monday February 19: Discussion protocol by Donald V. McGranahan
Thursday March 7: Wilbert E. Moore
(Exact date not known): Rainer Schickele
Saturday April 13: Alfred Schütz
Thursday April 25: Robert Waelder

[2]According to Richard Swedberg, it was a paper on rationality by Chester I. Barnard that triggered Schumpeter's decision (see Swedberg 2006, 72), although we believe that his recognition of Parson's critique of utilitarian economic theory in *The Structure of Social Action* was an important background factor. Barnard was president of the New Jersey Bell Telephone Company and also an intellectual who exchanged ideas with economists and Parsons himself at Harvard. His *The Functions of the Executive* (Cambridge: Harvard University Press, 1938) long remained an influential work. Parsons taught it in some of his classes as late as the mid-1970s.

[3]According to notes by Rainer Schickele.

Notes on the Presenters and Other Participants

Besides Joseph A. Schumpeter, Talcott Parsons, and Alfred Schütz, there were presentations by Harvard students from different departments:

Donald V. McGranahan (1917–2001) studied experimental psychology at Harvard. He was later the founder and director (1967–1977) of the United Nations Research Institute for Social Development. His most important book was *Measurement and Analysis of Socio-Economic Development.*

Wilbert E. Moore (1914–1987) was a PhD student of Talcott Parsons who became well known as coauthor of a premature formulation of a functional theory of social stratification and for early analyses of sociological aspects of economic modernization. He became professor at Princeton University and later the University of Denver. He became sufficiently prominent to be elected President of the American Sociological Association.

Rainer Schickele (1905–1989) became a noted agricultural economist. His most famous work is *Agrarian Revolution and Economic Progress.* He worked for the United Nations Food and Agriculture Organization and later joined the faculty of Institute for Regional Studies at North Dakota State University. The Rainer Schickele Papers are collected at the University Archives of North Dakota State University. Schickele was also the father of the well-known composer, musician, and humorist, Peter Schickele, also known as P.D.Q. Bach.

Robert Waelder (1900–1967), not a student, was an Austrian psychoanalyst and member of the Vienna Psychoanalytic Society who had trained under Anna Freud. In 1938, he immigrated to the United States. He taught for many years at the Boston Psychoanalytic Institute, where Parsons later became his colleague. From 1963, he was Professor of Psychiatry at Jefferson Medical College in Philadelphia and a prominent member of psychoanalytic circles in that city.

There were several other participants whom Schumpeter and Parsons later invited to contribute to a publication that they planned to develop on the basis of the seminar:

John T. Dunlop (1914–2003) was a labor economist and Harvard economics professor (1938–1984) who later served, among other positions, as the US Secretary of Labor. His most important book is entitled *Industrial Relations Systems.*

Gottfried Haberler (1900–1995) was an Austrian-American economist who emigrated to the United States in 1936 and became Professor of Economics and a close colleague of Schumpeter at Harvard. He is best known for his books, *Theory of International Trade* and *Prosperity and Depression.*

Paul Sweezy (1910–2004) was, at the time of the seminar, teaching assistant to Schumpeter. He later became famous for integrating marginal utility analysis into socialist economics. He was also the founder of the socialist publication *Monthly Review.*

Other confirmed participants include:

Abram Bergson (1914–2003) brought expertise in welfare economics to the seminar and later became perhaps the leading American scholar of the Soviet economy. He also served for a time as Director of the Russian Research Center at Harvard.

Wassily Leontief, (1905–1999) had joined the Harvard Department of Economics in 1932 after having earned his doctorate in Germany under Werner Sombart with a dissertation on *The Economy as Circular Flow*. From 1946, he served as Professor of Economics at Harvard and became famous for developing the theory of input–output analysis among sectors of the economy, a model that was later to influence Parsons' analysis of the dynamic relations between pairs of subsystems of society. Leontief was awarded the Nobel Memorial Prize in Economics in 1973. Several of his students have also been awarded the Nobel Memorial Prize in Economics.

We believe the "Jones" mentioned as a participant by McGranahan was likely Howard Mumford Jones, a prolific scholar of American culture and a person of wide-ranging interdisciplinary interests who was Professor of English at Harvard. Jones served as President of the American Academy of Arts and Sciences from 1944 to 1951. In 1965, his book *Strange New World* about early American culture won the Pulitzer Prize for General Nonfiction. It remains the best known of his many published books. Jones was also notable for teaching popular undergraduate courses and for the large number of later prominent scholars who studied under his supervision for doctoral degrees in English and Comparative Literature.

The "Friedrich" mentioned in a letter of Schickele to Talcott Parsons, February 8, 1963, was almost certainly Carl Joachim Friedrich, 1901–1984, who was Professor of Government at Harvard, some years senior in status to Parsons. Born into a wealthy industrialist family in Germany, Friedrich had studied both in the United States and under Alfred Weber at Heidelberg, where he received his degree in 1925. He then became an advisor to the German Academic Exchange Service, for which he assigned Parsons to Heidelberg University for the fellowship year of 1925–1926. Through that connection, fateful for Parsons' career, the two became close personal friends at Harvard. Friedrich was a wide-ranging scholar of politics and political philosophy, but is perhaps best known for his text, *Constitutional Government and Democracy*, and for *Totalitarian Dictatorship and Autocracy*, coauthored with his protégé Zbigniew Brzezinsky, later US National Security Advisor from 1977 to 1981.

Participants we have not been able to identify include "Trotter" mentioned by McGranahan, and "Pettie" and "Gordon," both of whom were mentioned in the discussion protocol.

Seminar Presentations and Discussions

The concept of the seminar was not for the presenters to advocate for complete, finished, and exclusive conceptions of the role of rationality in social scientific thought, but to convey to others open perspectives or lines of inquiry on a topic that all agreed to be fundamental. The goal for the speakers was to articulate distinctive theses and ways of clarifying basic concepts, often by extension of previous works, as grounds for open discussion in a workshop setting.

Joseph A. Schumpeter

The seminar started with Schumpeter as the first presenter. His thoughts on "Rationality in Economics" were presented and then discussed in two sessions, the second evidenced by a discussion protocol written by an unidentified author. Schumpeter's paper for presentation carries the title "The Meaning of Rationality in the Social Sciences." Immediately below the title, Schumpeter noted in parentheses: "Still only a sketch." The paper advances essentially three theses, which rest on conceptual distinctions by which Schumpeter sought to resolve the semantic complexity implicit in the concept of rationality.

The first thesis relates to what he calls the *observer's rationality*. Scientific observation of empirical facts is characteristic of *the logic of observation* in the sciences generally and therefore does not differ by various object domains. Succinctly formulated in the paper: "...rationality in the social sciences does not differ from scientific rationality in general." Schumpeter then tries to identify the most important components of the logic of observation. Referring to Kirchhoff's definition of mechanics, he takes up the concept of an "economy of description," including especially the rules of logic and prediction, as discussed in the early twentieth century based on implications of the theory of evolution.

Following a perspective similar to the sociology of knowledge, Schumpeter was fully aware that a prevalence of scientific rationality in the social sciences and humanities emerges only in social and cultural settings with a general affinity to rationality. Quite in line with arguments advanced in the sociology of knowledge, Schumpeter notes that components of values are inherent to rational observation. Therefore, rational procedures cannot be said to have pure or isolated absolute validity. The "assigned degree of accuracy" in a social science discipline is ultimately a matter of evaluation. Judgments about rationality are bound to the state of knowledge of the observer. However, these value dependencies do not, according to Schumpeter, collide with the famous postulate of value freedom for scientific inquiry as advocated by Max Weber. The postulate simply determines empirical judgments to be illegitimate if they are based on what is believed to be desirable in the object under investigation. Here, again, there is no difference in logic between the natural and the social sciences.

Finally, Schumpeter raises the question of whether a rational method produces propositions that can be relied upon as true. For him, rationality of method is a necessary, but not a sufficient condition for truth. Rationality and truth are mutually related, but they are not semantically congruent.

The issue of a rational scientific approach to the object world is quite independent of questions that the social sciences may raise of the rationality of objects under investigation, whether social actors or processes of action. On the basis of this proposition, Schumpeter formulates his second thesis: rationality of the observer is in most cases sufficient, and thus economic and sociological research hold the same status as the natural sciences. As an illustration of this thesis, Schumpeter considers the analyses of time series. They allow for the discovery of regularities and analysis of relations among variables, and thereby the identification of social mechanisms. Time series analyses lead to essential economic and sociological insights without the necessity of presupposing the rationality of action itself. Even if further analysis may determine that individuals or groups have acted rationally, or irrationally, the rationality of an analysis is not altered. The analysis is therefore independent of the rationality or lack of it on the part of actors; it rests on a logic of its own. Schumpeter summarizes his second thesis with the statement: "Wherever we have entities that can be quantitatively expressed and display regular relations to other such entities, we can get some 'laws' out of them in much the same way in which the physicist does and, again, the epistemological problems that may arise, do not seem to differ from those inherent in scientific procedure in general."

Although the first two theses clearly distinguish rationality of the observer from questions of the rationality of the observed action, hence assume the scientific self-sufficiency of the rational observer, it would be a mistake completely to ignore the rationality of actors as some epistemological positions postulate. This would involve giving up "the most powerful methodological tool" that is *not* at the disposal of the natural sciences.

Schumpeter demonstrates this point with the example of marginal revenue and marginal cost curves. The point of intersection of the two curves marks the instantaneous maximum of profit. It obviously models, first, the observer's rationality and in that respect does not differ from models of the physicist. The model does not say anything about the real decision-making of business owners or managers because they would not act according to the model in their own subjectivity and consciousness. But, and here there is a difference from models in physics, the relationship of an actor's behavior to economic laws is based on a subjective aim or norm, the meaning of which must be "understood." Thus, marginal revenue curves imply assumptions about the meaningful rationality in a person's orientation, and the usefulness of the model depends on the accuracy of these assumptions. The analysis of social action is bound as much to the "logic of an end" as it is to the "logic of a cause."

Schumpeter notes that the model is not based on something simply existing, but on something for which he uses the German term, *Geltung*. The term means a norm that is a valid rule of conduct, one that must be obeyed in the sense of a legitimate expectation or an institutionalized pattern. The implication is that the end or purpose that an actor pursues has to be *understood* by the social scientist, as is also the case in our orientations to one another's conduct in everyday life.

The reference to meaning, norms, and ends further complicates the determination of whether an act can be regarded as rational. Since there can be an "infinite variety of cognate ends" (e.g., an immediate profit versus a series of profits over periods of time), what might appear rational in one case might appear irrational in another. A further complication stems from the fact that there may be a multiplicity of simultaneous ends. Schumpeter gives the examples of class interests versus individual interests and interests of business corporations as wholes versus the interests of their executives, to which one might add also the interests of their workers and investors. Another challenge to the theory of rational action is the difference between rational behavior and irrational results. The rational behavior of an individual may result in collective chaos or, we may add, vice versa. Judgments about actions in distant times or locations present further challenges of understanding. Such judgment requires empathy with and understanding of a "Sinnzusammenhang"—a complex of meaning—that may seem very foreign to the culture of the analyst, yet needs to be addressed.

To summarize, Schumpeter draws a clear distinction between *subjective rationality*, or conformity of an actor's mental processes to a rational scheme, and *objective rationality* or the applicability of a rational scheme to the behavior of an actor. Schumpeter regarded subjective rationality as generally overrated and the two forms as often mistakenly confused. Keeping the distinction in mind may help us understand why empirical data deviate from rational models. Yet, knowledge of subjective rationality may facilitate better understanding and more accurate predictions. But even here subjective rationality and rationality of the observer lay on different planes that require further conceptual distinctions. Using German terms, Schumpeter contrasted "real reason" (Realgrund), describing the rational motives of actors, with "epistemic reason" (Erkenntnisgrund).

Schumpeter's evaluation of subjectivity was contradicted in seminar discussions, motivating him to change his terminology in a footnote of his paper. Instead of "subjective rationality," he used the term, "personal rationality." He noted that conscious awareness is not a necessary criterion of personal rationality, as habituation may result in continuation of a rational pattern without conscious reflection.

In his concluding section, Schumpeter addressed philosophical movements in the history of economics, although he saw their influence on actual economic models as quite limited. He started with the Physiocrats, whose major achievement, he argued, was to develop a conception of the economy "as a self-contained process reproducing itself in circular flows." With respect to rational action, however, they failed to distinguish what is from what ought to be and thus advocated an extra-scientific "idea of an ideal state of things" with effects on later movements, such as socialism. Their quasi-religious conception of a natural order implied "the useful truth that the economic process is a cosmos and not a chaos." It later led to a rationalistic philosophy with consequences for an economics based on the rationality of the observer, but which refrained from assuming a subjective rationality of economic actors.

English utilitarianism was then discussed as another example of a rationalistic system of thought. It, too, conceived of an ideal state, but also placed unlimited faith in the rationality of human individuals: in Schumpeter's words, "Thomistic rationalism has descended from the clouds, but only to reign supreme in the sphere of social action." For Bentham, the "greatest happiness for the greatest number" was the ultimate end. But, Schumpeter objects, "happiness of the greatest number" cannot be a real force in the way that the pursuit of happiness by an individual may possibly be. By failing to differentiate between objective and subjective rationality, utilitarians arbitrarily connected hedonism with rationalism.

By contrast to both physiocrats and utilitarians, Marx was not rationalistic. In the wake of Hegel, he relied on rationalism, but did so in an exterior way. His theory of social evolution propelled by class struggles included facets that enhanced the perspective of rationality of the observer. One facet was his conception of ideologies as rationalizations resulting from value judgments that hide underlying realities. Schumpeter regarded this idea as a great achievement, which might yet turn against the creator of the theory: "Such fire is dangerous to kindle... that burns more things than Marx had intended.... and class struggles...are after all nothing but another ideology."

Schumpeter closed by discussing the classics of economic theory at the turn of the twentieth century. Older theories had treated rational action not only as modeling action in general but also as providing a general solution for economic and social problems. By contrast, the newer theories had perceived more and more restrictions on rational action. Doubts had arisen that businesses acting in accord with rational patterns were necessarily more successful, and, even more certainly, that this was so for "the *social* results of rational business action." The task of generalizing the rational action model was replaced by a need to elaborate its specific instances or settings of its application. In this vein, Pareto suggested that *homo economicus* is only one of many "*homines*." Schumpeter's comment was that "by the absence of any rationale rule of combination," such a multiplication of models only shows "that life is ontologically irrational, at least as much as nature."

The discussion protocol for the two sessions on Schumpeter's paper begins by summarizing the conceptual distinctions he had developed. It then notes the objections to and further thoughts on Schumpeter's concepts as expressed by the participants. The discussion centered especially around the rationality of the observer and empirically observable deviations from rational action. Specific points were also placed in the context Schumpeter had provided of such historically important figures as Bentham, Marx, and Pareto as well as more general methodological and philosophical traditions.

Talcott Parsons

The second presenter to the seminar was Talcott Parsons. His sessions took place on November 27 and December 11, 1939. Notes by Rainer Schickele indicate that on the first of the two meetings the discussions were linked as well to the previous presentation by Schumpeter. The title of Parsons' paper is "An Approach to the Analysis of the Role of Rationality in Social Action," but it is quite short, only seven pages in length, despite the generality of its topic. Its brevity makes its argument somewhat cryptic, and so we will introduce it with a discussion of the conceptual scheme presented in Parsons' *The Structure of Social Action*, published two years earlier, which is presumed as a basis of his paper.

We surmise that Schumpeter's views of *The Structure of Social Action* and desire to come to terms with its critical perspective on economic theory was not only a reason for convening the seminar but also a reason that Parsons' presentation remained within the conceptual framework of his published book. That point is notable, because we now know, as referenced in the essay by Professor Endress in the second section of this volume, that the first major reformulation of Parsons' own theory, presented in the monograph, *Actor, Situation and Normative Pattern* (see: Lidz and Staubmann eds. 2010), was already well advanced, if not completed. On other occasions throughout his career, Parsons used his teaching, informal or formal discussions with colleagues, lectures at professional meetings, and guest presentations at other universities to try out his most recent ideas and to solicit feedback on them. That he held his most current thinking back from the seminar was an uncharacteristic course of action on his part, and it may also have been a factor in his apparent reluctance later to publish collected papers from the seminar.

At any rate, the starting point of Parsons' paper was the voluntaristic theory of action, as he had labeled the early systematic formulation of his frame of reference or basic conceptual scheme. The voluntaristic theory was based on the premise, confirmed in the first paragraph of his paper, that processes of action always involve choices between different possible courses of action—a premise that, contrary to some secondary accounts, remained a consistent element of Parsons' theorizing down to the end of his long career. The element of voluntaristic choice that, Parsons emphasized, enters all processes of action means that his theory "is . . .incompatible with purely mechanistic metaphysics." Rather, action involves, in every instance, elements of ends or goals, means to be used in attaining goals, norms (or rules, generally legitimated by underlying values) that regulate the permissible ends and uses of means, the given conditions of a social situation, such as, time, place, physical surroundings, and given social others, and, in some of Parsons' formulations, effort that must be expended to pursue specific ends. Following Durkheim especially, Parsons argued that the nature of normative regulation of action carries with it the implication that voluntarism is intrinsic to action, because there is always the choice between adhering to a rule and violating it. Similarly, the end of a course of action is always chosen over some potential alternatives, and it is a limiting case in which a selected goal or end can be pursued only through predetermined rather than chosen means. Parsons' voluntarism was thus thorough-going and contrasted radically with the behaviorism in both psychology and sociology that, at the time he wrote *The Structure of Social Action*, was a common, if not predominant, perspective, with its ambitions, however unrealized, to develop mechanistic explanations of human conduct.

In emphasizing voluntarism, Parsons eschewed the ideal of attaining a certain degree of predictability in the analysis of social action and its consequences. He accepted Weber's proposition that processes of social action are most predictable when actors conduct themselves rationally (Parsons 1981). Weber gave the familiar example of Gresham's law, the economic principle that a weaker currency drives a stronger currency out of circulation, because actors, being rational in their expenditures, will make purchases with the weaker currency while saving the currency that better retains its value. Generalizing the point, we can see that rationality on the part of a social actor is most readily understood by the social scientist who commands the ability to weigh considerations of rationality and logical consistency. Rationality thus enters the domain of empirical knowledge in a sort of privileged manner as compared with other standards of action.

Economic theory in the utilitarian tradition, from Adam Smith's emphasis on the rationality of the free market to the more refined marginal utility theories of Alfred Marshall and his Austrian contemporaries, Carl Menger and Eugen von Boehm-Bawerk, emphasized both voluntarism and rationalism. For them, economic action in its pure form involved choices that balance costs and utilities, the value of what must be given up in an exchange or other form of action relative to the value of what may be gained. In Parsons' terms, these utilitarian theories used only ends, the things of value to be gained, and means, the things of value to be given up or used up to obtain the ends. The economists adhered to a voluntarism in perceiving economic actors as making free choices, and Parsons acknowledged, as we have noted, that his own voluntarism derived from the tradition of economic utilitarianism. However, the economists viewed actors as intrinsically acting rationally, due to the powerful inclination always to enter exchanges or plan other conduct in order to gain things of greater value than the things given up in the course of their action. By contrast, Parsons argued that rational action is based on specific norms, and their underlying values, that establish expectations for actors in certain situations that they should conduct themselves in a rational manner. The rationality is thus not intrinsic, but normatively established, and in his paper Parsons emphasizes that the normative regulation of social action, including rational action, is often complex, involving multiple levels of ontological principles, values, and regulations. Thus, rationality predominates over other modalities of utilizing means to pursue ends only where social institutions impose highly structured norms of rationality.

Moreover, the rationality in social life includes a number of different modalities: not only economic rationality, which is based largely on calculations of costs, but also scientific rationality, resting largely on standards of empirical proof and logical consistency, as in Schumpeter's rationality of the observer, and technological rationality, with its focus on developing or selecting means from a stock of possible, but often difficult to use, means to pursue complex ends most effectively, to name only some key types.

Parsons also followed Weber in emphasizing that in many social situations norms impose not rationality, but expectations of traditionally "correct" conduct or of affectively or emotionally satisfying behavior, as in love relationships. In his paper, he notes that traditional norms close off the scope of consideration of ends and means to impose certain established ends-means relations, thereby precluding actors from conducting themselves in a rational manner. In later writing, Parsons argued that the pursuit of some types of rational conduct involves adhering to very stringent standards of affective motivation, as in the discipline expected of the surgeon in complex surgeries, the military officer commanding troops in the heat of battle with the lives of many soldiers at risk, or the investment banker making decisions during a collapse of a stock market. In situations such as these, rationalities of different types are normatively expected, but may be very difficult to maintain. We should also note that it is by understanding of the norms and institutions that are operative in these different settings that the social scientist can "predict" how actors will likely conduct themselves and what difficulties they are likely to experience in carrying out their conduct.

In sum, Parsons treats rationality as a special "mode of integration" of a number of elements of action, ends or goals, means, norms and their legitimating patterns of evaluation, conditions, and effort or affective dispositions or motivations. The integration of elements takes place on the individual level within given situations of action, but also involves the patterning of values, norms, and various conditions at the level of an action system as a whole, even the level of an entire civilization. Thus, in *The Structure of Social Action*, Parsons discusses at length Weber's analysis of the different "directions" of rationality, and hence the rationalization of institutional structures, in the great civilizations of the world, especially China and India as contrasted with the modern West. In his paper, he only mentions in passing that in traditional Chinese civilization the underlying premises of the value system were so different that "rationality" in economic activities took on very different forms from enterprise in the modern West. These materials provide additional depth to his main analysis in the essay of the complex respects in which rationality, especially the economic rationality that is the core reference of most of the other seminar papers, is not an intrinsic quality of actors or the action process, but a complexly shaped matter involving normative orientation. To act rationally always involves voluntaristic conformity to normative standards of rationality, standards that should be seen as relative not only to specific categories of social situation—economic, political, scientific, technological, and so forth—but also as relative to, and varying profoundly with, characteristics of the encompassing civilization.

Parsons' paper stresses emphatically the importance of rationality as a type of action and as a form of action essential to the institutional organization of entire societies or civilizations, but at the same time he also emphasizes its limitations. Rationality as a type of action is limited in the sense that it must be probed to understand both the complexity of its composition or makeup and its variation across different kinds of social settings. Moreover, we must understand that as a type of action the rational stands off against a number of other types, including the irrational, in which humans act in deviance from or in violation of normative patters of rationality, the traditional, the affective, and the non-rational, in the sense that standards of rationality do not apply to them, as in religious, philosophical, or, more broadly, existential conduct or action.

Similarly to Schumpeter, and in general accord with his discussion, Parsons devotes the last section of his paper to assessing Pareto's treatment of a comprehensive social system of rational action. He focuses especially on the famous conceptual distinction between "ophelimity *for* a collectivity" and the maximum of utility. The former is the situation in which the limit of benefits is attained for each member of the collectivity past which an increase in the utility of any one member could be achieved only by a reduction in the utility allocated to another member or other members. But in real social life, some members of society receive benefits at the cost of other members, and so there must be norms of justice that stabilize such conditions of unequal outcomes or, more generally, social inequality. The maximum of utilities is quite different from the standard of ophelimity, thus showing that the rational maximizing of utilities, when viewed across a society, depends on a complex normative order through which economic activity is embedded in a much more comprehensive social system. Parsons' brief discussion of Pareto's analysis thus leads to the conclusion that not only is rationality just one mode of integration of action systems, but rationality, even the pure case of economic rationality, depends on a broader normative or institutional structure. Thus, Parsons concludes, as Schumpeter did, with a warning against misplaced generalizations of models of rational action. In particular, the use of rationality to understand fields such as religion or art "results in severe distortion of the facts and gross misinterpretations."

Donald V. McGranahan

The meetings of the rationality group continued on February 12 and 19, for which Donald V. McGranahan wrote a protocol. It starts with a brief summary of a presentation delivered at the last rationality group meeting, which had again addressed issues of the definition of rationality. The question had been raised whether the criterion of rational action is a matter of thinking or a matter of a judgment of specific acts. The difference between rationality and truth was also emphasized. Further discussion noted that rational conclusions can be drawn from irrational premises and rational behavior may be grounded, as Parsons had emphasized, perhaps following the analysis of Weber's *Protestant Ethic and the Spirit of Capitalism*, in non-rational ultimate ends.

The main part of the protocol focused on "pseudo-rational explanations," such as ideologies with factual distortions of social reality or psychological "rationalizations", a major theme in psychoanalytic thought. These examples raised the question of how the real forces and motives behind such constructs could be explored. Psychoanalysis was mentioned as a suitable methodology as well as long-term observation through which inconsistencies in thought and belief might be revealed. Four conditions were identified for pseudo-explanations: Ignorance, conscious deception, emotional fixation, and rationalization. The question was raised if Pareto's "need for logical explanation" is grounded in a non rational need for legitimation similar to Thorstein Veblen's "instinct of idle curiosity" or Bronislaw Malinowski's concept of anxiety in the face of danger as a source of religious concepts and practices. Another example discussed in this context was the Marx–Engels thesis that ideologies are essentially false consciousness with the function of legitimating the pursuit of class interests.

Wilbert E. Moore

On March 7, Wilbert E. Moore, a former student of Parsons, presented a paper entitled "The Role of Ideas in the Extension and Limitation of Rationality." The presentation was obviously based on Moore's dissertation (Moore 1940), which carried the subtitle *Study of the Relations between Ideas and Institutions.*

Moore's basic proposition was that, contrary to the understanding that modern history has involved a natural increase in rationality, the status of rational action depends on the ideas of a given society and, within it, specific social situations. "There is no reason to assume that a rational orientation to the empirical world is any more 'natural' or 'basic' than the magical or traditional." One famous point of reference is Max Weber's thesis that the Protestant ethic was an important source for the development of modern rational economies. For modern society, however, it was not only Protestantism, but also a "climate of opinion" in which philosophical rationalism, as in the ideas of natural law and natural order, became characteristic.

Moore advanced his basic thesis by comparing "primitive" and "advanced" societies. Cultural patterns of rationality clearly differ considerably across societies, with their basic ideas and premises highly significant for norms of rationality in social life. Mode of orientation to the empirical world is especially important. However, there have been two contradictory views on the status of rationality in "primitive" societies. One view has held that, due to scarce technological means in the struggle for survival, early cultures were a kind of prototype of the rational *homo economicus*. In the opposing view, primitive thinking has had a pre-logical, mystical quality and, hence, a characteristic undifferentiated irrationality. Moore rejected both views as empirically not tenable. He cited studies by Bronislaw Malinowski and Raymond Firth as showing that the simplest societies have both non-economical elements such as religious rituals, but also rational practical technologies. Thus, he recounted Malinowski's observation that the Trobriand Islanders, on the one hand, had rational techniques for making their dugout canoes and, on the other hand, employed a variety of magical practices to improve results when they fished from their canoes.

Rainer Schickele

Rainer Schickele's presentation, "The Rational Means-End Schema as a Tool for Empirical Analysis of Social Action", began by arguing for the necessity of a clear definition of rationality. Because concepts, such as, rationality, are understood to be epistemic tools, they should be defined with clarity and in ways that relate to their purposes. In economics and sociology, the concept of rationality serves the analysis of action choices guided by reasoning. Such reasoning implies conscious reflection on facts to guide choices among potential means for attaining given ends. For adequate judgment of the rationality of action, the observer and the actor under study need to have reference to the same factual knowledge. A further criterion concerns the possibility of verification, which means that the ends of rational action must be real, not ultimate or transcendent ends.

The outline of the following arguments is closely oriented to Parsons' action frame of reference. Schickele treats the basic components of the unit act as actors, ends, means, and conditions, but, notably, not including norms as independent elements. Thus, he assimilates non-rational factors, such as tradition, ideologies, and, so forth, to the category of conditions. He then applies this theoretical frame to the analysis of capitalistic enterprise, including both individual actors and industry with collective actors. His examples lead him to his main conclusion, namely, that restricting analysis to the rational means-end schema is not sufficient. An account of norms and values as well as institutional and ideological conditions is indispensable for the analysis of rational action.

In the archives, there are two text-identical versions of the paper, one obviously prepared for the seminar presentation and the other for publication. At a much later stage, on February 8, 1963, Schickele sent a letter to Talcott Parsons with an inquiry about the Free Press as possible publisher for his book *Agricultural Policy*. The letter makes a reference to the rationality seminar: "I might mention also that the approach of this book is very much along the lines of a socio-political economy of agriculture and has in many parts been directly inspired by my association with you during 1939–1940 in Harvard. I was fortunate enough at that time to be one of the small group including you, Schumpeter, von Haberler, and Friedrich, who discussed the concept of rationality as a principle of motivating people in various fields of activity. More specifically, I have adapted your original conception of a means-end schema to the analysis and evaluation of national agricultural policies." Parsons replied on April 16, 1963: "I indeed remember knowing you many years ago in the connection which you mention toward the end of your letter. In particular I remember the discussions with Schumpeter on the problem of rationality. I only regret that more did not come out of this."

In the months after the seminar, Schickele had sent his paper for comments to several colleagues. He received a lengthy reply from Clarence Edwin Ayres, a prominent exponent of institutional economics, who had been a teacher of Talcott Parsons at Amherst College.

Alfred Schütz

In January 1940, Talcott Parsons sent two letters to Alfred Schütz (see Part 3 of this volume) inviting him to participate in one of the two scheduled February sessions of the rationality seminar. It was Gottfried Haberler who had told Parsons about Schütz (see Eberle et al. 2010, p. 201). Schütz had studied the works of Edmund Husserl intensively and had undertaken to develop a phenomenology of social life based largely on Husserl's work, but also on the sociology of Max Weber, to which he had given serious study even before turning to Husserl. In 1932, he had published in Vienna *Der sinnhafte Aufbau der sozialen Welt* (Schütz 1960), a major and highly innovative work, translated to English only in 1967, as *The Phenomenology of the Social World* (Schüüütz 1967). Although little known in the United States in 1940, he was in fact a major scholar and one who might properly feel that he and Parsons shared interests. Schütz had in fact been familiar with Parsons' *The Structure of Social Action* and became convinced that there was a close intellectual affinity between his own work and that of Parsons. Presumably, he had noticed his own volume cited in Parsons' book as a secondary work on Weber's methodology. As Eberle, Dreher, and Sebald write, Schütz regarded Parsons as his alter ego in the American scholarly world, viewing him as a Weberian and, through misperception, as "a sociologist of phenomenological persuasion."

The personal encounter between Schütz and Parsons, as well as later exchanges, quickly turned up deep differences in their respective understandings of theories of action, both in substantive and in methodological aspects. The exchanges between Parsons and Schütz have previously been well documented in the English volume edited by Richard Grathoff (1978) and a German version edited by Walter

M. Sprondel (1977). Helmut R. Wagner's intellectual biography of Schütz devotes several pages to the failed intellectual relationship between Parsons and Schütz, but only several lines to the latter's participation in the rationality seminar, even though his paper, when published, became a landmark contribution to the developing school of phenomenological sociology.

Although he did not yet acknowledge it, the depth of Schütz's differences with Parsons is quite apparent in his presentation to the rationality seminar, which finally took place on Saturday, April 13, 1940. His point of departure was the shared conviction that rationality and rational action belong to the core issues of a methodology and epistemology of the social sciences. However, Schütz emphasized the ambiguities of the meaning of rationality. He sought in particular to distinguish it from the practical reasoning that takes place in the naïve engagement of the actor with the everyday realities, including the social realities, of routine life. He sharply isolates such practical reasoning of an "actor within the world" from "the scientific observer of it." His essay explores the complex set of consequences that this distinction implies for the conceptual schemata of the social sciences. Social scientists, he argued, frequently mix up these two levels. There is a radical difference in the subjective construction of the social world between reasoning as conducted in everyday action and the logics of a systematic scientific observer.

Schütz states the crux of his argument by contrasting the commonsensical reasoning of the person who seeks to find his way about a city in the course of his routine activities with a cartographer's methodical construction of knowledge about the same city in the process of mapping it. While the cartographer may start with an aerial map of the city or with geometric studies of angles and distances among various points, the everyday actor starts from a personal center, typically his home, and uses knowledge of selected streets to walk, drive, or take public transportation to specific other places, for example, a store, a workplace, or the home of a friend. He thinks in terms of his personal experience with the route, for example, avoiding streets that may have a great deal of traffic at a given time of day. He uses typifications of individuals or groups he may encounter on the way, for example, a salesperson in a store, a police officer guiding traffic, or a ticket seller at the subway station, each of whom is viewed, and treated, as an instance of a type. He does not try to engage such persons as he would a spouse or other individual in whom he has a romantic interest, nor would he try to form detailed, methodically observed, logically organized knowledge of them, as would a social scientist undertaking research.

Schütz also notes that even the scientist takes recourse to such commonsensical typifications when his professional work is concluded for the day and he turns to everyday relationships with neighbors, shopkeepers, or members of his family. Indeed, he must similarly rely upon commonsensical reasoning to maintain cooperative relationships with his scientific colleagues. Knowledge of cellular biology, for example, provides no guidance in how to collaborate fairly and decently with fellow staff members of a laboratory. In emphasizing the importance of the naïve commonsensical attitude toward everyday life, Schütz radically relativizes the conception of rationality as he understood Schumpeter's idea of the understanding of the scientific observer as well as Parsons' formulations.

In Schütz's conception, the commonsensical understandings of everyday conduct are reasonable, but cannot be considered deliberate, rational action. They are not subject to logic in a strict sense nor are they based on methodical observation or calculated empirical predictions. They are not the result of disciplined, impersonal knowledge of situations, but are person-centered and based simply on practical encounters of people, places, and events. They consist of customs, habits, rules of thumb, typifications of previously encountered events, and so forth. They result in conduct and practices undertaken without conscious, reflective planning. Insofar as they result in knowledge, it has the form of "cookbook" or "recipe" knowledge, not methodical scientific knowledge.

The everyday world of contemporary society rests on the institutional complexes that Max Weber treated as rationalized, and they appear as such to the social scientist, who has undertaken to study them dispassionately and methodically, at "the level of theoretical observation and interpretation of the social world." Yet, the same world is encountered by the citizen in his rounds of activities as disenchanted, as lacking in sacred or charismatic meaning. It is thus that the citizen's attitude to the social world is one of mundane interests and of involvement in a variety of merely practical functions. Other actors are then viewed as embodiments of types and related to in terms of typifications of the settings and functions through which they are encountered—as shopkeeper, police officer, or ticket seller. The typifications provide the subjective means of anticipating events, including the activities of others. However, such anticipations differ in form and intellectual status from the predictions made by scientists on the basis of methodical empirical knowledge.

The social scientist, in attempting to understand the contemporary social world, must, then, gain access to the schemes of types and typifications with which actors engage their respective everyday worlds. Schütz suggests that the social scientist can accomplish a realistic analysis by creating conceptual "puppets" that react in typical ways to typical situations of various kinds in order to master ordinary social life. Even a rational action in the conceptual frames of classical economics, of the utilitarian principle, or of the marginal calculations of modern economics should be viewed as a puppet in this sense.

It should be noted that, as phenomenologist, Schütz's theoretical interests focused on understanding the subjectivity of individual actors. His mode of abstraction from the data of rational and commonsensical thought and action thus differed from the analytical perspectives of Schumpeter, Parsons, and the others. Yet, his account of practical, commensensical reasoning, as distinct from strict rationality, has come down to our times as a very influential contribution to social science—indeed, as perhaps the most important product of the rationality seminar.

Robert Waelder

The final meeting of the seminar took place on April 25, 1940, with a presentation of Robert Waelder entitled "Psychoanalysis and Rationality in Social Action." The following passage is a transcript of notes, Rainer Schickele made on Waelder's presentation[4]:

1. Model of Action
2. Rationality: Integration
3. Rationality: Natural world images
4. Significance of problem of rationality

(1) Motivation from conscious to unconscious, defined by accessibility to self-observation.

Three agencies of the mind: id, ego, super-ego.

Id = instinctual drives, urges emanating from biological nature.

Ego = our perception of reality, ability of anticipation of future events. Realization of danger and fear, meeting demands from the outside world as well as from urges inside.

Super-ego = conscience, self-observation, moral conduct.

Id as well as super-ego suggest to ego, and ego acts in compromise.

Ego-syntonic (*ich-gerecht*): actions accepted by ego.

(2) Limitations of rational "choice": a morphinist struggling sincerely against indulgence: the motives are on different levels, and there may be no choice.

Rational choice should apply only to ego-syntonic actions. In ego, various motivations meet (word not readable, Eds.), synthetic function of the ego.

Basic principle of psychoanalysis: undo repressions and reestablish the synthetic function of the ego.

(3) Query of Plato: *Lehrbarkeit der Tugend.*[5] If the veiled contradictions were removed, would all people become alike? Would knowledge remove all sources of conflict? Waelder doubts; it would boil down to which is more powerful: love or aggression? Merchant wishing (word not readable-eds.) on average as his wishes are doubtly fulfilled to his competitors.

Is his action rational or not?

(4) The significance of the rationality problem is a symptom of uncertainty of the Christian value system.

Publication Efforts

Letter Exchange on the Planned Publication

The third part of this volume begins with the letters concerning the seminar and the plan for publication. The letters indicate that Schumpeter was clearly the driving force both behind the seminar itself and then the plan to collect the presented papers

[4]With courtesy of the North Dakota State University Archive.

[5]Teachability of virtue (eds).

as well as additional papers by other seminar participants for a volume under his and Parsons' joint editorship. As of May 15, 1940, the publication plan was for June 15 to be a deadline for the submission of manuscripts by the presenters and September 1 by the non-presenters. A review process by the editors was then to follow in September. By October 9, however, the editors had received only three completed manuscripts, and therefore a new submission deadline was set for December 1. The editors also intended to organize a meeting of the group shortly after Christmas to discuss next steps. On March 2, Schumpeter asked Parsons when he was going to do something about the project. In his reply, Parsons complained that several of those asked to contribute had not responded.

From the letter exchange, it is obvious that the primary reason that the publication plans were not carried out was simply the reluctance of the invited contributors to submit their anticipated papers. In retrospective comments on the cooperation with Schumpeter and the publication plans in particular, Parsons noted in an autobiographical statement that there were other reasons for him to let the project die. As he expressed it: "There was another interesting episode which might, at a relatively late time, have turned me at least farther in the direction of economics. After my formal transfer to sociology, Schumpeter organized a small discussion group with younger people, mostly graduate students, on problems of the nature of rationality. After a few meetings he proposed to me that the group should aim at producing a volume, of which he and I should be at least coeditors, if not coauthors. Though not specifically rejecting the proposal, at least immediately, I remember having reacted rather coolly, and in fact I let it die. I am not wholly clear about my motives, but I think they had to do with the feeling that I needed a relatively complete formal break with economics" (1977, 32–33).

Interesting as this comment is, we might note that Parsons had actually left the Department of Economics nine years before the rationality seminar was initiated in 1939. He had also published *The Structure of Social Action* as a sociologist two years before the seminar. Thus, the explanation that his motivation for allowing publication to fall through was a need to consolidate his separation from economics seems less than compelling. We propose that a more immediate reason may have been that his own theory had evolved past the formulations of *The Structure of Social Action*, which were the formulations considered in his own and other presentations to the seminar. By 1940, he had completed the monograph, *Actor, Situation and Normative Pattern*, which, though he withheld it from publication, he was already using in his teaching. That monograph initiated a sequence of changes in Parsons' theory of social action that would not be consolidated until his major publications of 1951, the long essay "Values, Motives, and Systems of Action," written with Edward A. Shils, in Parsons and Shils, editors, *Toward A General Theory of Action*, and *The Social System*.

Alfred Schütz published a shortened version of his paper under the title "The Problem of Rationality in the Social Sciences" in *Economica*(1943). The paper was later included in the *Collected Papers*, volume II, as "The Problem of Rationality in the Social World," and the original version was posthumously published in *Collected Papers*, volume IV (1996). In the present volume, the version is the one authorized for publication by Schütz, himself. Schumpeter's paper was published posthumously as "The Meaning of Rationality in the Social Sciences" in *Zeitschrift für die gesamte Sozialwissenschaft/Journal of Institutional and Theoretical Economics* (Schumpeter 1984; see also Stolper and Richter 1984) without the introductory section. The complete paper was published by Richard Swedberg in *The Economics and Sociology of Capitalism* (Swedberg 1991; Schumpeter 1991a).

Exchange Between Talcott Parsons and Richard Grathoff/ Walter M. Sprondel

Following their meeting in the seminar, Talcott Parsons and Alfred Schütz started an exchange of thoughts on fundamental theoretical issues. Schütz wrote an extensive review of *The Structure of Social Action*, which stimulated a letter exchange that lasted until spring of 1941.

The two German sociologists, Richard Grathoff and Walter M. Sprondel, edited and published the Parsons/Schütz letters in the 1970s. In the course of the preparations for their edition, they sent several inquiries to Parsons, which are included in this volume together with Parsons' replies. Their first letter to Parsons is dated December 4, 1973. Parsons replied extensively to their specific questions on the seminar and the relationship with Schütz. Parts of this letter are included in their editions (English version with Grathoff as editor, 1978, and a German version under the authorship of Schütz and Parsons and with Sprondel as editor, 1977) as Parsons' retrospective view after 35 years. In our volume, Parsons' whole letter is published for the first time.

Parsons interpreted the main difference in the phenomenological concept of "'experience' of phenomena which are attainable without mediation of ... a conceptual scheme" and his own conviction that the analysis of a "state of a mind" presupposes an *a priori* frame of reference. "If this is correct, as Kant held, about knowledge of objects in the external world, it seems to me it is *mutatis mutandis* correct about the observation of the 'motives' of other actors and the self-observation of acting individuals." The epistemological differences of the two approaches to social research became even more relevant in the history of the social sciences since their dispute and Parsons' afterword. The letter is also of interest as Parsons commented on his view on the seminar topic of rationality. His understanding had changed considerably, not in the sense of a falsification of his early view, but of a broadening and an account of decisive theory developments and their inclusion in his later theory, such as cybernetics.

In the course of the exchange on the Parsons–Schütz relationship, the idea came up to start a second attempt at publishing the presented seminar papers. The project became concrete, and an assistant to Richard Grathoff, Dr. Peter Zernitz, was sent to Harvard and had several meetings with Parsons, as mentioned in Parsons' letter of March 27, 1979. The plan then expanded even to including the idea of having another colloquium on the seminar topic. It is not clear why that plan was not realized.

Nearly 40 years later, the volume at hand is the third, and this time successful, attempt to publish the seminar papers and discuss them from a contemporary perspective.

Current Perspectives

Rationality in the Social Sciences—The Schumpeter/ParsonsSeminar in Current Perspectives was the title of a session at the biannual meeting of the Austrian Sociological Association held in Innsbruck in 2015, which was organized by the first editor of this volume. Presenters were Andreas Diekmann (professor at ETH Zürich with a research focus on quantitative methodology and game theory), Antonio Strati (professor emeritus at Università degli Studi di Trento, who is a leading expert on the topic of organization theory and aesthetics), and Raf Vanderstraeten (professor of sociology at Ghent University and director of the Social Theory Center at Ghent University). Additionally, the University of Innsbruck had invited Victor Lidz to give the Boehm–Bawerk Lecture and speak on the topic of rationality in the social sciences. His talk was also included in the conference program as one of the plenary sessions.

The papers resulting from these presentations provided the basis for invitations to additional prominent scholars to contribute to this volume. The editors have chosen sociologists who represent important theoretical movements in the current state of the discipline to write essays complementing the original set of papers. Dieter Bögenhold (professor of economic sociology at Universität Klagenfurt) is a board member of The International Joseph A. Schumpeter Society. Martin Endress (professor of sociology at Universität Trier) is a phenomenologist who served for ten years as editor of the *Alfred SchützWerkausgabe* (Collected Works of Alfred Schütz) published by UVK (University of Konstanz Press). Mark Gould (professor of sociology at Haverford College) is a theoretical economic sociologist and a former student and collaborator of Talcott Parsons. Christopher Winship (Diker-Tishman Professor of Sociology at Harvard University and a member of the Harvard Institute for Quantitative Social Science) focuses—besides his research on stratification and race issues—on econometrics, mathematical methods, and statistical models. The basic argument put forward in his chapter is "that the social sciences need multiple, potentially complementary models of action." His statement serves as a concluding summary of the spirit in which the editors have tried to put together diverse perspectives on the question of rationality. It is also a solid point of departure for further work in the field.

Conclusion

Rationality is a basic component of human action, and its understanding and explanation is—as we have seen—an intricate issue. In the history of social thought, two views stand in fierce opposition to one another. One was voiced by Fyodor Dostoyevsky, who in his early masterpiece, *Notes from the Underground*, formulated it bluntly: "In short, one may say anything about the history of the world—anything that might enter the most disordered imagination. The only thing one cannot say is that it is rational (Dostoyevsky 2003, p. 230)." There remain scholars in the contemporary humanities, social sciences, and even in economics who may still subscribe to such a formulation. Post-modern and post-structural currents of thought have revitalized similar views. However, a majority of contemporary scholars are committed in various degrees to an opposite view. Among them, the adherents of rational choice theory represent a strong movement within both sociology and economics.

We are deeply convinced that the concomitant contradictions are the result of conceptual frames that lack the necessary complexity. To resolve the paradoxes and contradictions requires conceptual differentiations and a refined and highly complex theory. As Alfred Schütz formulated it in his talk, it is a matter of bringing out "the concealed equivocations and connotations and to isolate the question of rationality from all the other problems surrounding it." The social sciences still have a long way to go to realize that achievement. We hope that publication of the Schumpeter–Parsons Seminar manuscripts along with evaluation of their key ideas from contemporary perspectives will advance that crucial endeavor.

References

Dostoyevsky, Fyodor. 2003 [1864]. *Notes from Underground, the Double, and Other Stories*. Trans. Constance Garnett. New York: Barnes and Noble Classics. http://www.pagebypagebooks.com/Fyodor_Dostoevsky/Notes_from_the_Underground/

Eberle, Thomas S., Jochen Dreher, and Gerd Sebald. 2010. Editorischer Bericht. In *Werkausgabe Band IV Zur Methodologie der Sozialwissenschaften*, ed. Alfred Schütz, 201–202. Konstanz: UVK.

Lidz, Victor, and Helmut Staubmann, eds. 2010. *Talcott Parsons: Actor, Situation and Normative Pattern. An Essay in the Theory of Social Action*. Vienna: LIT.

Moore, Wilbert E. 1940. *Slavery, Abolition and the Ethical Valuation of the Individual: A Study of the Relations Between Ideas and Institutions*. Dissertation, Harvard University.

Moss, Laurence S., and Andrew Savchenko, eds. 2006. My Life and Work – A Seminar with Talcott Parsons at Brown University. *American Journal of Economics and Sociology* 65 (1): 1–57.

Parsons, Talcott. 1937. *The Structure of Social Action*. 2 Vols. New York: Free Press.

———. 1959. A Short Account of My Intellectual Development. *Alpha Kappa Delta* Winter: 3–38.

———. 1977. On building social systems theory: A personal history. In *Social Systems and the Evolution of Action Theory*, 22–76. New York: Free Press.

———. 1981. Rationalität und der Prozess der Rationalisierung im Denken Max Webers. In *Max Weber und die Rationalisierung des Handelns*, ed. Walter M. Sprodel und Constans Seyfarth, 81–92.

Schumpeter, Joseph A. 1984. The Meaning of Rationality in the Social Sciences. *Zeitschrift für die gesamte Staatswissenschaft/Journal of Institutional and Theoretical Economics* 140: 557–593.

———. 1991a. The meaning of rationality in the social sciences. In *The Economics and Sociology of Capitalism*, ed. Richard Swedberg, 316–338. Princeton: Princeton University Press.

———. 1991b. Talcott Parsons' manuscript: Sociology and the elements of human action. To the committee on research in the social sciences. In *Schumpeter. A Biography*, ed. Richard Swedberg, 220–221. Princeton: Princeton University Press.

Schütz, Alfred. 1943. The Problem of Rationality in the Social Sciences. *Economica* 10: 130–149.

———. 1960. *Der sinnhafte Aufbau der sozialen Welt.* Vienna: Springer.

———. 1964. The problem of rationality in the social world. In *Collected Papers II Studies in Social Theory*, ed. Alfred Schütz, 64–88.

———. 1967. *The Phenomenology of the Social World.* Evanston, IL: Northwestern University Press.

———. 1996. The Problem of Rationality in the Social World. A Lecture Delivered at the Faculty Club of Harvard University on April 13th, 1940. In *Collected Papers* IV 1996-I-1, S. 6–24.

Stolper, Wolfgang F., and Rudolf Richter. 1984. Editorial introduction to Joseph A. Schumpeter The Meaning of Rationality in the Social Sciences. *Zeitschrift für die gesamte Sozialwissenschaft/Journal of Institutional and Theoretical Economics* 140 (4): 577–578.

Swedberg, Richard. 1991. Introduction: the man and his work. In Swedberg R, Joseph A (eds) Schumpeter: the economics and sociology of capitalism. Princeton University Press, Princeton, NJ.

———. 2006. On teasing out sociology from economics: A brief note on Parsons and Schumpeter. *American Journal of Economics and Sociology* 65 (1): 71–74.

———. 2015. Schumpeter and Talcott Parsons. *Journal of Evolutionary Economics* 25: 215–222.

Part I
Original Papers of the Schumpeter/Parsons Seminar

The Meaning of Rationality in the Social Sciences

Joseph A. Schumpeter

I

My first thesis is that, as far as the logical quality of the analyst's fundamental attitude is concerned, rationality (rational procedure) in the social sciences does not differ from scientific rationality in general. That is to say, the scientific analyst or observer of any set of phenomena will always try to behave rationally toward the subject matter of his research whatever that subject matter will be, and his fundamental procedure will always be amenable to description by rules that apply to all cases of analytic endeavor. This we shall call observer's rationality.

What that common scientific rationality consists in, I am not going to analyze beyond noting a few surface features which I will try to keep as non-committal as possible. In the main, I shall, wherever this subject intrudes into the argument, rely on our every-day familiarity with it.

Generalizing Kirchhoff's definition of mechanics I shall define science in general as the endeavor to describe phenomena we happen to be interested in, in the way most economical with reference to an assigned degree of accuracy. The element of rationality enters by means of that minimum condition which may, I think, be so interpreted as to also include, to some extent at least, the element of predictability of future phenomena: in other respects predictability is merely a *test*, while in still others it refers to important, but logically extraneous, considerations of usefulness.

It follows that scientific procedure must necessarily reject all forms of thought that are in conflict with the rules of logic or cannot, in principle at least, be tested by these rules. But it does not necessarily follow that it also excludes reasoning on anything except verifiable "facts." Aversion to introducing any entities that cannot

---

This contribution is published with permission of the Harvard University Archives, Talcott Parsons Papers.

The author was deceased at the time of publication.

H. Staubmann, V. Lidz (eds.), *Rationality in the Social Sciences*,
DOI 10.1007/978-3-319-62377-1_2

be observed or experimentally produced is part of the scientific attitude only so far as it is based on the principle of economy in description. If the hypothesis that planets are moved by angels, opened the shortest way to describing their motions, there could be no objection to it on grounds of scientific rationality.

Both the scientific attitude and that aversion to extra-empirical cognition are, of course, sociologically related. They are both the products of "rationalist" civilizations. But logically they should be kept distinct. So should scientific rationality and rationalism in another sense that may be best visualized in the context "rationalist philosophy." Although it comprises a great number of types – among which I believe, scholastic philosophy and St. Thomas' philosophy in particular – the relevant point may be instanced by Hegelianism.[1] Illustrative examples and still another meaning will be noticed later on.

I have defined scientific endeavor with reference to "an assigned degree of accuracy." It is obvious why that was necessary. What is the most economical way of description or, in other words, the optimal way of explaining a phenomenon, cannot be determined until we have made up our mind how deeply we wish to go into it. But this is part of our choice of the goal to aim at which in itself, *and aside from questions of consistency of any particular goal with others we may at the same time wish to reach*, is not a question of rationality at all, but of "valuation."

Scientific rationality is also relative to the horizon of the analyst, that is to the information and mental equipment at his command. What behavior is rational for a given analyst or observer can only be determined if we know what he knows. For the social sciences this entails particularly intriguing consequences, but the fundamental point holds for any science and must be noted at once. An example will illustrate it. When using infinite series, the mathematicians of the eighteenth century – until Cauchy in fact, I think – did not bother much about conditions of convergence, and only their sound horse sense (or the instinct of genius if you so please) prevented them from falling into very serious error. A modern mathematician would, if he neglected to test his series for convergence, be voted most irrational. But were the old masters any less irrational? One feels greatly tempted to say they were, and to resolve the obvious dilemma by adding that they were "objectively" irrational. Since, however, such a judgment is only arrived at by comparing their equipment with ours and since the latter has no title to "absolute" validity – whatever that may mean – we must recognize the fact that we are, in this as in other matters, acting as self-appointed judges whose verdict sometimes is and sometimes is not upheld by other equally self-appointed judges. This means more than that a strong personal equation unavoidably enters into any pronouncement about the rational quality of a given attitude or act. It means that that rational quality is by nature relative to the information and mental equipment we individually happen to possess or, if I may venture that far, which we *could* possess if we

---

[1]Rationalism as a philosophy (or theory of the world) is in Hegelianism wedded to the use of rational models so as to make the two practically synonymous. This is well expressed by the two famous propositions in the preface to Hegel's *Philosophy of Natural Law*: (1) What is rational is actual, (2) What is actual is rational.

availed ourselves of all the facilities at our disposal as seen by a self-appointed judge of "higher" rank.

Value judgments enter into all this, of course. But this is not denied by anybody who, like myself, stands for excluding them from the realm of the social sciences. What is meant by "Wertfreiheit" is merely freedom from value judgments of a particular kind, viz. from judgments about how it would be *desirable* for the phenomena under study to behave. This means positing ultimate ends and, though I admit that it is more difficult in the social sciences than it is in others to prevent our ends or sympathies from influencing our results – "wishful thinking" – I cannot see that the logical position of those ultimate ends is any different in the social field. All that can be legitimately claimed for them, on the scientific plane, reduces to, first, the task of working out the consequences that action taken in order to realize any given ultimate end would have; second, the task of explaining why given people at any given time and place should feel about any given ultimate ends as they actually do. And both tasks wholly fall within the scope of scientific rationality.

Paul Sweezy raised the question whether there are "ultimate ends" at all. Their existence seems, however, to follow from a consideration of argumentative technique: Any proposition containing a value concept necessarily leads back to another proposition of the same nature – value judgments never reduce to anything else but value judgments; and since we must eventually break off this recursus – which cannot be circular – at some point, there will always be one value judgment that, for the purpose in hand, will take the position of the "ultimate" one. But as a matter of practice, it is quite true that ordinarily we do not meet with ultimate values and that the valuations we do meet with are usually intermediate ones, i.e., really refer to means to an end not itself under discussion. That is why, in apparent contradiction to the opinion submitted, we can so very often speak of the *rationality or irrationality of an end.* I will emphasize at once that this seems to me the only justifiable meaning of the phrase. But there is such a thing as *normality of an ultimate end* which it is not always easy to distinguish from rationality and which, I believe, accounts for the fact that many people are so averse to accepting the extra-rationality of ultimate ends and to seeing the difference between a madman and an ascetic.

I may as well conclude this part of my argument by pointing out what seems to me the relation between rationality of analytic procedure and rationality of the result which, as long as we speak of observer rationality only,[2] may simply be equated to "truth." Obviously rationality of procedure is a necessary condition for rationality of the result if we except the case of chance coincidence of irrational procedure with a "true" result, such as the case of a true proposition's resulting from a formally wrong syllogism from wrong premises. No less obviously, however, rational procedure is not a sufficient condition for the emergence of a "true" result,

[2]This is intended to exclude not only pragmatic rationality of results *ex visu* of the observed individuals or groups, (see infra) but also the ontological truth of, say, prophecy which might be arrived at by non-rational means.

unless we include correctness and adequacy of both the material and the equipment at the command of the analyst which we cannot do if we admit varying horizons. While there is thus a relation between rationality and truth, there is not congruence.

II

So far all there is of rationality in social science emanates from the analyst. It is imported into the facts from the analyst's mind and the rationality of the processes of the latter is all that matters. We will emphasize at once that this observer's rationality has in itself nothing whatever to do with the presence or absence of rationality in the human types or human actions observed, or even with the applicability of the concept of rationality to the subject matter under investigation.

Now my second thesis is that there are many and important cases in which that is all, and in which the attitude of the analyzing economist or sociologist remains all along within the processes of thought that are used by the analyst of a biological species or the analyst of mechanical or electrical phenomena. Since in modern economics this type of investigation has of late acquired additional importance, I shall choose my example from that field. Everyone knows that statistical material is often presented in the form of time series, that is to say, of sequences of data, ordered in historic time. If we plot a number of such series over the same time axis, we immediately observe that there are disturbed, yet very definite relations between them. These relations can be measured and expressed analytically and this in itself suggests to us the conception of a mechanism that can be investigated as such. But we can go farther than this. We can choose these time series in a way that seems meaningful to us, replace the time series by the concepts that correspond to them, and build a rational model or theory that will display in the abstract some features of those relations and stand to reality as does, say, the scientific model of astronomy. For instance, I can take *indices* of total production, of the price level, of interest rates and of demand deposits, and look upon the state of the economic system as characterized by them. And I can also take the *concepts* of total production, price level, interest rates and demand deposits, and impose conditions on their behavior as against each other. These conditions I derive either directly from the statistical observation or more directly from relations that I, from other sources, know to subsist between these quantities or their rates of change.

Never mind whether such a theory, working with those four variables only would be satisfactory or not, that is whether it would or would not describe or account for, those phenomena for the sake of which I constructed that setup. The essential point is that here we have objectively observable quantities which do not, or at least need not, directly imply anything about human behavior and with which I can, nevertheless, derive significant economic results. It is true, of course, and has been pointed out by Professor Parsons, that further analysis of those entities and the relations that I might set up between them, would inevitably lead to acting men. But this doesn't alter the fact that meaningful arguments can be framed without such further analysis and that the mechanism of my four quantities is to a certain extent a logical world unto itself. If it is not absolutely self-contained, it shares this property with any other scientific model or theory which must always have boundaries that cut through real, as distinguished from analytic, relations. No doubt our time series have their peculiarities which are not exactly paralleled in any other material. In particular, their relations are infinitely less stable than relations are in say, physics, and the elements of disturbance and error play a role that, for the practice of research, amounts to a difference in kind. But all this does not seem to me to be relevant to the question of principle involved. In particular, if we find a certain relation between price level and total production, it is for this kind of research completely immaterial whether or not this relation can be reduced to reactions of firms that appear to us rational or not. As what I am going to say will amply prove, I do not mean that this is irrelevant from every conceivable standpoint, but it is irrelevant for the type of analysis I am now envisaging and which, of course, is not confined to economics. Wherever we have entities that can be quantitatively expressed and display regular relations to other such entities, we can get some "laws" out of them in much the same way in which the physicist does and, again, the epistemological problems that may arise, do not seem to differ from those inherent in scientific procedure in general.

III

It might seem (and some economists as well as some sociologists of the behavioristic type come near to holding this view) that we ought to confine ourselves to such objective and measurable relations as we have just been considering. My third thesis is, however, that doing so would amount to throwing away a most effective tool of analysis, the value of which is not at all impaired by the fact that it is not available in the physical sciences. Again, the tool in question can best be displayed by means of an example.

Consider a firm that produces a commodity which cannot be substituted at all and for which there exists a demand schedule which that firm cannot expect to influence. Further assume, for simplicity's sake, that there is only one way open to the firm of producing that commodity. We can construct what economists call marginal revenue and marginal cost curves, and determine from their point of intersection that quantity of output which will maximize the instantaneous profits of the firm. This is the classic case of monopoly and a number of propositions about monopoly price and monopoly output can be readily proved. Now what is the nature and the use of such a construct?

First of all, observe that we are still within the sphere of observer's rationality. The model just described is the product of the analyst's mind as much as any physical theory is, and does not in itself say anything about reality or about anybody's actual behavior or rationality. It is of particular importance to note that even if the model should fit anyone's behavior this does not mean that the individual in question consciously aims at the result and still less that he arrives at it by processes at all similar to the analytic procedure. Most businessmen, of course, do not know what a marginal cost and a marginal revenue curve is; most of them would not know how to construct them, even if they knew what they meant; and it is safe to say that not a single businessman's subjective processes are correctly described by saying that he is hunting for their point of intersection. But nothing of this is necessary for the model to have sense and to be useful. For a man's behavior may conform to it and be economically described by it, even if its contents are as foreign to his mind as the law of gravitation is foreign to a stone.

Yet, second, there is a difference between the relation of the stone to its law of motion and the relation of our firm to the law of its economic behavior. In the first case we describe observed facts directly although we subject them to a purifying process of abstraction (no friction and that sort of thing). In the second case we also aim at describing observed fact but we chose a detour. We take a preliminary step which consists in setting up a norm of behavior. And this norm is not a norm in the statistical sense but a norm in the sense akin to that of a logical rule or, possibly, even to that of an ethical imperative. In order to set it up we need not only a number of factual data, *but we need also to understand a meaning*. We are setting up a model that embodies a meaning in the sense that it gives the conditions under which a certain given goal, the maximization of profits, would be attained. Such a model may serve the purposes of description by giving us a standard with which to compare actual behavior or it might, in the most favorable case, help to describe actual behavior by giving its rationale. But in either case an element enters which is extraneous to the description or analysis of the physicist. Although the whole thing is, as has been said, still a product of the rationality of the observer, the latter makes in constructing it an assumption about a rationality present in his subject matter and the whole usefulness of the model will depend on the degree to which that hypothesis is justified by facts. To be sure it is quite sufficient that what firms want is to make money and that they would rather make more than less of it. Also we can take account of any amount of deviations as we must anyhow do also in the case of physical sciences. But that doesn't alter the fact that we have to do with the logic of an (intermediate) end and not only with the logic of a cause. The case is one of a setup that is itself supposed to be rational – of an objective rationality (rationality in the object) seen through the rationality of the observer.

The importance of models of this nature is enormous and extends far beyond the scientific sphere. We could not go through a single day if we had not constant recourse to this method of constructing, however imperfect, models that are rational in this sense. It is not too much to say that that understanding of non-physical things which enables us to act in daily life, entirely rests upon such schemata of rationality. Objections to them can be founded only on the imperfections of a particular case or on an abuse of them. But abuses can only be found out by trying. And this brings up a question of fact.

A few comments will be useful:

1. To begin with, let us restate what I meant to convey by "rationality of the object seen through the rationality of the observer." The observer visualizes an end, the instantaneous maximization of profits, which he understands and, putting himself in the place of an imaginary individual that clearly perceives, and aims at, this end, he states the means (or, in this case, conditions) that seem to him – the observer – conducive to, or logically implied by, the end (or, the conditions action would have to fulfill to produce it). If he has succeeded in "understanding" the end and if he has correctly set out its implications then he has, as we have styled it, derived a "norm" which is "valid," whether there are any facts conforming to it or not (whether it is "verified by facts" or not). This is the situation which has given rise to the distinction between what in German is referred to as *Gelten* und *Sein*. But, potentially at least, this norm is visualized as something capable of being realized by the firms which are the objects of analysis. This is an additional assumption which, e.g., the mathematician need not make. That is what I mean by rationality in the object and what distinguishes a type of rational schemata in the social sciences from "*mécanique rationnelle*," i.e., rational schemata in the physical sciences (as well as from other types, mentioned before, of rational schemata in the social sciences).
2. The end need not, of course, be shared by the analyst, but we have said that it must be understood by him. For his understanding of the end is the necessary prerequisite for setting forth its implications as to means. This brings us up to the difficulty in application inherent in what I will call the infinite variety of cognate ends. Any such end like maximizing profits is not uniquely determinate. That is why I have added the world "instantaneous." The old Cournot-Marshall theory of monopoly only holds for that subcase – that is to say, practically never – and is not applicable to the cases in which monopolists wish to maximize profits over a (considerable) period of time (a case dealt with by Evans, Roos, Smithies et al.). Dissatisfaction with rational schemata in economics seems to me mainly due to the difficulty of picking appropriate rational models. Here, then, questions of fact enter after all – the rationality of a model must be supplemented by the rationality of its application which is part of the analyst's task. Many types of behavior are looked upon as irrational (not conforming to a schema of rational action) and the range of rationality in action is in consequence often underestimated because the tests of rationality have been made by means of models that failed to fit, not because they were rational but because they did not catch the right type of "Zweckrationalität."
3. Conflicting ends, modifying each other, afford another kind of instance for the same truth. An individual's or group's behavior may ideally conform to the rules of rationality and yet not seem to do so if tested by a schema embodying one end only. A social class would not consistently act according to its economic interests even if these were uniquely determined at any given point of time – which they never are – because it has also other interests to which it attaches varying weights. At a time, when the agrarian interest was dominant in the class

that formed English political society, the duties on foodstuffs were abolished. This was contrary to the economic interests of that class and might easily be interpreted as, from its standpoint, irrational. But a ruling class's first and foremost interest is to rule and from this angle that action was perfectly rational. The conflict of ends is well illustrated by the fact that the conservative party actually split on that issue.

The same example also illustrates another important cause of what might be called spurious failure of rational models: the faulty construction of the agent, "into the place of which" the analyst should put himself. A class never acts as such. It acts through politicians whom it "supports." But the personal success of politicians depends also on other things than the class interests of their supporters. Often it is best served by selling the latter down the river. And what looks very refractory to rational schematization if made to turn on class interest, may yet fit excellently into a schema of rationality if the analyst constructs his agent correctly. Such examples abound: the interest of a business corporation vs. the interests of the executives, the interests of the working class vs. the interests of trade-union officers are cases in point.

4. For many obvious reasons it is very important to distinguish between rational behavior and rational result. Behavior can ideally conform to a rational schema and yet produce or help to produce a result which is rational only in the sense that the analyst can understand it by means of rational processes of mind but in no other. This may best be illustrated by all those cases in which the mass effect of actions, each of which may be described by a strictly rational model, spells chaos and produces results most irrational from the standpoint of the ends of the actors. Every economic crisis may be cited in verification. This illustration is particularly interesting because, far into the nineteenth century, economists used to argue that unfettered economic self-interest of individuals is bound to produce the maximum of welfare for all, *because* every individual strives to maximize his own. Such slips, by the way, may have much to do with the discredit that no doubt attaches to analysis by means of rational models in our sense.
5. Beyond very simple cases which we may hope hail from an almost universal pattern of human behavior, understanding an end and judging rationality of means often requires that the analyst "puts himself" into places very far distant from his time and social location. Sometimes he has to transplant himself into another cultural world. It might well be asked what justification there can be for such "*Einfühlung*" into Brahmanism behavior or Hannibalian strategy, and whether sociologist or historians are writing anything else but novels. Into this I cannot go. But if we admit that when venturing into the "*Sinnzusammenhang*" of things so far removed from our own personal experience we are not merely stepping on clouds, we must at least recognize the risks inherent in such undertaking. Max Weber affords a good illustration of the dangers I mean to refer to, when he denies rationality to the ancient Chinese mind on the ground, among others, that examinations in classical literature were tightened as a remedy for shortcomings the bureaucracy displayed in dealing with catastrophic floods.

IV

Workers in the fields of the Social Sciences have, explicitly or implicitly, gone beyond rational schemata of the type we have been considering so far by assuming that the individuals under research – sometimes even "the people" as such – are themselves actuated by clearly perceived motives, and regulate their behavior with conscious rationality working in the full daylight of their ego's (subjective rationality). In doing so, those analysts, especially those of bygone generations, have almost invariably overrated the actual range of consciously rational action. Moreover, they so formulated their propositions as to lay them open, quite unnecessarily, to objection whenever it could be shown that their concepts were entirely foreign to the individuals whose behavior they tried to describe, whereas we have seen that, for instance, the fundamental theorem about monopolistic pricing is independent of whether or not the monopolist has any notion of marginal revenue or marginal cost curves. Finally, they almost completely overlooked the fact that the conscious motives that a man will tell himself and others are largely "rationalizations" of impulses he either is unable or unwilling to diagnose or to admit. But this does not dispose of the question whether or not the distinction between objective rationality (applicability of a rational schema to the actor's behavior) and subjective rationality (conformity of the actor's mental processes to a rational schema) is completely otiose.

I answer in the negative. No doubt, the distinction *is* otiose in many cases and for many purposes. Wherever it is and where in consequence the introduction of subjective rationality owes its introduction into our analysis merely to the failure of analysts to perceive the fact that models of rational action do not necessarily imply conscious rationality on the part of the actors, it is sound method to discard what then turns out to be a redundant hypothesis. But all the same I believe that there are other cases and other purposes for which presence or absence of subjective rationality is not a matter of indifference. My reasons are as follows.

I have been at pains to emphasize that the propositions such as the one about the monopolist's profit maximum are independent of the subjective rationality of individual monopolists. But that is true only so long as we are interested in that proposition as such and in nothing else. If, however, we apply it as an interpretative schema, it may occur to ask *why* it does or does not fit the facts of the particular case in hand. Taking the first alternative, subjective rationality on the part of the monopolist concerned would afford a very obvious *explanatory hypothesis*: the monopolist's conscious calculations of his own pecuniary interest would then constitute a real force ("Realgrund" as distinguished from "Erkenntnisgrund" – sorry, but for these things there are no perfectly adequate English terms). The value of that hypothesis may be inferred from the fact that if, for some reason or other, we do not feel justified in adopting it, conformity of behavior to the rational pattern becomes a puzzle, solution of which is both a laborious and a difficult task.

But the question why it is that reality sometimes conforms to rational schemata is by no means uninteresting. The answer makes a difference to diagnosis and especially to prediction: we control a pattern more fully, understand it *better*, handle it with more confidence, forecast its reactions to a given disturbance more surely, if we know that answer. If the monopolist acts with conscious rationality his behavior, say, in a period of rapid change will not only be easier to foretell than if he does not but it will be different from what it would be if other factors accounted for his conforming to the rational schema. In particular his – or anybody's – reactions to the element of *expectations*, especially his speed of reaction, will to a considerable extent depend on the degree to which he is "consciously rational." Of still greater importance than in the cases of often repeated every-day actions is subjective rationality in the cases in which our observations are few or refer to exceptional or even unique circumstances. Suppose the task is to interpret American foreign policy. Few will deny that up to 1914, the actual behavior of the American government with respect to its relations with foreign nations almost ideally fits into a very simple rational schema. Excepting the war with Spain, we shall not be contradicted by any major factors, if we say that the "people" wanted a very understandable thing and that they rationally acted according to the implications of that goal: first they wanted independence; then they wanted to buttress it by suspiciously watching their former master and fighting him whenever there was any occasion to do so; finally they capped their policy by the Monroe doctrine and stoutly stood for it and all its implications for the rest of the period. We have here the picture of a nation that wants to be a world unto itself – to be left alone and to leave alone, and if ever rational schema fitted any political events it does so in this case. But it makes a lot of difference for our understanding the past and for our predicting the future, whether that behavior was due to conscious rationality working for a clearly seen end or to environmental conditions, group interests and so on that so happened to mold things as to produce, for that period, what will bear description in terms of a rational model.

The best instance for what I am trying to convey is the theory of democracy. The old theory of democracy as formulated in the seventeenth and eighteenth centuries *presupposes* degrees of awareness of one's interests, clearness of ends, rationality in the perception and use of means and, most important of all, accessibility to rational argument which are altogether unrealistic. A reformed theory of democracy could still use, to a considerable extent, rational schemata, but it would have to drop, not wholly but also to a considerable extent, the hypothesis of conscious rationality; and it would, in consequence of this, arrive at a totally different picture of democratic processes, particularly as regards the role to be assigned to rational arguments. And in such a theory the precise range of subjective rationality would constitute a vital part.

Two things must be noted here. First, it is not necessary that the subjective rationality of actors works in the same way as the rationality of the observer. The theorist of monopoly will describe the behavior of even a rational monopolist in ways that more or less differ from the actual methods by which the monopolist arrives at his decisions. We have here the germ of another distinction and another task which, however, need not detain us.

Second, it might be objected that whatever we may find out by means of subjective rationality can always be embodied in our "objectively rational" models so that there is no reason after all to stress what of subjective rationality might be in the actors we observe. I think that my examples suggest this is *not* always so. But even if it were that would only amount to saying that once we have gained full analytic control over a phenomenon we can discard conscious rationality. Heuristically, however, and so long as we are trying to gain analytic control but have not yet gained it, that hypothesis may nevertheless render valuable service. If we know how firms actually react to expectations of future prices and profits, we need perhaps no longer worry about what the subjective rationality of managers has got to do with it. But while we are trying to find out, our task will be rendered easier if we do not refuse to utilize what we may know about their subjective rationality. Similarly, modern economic theory dispenses with the concept of utility, replacing it by a few postulates about choice. But that does not alter the fact that the old marginal utility has in the past proved to be a very helpful piece of scaffolding.

The relevance of subjective rationality to analysis in the social sciences stands out perhaps still more clearly in cases in which rational schemata do not fit. Diagnosis of the reasons for the discrepancy then becomes an obviously unavoidable task of analysis. Into this diagnosis the element of subjective rationality enters, so it seems to me, in two ways. First, deficiency in subjective rationality may directly be the reason we seek, or one of these reasons. In this case it ipso facto presents its credentials as a relevant factor and, moreover, points the way to remedial interference. Secondly, investigation of subjective rationality may put us on to the track of other reasons and even help us to identify the right "objectively rational model." This can be best shown by an example.

Suppose we have before us a firm which neither in the method of production used (in its economy of heat and power for instance), nor in its location, nor in its cost calculation, nor in its price policy conforms to the model by which we are trying to "interpretatively describe" its behavior. In the first place, this lack of objective rationality *may* be due to lack of subjective rationality in the management, and might be remedied by an efficiency expert's pointing it out to the management.[3] In the second place, whatever the lack of objective rationality may be due to it is often easier to find the hitch with than it would be without the use of the concept of subjective rationality. For instance, the irrational situation may have arisen from one that perfectly conformed to the rational model applied but ceased to do so owing to a change in the commercial, technological and so on data. Now, the firm

[3]I suspect that part of the opposition my theory of subjective rationality met in our group, especially from Professor Parsons, is due to my infelicitous terminology. Perhaps I should speak of personal rationality – meaning thereby rationality residing in a man rather than in a pattern – and I should not have used the word "conscious" since automatization of often repeated actions will make forms of behavior subconscious which are, nevertheless, included in my conscious rationality: if a mathematician solves a differential equation in the best known manner he is being "consciously rational" in my sense if, in a particularly simple case, he writes down the solution quite mechanically.

may have failed to adapt itself, because it had as yet no time to do so or because the management is traditional, lazy, lethargic or because it thinks that the change responsible for the discrepancy is but temporary. In the latter case, if the management is right – which only means that the analyzing economist is of the same opinion – the case, though not conforming to the rational model applied, may yet be brought within the precincts of rationality by means of another model. But which we are to choose will be much easier to determine – as will in general the right one of all those varieties I have discussed before under the heading of objective rationality – if we know something, from direct observation of the types we have to deal with, of the nature, time-span, and so on of the subjective rationalities involved.

Our model may not fit a given firm also for another class of reason. The technology of its productive process may rouse the contempt of the consulting engineer, and yet the setup as a whole be quite rational because it may not pay the leading man to bother about technology: he may have such a flair for fashions for instance and be so excellent a salesman and so entirely absorbed by filling these functions successfully that it would be sheer waste of effort for him to worry about whether or not his plant is economical of, say, power of labor. I mention this class of cases – of conflict between engineers' and economic rationality – not only because they are in themselves important and the source of much inadequate interpretation, but also because at least the engineer's rationality is so excellent an example of subjective rationality and for the importance of attending to it. Engineers' rationality turns on ends perceived with ideal clearness. It goes about devising means by ideally rational and conscious efforts. It reacts promptly to a purely rational new impulse – e.g., a new calculation published in a professional periodical. It is comparatively free from extraneous considerations. That is to say, it functions in a particular way *because* of its "conscious" quality of its intentional struggle for rationality. All the sectors in which that is the case – medicine is another example – are intimately associated with what is usually referred to as "material progress" and display mechanisms that powerfully affect the states and the behavior of social groups. They reveal the action of a distinct factor or "social force." Incidentally, they also supply an answer – which is partial only, but *almost* sufficient – to the question how we are to satisfy ourselves whether and to what extent we are in the presence of subjective rationality.

If our firm failed to adapt itself to the new environmental conditions from habit, laziness, lethargy, its behavior may, from the standpoint of its manager, yet conform to a rational model – he may be maximizing his welfare by not bothering. Now, just as in the case of altruistic behavior practiced from an "egotistical" wish for the satisfaction such a behavior yields or, in the case of energetic and aggressive activity pursued "hedonistically" – because it gives pleasure – so we are in cases such as the one of the lazy manager in danger of losing our criterion of rational behavior: all behavior, so it seems, would have to be looked upon as tautologically rational *ex visu* of suitably chosen ends and horizons. The ways to encounter this danger – which, if not successfully encountered would limit us to observer's rationality – may be many. But recourse to subjective rationality seems to me to be one of the most feasible ones.

The greatest of all the services that research into the facts of subjective rationality can render is the – possibly – melancholy one of showing up the narrow limits of its range. These limits have been sufficiently emphasized during the last half-century by writers of the most varied types, among leading economists principally by Pareto. What has not been sufficiently emphasized is that the scope of objective and of subjective rationality in action, while immeasurably smaller than our predecessors in economic and political theory thought, is at the same time wider than some of its critics would have us believe. If my points be scrutinized from this angle, it will be seen that every one of them extends the range of application of rational models in one way or another. It is hardly necessary to add that this puts us in a better position for dealing with the subject of Error in History and with the subject of faulty practice[4] and its persistence or elimination (Taylorism).

V

Some of the points I have touched upon may possibly be instanced and clarified by going quickly over a few of the general "systems" with which economics is usually credited. When we try to reconstruct the social world of an economist from his writings, we are likely to fall into two errors. First, we may forget that the construction of a general schema of action is not the economist's business. His schemata are devised for certain special uses and must be judged by their success in actual application, and not without reference to it. This is all the more important because the older economists have had the unfortunate habit of adding semi-philosophical orbiter dicta, most of which sound horribly trite, and may easily reflect discredit on what they had really to say, especially in the eyes of a layman. Secondly, even where economists did construct, or adopt, what was intended to be a social philosophy, we mustn't take it for granted that they were much influenced by it in their professional work. Nobody judges Newton's performance in the world of mathematics and physics by his utterances on theology. Nobody reproaches Joule

[4]By faulty practice, as distinguished from error, I mean practice conforming to standards of rationality in use at the relevant time and place that themselves deviate from the correct implications of the end pursued. Example: in order to make money, a firm stands in need of correct methods of cost calculation; as a matter of fact none of the methods actually in use are correct and business decisions, that are otherwise rational and even consciously so, are often vitiated by them. Of course not everything is really irrational that appears to the economist to be so. For instance, economists often state that it is irrational for firms to insist always on charging prices that will cover overhead charges rather than to take what they can get. But big business that knows itself to be unpopular, will often be driven to that course from a fear that it will not be allowed to put prices up again after having lowered them and from a desire to charge prices that can be easily "justified." This, of course, is one of those cases in which a model fails from taking inadequate account of the data before the actor and of the ends he actually pursues.

for giving as one of his reasons for belief in the conservation of energy, that it would be derogatory to God to think that anything in the creation could get lost. Similar justice must be rendered to economists and sociologists.

We will begin with the physiocrats whose positive achievement was the clear conception of economic life as a self-contained process reproducing itself in circular flows. But they looked upon their theory as an explanatory schema of the social world as a whole, with a general philosophy thrown in. The distinction between analyzing what is and postulating what ought to be, was as far from their minds (and the minds of their contemporaries) as it was from the mind of Plato. There was an ideal state of things, preordained in God's plan which at one and the same time was the natural state and yet not the existing one but one that had still to be realized. The way to realize it was to allow everyone to act according to his own self-interests while (so we ought to add) conserving the fundamentals of the existing institutional framework, in particular the landowning class. We need not go any farther for our purposes. The case illustrates to perfection a certain number of points which keep on turning up, however the particular garb may change.

There is first that idea of an ideal state of things which, if once realized, would indefinitely continue to exist. In itself such a belief, nowadays mainly harbored by socialists, is clearly extra-scientific, which in the case of the physiocrats is made particularly obvious by the theological character impressed by them upon the *ordre naturel*.[5] But from the standpoint of the actual use made of this conception, it merely looks like a descriptive device for expressing the useful truth that the economic process is a cosmos and not a chaos. What really depends upon the concept of the ideal state and its divine sanction is only a series of value judgments which we can easily dispense with. Of course, once one believes in such an ideal state, any element of an actual state can be unequivocally labelled as right and wrong. Beyond that however, since all the Deity was supposed to do was to lend the weight of its authority to the theorems propounded by the physiocrats, there was no theological influence whatever. Nevertheless, we have here a typically rationalist system. That is to say, a system built upon the belief that there is, underlying the empirical world, a plan or order that human reason can reveal by propositions, acceptance of which can be logically enforced. In their economic theory they clearly used a rational schema of the sort which we have tried to individualize by the phrase "rationality of the subject matter seen through the rationality of the observer." But as far as I can see no assumption about subjective rationality was necessarily involved although in common with all the thinkers of their time they certainly greatly overestimated its range of application.

Let English Utilitarianism be our next example. Here, the theological note is absent but otherwise the case is exactly similar to the preceding one. Again, there is an ideal state, which is natural though it doesn't exist, and which when reached will persist indefinitely. There is a well-nigh unlimited belief in the actual rationality of man. Most of the economic propositions of the economists of the group, Bentham

[5]See in particular Francois Quesnay's *Droit Naturel*.

himself included, could I suppose be stated in such a way as to avoid the hypothesis of conscious rationality. But the political theory of Benthamism could not. The recipe: educate people and let them vote freely and equally, presupposes, if intended to be the remedy for everything the Benthamites did not like and the key to everything they did like, that everybody knows or can be made to know what he wants and is able and willing to work for it and to discuss it with ideal rationality: Thomistic rationalism has descended from the clouds, but only to reign supreme in the sphere of social action. Uncompromising intellectualism, aptly wedded to associative psychology by James Mill, is the backbone of Benthamite sociology. The observer's rationality welds with the *ratio* in the subject matter and this *ratio* is, potentially at least, subjective rationality producing, and accounting for, the objective rationality in the social patterns. Everything is conscious and what is not is being covered by a fig leaf: English tradition became so firmly set that even so modern an author – is he so very modern though? – as Professor Pigou defined welfare as a state of consciousness.

The gulf between what is and what ought to be on the one hand, and between ultimate ends and means on the other hand, is not of course narrowed thereby. But it looks smaller from the Benthamite standpoint than from almost any other. The ultimate end remains an improvable postulate but Bentham saw a particular ultimate end so ardently that he almost thought he could prove it and condemn the dissenter logically as well as ethically. What he considered a normal ultimate end became for him the ideal ultimate end. As everyone knows, that end was the principle, greatest happiness of the greatest number, of which Bentham speaks with the reverence of religious belief.[6]

Now the proposition that everyone seeks happiness might be considered as a factual assertion although it can be made true only at the expense of being made a tautology. But there is no real "force" that tends to realize the greatest happiness of the greatest number of people which has therefore to be realized, if at all, as a by-product of "forces" aiming at other goals. This is in fact what Bentham tried to deduce from the action of unfettered self-interests in a way so uncritical as to arouse the just criticism of the historical school. These critics were, however, primarily moved to contempt by the philosophy of life that was at the back of his value judgments and by that union of rationalism and hedonism which was of the essence of that philosophy: logically, rationalism and hedonism have nothing to do with each other; but Benthamite rationalism is essentially hedonistic, reducing as it does to a logic turning on pleasure and pain, to a logic that makes a last desperate attempt to conquer the world of ultimate ends.

Next, we will cast a glance at Marx. If we took at face value some of his Hegelian professions and then turned to the Master himself in order to allow ourselves to be impressed by the dialectic process by which Reason progresses in the Consciousness of Freedom by thesis, antithesis and synthesis – or by the Idea

[6]Doubtless through ignorance, I am unable to trace that "principle" (*with full realization of its implications*) farther back than to Beccaria's *Dei delitti e delle pene*.

which, having Being, is Nature – and that sort of thing, we might feel that we shall have done all there is to do, if we simply state that we have before us another rationalist system of the kind defined apropos of one comment on the doctrine of the physiocrats. But that would be quite wrong. For Hegelian is only Marx's garb and not the body of his thought. He tells us as much himself in the preface to the second edition of the first volume of *Das Kapital* and the ease with which that garb can be stripped off the body shows conclusively that he did not mistake the nature of his argument. In economics Quesnay and Ricardo, in sociology a number of French historians have left much clearer traces in his writings than Hegel's thought did as distinguished from Hegel's phraseology.

Marx primarily envisages a process of social evolution. The protagonist in this process is the struggle of classes, and all other factors in it are strictly impersonal too. Even economic value is carefully made so, even the labor force is. The conceptual schema is *intended* to be severely objective. Rationality enters the process to be described, in the first instance, merely as observer's rationality – it is the observer who, rationally analyzing, *understands* how blind and chaotic forces, like geological eruptions procreate and disrupt one state of society after another until the socialist goal shall be reached. But this goal is not a teleological one nor one to be realized because it is a worthwhile ideal. That was the view of what Marx felt to be "utopian" socialism from which he was anxious to distance his own, the "scientific" socialism – the socialism which is to be understood, by means of scientific analysis, as the necessary outcome of the observed social process.[7]

Nevertheless, rational schemata enter the Marxian structure by several doors. The two most important ones may be noted. First, rational patterns are implied in many of his statements even if they are not made explicit. For instance, among the conditions under which his law of value would directly apply to actual relative prices, is the condition that all commodities are produced according to the rules of economic rationality – all firms behaving according to the ordinary classical schema as it would work out in perfect competition. This might, however, be objective rationality only. Second, when Marx attempts to explain how resources are allocated in such a way as to equalize the rate of profit on total capital he again argues from conditions of perfect competition. But in doing so he uses language which strongly suggests that he is thinking of the subjective rationality of actors who bring about that equal rate because they imagine (sich einbilden) that this must be so.

An astounding performance remains to be mentioned – it is astounding if we consider the mentality of his time and the success with which, in this point, he anticipated later thought. The word rationalization has by now acquired other meanings, but one type of rationalization and its baleful influence on the analysis

---

[7]Barring the one definite goal, his theory may in fact, as he himself suggested, be likened to that of Darwin. At any rate, he conceived of evolution not in a rationalist spirit but in the spirit of empirical science. Of course, evolution *may* also be looked upon as transcending the means of empirical science (*évolution créatrice*) and Marx and Darwin may both be wrong. I believe they are. But that is another matter.

of social phenomena he perceived with unsurpassable clearness – the type referred to as ideologies. He never ceased to preach that people invariably misconceive the events of their own time and that they do so not at random but in a systematic way: they look upon their struggles as struggles about some ideals or values and never get at the social realities below. Now, these ideologies are mostly rational schemata devised in order to marshal events into readily understandable units. To point out their treacherous character, to uncover what underlies them, to show up one kind of disservice that attempts at analysis by means of rational schemata may render – all that meant a great step forward. Such fire is dangerous to kindle however. It may well be that it burns more things than Marx had intended it to burn, and that the class struggles by which he meant to replace what he considered as pseudo-explanations, are after all nothing but another ideology.

Finally, a word or two should be said about the use of rational models by the economists who, mostly in a derogatory sense, are now looked upon as "classics." Into the modern phase I will not enter because advance, destructive and constructive, is rapid enough to have produced chaos for the time being much as – *si licet parva componere magnis* – it has done in physics. Suffice it then to say that in spite of the spread of the analysis that, as mentioned before, work with time-series material and with concepts designed to fit corresponding theoretical requirements, rational models in our sense have not gone out of fashion entirely. The theory of monopolistic competition, the theory of economic behavior oriented on profits over time, the theory of location and other examples could be cited in support of that statement. The only thing I should like to advert to is that modern schemata of rationality in action increasingly tend to strip the "rational" patterns of a connotation so obvious in older theory: older theory almost invariably implied that if a firm acted according to the rational pattern, such action would in fact tend to realize the goal it aimed at or, at least, would not fire back upon the actor. We are less optimistic about that and still less so about the rationality of the *social* results of rational business action.

But we will confine ourselves to the state of things in, say, 1900 or thereabouts. Very roughly, methods and results of economics may, as of that year, be identified with the teachings of Alfred Marshall and of Knut Wicksell.

Both used rational schemata very liberally and without displaying any symptoms of doubts or of compunction. Marshall indeed professed to study humanity in its ordinary business pursuits and actually did provide tools and suggestions for the handling of deviations from rationality. All the same a rational schema, or rather a system of rational schemata for the behavior of individual households and firms, is the skeleton of Marshallian economics – the skeleton worked out much more fully by Léon Walras. Interrelations between these schemata supply the "social" results. The same holds for Wicksell.

Both also expressed themselves in a way which suggests excessive reliance on *subjective* rationality. Marshall's producers "each governed under the sway of free competition by *calculations* (my italics) of his own interest will *endeavor* (my italics) so to regulate the amount of any commodity ... that this amount shall be just capable on the average of finding purchasers ... at a remunerative price." His speculators analyze situations rationally on the basis of strictly logical considerations. His savers save under the influence of forethought, rationality of which is implied. And so on.

Much (though not all) of this could no doubt be formulated in terms of objective rationality and freed from the hypothesis of subjective conscious rationality. But it is fair to suppose that this distinction did not occur to either Marshall or Wicksell and that they simply identified the two. After all, though conscientious and neat analysts, they were in no mind to bother about epistemological niceties. And they paid the penalty for this, as they did for language suggestive of hedonist premises.[8] Institutionalist critique in this country, not staying to ask how much of all that was essential and how much only a façon de parler, bombed the whole structure on those grounds – with more success than was fair.

It should be observed that the reform primarily associated with the name of Pareto, though it did much to remove the hedonist stigma and though it reduced the emphasis on conscious rationality quite a lot, yet retained in service the objective rational schema.[9] And this turned around the profit motive. We have, it is true, seen that it is not essential for the applicability of the hypothesis of rationality in action to assume any particular end. But in practice, it is almost necessary to construct a rational schema with a view to a single end – otherwise the construct loses its main raison d'être, simplicity. Hence the *homo economicus* turned up again. Marshall obviously did not like him. But Pareto accepted him, comforting us with the assurance that another time we would consider the *homo religiosus*, the *homo eroticus*, and so on in turn. This, however, only shows up a very serious limitation. Even if I could – I cannot – visualize the laborious life of a *pure* homo eroticus, any attempt at combination of all those homines would only serve to show, by the absence of any rational rule of combination, that life is ontologically irrational, at least as much as "nature."

[8]Those, of course, are still more in evidence with Jevons who had no hesitation about talking, in the best Benthamite form, about economies as "calculus of pleasure and pain."

[9]Removal of the utility concepts did not, so I think in spite of what one should think at first blush, alter the situation in the respect in which we are interested.

Discussions on the Meaning of Rationality in Action

(Unknown Author)

I. Schumpeter on *Rationality in Economics*

October 27 and November 13, 1939

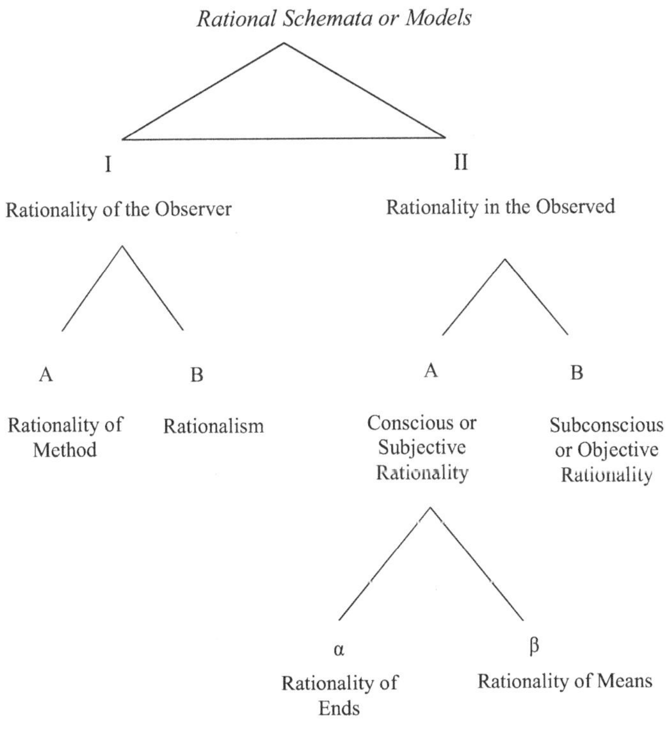

This contribution is published with permission of the Harvard University Archives, Talcott Parsons Papers.

H. Staubmann, V. Lidz (eds.), *Rationality in the Social Sciences*,
DOI 10.1007/978-3-319-62377-1_3

No claim is made for the above schema except that it is a convenient skeleton for the speaker's comments. Criticism is nevertheless invited and one made by *Haberler* may be mentioned at once: Rational behavior of the observer is, of course, not less required sub II than sub I where it stands alone.

The division I A simply stands for the class of all cases in which there is no suggestion of any rationality being attributed to the subject matter of research. In the discussion the points have been raised what the criteria of rationality of the observer's behavior are, how this rationality can be tested and whether it differs from truth of the result. But these points, however interesting, are not really germane to the subject of these discussions.

In *I A* belong all the methods of the physical sciences in the term's widest acceptance. But there are problems and methods in the social sciences and in particular in economics that can be treated in the same way. The example has been given of a study of the behavior relatively to each other of the time series of price level and some rate of interest. Certain relations can be established and certain prognoses can be made without any assumption about human behavior in general or rationality of human behavior in particular. To this *Parsons* replied that further analysis would inevitably lead up to both. That is so. But this doesn't seem to impair the significance of the fact that a theory of the contour lines of the economic process, though possibly only an inadequate one, could be constructed in that way, and that the problem of rationality in action does not enter into all economic models.

Division *I B* has been inserted only to be dismissed. By rationalism, the speaker intended to indicate the philosophical view, that there is underlying the empirical cosmos an order or plan that is rational from any of very many standpoints. One of these standpoints is indicated by God's purpose and on the other end of the scale there is the metaphysical belief in universal determinateness which is as religious in character as any other such belief. Teleology was mentioned in this connection. It is the connecting link between *I A* and *I B*. Its heuristic value is great enough to comfort us in many cases in the face of the fact that there is no methodological foundation for it.

Division *II A α* owes its existence to the fact that we often formulate value judgments about ultimate ends. For instance many of us call it reasonable if a government strives for access to the sea and unreasonable if it strives for victory for victory's sake. Ends incident to an ascetic view of life some people call unreasonable as they would also call the wish for immediate enjoyment regardless of the hygienic consequences. In economics such judgments abound and it is, therefore, necessary to emphasize that they cannot have any place in science except as subjects of research and explanatory argument: it is, of course, perfectly legitimate to try to explain why certain people in certain environments should develop just those ultimate ends which they happen to have and no others.

Sweezy raised the question whether there are any ultimate ends. The answer given was that the analysis of ends and values never leads up to anything else but other ends or values, and that in the nature of things such a recursus cannot be infinite or circular.

Pettie raised the objection why an ascetic should not be voted irrational if a madman is. The answer is that the madman is not voted irrational unconditionally but only in two cases: first, if his behavior or argument rests on assertions of fact which can be proved to be not true; second, if his inference from those facts does not proceed according to the rules of logic. Thus a man suffering, say, from depressive mania is not necessarily irrational if he doesn't assert non-existent facts but simply takes an abnormally gloomy view of them and thereupon reacts with corresponding violence. Irrational, however, is the madman suffering from paranoia, the sort of man who will for instance reason: "The world is a camel because I have killed my child."

Heading *II A β*. The rationality of means, in German - *Zweckrationalität*, is of course the main center and domicile of what may be termed the hypothesis of rationality in economics. It raises the question how far economic behavior is as a matter of fact governed by conscious rational processes of the mind. In judging the use of this hypothesis if actually made in economics the following points must be observed.

(1) The heuristic value of this hypothesis is of course very great. The falling stone can only be observed, man in action can be understood.
(2) In order to use the hypothesis it is not necessary to assume that people actually observe the rules of rationality in all cases and to 100 per cent. It is only necessary to assume that they attempt to do so and that a theoretical model embodying the rule of rationality will be sufficiently significant to serve as a norm, elucidating the logic of what people want to do.
(3) This raises the question of deviations whose quantitative importance is an essential object of research. Some important classes may be mentioned:

(a) Errors are one such class, the relevant question with respect to them being how far they can be treated as errors in the statistical sense and how far they tend to cumulate on the one hand and to occur mass-wise on the other.
(b) From error in this sense must be distinguished systematically faulty practice. For instance the methods in actual use of providing for the depreciation of durable assets, machinery, for example, are practically all of them indefensible from the standpoint of rationality. What then is the meaning of setting up a rational model for this if it has nothing to do with actual practice?
(c) Since it has been held that there is no meaning to value judgments about ultimate ends, a firm may look extremely irrational to the engineer or efficiency expert and yet be perfectly rational from the standpoint of the owner-manager who wants an easy life. This type of case is extremely serious because it tends to obscure the practical distinction between what is rational and what not.

(4) In appraising rationality it is essential to get hold of the right period of time, that is the period with reference to which the individual under observation means to act. Behavior that would constitute evident deviation from rationality if a man wants to maximize his profits for the current month, might be perfectly rational

if he is thinking of a decade. Like most of these points this is also very important for the purpose of political interpretation.

(5) Inadequate interpretation in general and a mistaken appraisal of rationality in action in particular often results not only from an ignorance of the purposes the acting individual intends to serve, but also from misjudging the data which were actually before that individual. An economic instance of the first type is the principle many business men profess of always charging average total costs. This may easily seem irrational even in cases in which it is not so at all. For instance, in the case of unpopular big concerns, which have a strong motive to follow a policy which is justified in the eyes of the man in the street. In passing we may notice those interesting cases in which behavior, perfectly rational from the standpoint of an individual firm, will lead to results that are highly irrational from the standpoint of all the firms taken together.

Under *II B* are the cases in which behavior will fit a rational schema, which according to such tests as it is in our power to apply are not present in the mind of the acting individual. For instance it is a well-known theorem that the output which will maximize net gain is the one that corresponds to the intersection of his marginal revenue and marginal cost curves. It is sometimes held that nothing is farther from the mind of a business man than trying to find that point of intersection. But this is quite unnecessary. If the business man merely wants to make money his behavior will fit that rational schema. The reason for this is of course that experience is handed to us not by the rational procedures of the classroom but in the form of rules of the thumb which we never bother to analyze but which may be perfectly rational all the same. That is why we cannot as a rule hope to arrive at the meaning of anyone's behavior and of the *Sinnzusammenhang* involved, by the naive method of interviewing people. But the range of rational schemata, nevertheless, reaches much farther than we would believe at first sight.

From the standpoint of those principles, brief analyses were offered of the physiocratic and the Benthamite system, of the teaching of Karl Marx, and of more modern methods of handling rational schemata. In the opinion of the speaker of the objections on principle against rationalism in the sense defined and against over-estimation of the range of conscious rationality in action can be taken account of satisfactorily and the essential results, even of older doctrines, are not substantially affected by them. The general philosophy of the natural order of the physiocrats can be brushed aside and all that really matters in their teaching can still be retained. But the fundamental difficulty of rational interpretations still remains: since on the one hand that rationality can only be rationality from the standpoint of the acting individual and since on the other hand the rational schema of his behavior can only be constructed by the observer, the procedure presupposes, first, that on principle there is meaning to our trying to place ourselves on the standpoint of another human being, possibly one that lived long ago in a completely different cultural environment and, secondly, that as a matter of fact we can successfully do so.

Further Points from the Discussion

Parsons emphasized the distinction between rationality of procedure and rationality of the product. He also said that the distinction between conscious and non-conscious did not seem to him important from the standpoint of an operational attitude. As long as the rational coat fits it is a matter of indifference whether the observed individual ontologically acts rationally or not.

McGranahan argued against chains of valuations.

Bergson made the rationality of a proposition about relations depend on the use to be made of that relation.

Gordon pointed out that the above definition of the rationality of the observer is not applicable to the rationality in the observed. Another remark of his which the reporter remembers to have thought important can unfortunately not be reconstructed from his notes. The same is, he regrets to state, true of *Leontief's* contributions to the discussion.

Schickele commented on certain difficulties incident to the concept of rational procedure and gave spurious correlation as an example. He also insisted on the philosophical character of the problem of the relation between a model and reality. He also held that philosophical standpoints are necessarily implied in the way in which we select our data.

An Approach to the Analysis of the Role of Rationality in Social Action

Talcott Parsons

The concept of rationality as here treated is part of a generalized conceptual scheme which is applicable to problems in the description and analysis of systems of human action in society. Insofar as action is conceived in these terms, the central point of departure is the conception of choice between alternative courses of action. The conception of choice itself implies that in some sense the probable consequences of two or more alternative courses of action are foreseen or predicted. If such prediction is conceived as rational, it is arrived at by the application of "empirical knowledge". Knowledge in this sense may range all the way from the crudest common sense to the most refined technical science. It seems, however, that its core can always be treated as consisting on one hand of statements of observable fact, subject to empirical verification, and of logical reasoning. One of the important criteria of logical adequacy of knowledge is the precision or lack of ambiguity of concepts and propositions. Furthermore, knowledge that consists of more than one proposition is rational only insofar as the various propositions that make up the content of knowledge are logically consistent. Hence, perhaps, the three criteria of verifiability by observation, precision and consistency, are the primary criteria of the rationality of knowledge.

Mere prediction of the probable consequences of proposed alternatives is not, however, a sufficient basis of choicc. It is, in addition, necessary to have criteria on the basis of which one alternative is preferred to another. This involves some kind of normative standards that define the grounds of preference. It is perhaps sufficient for present purposes to say that choice involves the balancing of "advantages" or "utility" in Pareto's "sociological" sense, and "disadvantages" or "cost." The analysis of what underlies these conceptions is decidedly complex, but at least a satisfactory general outline can be worked out in terms of the theory of social

This contribution is published with permission of the Harvard University Archives, Talcott Parsons Papers.
The author was deceased at the time of publication.

H. Staubmann, V. Lidz (eds.), *Rationality in the Social Sciences*,
DOI 10.1007/978-3-319-62377-1_4

action. It may be said here merely that utility involves a normative component or, in other words, an element of "value" and an affective component, the two being, in the rational case, integrated with one another. Much the same is true of cost, except that the value component enters in a negative role. It is the sacrifice of potential values that constitutes cost. The structure of affects or emotions, on the other hand, appears to be of a polar character, so that cost may involve both the sacrifice of positive emotional satisfaction, and the incurring of negative affects, such as "pain."

Rational choice, then, is on the one hand a process of the application of empirical knowledge to the clarification of alternative courses of action and their consequences. On the other hand, in the light of this knowledge, and of the balancing of utility and cost, the rational choice is the one that yields the most favorable utility-cost balance. It cannot be adequately described either as the maximization of utility or the minimization of cost, since neither element can be isolated from the other.

There is probably a sense in which the concept of rationality thus defined implies "free will." Its use in this manner, however, is not a matter of deduction from a metaphysical theory of the will. On the contrary, the definition of choice is theoretical in the scientific sense and is analogous to that of force in mechanics. It is no more necessary for us to know what the will "really is" than it is for the physicist to know what force "really is." The primary relevance of philosophy to this conceptual scheme is negative. It is quite true that it is incompatible with purely "mechanistic" metaphysics, which defines all reality as a mechanical system in the Newtonian sense.

Of considerably greater scientific significance than the question of free will is the fact that rational choice implies what may be called the "normative orientation" of action. This is true in two different senses. On the one hand, the conception of rational knowledge is of a normative character. By no means all propositions that purport to be of empirical application constitute empirical knowledge. They may be erroneous on the level of observation or may involve ambiguities and logical inconsistency. Hence, in this sense, to act rationally is, so far as knowledge is relevant, to conform with the norm of "truth." Rational action is oriented to norms, secondly, in that the criteria of choice as between correctly understood alternatives involve reference to normative patterns, notably to the values which the actor accepts as binding. It follows from this fact that a description of the course of rational action may be used in either of two ways. It may itself be a normative pattern, setting forth what in a given situation and from a given point of view *ought* to be done. On the other hand, it may be used in an explanatory context to contribute to the explanation of what has been done or probably will be done. This double significance of the conceptual scheme of action runs through all phases of it.

Seen from this point of view, rationality is essentially a mode of organization or of integration of the elements of a system of action. It is a way in which different elements are related to each other in certain ways that we describe as "comparing" and "balancing." It follows from this way of looking at the problem that there are three different kinds of limitations on rationality. In the first place, action may be "irrational," i.e., it may *deviate* from the pattern that is normatively defined as a rational pattern. Insofar as, in terms of the relevant values, criteria of empirical knowledge and situational data, the actor may be said to accept the normative pattern as binding and yet his action fails to conform with it, he is acting irrationally.

Secondly, there is the question of the scope of the system which may be considered to be organized or integrated in this way. The fact that a system is limited in rationality through the removal of certain elements of it from any process of balancing in relation to advantage is not a sufficient basis for calling it irrational, unless there is ground for imputing a normative pattern that would include these elements to the actor. One extremely important case of this type of limitation of scope is that in which certain elements relevant to action are "traditional," i.e., are accepted as fixed and not subject to calculations of utility and cost.

Third, it is logically inherent in the conception of rationality here advanced that the ultimate elements which are rationally organized in a system of action are not themselves rational, nor, of course, are they irrational. They are simply "given" from the point of view of analysis in terms of rationality. It is convenient to borrow Pareto's term in this connection and refer to them as "non-logical." A minimum catalogue of the logically essential non-logical elements of any rational system must include, on the one hand, the facts of the situation in which the actor is placed, on the other, the primary ideal patterns or modes of normative orientation which are binding for him. The latter includes specifically defined ultimate ends, various types of regulatory patterns, or systems of rules, and diffuser "value attitudes" which, while not describing specific mode of action, define general directions and exclude some possible modes as incompatible with them. These non-logical elements of rational systems do not, however, become significant to action except in a close relation of interdependence with the elements of rationality. In the first place, the facts of the situation do not enter into rational systems, except insofar as they are empirically known. Furthermore, even though a system of ultimate ends and values is not as such a system of empirical knowledge, it involves a cognitive element which is subject to rational standards, notably of precision and consistency. Finally, it is a matter of empirical experience that systems of ultimate ends and values are closely interdependent with systems of cognitive orientation to the non-empirical aspects of human experience. This involves, on the one hand, ideas that we would class as systems of metaphysics and ontology, on the other hand, ideas centering about the various aspects of the "problem of meaning," of which the "problem of evil" may be taken as an example.

There are a variety of different levels on which the conceptual scheme of rationality may be employed. The problem is always that of the significance of rational elements in understanding variations as between different individual cases of action. Sometimes on a relatively concrete level, certain elements do not come within the scope of the rational system at all, but must be treated as non-logical elements of the "definition of the situation". This would be true, for instance, of the kind of basic attitude toward vocational activity that has, on the one hand, been dominant in China, on the other hand, in the modern western world. Most actors, indeed, are totally unaware that these elements could possibly be subject to rational consideration. But seen in terms of a sufficiently broad comparative historical perspective, it becomes clear that they are variable over a wide range and that this variation is related to the fact that, at certain points in their history, they have been significantly included within the range of the rational mode of organization of the systems in question. It is thus clear that the scope of the rationality of a system of action is not determined on an ontological basis, but will differ according to the character of the problem and the perspective in which it is treated.

So far, however, as a system can be analyzed in terms of rationality at all, rationality is to be treated as a mode of integration of the system as a whole. It is impossible to define cost in either the technological or the economic sense without reference to the whole system that is treated as in any sense rational, and to its basic data on both the situational and the normative sides.

Pareto's theory of social utility may be considered to be an attempt to formulate the concept of a total social system of rational action, including its non-logical elements.

1. He takes the most elementary "technological" level of analysis for granted. He starts his own explicit discussion on the economic level, which presupposes that action is rationally integrated in relation to a coherent system of ends for each individual.
2. He then points out that the doctrine of maximum satisfaction involves certain non-economic assumptions that define a particular mode of interpersonal integration of the social system.
3. To approach a more generalized social statement, it is necessary to drop this assumption. When this is done, it is possible in purely economic terms to define what he calls a maximum of ophelimity *for* a collectivity. This, relative to a process of change, is a point up to which the ophelimity of every individual increases, but beyond which further change in the same direction would increase the ophelimity for some individuals, but decrease it for others. It is treated as a maximum, regardless of the numbers of persons on each side. On the economic level, he says, the concept of a maximum of ophelimity *of* the collectivity as a unit is nonsensical.
4. The conception of the maximum of utility as distinguished from ophelimity *for* a collectivity involves the integration of its members on a distributive level. Put somewhat differently, it is only meaningful insofar as there is a distributive standard, according to which it is held to be *just* that one individual or group should receive while others do not, or that divisible goods should be distributed according to any particular rule, whether it involves equality or any particular kind of inequality. Such a standard cannot be derived from considerations of economic rationality, but must be treated from this point of view as a non-logical datum.
5. A standard of distributive justice would be part of a system of normative orientation, but for Pareto's purposes this is not sufficient to define a social system. In addition, it is necessary to consider what is involved in the conception of a maximum of utility *of* a collectivity considered as a unit. This conception apparently involves, in addition to those already treated, two other elements. On

the one hand, there are those elements that are essentially necessary for the survival of the collectivity as a unit, in respects which cannot be analytically segregated as applying to the survival of the members distributively. Thus, there are factors affecting the survival of a state or nation as a unit which cannot be allocated to its individual members. The great majority of the members might survive, while the state is destroyed. On the other hand, there is an element that is formulated by Pareto as "the end which a society pursues." This is essentially a matter of *common* values, in which the individual members of the community participate, but which cannot be said to be values of the individuals as individuals. Thus, to take the political example again, the various citizens of a state participate in its prestige, but that prestige cannot be distributed among them.

This is an exceedingly condensed sketch of Pareto's scheme. It is, to my knowledge, by far the most ambitious attempt to achieve a generalized formulation of a total social system of rational action in the literature. It should, however, be clearly realized that even this is abstract in relation to concrete social systems, for there is a great deal of evidence that rationality is only one of the modes in which systems of action are integrated. The attempt to fit action in such fields as religion, magic, art and perhaps various others entirely into the conceptual scheme of rationality, results in severe distortion of the facts and gross misinterpretations. It is one of the principal factors responsible for the wide currency of anti-intellectualist theories that purport to demonstrate the predominant irrationality of most of human action. Much of what has been interpreted as irrational is better treated as non-logical.

Rationality in Action: (Discussion Protocol of the) Meeting of Monday, Feb. 19, 1940

Donald V. McGranahan

The speaker having first summed up his argument presented to the meeting of February 12, it will be useful to re-state a few of the points that were made then. The rationality of the acting individual refers primarily to his thinking and only in the second place to his action or behavior. Moreover, it proved necessary to distinguish strictly between rationality and truth (=objective validity as understood by the observer). Conclusions can, in a rational way be derived from irrational premises, and something that is false can be true from the standpoint of false premises, which fact offers an alternative theory of primitive thought. On the other hand, it has been stressed that rational habits and command of factual information have, after all, something to do with ultimate values because ignorance gives free sway to emotionality. To contrast rationality considered as thinking determined by reason and irrationality considered as thinking determined by emotion, was thus seen to be a doubtful matter. The rationalizing effect of the task motive, which works towards solution in terms of logical and empirical means, was particularly recognized and so was the anti-rational tendency of any other kind of motive. The material of irrational thought was divided into an affective and into a pseudo-explanatory group. Wishful thinking.

Pseudo-explanations were divided into rationalizations (comments by Trotter and Jones), ideologies and derivations, the latter concept lacking the element of repression that enters more or less into the former two.

Methods for discovering "real" motives behind rationalizations and ideologies:

1. The psycho-analytic method working through free association.
2. The method of eliminating the condition which accounts for the wish to repress.
3. The method of observing the individual or group under study for a prolonged period, when it will very often become obvious whether a given declaration of

---

This contribution is published with permission of the Harvard University Archives, Talcott Parsons Papers.
The author was deceased at the time of publication.

H. Staubmann, V. Lidz (eds.), *Rationality in the Social Sciences*,
DOI 10.1007/978-3-319-62377-1_5

motive is consistent with the general picture of the individual's or group's reactions or not. Sometimes the mere perception of the existence of a strong motive other than that implied in the argument put forth will be sufficient. It must not be forgotten, however, that it is sometimes precisely the ideal motives that are repressed and also that, objectively, self-interest is something so subtle and elusive, and works so differently according to the period of time for which consequences are taken into account, that difficult problems of interpretation may arise even in the most favorable cases.

The speaker expressed the opinion that pseudo-explanatory statements always rest on one or more of the following four conditions:

1. Limitation by ignorance: inadequacy of explanation is in this case due to the individual's lacking the necessary background, although within his limitations he may think correctly. Thus primitive thought has fewer rules and hence fewer restrictions.
2. Conscious deception (lying; propaganda).
3. Emotional fixation, not involving repression.
4. Rationalization: The actual reason is here known or knowable but repressed, and another is offered that is believed to be more acceptable. These rationalizations often prove highly variable and this element of variability connects them with ideologies and derivations. The fact, however, of the frequent presence of actual multiplicity of motivation will generally stand in the way of our finding a single motive that is being repressed or otherwise removed from the surface.

Pareto stresses the need for logical explanation. A discussion arose on the question whether this need should be primarily interpreted as a need for justification, particularly for justification in the face of challenge. Against this view was urged the fact of scientific or simply idle curiosity (Veblen's instinct of idle curiosity; the child worrying about the causes of everything). There is also the element of anxiety in the face of the dangers harbored by the environment (Malinowski's theory of religion).

There was discussion on the meaning and interval of application of the Marx-Engels theory of ideologies. Although ideology does not necessarily imply this, Marxian ideologies are essentially systems of explanations which are not true or at least do not go to the bottom of things. The real nature of historical struggles is in this sense always veiled by their representation as struggles over values. The value systems, according to the theory, merely express and justify conditions or actions. Of course this meaning of ideology has nothing to do with ideology in the sense of normative systems, or in the sense of Weber's ideal types.

The Role of Ideas in the Extension and Limitation of Rationality

Wilbert E. Moore

In the comparative studies of various cultures it is a commonplace observation that rational thought and action[1] are not everywhere equally extensive. A variety of more or less general explanations of this observable variation have been advanced, some of which it will be necessary to examine in the course of the present discussion. But throughout the literature dealing with the comparative study of social systems, there is scarcely any mention of the possibility that certain basic ideas to be found within the cultures examined might have some relation to the relative importance of norms of rationality in the society.

The role of ideas in relation to action may be approached from numerous points of view. Among these at least two may be distinguished.

1. The relation between "ideas" and concrete "means" and "ends". Several possibilities of relationship may be briefly indicated.
   (a) Ideas may involve specific ends in rational action within an institutional framework. For example, the "advancement of science" or "preservation of learning" may stand as more ultimate, and diffuse, ends or culture goals, held in justification of systems of rational action.
   (b) Ideas of a general or diffuse nature may limit possible variation in concrete ends, yet depend upon institutional definitions of the situation and normative prescriptions for determination of what the given concrete ends within these limits shall be. An example of this type of relationship may be found in the "ethical valuation of the individual." Such a general idea stands in no neatly determinate relationship to particular institutional structures. Yet if such an

This contribution is published with permission of the Harvard University Archives, Talcott Parsons Papers.

The author was deceased at the time of publication.

[1]The criteria of rationality developed in Professor Schumpeter's paper are adopted in this discussion.

H. Staubmann, V. Lidz (eds.), *Rationality in the Social Sciences*,
DOI 10.1007/978-3-319-62377-1_6

idea be widely held as a basis for social relationships, limitations are imposed on possible variations in concrete structure of the society, beyond which limits the goals or institutional patterns will be recognized as manifestly out of harmony with the diffuse sentiment. It may be pointed out in passing that the more general and abstract the idea the less determinate is its relation to and bearing on the concrete social structure, and the more probable that *conflicting* concrete interests and claims to loyalty may be offered as in keeping with or as contributing to the diffuse sentiment.[2]

(c) Ideas, notably religious ideas, may limit possible variation in concrete action in reference to them through a (more or less arbitrary) symbolic fitness of means to ends. Thus, a wide variety of religious systems include forms of ritual washing to symbolize spiritual cleansing. It may be noted that such "symbolically appropriate" ritual actions in reference to ideas in the realm of the sacred involve analogies of both idea and action to a concrete means-end relationship in the profane world.

2. The basic mode of orientation to the empirical world. It is this problem which is of chief interest in the present discussion. The question of chief interest then becomes that of the role of ideas in determining the concretely observable variation in importance of rational action and the norm of rationality in various social systems. This may have implications for the problem of using the criteria of rationality in the analysis of social action, and perhaps make possible an indication of some of the additional areas into which it is necessary to move.

The question immediately to be considered therefore is that of the influence of the basic orientation or "system of truth" upon the orientation of the actor to his situation and various specific ends. This question may be approached in at least a preliminary way by reference to some of the empirical evidence on the extension and limitation of rationality in several societies, in relation to certain features of the "basic orientation" to the empirical world prevailing in the respective societies. The first instructive body of evidence which may be considered concerns the extent of rationality in "primitive" (relatively simple and non-literate) societies.

One extreme interpretation of the importance of rationality in primitive society has now largely gone by the boards. This interpretation may be styled the primitive struggle-for-existence theory. Simply stated, this view holds that of all living people, the primitives or savages, having small material resources and meager technology, must of necessity be continuously engaged in wresting the minimum essentials for existence out of the soil. According to this view the primitive is the type economic man. Civilization is then explained by the "surplus" theory, that is, that the non-economic interests of civilization depend upon the accumulation of an economic surplus and a leisure class. This view has a certain ethnocentric

[2]*Cf.* Wilbert E. Moore, *Slavery, Abolition, and the Ethical Valuation of the Individual: a Study of the Relations between Ideas and Institutions*, unpublished doctoral thesis, Harvard University, 1940.

plausibility, but unfortunately fits *no* available evidence concerning primitive behavior. For example, even among the native Australians, who apparently have the most meager material level of living known, the social structure includes a large variety of non-economic elements, including religious rituals and ceremonial dancing.[3]

Faced with this type of evidence, certain theorists adopted another interpretation which in some respects is at the opposite pole from the first. This we may call the theory of "undifferentiated irrationality" among primitives. Its most extreme formulation has come from the pen of Lucien Lévy-Bruhl. In a series of books, the basic thesis of which remains the same,[4] Lévy-Bruhl has maintained the position that primitive mentality may be aptly characterized by the term "pre-logical". Briefly stated, Lévy-Bruhl's position is that the primitive does not think logically, but rather mystically and symbolically. The primitive pushes the law of agreement beyond its proper bounds, and is unaware of the law of contradiction. Chance associations between elements of the empirical world are thought to be due to a mystical connection, and magical actions designed to control these elements rely upon "contagion". Now, aside from the linear evolutionary bias revealed in Lévy-Bruhl's very terminology, some further remarks may be made in regard to this general theory. Dr. McGranahan has previously suggested in this group that the theory may have some validity in so far as the primitive has fewer laws or principles of logic, and is therefore freer to think emotionally.[5] Accepting this suggestion for the moment, we may yet distinguish other variable elements.

It may very well be true – in fact, certainly is true – that the "horizon" of the primitive actor in reference to factual information is more limited than is generally true in modern Western society. In view of the very real necessity of making *some* orientation to meaningful[6] aspects of the empirical world, it may therefore be

[3]*Cf.* W. Lloyd Warner, *A Black Civilization*, New York, Harper and Bros., 1937. It has been one of the services of the "functionalists" among the anthropologists to indicate the importance of the interrelation of various aspects of the social organization in primitive societies, and the high importance of rituals, traditions, and myths in maintaining group solidarity.

[4]*Cf.*, for example, *L'expérience mystique et les symboles chez les primitifs*, Paris, F. Alcan, 1938; *Primitive Mentality*, New York, The Macmillan Co., 1923; *The Soul of the Primitive*, London, Allen and Unwin, 1928; *Le surnaturel et la nature dans la mentalité primitive*, Paris, F. Alcan, 1931.

[5]See also D. V. McGranahan, "The Psychology of Language," *Psychological Bulletin*, 33: 178-216, 1936.

[6]This is a necessary qualification which is too often overlooked by ordinary "environmentalist" discussions. Even in regard to modern science, the concrete data of the empirical world are for all practical purposes inexhaustible. For the layman in *any* society, only certain, and often fairly limited, aspects of external reality require modes of adjustment or control. It is also necessary, of course, to distinguish levels of knowledge and control. The knowledge of primitives in regard to food supply, habits of game animals, seasons, etc., is often *more* detailed than is that of the ordinary layman in Western society, because the former's control over these important elements is less adequate. It is thus paradoxically possible for the primitive to be required to know more, because he has less knowledge at a higher level.

expected that the actor in non-literate society will reach the limits of a rational orientation more quickly – that is, in reference to fewer empirical elements, and, possibly, in reference to a smaller proportion[7] of empirical elements.

It is especially true that in any social system some sort of orientation must be made to those aspects of external reality which involve uncertainty and risk. It is at this point that Lévy-Bruhl's thesis breaks down, for he fails to distinguish types of social action. Much of his data clearly has reference to symbolic and ritual behavior, not to rational action in social systems. Now, in view of the foregoing considerations, it may be proper to expect magical and ritual behavior to appear "sooner" in a primitive society – that is, rational orientation is more quickly exhausted – than in a society with a high development of knowledge and technology.[8] But, in view of a great amount of evidence to the contrary, it would be a mistake to maintain that the primitive neglects rational action, at least in the form of a practical technology. When Lévy-Bruhl turns to the evidence concerning primitive technology, he flounders rather badly and attempts unduly to minimize its importance. It has been one of the chief contributions of Malinowski, Firth, and others to point out that the primitive by no means neglects even economic rationality, and that he pretty clearly distinguishes such action from the non-rational.

A simple example from the work of Malinowski,[9] which may serve to point up the issue, is to be found in canoe-building and canoe-magic in the Trobriand Islands. The evidence is clear that the Trobriander knows well enough that no amount of magic will build a canoe for him. The rational technology of canoe-building, which in turn is related to the economic activity of fishing, is fairly well developed. But the Trobriander also knows that no possible extension of rational orientation will provide control over all important elements in the concrete situation. Among these elements are the weather and the supply of fish. He ekes out his rational orientation with magic and ritual. This is one indication, among many, that the primitive no more lives in a world made up exclusively of spirits or mysterious forces than does the modern man live in a situation to which at all times his adjustment is rational.

The fact that members of primitive societies are in fact expected to conform to the norm of rationality in certain respects does not, of course, mean that the areas of

---

[7]The considerations advanced in the previous note make it clear that there is a possible variation in the number of aspects of the empirical world meaningful to the society as a whole. In general, the less complex the society, the fewer are the aspects of empirical reality to which it is necessary to make an adjustment.

[8]This set of considerations may be one basis for the commonly assumed relationship between ignorance and what we call superstition.

[9]*Cf.*, Bronislaw Malinowski, *Argonauts of the Western Pacific*, New York, E. P. Dutton and Co., 1922; *Coral Gardens and Their Magic*, New York, American Book Co., 1935, 2 Vols.; "Magic, Science, and Religion," in Joseph Needham, ed., *Science, Religion, and Reality*, New York, The Macmillan Co., 1925, pp. 19-84. The relations obtaining between rational and non-rational action in primitive society are perhaps most clearly set forth by Malinowski in his article, "Culture," *Encyclopedia of the Social Sciences*, 4: 621-646, especially pp. 634-639.

orientation covered by the norm of rationality are equally extensive in all societies. The importance of the difference in available knowledge has already been noted. But this alone is not an adequate explanation for observed differences in the extensity of rationality. There are positive limits to the application of rational knowledge, and, *a fortiori*, to the acquisition of that knowledge. This is readily understandable in view of the functional necessity in any society of institutional controls governing systems of rational action.[10]

There is no reason to assume that a rational orientation to the empirical world is any more "natural" or "basic" than the magical or traditional.[11] Thus, *interest* in rationality is of utmost importance in determining the relative weight attached to such an orientation in any society. The supposed "irrationality" of the primitive (which is always limited) is consequently not only a result of inadequate knowledge, but the emphasis upon both knowledge and rational technology are limited in view of a difference in interest.[12]

Since the extension of rational knowledge and techniques is no more natural than the emphasis on other modes of orientation, interest in such extension must be positive. This means that the role of ideas in relation to the emphasis on rationality cannot be interpreted simply as a removal of traditional barriers – the "cake of custom" – to allow the natural progression of science and technology to resume its course. Nor is interest to be taken as given; it is determined by ideas prevalent in the society.

The foregoing line of interpretation is borne out in the examination of other societies. A brief consideration of the "basic orientation" of Chinese thought, which can scarcely in any evolutionary sense be called pre-logical, may clarify the role of

---

[10]Cf. Talcott Parsons, *The Structure of Social Action*, New York, McGraw-Hill Book Co., 1937, pp. 51-125, and *passim*. Raymond Firth has pointed out (*Primitive Polynesian Economy*, London, George Routledge and Sons, 1939, p. 361) that traditional elements of control do not allow the primitive to treat the norm of rationality as the "universal, unique, and dominant imperative" in his adjustment to the empirical world. (*Cf.* also his *Primitive Economics of the New Zealand Maori*, New York, E. P. Dutton and Co., 1929)

Although it is the central thesis of this paper that there are observable differences in the importance attached to rationality in various societies, this is a matter of degree and not of kind. It should be noted that pushing rationality beyond immediate necessities of productive efficiency and cognitive orientation (given a certain functional integration of the social system) need not contribute to greater "efficiency" or social stability, but rather to its opposite. This is associated with the difficulties engendered when social scientists examine non-rational elements of the social structure. Although, ideally, the scientific approach cannot be one of attack, treating sacred things in a profane manner may still be interpreted as contrary to social order. It may perhaps be safely asserted that every society makes certain limitations upon rational knowledge and technique, when this knowledge or technique manifestly runs counter to social order.

[11]Pareto gives extensive documentation of this statement. A large portion of his *Trattato di Sociologia generale* (translated as *The Mind and Society*, New York, Harcourt, Brace and Co., 1935, 4 Vols.) is devoted to a consideration of non-rational theories and actions, and their importance in the social structure.

[12]This has been implicitly recognized by Malinowski in his "Magic, Science, and Religion," loc. cit., p. 36.

the varying emphasis upon rationality. Marcel Granet in his *La pensée chinoise*[13] has pointed out that although the general orientation of the Chinese has many superficial similarities to that of the Western world, it is basically different. The orientation is rationalistic; that is, the focus of interests is not transcendental. But the worldly orientation is definitely limited. Rational action – shrewd, practical, conservative, has become traditionalized within limits, and one does not ask questions beyond those limits. The order of nature is a mystical order (involving the conceptions of Yin and Yang,[14] and the mystical association among directions, winds, seasons, colors, etc.) and the approach of the cultured gentleman to that natural order is anti-analytical. Thus in an old and apparently rationally oriented culture there has been very little development of natural science. Again, therefore, the area of social action which is amenable to analysis according to the criteria of rationality is definitely limited, and the source of this limitation is to be found in the realm of ideas.

The role of ideas in the extension of rationality has been most fully developed in the work of Max Weber.[15] Although it is impossible to review in detail even the main lines of the investigation, it may be noted that Weber found both logical and genetic connections between certain ideas of Protestantism, especially of Calvinism, and the development of modern rational capitalism. The Calvinistic doctrine of salvation by election (predestination) meant that nothing the individual could do would make a difference in his status in eternity. But each individual was expected to glorify God, whether saved or damned. Moreover, the conception arose that God gave signs of election by prospering those who were among the elect. The individual was therefore expected to pursue worldly gain in an impersonal devotion to a calling as a means of finding out about salvation. This mode of orientation Weber called "worldly asceticism" – an active domination over the evil of the world. A shrewdly rational technology was therefore enjoined. Merton has shown[16] that the influence of Protestantism was not confined to economic pursuits, but extended to those learned fields upon which a complicated economic structure depended: in the first instance on science and technology. Great importance was placed on rational knowledge of the world in order to *use* the world for the greater glory of God. The "Protestant Ethic" would thus seem to have a bearing not only upon the great importance attached to economic rationality in our society, but also upon the

[13]Paris, *La Renaissance du Livre*, 1934.

[14]Yin and Yang are terms applied to dichotomous groups of empirical elements. Thus, any observable entity or quality belongs either to one category or the other. They are mutually exclusive and conceived of as opposites.

[15]Max Weber, *The Protestant Ethic and the Spirit of Capitalism* tr. by Talcott Parsons, New York, Scribners, 1930. Cf. Talcott Parsons, op. cit., pp. 500-578, especially pp. 533-538.

[16]Robert K. Merton, *Science, Technology and Society in Seventeenth Century England*, in the series *Osiris*, Vol. IV, part 2, pp. 357-362, Bruges, Belgium, The Saint Catherine Press, 1938. See especially pp. 414-495.

general expectation of a rational orientation to the empirical world, which, in our society, comes close to being a cult of rationality.[17]

This interpretation of the available data has been the center of a good deal of criticism. Some of this is reviewed by R. H. Tawney in his "Foreword" to the translation of *The Protestant Ethic*.[18] One line of criticism maintains that this is not a causal relationship but a functional one. This Weber by no means denied. But another type of criticism denies that ideas had any importance – that is, that the development of modern rational technology and science was "natural," and the associated ideas "mere ideologies." This interpretation not only does not take account of all the available evidence concerning this particular relationship,[19] but also transgresses certain basic considerations previously indicated – namely, it assumes the point to be proved (a point which cannot be proved in view of the evidence), that a rational orientation to the empirical world is "natural," and technology naturally accumulative.

It is not meant, of course, to imply that the "Protestant Ethic" was the sole significant "idea" which has been of importance in the modern Western basic orientation. Certainly older conceptions of an "order of nature," natural law, and philosophical rationalism are important. These elements of the general "climate of opinion," however, are all in the realm of ideas, and are peculiarly Western.

From this too brief survey it may in general be concluded that the amount (or proportion) of social action which is amenable to analysis by the rationality schema is variable between cultures. That is, not only is there a variation in terms of knowledge, and in terms of ignorance and error, but also of the importance of rational action in total social systems. The explanation of this variation in importance is not adequately accomplished by reference to the prevailing store of knowledge and technology itself, but is dependent upon variations in the "interest" in rationality involved in the basic orientations of the societies in question.

These considerations have certain important bearings on the problem of the usefulness of the rationality schema as an analytical tool for the interpretation of concrete social systems, for the schema is dependent upon the actual or imputed rational orientation of the individual actor.[20] In reference to any concrete system of social action it is therefore necessary, for analysis in terms of the mode of

---

[17]This suggests that Pareto's sub-class of residues which he calls the "need for logical developments" (I-ε) may be simply the need for linguistic conformity, which in *our* society emphasizes conformity with the norms of rationality. Pareto himself (*op. cit.*, vol. II, p. 591 [Sec. 974] states that it is not to be found among "savage peoples." *Cf. op. cit.*, Secs. 972-975.

[18]Pp. 1(a)-11.

[19]For example, just as Weber pointed out that the rising *bourgeois* capitalists were drawn from the social classes espousing the various branches of Calvinism, Merton has shown that the religious affiliation of the leaders in science and technology was predominantly Puritan – far beyond chance expectation. *Cf.* Weber, *op. cit.*, pp. 35-46; Merton, *op. cit.*, pp. 471-495.

[20]*Cf.* the discussion of "rationality of the actor" in Professor Schumpeter's essay in this series. It is not meant to imply that this is a limitation upon the scientific observer's rational knowledge about the various modes of orientation prevalent in divergent societies.

orientation, to ask not one, but a series of questions. The more important of these may be indicated in outline form:

I. What action conforms to the criteria of rationality?
II. What action is amenable to analysis in terms of these criteria, but fails to conform?
   A. What are the sources for this lack of conformity?
      1. Ignorance?
      2. Error?
      3. Lack of interest (i.e., orientation of action in conformity with other criteria: traditionalism, ritual, symbolic behavior)?
III. What action is not amenable to judgment in regard to its rationality?[21]
IV. What are the sources and significances of this particular weighting of types of action, in reference to the basic orientation of the entire social system?

Finally, it must be noted that filling out the "answers" to any such outline, however elaborated, will not give anything approaching a complete description of the various social systems, but rather an indication of certain elements and relationships within terms of a particular conceptual scheme: social action. The principal thesis of the present essay has been that in terms of the action schema not only are there variations in the degree of conformity to the norms of rationality of action in various societies, but that these variations can be accounted for in terms of other norms and ideas obtaining in the several societies.

---

[21]In general, action oriented to super-empirical ends, chiefly religious action. Such a mode of orientation is, strictly speaking, *non*-rational.

The Rational Means-End Schema as a Tool for Empirical Analysis of Social Action

Rainer Schickele

A Working Concept of Rationality

Content and Area of the Concept

Using a concept without controlling its two basic dimensions of content and area, is like shooting with blank cartridges: one hears the bang, but fells no game. The content of a concept is designated by the characteristics according to which things are subsumed under it; the area covers all the varieties of things included in it. Content and area of any concept vary in inverse relation: the more characteristics are contained in a concept, the fewer things are included in its area, since the addition of each new criterion excludes a number of things from the concept.

In social science discussions, the amount of confusion traceable to the neglect of these elementary facts concerning the structure of a concept is amazing. Imagine the confusion into which zoologists would plunge if they were to use such terms as homo sapiens, fauna, vertebrates and orang-outang synonymously; yet, this is exactly what we often do in the Social Sciences when we talk about capital, institutions, or rationality.

The content of a concept determines the degree of generality, the level of abstraction, on which it must be operated. For any specific analytical context there exists on the scale of the content-dimension a point where a certain relevant concept has an optimum operational usefulness. Moving from this point in the direction of either higher generality by dropping more and more differentiating criteria and adding more and more things to the area of the concept, or in the

---

This contribution is published with permission of the Harvard University Archives, Talcott Parsons Papers and the North Dakota State University Archives.

The author was deceased at the time of publication.

H. Staubmann, V. Lidz (eds.), *Rationality in the Social Sciences*,
DOI 10.1007/978-3-319-62377-1_7

direction of lower generality by adding criteria and dropping things from its area, is apt to diminish its operational usefulness in the particular problem in question.

Such very general, highly abstract concepts like life, matter, mind, action, society – are very useful for taxonomic purposes, for establishing an intelligible order in the vast complexity of phenomena by means of classification, but their operational value as analytical tools is practically nil. The statements that can be based on them almost necessarily partake of the character of truisms. They form the bulk of the conceptual material which makes up much of the books on "pure" economic theory.

At the other end of the scale of levels of abstraction concepts are found whose content is so large as to include many characteristics irrelevant to the problem under study, and hence to preclude the formulation of generalized functional relationships. They form the bulk of the conceptual material which makes up much of the merely descriptive empirical studies in industrial and agricultural economics as well as in the sociological case studies of recent years.

The content of a concept represents its sharpness as an analytical tool for any given problem. The tools may be too sharp or too dull. Nobody would want to fell trees with a razor blade, or shave with an axe.

The Criteria of Rationality in Social Action

One cannot forge a tool without knowing precisely to what purpose it is to be put. Rationality is a generic term whose specific content must be geared to the purpose it is to serve. A psychologist needs another concept of rationality than a philosopher. For the purpose of this discussion, the concept is to apply to socio-economic empirical phenomena.

In the following, the concept of *rationality* shall refer to those elements in socio-economic *actions* of people which are governed by "*sufficient reason*" applied to problems of *choice*. Rationality implies conscious reasoning from facts upon which to act in deliberate choice between alternative means to attain given ends.[1]

By this definition, "subconscious" rationality is ruled out. Reflexive or traditional elements in action are not covered by our term rational. The appropriateness of means-end relations is, therefore, a necessary, but not sufficient, condition for rationality of action. Pulling my hand away from a hot stove is certainly appropriate to the end of not getting burned, but this action is not rational as it does not involve a

[1]Note the voluntaristic character of rationality. It is meaningless to say that a triangle acts rationally by making its angles add up to 180 degrees; or a stone by falling at a certain rate of acceleration. These are phenomena which must be analyzed by concepts of "natural law", explaining events by "efficient cause" determining mechanistic relationships between factual elements. Similarly, it is meaningless to say that a business man's profits are determined by the variously priced production factors interacting according to certain natural laws (although many distinguished economists came very close to saying just that).

I do not deny that there are higher levels of abstraction where this dichotomy of voluntaristic and "natural" concepts is resolved into uniformities of higher generality; but in this discussion I propose to learn these ultimate epistemological problems of causality and free will alone.

process of reasoning and deliberate choosing. (I ask the reader to gaily join me in jumping the epistemological hurdle of defining the borderlines of consciousness lest we get awkwardly entangled in its meshes).

But we need further restrictions. In order to apply the concept of rationality to empirical phenomena, the appropriateness of means-end relations must be observable, capable of being tested. Hence, means shall be considered "appropriate" if they have a relatively high probability of achieving the ends in the judgment of *both* actor and observer. Hereby, purely "subjective" rationality is ruled out of the area of our concept.

The question arises: how should the differences in horizon, or extent of knowledge, between the actor and the observer be accounted for in the analysis of rationality of action? The answer I suggest is: let us restrict the term rational to cases where the knowledge of relevant facts possessed by the actor and observer is of comparable magnitude, and where both look at the situation essentially from the same viewpoint. If they don't, chances are that the means and ends of the action under consideration are evaluated differently by actor and observer. In such cases, the question should be reformulated, or the evidence drawn upon should be recast until the viewpoints and frames of reference of both actor and observer roughly coincide, before a statement about the rationality of the action is made.

The criterion of testability of the appropriateness of the means to their ends involves another characteristic which restricts the area of rationality still further. The ends of rational actions must be "real", their attainment subject to empirical verification by the observer. Actions directed toward the achievement of transcendental (or "ultimate") ends are thereby excluded from the category of rational action, unless empirically observable ends can be substituted as stand-ins for ultimate ends. This problem will be discussed more fully below.

To summarize: a socio-economic action (or phase of complex action system) shall be called rational, if

(a) the actor applies conscious reasoning from facts to arriving at a deliberate choice between alternative means appropriate to a given end.
(b) the appropriateness of the means can be tested, and their probability of achieving the ends is considered high by both actor and observer.
(c) the degree of attainment of the end is empirically verifiable by the observer and found sufficiently high in the light of the appropriateness of the means employed and other relevant circumstances of the situational context.

This rather narrow definition of rationality is not meant to claim general validity and acceptance. It can be justified only on the ground that it is more useful and convenient than a more general one for the specific purpose of analyzing complex systems of socio-economic action. It coincides fairly well with Pareto's definition of "logical action". To all those actions, or elements of action complexes, whose ends are not objectively verifiable, and which do not involve processes of teleological reasoning, a different set of conceptual tools must be applied.[2]

[2]It is my impression that Pareto left that set of tools in a rather confused and crude state of affairs. He might serve as a warning against toe great a pedantry on the one hand, and too sweeping a use of iridescent terms on the other. See Talcott Parsons, "Structure of Social Action", Ch. V.

The Analytical Significance of the Means-End Schema of Action[3]

The Elements of the Schema

A concrete system of action can be conceived as a complex of "unit-acts" analytically separable, but empirically integrated into an organic whole. Methodologically, the separability of the unit acts rests upon their independent variation within the action system.[4] The independence of these unit-acts need not be, and indeed hardly ever is, existent in the concrete system; it is only necessary that such an independence of variation *within a narrow range* can logically be assumed without departing too far from reality. The "unit-act" is an analytical device, not an empirical fact. It is essential, of course, that the schema of the unit-act is relevant to the problems of the concrete action system under consideration, and that its relations to the system as a whole are appraised throughout the course of the analysis.

For our present purpose, the basic structural elements of the action schema (of a unit-act) are:

(1) the *actor*, which may be an individual or a collective group;
(2) the *end*, which the actor pursues; it should be defined as unambiguously as possible;
(3) the *means*, which are available to the actor for the pursuit of his end. They form that part of the situation which is amenable to his control and manipulation;
(4) the *conditions*, which form that part of the *situation* that lies outside the actor's control and is taken by him as given; they include normative patterns of behavior, institutions, general state of empirical knowledge, technology, economic organization etc.

This is not the place to trace out the epistemological intricacies of such a schema in detail; they are perplexing, indeed. But on the whole I believe they are not so serious as to vitiate its usefulness as an analytical device. A few clarifying comments, however, are indispensable.

This means-end schema is applicable to rational action, as defined in the preceding section, and to a unit-act within a broader system of action. But – and this is all-important – its relation to non-rational action elements and to other unit-acts of the action system must also be subjected to our scrutiny lest our analysis becomes purely formalistic and loses its relevance to the concrete problem in hand. To avoid unmanageable complexity of the analytical operations I suggest that we conceive of the non-rational elements entering the means-end schema by way of the "conditions",

[3]The entire following discussion represents the precipitate of my association with Professor Parsons in his seminars, writings and personal conversations. Whatever merits may be found in the following discourse should be credited to his pioneer work, while the responsibility for its demerits must be put squarely upon me.

[4]See T. Parsons, ibid. p. 737 ff.

and the repercussions of other unit acts entering by way of the "means". That is to say for any empirical phase of a concrete action system under study, (1) such non-rational elements as institutions, traditions, ideologies, and transcendental value systems are thought of as determining or affecting the "conditions" which are not readily controllable by the actor and limit or condition the means and ends of his action; and (2) the ends of other unit-acts are thought of as modifying the "means" of the unit-act under study, by impairing the effectiveness of these means in case of conflicting ends, or accentuating it in case of converging ends.[5]

The Relation of the Unit-Act to the System of Action

The rational means-end schema of the unit-act requires, according to our specific definition of rationality and of the structural elements of the schema, that the end be empirically observable and homogeneous. Any concrete system of social action involves a complex hierarchy of ends where many of the ends, and, indeed, all "ultimate" ones, transcend the possibility of objective verification. This, however, does not mean that all the important actions related to transcendental ends fall outside the pattern of rational behavior. These ultimate ends are the last links of chains of "intermediate" ends many of which are empirically observable and suitable for incorporation in rational means-end schemata of unit-acts.

For instance, we cannot directly observe the happiness of a society, undoubtedly an ultimate end of many social actions. But we can assume that part of the action directed at happiness is designed to achieve satisfaction of wants through material goods and services as an intermediate end, and that some correlation is likely to exist between social welfare (happiness) and the observable amount and distribution of goods and services in a society.

We can develop fairly reliable indicators which reflect the relative degree of success of given actions in attaining respective transcendental ends[6], and by means of which the rational action schema can be made to apply throughout a vast sphere of social action. The question 'does democratic party-politics maximize the people's happiness', cannot be answered by the use of a rational means-end schema; the question involves a whole complex system of action in which the end is transcendental. But the question: 'to what extent does democratic party politics, now and here, succeed in compromising conflicting interests in the formulation of public policy', can probably be answered, at least by approximation, since the various conflicting ends of social groups, the means they employ, and the public policy that

[5]The reason for the impact of other unit-acts upon the one under study being absorbed by the "means" is to keep the "end" of the schema as homogeneous and clearly defined as possible. The alternative of accounting for other unit-acts by dealing with a multiplicity of ends in our schema is apt to cause confusion and eventual break-down of the analytical process.

[6]For instance, suicide and divorce rates, migration, compliance with moral standards, etc., can be used as such indicators.

emerges are empirically observable, and can be ordered into a set of unit-acts which are oriented with reference to the empirical context of the socio-political situation of a given country at a given time.

A prime criterion of rationality in action is the appropriateness of the means to the end. Since an empirically observed act is usually the resultant of several conflicting ends, the appropriateness of the means depends upon which of the ends is chosen as element of the action schema. Even a perfectly simple empirical act may be judged rational with reference to one schema, non-rational with reference to another. It is exceedingly important to keep always in mind that any empirical action may have a multiplicity of ends, and if it does, there are as many possible unit-act schemata applicable to it as there are ends.

A simple example: I pull my hand away from the knife of a surgeon. This is the empirical act. If the end entered into the schema is to get rid of my wart, the means of pulling my hand away is inappropriate, and the act not rational; if the end is to avoid pain (in a different unit-act!) the means is appropriate, and the act rational. This example should show up strikingly the danger of confusion the means-end schema of a unit-act with the empirical action itself.

Hence, the statement that an actor behaves not rationally can refer only to a certain means-end schema. If, in the judgment of the observer, the means employed by the actor have such a low degree of probability of success (appropriateness) that the choice of picking those means in pursuit of a given end is not based upon rational grounds, it may well be that these very means are quite appropriate to advance a different end which is in conflict with the other. The first verdict can stand only if it is demonstrated that no such conflicting ends exist in the empirical action. For instance: an entrepreneur A uses production methods yielding him a handsome profit, while entrepreneur B uses other methods and sustains a loss. Now, B's action can be called not rational only if (1) he really had the same end in view as A, and (2) he had the choice of alternative means which could have yielded a profit. If B's action reflected a compromise between 2 conflicting ends, e.g. making the maximum profit for this year (A's end) and enjoying more leisure, it may well have met the requirements of rationality. The position of the unit-act in A's action system is, then, not the same as in B's case because of differences in the ends pursued.

For this reason it is of paramount importance to connect any specific unit-act with the empirical action system as a whole, by subjecting the latter to a careful analysis of its multiplicity of ends. Note specifically that two unit-acts are often connected in such a way that the end of the one constitutes a means in the other.

The Role of the "Conditions" in the Means-End Schema

In the situational context of an empirical system of socio-economic action, the "conditions" of a component unit-act comprise all those elements and factors in the situation which are uncontrollable by the actor, yet relevant to his acting. They determine, in a broad sense, the limits within which the actor is free to choose his means in the pursuit of his end.

There are three main classes of conditions that are particularly relevant to social action:

(1) the innate or fairly permanent characteristics and capabilities of the actor (or collectivity of actors);
(2) the general state of knowledge and technique; and
(3) institutions, traditions, formal organizations, (political, economic, legal, etc.) and normative patterns of conduct (in brief "institutional conditions").

I shall confine myself to this last group of elements only as they are of special significance to our problem. It is clear, that these institutional conditions transcend the orbit of any specific unit-act; that the more fundamental ones among them are germane to the whole system of action, of which the various unit-acts under analysis are components. The institution of private property, for instance, is a relevant condition in most unit-acts belonging to systems of socio-economic action.

Furthermore, they influence the establishment of ends, as well as the selection of means. If ends and means become sufficiently incompatible with prevailing normative patterns of conduct to provoke restraining sanctions, the means become unavailable, the ends unattainable. These institutional conditions, therefore, tend to bring about an integration and coordination of unit-acts within an action system. They canalize the aspirations of actors into working toward fairly stable and standardized systems of ends, by employing fairly standardized sets of means. As they represent formally established patterns of social and economic relations between individuals and groups, they form an important basis for arriving at "legitimate expectations of the actions of others" on the part of the actor, an extremely vital function, indeed.[7]

Some of the institutional elements may become variables and enter as means into certain action schemata; namely if (1) the "actor" consists of a collectivity of actors, and (2) the action spans a considerable period of time. Institutions, laws, organizations do change, and sometimes they change quite rapidly. If they do, they become means employed by acting groups in pursuit of definite ends.

Ideologies and the Action Schema

By ideologies I mean, for our present purpose, systems of ideas concerning ethical norms and values and the cognitive orientation of men in the phenomenal world. They operate upon the means-end schema of action primarily through the institutional conditions and through the ends. These two structural elements of the action schema are suspended, as it were, from ideologies. Ideologies are *not* part of the

[7] See, T. Parsons, op.cit.

action schema, but they are reflected in the institutional conditions and the ends. Institutions, normative patterns of conduct and ends are empirically observable elements in the action system; but their norms and meaning are derived from ideologies, from systems of transcendental ideas not verifiable by objective observation. The relation between institutions and ideologies is in some respects analogous to that between symbol and meaning.

A major change in the institutional pattern implies a change in the relevant ideologies. Since ideologies are generally expressed in concepts of much higher abstraction than institutions which are concrete parts of the situation, considerable changes in institutional patterns may take place with no or only small changes in ideology. For instance, the empirical characteristics of the private property institution have undergone far-reaching changes with the expansion of corporate property during the last 100 years, while the ideology giving private property its meaning and moral justification has changed but little, at least until very recently. On the other hand, minor changes in ideology may take place without formal changes in institutions. For instance the ideology underlying the doctrine of state rights has changed quite a little, yet those changes are reflected in different judicial interpretations of constitutional law rather than in changing the constitution itself; new meaning is given to old symbols.

It is clear, however, that the divergence between institutions and ideologies cannot grow very wide before increasingly serious disruptive tendencies and tensions develop, until harmony or at least mutual compatibility between the two categories is reestablished.

To illustrate: from the viewpoint of the individual actor, the institutional pattern is not subject to his control; he can evade it, but not change it. Frequent violations of normative patterns by many actors can be taken as a dependable symptom of a change in ideology rendering the existing institution obsolete and inadequate. The Anti-trust Laws and their inefficacy in coping with widespread violations offer an example of a growing divergence between the ideology underlying the concept of "restraint of trade" sustained by the business community, and its corresponding concrete institution. The other door through which ideologies enter into the action schema is the end. I pointed out above that although the end in our rational means-end schema is a concrete empirical one; it very often is intermediate, representing a stage in a hierarchy of ends which transcends the realm of the empirical world. These "ultimate" ends toward which the empirical ends of the rational action schemata lead are elements of ideologies. The empirical ends of the concrete action system of a feudal-aristocratic government reflect a very different ideology and system of transcendental ends from that of a liberal-democratic government. It follows that the significance of rational action with respect to concrete social action systems, as well as its empirical content, are directly affected by the ideological contexts of these various action systems.

It is possible, and from a methodological viewpoint sometimes useful, to conceive of ideologies as forces of social integration. Undoubtedly, the "structuralization" of ends, means and normative patterns in the body politic is always associated with general, yet fairly definite ideologies accepted and sustained by the majority of the members of a society. It must not be overlooked, however, that there are conflicting ideologies as there are conflicting ends in any society.[8]

Sketch of the Action Schema Applied to two Specific Empirical Action Systems, and Appraisal of their Interrelation

In the following I shall draw a free-hand sketch of how the analytical operation so far outlined might be applied to type-cases of empirical action systems and what kind of conclusions might the analysis be expected to yield.

The Capitalistic Enterprise

The Capitalistic enterprise, the Firm, represents an empirical action system which can be analytically dissected into many unit-acts. These unit-acts are best designated by their respective ends, since, according to our schema, the end of any unit-act is defined as a single homogeneous end. For the present illustration, I choose the unit-act of maximizing profit; and the structural elements of its means-end schema are:

(1) the *actor*: an individual entrepreneur;
(2) the *end*: to earn a profit so high as to support his accustomed scale of living and provide in addition the highest possible amount for investment.
(3) the *means*: production and marketing factors and techniques available to the entrepreneur and offering him opportunities of choice between alternatives;
(4) the *conditions*: price relations between factors and goods, established patterns of contractual relations, institutions, laws and any other situational elements relevant to his enterprise and outside his control.

This schema meets all the formal requirements of rational action (see above). The rationality of the entrepreneur's action operates freely, through means logically appropriate to the end, and within the limits set by the conditions of the situation. To

[8]For the purpose of appraising the relation between ideologies and concrete action systems, it is not necessary to settle the question of primacy of these two categories in the causal nexus. We can start from the simple statement of fact that at any given time and place, there exist ideologies, and there exist situational contexts and systems of empirical ends, and social action is oriented to both. A detailed analysis of their interrelationship might well proceed by posing the three-fold query: (1) How do ideologies influence action in a given situational context?; (2) how does the situational context influence action within given ideologies; and (3) what is the character of the inter-action between ideologies and situational contexts operating through the medium of the actors? Much of Max Weber's findings can be interpreted in this light.

pronounce the empirical act described by this schema, or the actual behavior of the actor, as rational, the empirical content of the schema is subject to a further condition: the compatibility of the end with the conditions. Namely, if the empirical conditions (e.g. the cost-price ratios, or legal restrictions) are such as to consistently frustrate the entrepreneur's attempt to attain his end despite his competent application of technically appropriate means, his end cannot be achieved, his action falls short of the rational norm. Compatibility of the empirical end with the empirical situational context, under the assumption of average (or some standard of) competence of the actor, is a necessary requirement of rational action. If this requirement is not met, the conditions of the situation do not permit empirically appropriate means becoming available for the pursuit of the end. Entrepreneurs who continue to pursue that end in the face of a situational context persistently frustrating their attempts do not act rationally. They must either change the situational context which requires concerted action on the part of many actors and involves a change in ideology, or they must change their end.

For instance, if freedom of contract and private property rights became so restricted that a situational context develops which renders the end of profit maximization over and above living cost (as defined in the schema) for the individual entrepreneur incompatible with the situation, and hence unattainable, the action system would disintegrate, and readjustments in ideologies, institutional arrangements and ends would need to take place.

Since the conditions transcend the orbit of the particular unit-act, the relationship between the end and the conditions constitutes one connection of the unit-act with the concrete system, as I pointed out above. Another important connection between our specific unit-act and other unit-acts is established by the relationship between that specific end and other ends. If there are some which are in conflict with the first, the degree of achievement may be greatly impaired, without, however, necessarily signifying any incompatibility of the end with the conditions as was true in the previous case.

If our entrepreneur, besides pursuing the end of maximizing profit over and above his living expenses, simultaneously pursues the end of enjoying a certain amount of leisure, or of providing exceptionally good working-conditions for his employees, these other ends which belong to other unit-acts and require different means, are to some extent in conflict with the end of profit maximization. The size of his actual profit, in consequence, falls so low that no surplus above his living expenses remains, or even that he needs to reduce his scale of living. Here, the lower degree of achievement of the end in our unit-act is not the result of non-rational action, and does not produce a sense of frustration on the part of the actor.

It is obvious, how the identical empirical content of the means-end schema of a specific unit-act has completely different meanings and must be differently interpreted, depending upon the relationship between the unit-act and the concrete action system. In the first case, the rationality of the unit-act is impaired by the lack of compatibility between conditions and the end; in the second, the rationality of the unit-act remains intact, despite the insufficiency of the means to attain the end, because not lack of rationality in action, but other conflicting ends simultaneously pursued according to rational norms of acting, impair the attainment of the end of the specific unit-act under study.

I consider this method of interpreting the relationships between a unit-act and the action system, which I have sketched here only in broad outlines, of paramount importance in the analysis of social action.

The Capitalist Industry

From the action system of a capitalistic industry, a unit-act is chosen which is analogous in many respects to the one discussed in the preceding section. Its structural elements are:

(1) the *actor*: the collectivity of all entrepreneurs in a country;
(2) the *end*: to produce goods and services in such amounts as to support *all* members of society (including workers) at generally accepted scales of living and to achieve in addition the highest possible rate of capital accumulation;
(3) the *means*: production factors (including labor) and techniques; marketing organizations; and other formal and informal institutional arrangements fairly flexible through time and amenable to entrepreneurial control.
(4) the *conditions*: the scale of consumers' preferences for goods and services; a normative pattern of distribution of the social product among the members of society (including workers) based upon the marginal productivity and ownership of the factors; a minimum of restrictions upon the entrepreneur's use and disposal of production factors; and other institutional arrangements relevant to the economy, and fairly stable through time.

Again, let us posit the two-fold query regarding the connection between this unit-act and the action system: (1) to what extent is the end compatible with the conditions?, and (2) are there other ends in the concrete action system conflicting with the end of our unit-act?

There are two elements in the conditions which may readily frustrate the end. First, the normative pattern of distribution according to ownership and marginal productivity. It is conceivable that a situational context develops which would press the value of the marginal product of a considerable number of workers below the cost of living at an acceptable scale. If these workers do not own production factors other than their labor, they cannot support themselves, and the end of supporting *all* members of society is not attained. Nobody can deny that there is plenty of empirical evidence pointing to the actual existence of such a situational context in contemporary capitalistic economies.

The ideology underlying this normative pattern of distribution constitutes a central theme of the classical doctrine of liberalism and utilitarianism. But note: this normative pattern is not an end in itself; it is justified only on grounds that it is the best to permit the attainment of the end, i.e. that *all* people earn enough to live decently. And this end is part of the general ideology. Now, if the normative pattern of distribution as part of the institutional structure of the conditions interferes with the attainment of the end sufficiently to generate widespread discontent, changes must occur either in the end (ideology) or in the conditions (institutions) or in both, in the direction of reestablishing compatibility of these two elements of the action system. As a matter of fact, the rapid growth of social legislation in the capitalist countries during the last 20 to 30 years may well be interpreted as representing just such changes in the normative distribution pattern whose obstructive effects are being realized more and more.

The second element in the conditions apparently exerting a growing tendency to interfere with the end is the freedom of the entrepreneur to use and dispose of the productive factors he owns and acquires. In the ideology of classical liberalism the justification of this freedom rests upon the notion that private property in productive factors is the result of individual effort contributing to the collective end, and that a minimum of restrictions placed upon use, acquisition and disposal tends to maximize general welfare. If a situational context develops which leads to abuses of such unrestricted freedom of property on the part of the individual to the detriment of the collective end, an incompatibility emerges between end and conditions, and forces of readjustment are set in motion. The legal treatment of corporate wealth as private property, and the widespread separation of ownership and control are situational developments which are producing growing tensions between conditions and end. Institutional arrangement leading to a very high degree of inequality of income and preventing a reasonably full utilization of productive factors render the conditions in the rational means-end schema of our unit-act incompatible with its end.

Up to the Great Depression, the adjustments purported to eliminate these incompatibilities were primarily directed toward appropriate changes in the institutional conditions. Unfortunately, these adjustments moved much too slowly, were unable to relieve the frustration of the expectations of large masses of people. And in a growing number of countries adjustments occurred not only in the conditions, but even primarily in the ideology and the corollary ends of socio-economic action: through the growth of totalitarian anti-democratic ideas, which, in turn, were reflected in the situational context through the establishment of terroristic authoritarian regimes.

So much for the test of conditions-end compatibility. The second query concerns the examination of conflicting ends in the action system impinging upon the unit-act under analysis. The concrete action system in which the collectivity of capitalist entrepreneurs functions as actor consists of many other unit-acts differentiated by their respective ends. For instance, such ends may be the maximization of power in the body economic and politic; the improvement of working conditions for laborers; the enjoyment of leisure, recreation, conspicuous consumption. Any one of these ends may, to some extent, be in conflict with the end of providing a good livelihood to all members of society and in addition accumulating capital. What the major ends of a concrete action system are, and to what extent they conflict with the end of the particular unit-act under consideration, constitute an indispensable phase of the analysis. A rational means-end schema of a unit-act applied to an empirical concrete action system cannot yield reliable results unless the position of its end with reference to the major other ends of other unit-acts is at least approximately determined.

Evaluation of Some Interrelationships between Two Unit-Acts with Reference to a Common Action System

The two unit-acts outlined above have been treated in isolation; that is to say that they have been analyzed with reference to two different concrete action systems: the capitalistic firm, with the individual entrepreneur as actor; and the capitalistic industry, with the collectivity of entrepreneurs as actors. It is possible to study these two unit-acts with reference to a common action system of which they both form components; for instance, to the total system of socio-economic action in Western countries, to democratic-capitalist national economies. While the unit-act is designated first by the end, which is simple or homogeneous by definition, the action system is best designated first by the actor; any empirical action system is characterized by a multiplicity of ends simultaneously pursued by the actor, which renders the latter a better criterion for taxonomic purposes than the former. In the action system of western national economies, the collectivity of all members of society is the actor – a very complex actor indeed.

It would far transcend the scope this essay – not to speak of my analytical prowess – to carry this analysis through, even as cursorily as the two preceding schemata. But I shall venture a few suggestions which seem to follow from the previous analysis interpreted in the light of a common action system.

First, let us examine the question of the compatibility between conditions and ends. The action system of the firm is, in itself, devoid of any social aggregates. As long as the situational context is such that at least one entrepreneur, through at least one firm, can earn a satisfactory profit, the rationality of this unit-act is attested.

In the action system of the industry, however, it is social aggregates which form the elements of the unit-act: the collectivity of entrepreneurs, all of them, not just a few, is the actor, and an acceptable livelihood of *all* members of society, not just a few, is the end. If the conditions are such that a significant number of entrepreneurs go bankrupt, and a significant number of people go ill-fed, ill-clad and ill-sheltered, the rationality of this unit-act is impaired.

The conditions of both unit-acts stem from the same ideology, and are the same in their essential and relevant features. But the fact that their conditions are compatible with the end of the first unit-act pertaining to the action system of the firm is no guarantee that they are also compatible with the end of the second unit-act, pertaining to industry. There still are many economists who are utterly unaware of the differences between these two action systems and the empirical content of their respective means-end schemata. For instance, the normative pattern of distribution of the social product is governed by the principle that people should be rewarded according to their contributions to the social product. This empirical principle is a reflection of the liberal ideological concept of "just reward for effort and sacrifice", of man's right to "his" product. Since he contributes to the social product not only with his labor, but also with "his" capital and "his" land, the institution of private property has become an empirical corollary of this ideological concept. But the same ideology, referred to the action system of the political economy as a whole, also postulates the inherent harmony between individual and social interest, and essential equality of opportunity for all men. It follows that property titles as claims to income are only justified in so far as the size of property holdings of individuals varies as a function of their effort and sacrifice. It is difficult, indeed, to convince people today that this is so, because it is not so. This ideological conception of a just principle of distribution, confronted with a situational context, with institutional conditions, which do not meet these norms, goes far to explain the uneasiness of people in the face of a tremendous concentration of property in a few hands, greatly accelerated by the elaborate device of corporate finance; or the uneasiness of economists and politicians over interest and rent as incomes to holders of property titles, not involving commensurate efforts and sacrifice on their part. Henry George and Marx are still very much alive.

As indispensable rent and interest are to the optimum allocation of productive resources, as incompatible with the liberal ideology they are as sources of private income. The rising tide of social legislation effecting a redistribution of income to non-propertied classes, through graduated income taxes, relief and various kinds of subsidies, might well be interpreted as institutional adjustments designed to mitigate the incompatibility of the concrete capitalist pattern of distribution with the liberal ideology of just reward for effort and sacrifice. The far-reaching modifications in the institutional conditions of the democratic-capitalist economy testify for the perseverance of the liberal ideology.

Second, as to the question of conflicting ends. Even simple empirical ends of social action are associated with certain ideologies, as has been pointed out previously. In any complex empirical system of social action there always are considerable numbers of conflicting empirical ends which either belong to conflicting ideologies, or compete within the same ideology. I shall limit my remarks to the latter case.

The ideology of 18th and 19th century liberalism conceived of an inherent congruity of the ends of our two action schemata: the entrepreneur's end to maximize profits, and the collectivity of all entrepreneurs to maximize social product. In fact, the entrepreneur's end was thought of as intermediary and subservient to the collectivity's end. This ideology could not long stand the stress resulting from a serious conflict between these two ends in the empirical action system.

In preceding paragraphs I interpreted certain changes in institutional conditions as adjustments to the end and the liberal ideology associated with it. Here, I should like to suggest that certain changes in the liberal ideology and in the ends associated with it can be interpreted as adjustments to institutional and technological conditions.

With more and more small-scale entrepreneurs being driven out of business, with millions of workers chronically unemployed, the liberal ideological concept of the inherent harmony of individual and social interest, of the congruity of the entrepreneur's and the collectivity's ends in our unit-acts, is no longer accepted by the majority of people. This change in ideology has been reflected in a change of the end of certain categories of firms, e.g., public utilities, educational enterprises, cooperatives, etc. The lack of opportunities, for workers as well as investors has given increasing emphasis to security as an end in the social action system, often at the expense of income. There can be no doubt that important changes in many elements constituting the ideology of classical liberalism are taking place, and a newly re-constituted ideology of 20th century liberalism is in the making, in which the basic tenets of humanitarian ideas remain intact, but many subordinate doctrines are modified or re-interpreted so as to mitigate certain serious conflicts both between ends and between conditions and ends in the concrete systems of social action.

In conclusion, I should like to emphasize that the dichotomy of ideology and rational means-end schemata of social action is of analytical, not of genetic importance. For the purpose of this discussion and I believe quite in general, it is irrelevant which is ultimately cause and effect in a one-way causal chain, the idea or the situation. We have proceeded according to the methodological principle of keeping alternatively one factor constant while varying the other, fully realizing that in reality both are mutually interdependent and vary together. By restricting ourselves to the epistemological position of either extreme materialism or idealism we arbitrarily and unnecessarily limit the variety of analytical tools at our disposal, and withdraw wide ranges of evidence from our field of inquiry.

Applying this general reasoning to our specific subject matter, I suggest that it is convenient, for analytical purposes, to conceive of the ends and the conditions of rational action schemata as being associated with corresponding ideological conceptions. The character of this association is assumed to be one of mutual interaction.

This device enables us to keep all the structural elements of the rational means-end schema of specific unit-acts strictly on the plane of empirical observation, but at the same time to evaluate and interpret any unit-act in terms of its position relative to other unit-acts of the same concrete action system, and to other relevant action systems of which the former constitutes a part. Stresses, incompatibility and conflicts within and between action systems, then, are traced in the light of their ideological connotations, since they almost invariably derive from conflicting norms. Ethical norms governing social behavior, however, can be expressed only in terms of ideologies.

I maintain, therefore, that studying a concrete phenomenon of social action exclusively in terms of rational means-end schemata without reference to norms and values systems which are derived from ideologies, can yield no more than a meagre and over-simplified statistic description and can never answer really vital questions concerning the workings of social processes. Ideologies co-determine, together with material factors, the institutional conditions as well as the ends that enter as elements into the means-end schema. That is to say that rational action is oriented to ideological conceptions in two fundamental ways: in the selection of ends pursued and in the limits of choice of means set by institutional conditions. Any analysis of rational action is void of meaning and does not contribute to the understanding of social processes unless it is referred to these points of orientations.

The Problem of Rationality in the Social World

Alfred Schütz

I

The problem suggested by the terms "rationality" or "rational action" as used in current literature is most certainly central to the methodology and epistemology of the scientific study of the social world. The terms themselves, however, are not only used with many different meanings – and this sometimes in the writings of the same author as, for instance, Max Weber – but they represent only very inadequately the underlying conceptual scheme. In order to bring out the concealed equivocations and connotations, and to isolate the question of rationality from all the other problems surrounding it, we must go further into the structure of the social world and make more extensive inquiries into the different attitudes toward the social world adopted, on the one hand, by the actor within this world, and, on the other hand, by the scientific observer of it.

What is commonly understood by the term "rational action" is best shown by the definition of "rationality" or "reasonableness" given by Professor Talcott Parsons in his remarkable study on *The Structure of Social Action:*[1]

"Action is rational in so far as it pursues ends possible within the conditions of the situation, and by the means which, among those available to the actor, are intrinsically best adapted to the end for reasons understandable and verifiable by positive empirical science." Indicating in his usual careful manner the methodological point of view from which he contemplates his problem, Professor Parsons comments upon this definition as follows: "Since science is the rational achievement par excellence, the mode of approach here outlined is in terms of the analogy

This contribution is published with permission of the Harvard University Archives, Talcott Parsons Papers.

The author was deceased at the time of publication.

[1]New York, 1937, p. 58.

H. Staubmann, V. Lidz (eds.), *Rationality in the Social Sciences*,
DOI 10.1007/978-3-319-62377-1_8

between the scientific investigator and the actor in ordinary practical activities. The starting point is that of conceiving the actor as coming to know the facts of the situation in which he acts and thus the condition necessary and means available for the realization of his ends. As applied to the means-end relationship this is essentially a matter of the accurate prediction of the probable effects of various possible ways of altering the situation (employment of alternative means) and the resultant choice among them. Apart from questions relating to the choice of ends and from those relating to 'effort'. . .there is, where the standard is applicable at all, little difficulty in conceiving the actor as thus analogous to the scientist whose knowledge is the principal determinant of his action so far as his actual course conforms with the expectations of an observer who has, as Pareto says, 'a more extended knowledge of the circumstances.'"

This definition gives an excellent résumé of the widely used concept of rational action in so far as it refers to the level of social theory. It seems important, however, to make more precise the peculiarity of this theoretical level by contrasting it with the other levels of our experience of the social world. We must, therefore, start by examining what we really mean when we speak of different levels in observing the social world. Following this a short description of the social world as it appears to the actor within this world in his everyday life will give us an opportunity of examining whether or not the category of rationality becomes determinative for his actions. Only after these preliminaries shall we examine the social world as it is given to the scientific observer; and together with it we shall have to examine the question of whether the categories of interpretation used by the scientist coincide with those used by the observed actor. Anticipating our results, we may say at once that with the shift from one level to another all the conceptual schemes and all the terms of interpretation must be modified.

II

The fact that the same object has a different appearance to various observers has been illustrated by some philosophers by the example of a city which, though always the same, appears different to different persons according to their individual standpoints. I do not wish to over-work this metaphor, but it helps to make clear the difference between our view of the social world in which we naively live and the social world which is the object of scientific observation. The man brought up in a town will find his way in its streets by following the habits he has acquired in his daily occupations. He may not have a consistent conception of the organization of the city, and, if he uses the underground railway to go to his office, a large part of the city may remain unknown to him. Nevertheless, he will have a proper sense of the distances between different places and of the directions in which the different points are situated relatively to whatever he regards as the center. This center will usually be his home, and it may be sufficient for him to know that he will find nearby an underground line or a bus leading to certain other points to bring them all within his reach. He can, therefore, say that he knows his town, and, though this knowledge is of a very incoherent kind, it is sufficient for all his practical needs.

When a stranger comes to the town, he has to learn to orientate himself in it and to know it. Nothing is self-explanatory for him and he has to ask an expert, in this case a native, to learn how to get from one point to another. He may, of course, refer to a map of the town, but even to use the map successfully he must know the meaning of the signs on the map, the exact point within the town where he stands and its correlative on the map, and at least one more point in order correctly to relate the signs on the map to the real objects in the city.

Entirely different means of orientation must be used by the cartographer who has to draw a map of the city. There are several ways open to him. He can start with a photograph taken from an aeroplane; he can place a theodolite at a known point, measure a certain distance and calculate trigonometrical functions, etc. The science of cartography has developed a standard for such operations, elements the cartographer must know before he begins to draw his map, and rules he must observe if he is to draw his map correctly.

The town is the same for all the three persons we have mentioned – the native, the foreigner and the cartographer – but for the native it has a special meaning: "my home town"; for the foreigner it is a place within which he has to live and work for some time; for the cartographer it is an object of his science, he is interested in it only for the purposes of drawing a map. We may say that the same object is considered from different levels.

We should certainly be surprised if we found a cartographer in mapping a town restricting himself to collecting information from natives. Nevertheless, social scientists frequently choose this strange method. They forget that their scientific work is done on a level of interpretation and understanding different from the naive attitudes of orientation and interpretation peculiar to people in daily life. When these social scientists speak of different levels, they frequently consider the difference between the two levels as entirely and simply one of the degree of concreteness or generality. These two terms, however, are no more than chapter headings for much more complicated problems than those which they directly suggest.

In our daily life, as in our scientific world, we, as human beings, all have the tendency to presume, more or less naively, that what we have once verified as valid will remain valid throughout the future, and that what appeared to us beyond question yesterday will still be beyond all question tomorrow. This naive presumption may be made without danger if we deal with propositions of a purely logical character, or with empirical statements of a very high generality, though it can be shown that these kinds of propositions, too, have only a limited realm of applicability. On the other hand, at a so-called concrete level, we are forced to admit very many suppositions and implications as beyond question. We can even consider the level of our actual research as defined by the total of unquestioned presuppositions which we make by placing ourselves at the specific standpoint from which we envisage the interrelation of problems and aspects under scrutiny. Accordingly, passing from one level to another would involve that certain presuppositions of our research formerly regarded as beyond all question would now be called in question;

and what was formerly a *datum* of our problem would now become problematic itself. But the simple fact that new problems and aspects of facts emerge with the shift in the point of view, while others that were formerly in the center of our question disappear, is sufficient to initiate a thorough modification of the meaning of all the terms correctly used at the former level. Careful control of such modifications of the meaning is, therefore, indispensable if we are to avoid the risk of naively taking over from one level to another terms and propositions whose validity is essentially limited to a certain level, that is, to its implied suppositions.

Philosophical and in particular phenomenological theory has made very important contributions toward the better understanding of this phenomenon. However, we need not concern ourselves here with this very complicated problem from the phenomenological viewpoint. It will be sufficient to refer to an outstanding thinker of the English-speaking world, to William James and his theory of conception. It was he who taught us that each of our concepts has its fringes surrounding a nucleus of its unmodified meaning. "In all our voluntary thinking," he says, "there is some topic or subject about which all the members of the thought revolve. Relation to our topic or interest is constantly felt in the fringe of our concepts. Each word in a sentence is felt, not only as a word, but as having a meaning. The meaning of a word taken thus dynamically in a sentence may be quite different from its meaning if taken statically or without context." It is not for us to discuss here James's theory of the nature of such fringes and their genesis in the stream of thought. For our purpose it will be sufficient to say that already the connection in which a concept or a term is used and its relation to the topic of interest (and this topic of interest is in our case the *problem*) create specific modifications, of the fringes surrounding the nucleus, or even of the nucleus itself. It was also William James who explained that we do not apperceive isolated phenomena, but rather a field of several interrelated and interwoven things as it emerges in the stream of our thought. This theory explains sufficiently for our purposes the phenomenon of the meaning on a term being modified as we pass to another level. I think that these superficial references will be sufficient to indicate the nature of the problem we are dealing with. The term "rationality," or at least the concept it envisages, has, within the framework of social science, the specific role of a "key concept." It is peculiar to key concepts that, once introduced into an apparently uniform system, they constitute the differentiations between the points of view which we call levels. The meaning of such key concepts, therefore, does not depend on the level of the actual research, but, on the contrary, the level on which the research may be done depends upon the meaning attributed to the key concept, the introduction of which has for the first time divided what formerly appeared as a homogeneous field of research into several different levels. Anticipating what we shall have to prove later, we shall say that the level made accessible by the introduction of the term "rational action" as a chief principle of the method of social sciences is nothing else than the level of theoretical observation and interpretation of the social world.

III

As scientific observers of the social world, we are not practically but only cognitively interested in it. That means we are not acting in it with full responsibility for the consequences, but rather contemplating it with the same detached equanimity as physicists contemplate their experiments. But let us remember that notwithstanding our scientific activity we all remain human beings in our daily life – men among fellow-men with whom we are interrelated in very many ways. To be precise, even our scientific activity itself is based on the co-operation between us, the scientists, and our teachers and the teachers of our teachers, a co-operation by mutual influence and mutual criticism; but in so far as scientific activity is socially founded, it is one among other emanations of our human nature and certainly pertains to our daily life, governed by the categories of vocation and avocation, of work and leisure, of planning and accomplishing. Scientific activity as a social phenomenon is one thing, the specific attitude the scientist has to adopt toward his problem is another. Considered purely as a human activity, scientific work is distinguished from other human activities merely by the fact that it constitutes the archetype for rational interpretation and rational action.

In our daily life it is only very rarely that we act in a rational way if we understand this term in the meaning envisaged in Professor Parsons' previously quoted statement. We do not even interpret the social world surrounding us in a rational way, except under special circumstances which compel us to leave our basic attitude of just living our lives. Each of us, so it seems, has naively organized his social world and his daily life in such a way that he finds himself the center of the social cosmos surrounding him. Or, better, he was already born into an organized social cosmos. For him it is a cosmos and it is organized in so far as it contains all the comfortable equipment to render his daily living and that of his fellow-men a routine matter. There are, on the one hand, institutions of various kinds, tools, machines, etc.; on the other hand, habits, traditions, rules and experiences, both actual and vicarious. Furthermore, there is a scale of systematized relations which everyone has with his fellow-men, starting from the relations with members of his immediate family, relations with kinsmen, with personal friends, with people he knows personally, with people he met once in his life, through relations with those anonymous men who work somewhere and in a way he cannot imagine, but with the result that the letter he puts into the pillar box reaches the addressee in time, and that his lamp is lit by the turn of a switch.

Thus the social world with the *"alter egos"* in it is arranged around the self as a center in various degrees of intimacy and anonymity. Here am I and next to me are *"alter egos"* of whom, as Kipling says, I know "their naked souls." Then come those with whom I share time and space and whom I know more or less intimately. Next in order are the manifold relations I have with people in whose personality I am interested, though I have only an indirect knowledge of them such, for instance, as may be obtained from their works or writings or from reports from others. For example, my social relation with the author of the book I am reading is of this kind.

On the other hand, I have social relations (in the technical meaning of this term), though superficial and inconsistent ones, with others in whose personalities I am not interested, but who merely happen to perform functions in which I am interested. Perhaps the salesgirl in the store where I buy my shaving cream, or the man who polishes my shoes, are much more interesting personalities than many of my friends. I do not inquire. I am not interested in social contact with those people. I just want to get my shaving cream and to have my shoes polished by whatever means. In this sense, it makes very little difference to me whether, when I want to make a telephone call, an operator or a dial intervenes. Incidentally – and here we enter the remotest sphere of social relations – the dial, too, has its social function because it derives, as do all products of human activity, from the man who invented, designed and produced it. But if I am not guided by a special motive, I do not ask for the history, genesis, and construction of all the tools and institutions created by other people's activity. Likewise, I do not ask about the personality and destiny of fellow-men whose activity I consider as a purely typical function. In any case, and this is important for our problem, I can use the telephone with success without knowing how it functions; I am interested only in the fact that it does function. I do not care whether the result achieved, which alone interests me, is due to the intervention of a human being whose motives remain undisclosed to me or to a mechanism whose operation I do not understand. What counts is the typical character of the occurrence within a typified situation.

Thus, in this organization of the social world by the human being living naively in it, we already find the germ of the system of types and typical relations which we shall recognize later in its fullest ramification as the essential feature of scientific method. This typification is progressive in the same proportion as the personality of the fellow-man disappears beyond the undisclosed anonymity of his function. If we want to do so, we may interpret this process of progressive typification also as one of rationalization. At least it is envisaged by one of the several meanings Max Weber attributes to the term "rationalization" when he speaks of the "disenchantment of the world" (*Entzauberung der Welt*). This term means the transformation of an uncontrollable and unintelligible world into an organization which we can understand and therefore master, and in the framework of which prediction becomes possible.

In my opinion, the fundamental problem of the different aspects under which our fellow-men and their behavior and actions seem given to us has not yet received from sociologists the attention it merits. But if social science, with few exceptions, has failed to consider this kind of rationalization of its conceptual framework, each of us human beings, in "just living along," has already performed this task, and this without planning to do so and without any effort in the performance of his job. In doing so, we are guided neither by methodological considerations nor by any conceptual scheme of means-end relations, nor by any idea of values we have to realize. Our practical interest alone, as it arises in a certain situation of our life, and as it will be modified by the change in the situation which is just on the point of occurring, is the only relevant principle in the building up of the perspective structure in which our social world appears to us in daily life. For, just as all our visual apperceptions are in conformity with the principles of perspective and convey the impressions of depths and distance, so all our apperceptions of the social world necessarily have the basic character of perspective views. Of course the social world of a sixty-year old Chinese Buddhist in the time of the Ming dynasty will be organized in quite a different way from the social world of a twenty-year old American Christian of our own day, but the fact remains that both worlds would be organized, and this within the framework of the categories of familiarity and strangeness, of personality and type, of intimacy and anonymity. Furthermore, each of these worlds would be centered in the self of the person who lives and acts in it.

IV

But let us proceed in our analysis of the knowledge that a man living naively has about the world, the social world as well as the natural. In his daily life the healthy, adult, and wide-awake human being (we are not speaking of others) has this knowledge, so to speak, automatically at hand. From heritage and education, from the manifold influences of tradition, habits and his own previous reflection, his store of experiences is built up. It embraces the most heterogeneous kinds of knowledge in a very incoherent and confused state. Clear and distinct experiences are intermingled with vague conjectures; suppositions and prejudices cross well-proven evidences; motives, means and ends, as well as causes and effects, are strung together without clear understanding of their real connections. There are everywhere gaps, intermissions, discontinuities. Apparently there is a kind of organization by habits, rules, and principles which we regularly apply with success. But the origin of our habits is almost beyond our control; the rules we apply are rules of thumb and their validity has never been verified. The principles we start from are partly taken over uncritically from parents and teachers, partly distilled at random from specific situations in our lives or in the lives of others without our having made any further inquiry into their consistency. Nowhere have we a guarantee of the reliability of all of thcsc assumptions by which we are governed. On the other hand, these experiences and rules are sufficient to us for mastering life. As we normally have to act and not to reflect in order to satisfy the demands of the moment, which it is our task to master, we are not interested in the "quest for certainty." We are satisfied if we have a fair chance of realizing our purposes, and this chance, so we like to think, we have if we set in motion the same mechanism of habits, rules and principles which formerly stood the test and which still stand the test. Our knowledge in daily life is not without hypotheses, inductions, and predictions, but they all have the character of the approximate and the typical. The ideal of everyday knowledge is not certainty, nor even probability in a mathematical sense, but just likelihood. Anticipations of future states of affairs are conjectures about what is to be hoped or feared, or at best, about what can be reasonably expected. When afterwards the anticipated state of affairs takes some form in actuality, we do not say that our prediction has come true or proved false, or that our hypothesis has stood the test, but that our hopes or fears were or were not well founded. The consistency of this system of knowledge is not that of natural *laws*, but that of *typical* sequences and relations.

This kind of knowledge and its organization I should like to call "cook-book knowledge." The cook-book has recipes, lists of ingredients, formulae for mixing them, and directions for finishing off. This is all we need to make an apple pie, and also all we need to deal with the routine matters of daily life. If we enjoy the apple pie so prepared, we do not ask whether the manner of preparing it as indicated by the recipe is the most appropriate from the hygienic or alimentary point of view, or whether it is the shortest, the most economical, or the most efficient. We just eat and enjoy it. Most of our daily activities from rising to going to bed are of this kind. They are performed by following recipes reduced to automatic habits or unquestioned platitudes. This kind of knowledge is concerned only with the regularity as such of events in the external world irrespective of its origin. Because of this regularity it can be reasonably expected that the sun will rise to-morrow morning. It is equally regular, and it can, therefore, with as good reason be anticipated too that the bus will bring me to my office if I choose the right one and pay my fare.

V

The foregoing remarks characterize in a very superficial manner the conceptual scheme of our everyday behavior in so far as the term "conceptual scheme" can be applied at all. Are we to classify a behavior of the type just described as rational or irrational? In order to answer this question we must analyze the various equivocal implications which are hidden in the term "rationality" as it is applied to the level of everyday experience.

1. "Rational" is frequently used as synonymous with "reasonable." Now we certainly act in our daily life in a reasonable way if we use the recipes we find in the store of our experience as already tested in an analogous situation. But acting rationally often means avoiding mechanical applications of precedents, dropping the use of analogies, and searching for a new way to master the situation.
2. Sometimes rational action is put on a par with acting deliberately, but the term "deliberately" itself implies many equivocal elements.

(a) Routine action of daily life is deliberated in so far as it always relates back to the original act of deliberation which once preceded the building up of the formula now taken by the actor as a standard for his actual behavior.
(b) Conveniently defined, the term "deliberation" may cover the insight into the applicability to a present situation of a recipe which has proved successful in the past.

(c) We can give the term "deliberation" a meaning covering the pure anticipation of the end – and this anticipation is always the motive for the actor to set the action going.
(d) On the other hand, the term "deliberation" as used, for instance, by Professor Dewey in his *Human Nature and Conduct*, means, "a dramatic rehearsal in imagination of various competing possible lines of action." In this sense, which is of the greatest importance for the theory of rationality, we cannot classify as rational the type of everyday actions which we have examined up to now as deliberated actions. On the contrary, it is characteristic of these routine actions that the problem of choice between different possibilities does not enter into the consciousness of the actor. We shall have to come back to the problem of choice immediately.

3. Rational action is frequently defined as "planned" or "projected" action without a precise indication of the meaning of the terms "planned" or "projected." We cannot simply say that the non-rational routine acts of daily life are not consciously planned. On the contrary, they rest within the framework of our plans and projects. They are even instruments for realizing them. All planning presupposes an end to be realized by stages, and each of these stages may be called, from one point of view or another, either means or intermediate ends. Now the function of all routine work is a standardization and mechanization of the means-end relations as such by referring standardized means to standardized classes of ends. The effect of this standardization is that the intermediate ends disappear from the consciously envisaged chain of means which have to be brought about for performing the planned end. But here arises the problem of subjective meaning which we have mentioned before. We cannot speak of the unit-act as if this unit were constituted or demarcated by the observer. We must seriously ask: when does one act start and when is it accomplished? We shall see that only the actor is in a position to answer this question.

   Let us take the following example: Assume the professional life of a business man to be organized and planned to the extent that he intends to continue with his business for the next ten years, after which he hopes to retire. To continue his work involves going to his office every morning. For this purpose he has to leave his home at a certain hour, buy a ticket, take the train, etc. He did so yesterday and he will do so to-morrow if nothing extraordinary intervenes. Let us assume that one day he is late and that he thinks: "I shall miss my train – I shall be late at my office. Mr. 'X' will be there already, waiting for me. He will be in a bad humor, and perhaps he will not sign the contract on which so much of my future depends." Let us further assume that an observer watches this man rushing for the train "as usual" (so he thinks). Is his behavior planned, and if so, what is the plan? Only the actor can give the answer because he alone knows the span of his plans and projects. Probably all routine work is a tool for bringing about ends which are beyond routine work and which determine it.

4. “Rational” is frequently identified with “predictable.” It is not necessary to return to this question. We have already analyzed the specific form of prediction in everyday knowledge as simply an estimate of likelihood.
5. According to the interpretation of some authors, “rational” refers to “logical.” Professor Parsons’ definition is one example and Pareto’s theory of non-logical action to which he refers is another. In so far as the scientific concept of the rational act is in question, the system of logic may be fully applied. On the level of everyday experience, however, logic in its traditional form cannot render the services we need and expect. Traditional logic is a logic of concepts based on certain idealizations. In enforcing the postulate of clearness and distinctness of the concepts, for instance, traditional logic disregards all the fringes surrounding the nucleus within the stream of thought. On the other hand, thought in daily life has its chief interest precisely in the relation of the fringes which attach the nucleus to the actual situation of the thinker. This is clearly a very important point. It explains why Husserl classifies the greater part of our propositions in daily thought as “occasional propositions,” that means, as valid and understandable only relative to the speaker’s situation and to their place in his stream of thought. It explains, too, why our everyday thoughts are less interested in the antithesis “truefalse” than in the sliding transition “likely-unlikely.” We do not make everyday propositions with the purpose of achieving a formal validity within a certain realm which could be recognized by someone else, as the logician does, but in order to gain knowledge valid only for ourselves and to further our practical aims. To this extent, but only to this extent, the principle of pragmatism is incontestably well founded. It is a description of the style of everyday thought, but not a theory of cognition.
6. A rational act presupposes, according to the interpretation of other authors, a choice between two or more means toward the same end, or even between two different ends, and a selection of the most appropriate. This interpretation will be analyzed in the following section.

VI

As Professor John Dewey has pointed out, in our daily life we are largely preoccupied with the next step. Men stop and think only when the sequence of doing is interrupted, and the disjunction in the form of a problem forces them to stop and rehearse alternative ways – over, around or through – which their past experience in collision with this problem suggest. The image of a dramatic rehearsal of future action used by Professor Dewey is a very fortunate one. Indeed, we cannot find out which of the alternatives will lead to the desired end without imagining this act as already accomplished. So we have to place ourselves mentally in a future state of affairs which we consider as already realized, though to realize it would be the end of our contemplated action. Only by considering the act as accomplished can we judge whether the contemplated means of bringing it about are appropriate or not, or whether the end to be realized accommodates itself to the general plan of our life. I like to call this technique of deliberation "thinking in the future perfect tense." But there is a great difference between action actually performed and action only imagined as performed. The really accomplished act is irrevocable and the consequences must be borne whether it has been successful or not. Imagination is always revocable and can be revised again and again. Therefore, in simply rehearsing several projects. I can ascribe to each a different probability of success, but I can never be disappointed by its failure. Like all other anticipations, the rehearsed future action also has gaps which only the performance of the act will fill in. Therefore the actor will only retrospectively see whether his project has stood the test or proved a failure.

The technique of the choice is this: The mind of the actor runs through one alternative and then through the other till the decision falls from his mind – to use the words of Bergson – as a ripe fruit falls from the tree. But it is a prerequisite of all choice that the actor have clearly in mind that alternative ways of applying different means or even alternative ends do actually exist. It is erroneous to assume that consciousness of such alternatives and therefore choice is necessarily given before every human action and that in consequence all acting involves deliberation and preference. This interpretation uncritically confuses selection in the sense of just singling out without comparison of alternatives, and choice in the sense of electing the preferred. Selection is, as has already been pointed out by James, a cardinal function of human consciousness. Interest is nothing else than selection, but it does not necessarily involve conscious choice between alternatives which presupposes reflection, volition, and preference. When I walk through a garden discussing a problem with a friend and I turn left or right, I do not choose to do so. I have no alternative in mind. It is a question for psychology to determine the motives for such behavior, but I cannot say that I prefer one direction to another.

Undoubtedly there are situations in which each of us sits down and thinks over his problems. In general he will do so at critical points in his life when his chief interest is to master a situation. But even then he will accept his emotions as guides in finding the most suitable solution as well as rational deliberation, and he is right in doing so, because these emotions also have their roots in his practical interest.

He will also appeal to his stock of recipes, to the rules and skills arising out of his vocational life or his practical experiences. He will certainly find many systematized solutions in his standardized knowledge. He may perhaps consult an expert, but again he will get nothing else than recipes and systematized solutions. His choice will be a deliberated one, and having rehearsed all the possibilities of action open to him in the future perfect tense, he will put in action that solution which seems to have the greatest chance of success.

But what are the conditions under which we may classify a deliberated act of choice as a rational one? It seems that we have to distinguish between the rationality of knowledge which is a prerequisite of the rational choice and the rationality of the choice itself. Rationality of knowledge is given only if all the elements from which the actor has to choose are clearly and distinctly conceived by him. The choice itself is rational if the actor selects from among all means within his reach the one most appropriate for realizing the intended end.

We have seen that clearness and distinctness in the strict meaning of formal logic do not belong to the typical style of everyday thought. But it would be erroneous to conclude that, therefore, rational choice does not exist within the sphere of everyday life. Indeed, it would be sufficient to interpret the terms clearness and distinctness in a modified and restricted meaning, namely, as clearness and distinctness adequate to the requirements of the actor's practical interest. It is not our task to examine whether rational acts corresponding with the above-mentioned characteristics do or do not occur frequently in daily life. There is no doubt that "rational acts" together with their antithesis, defined by Max Weber as "traditional" or "habitual" acts, represent rather ideal types which will be found very seldom in their pure form in everyday action. What I wish to emphasize is only that the ideal of rationality is not and cannot be a peculiar feature of everyday thought, nor can it, therefore, be a methodological principle of the interpretation of human acts in daily life. This will become clearer if we discuss the concealed implications of the statement – or better, postulate – that rational choice would be present only if the actor had sufficient knowledge of the end to be realized as well as of the different means apt to succeed. This postulate implies:

(a) Knowledge of the place of the end to be realized within the framework of the plans of the actor (which must be known by him, too).
(b) Knowledge of its interrelations with other ends and its compatibility or incompatibility with them.
(c) Knowledge of the desirable and undesirable consequences which may arise as by-products of the realization of the main end.
(d) Knowledge of the different chains of means which technically or even ontologically are suitable for the accomplishment of this end, regardless of whether the actor has control of all or several of their elements.
(e) Knowledge of the interference of such means with other ends or other chains of means including all their secondary effects and incidental consequences.
(f) Knowledge of the accessibility of those means for the actor, picking out the means which are within his reach and which he can and may set going.

The aforementioned points do not by any means exhaust the complicated analysis which would be necessary in order to break down the concept of rational choice in action. The complications increase greatly when the action in question is a social one, that is, when it is directed towards other people. In this case, the following elements become additional determinants for the deliberation of the actor:

First: The interpretation or misinterpretation of his own act by his fellow-man.

Second: The reaction of the other people and its motivation.

Third: All the outlined elements of knowledge (*a* to *f*) which the actor, rightly or wrongly, attributes to his partners.

Fourth: All the categories of familiarity and strangeness, of intimacy and anonymity, of personality and type, which we have discovered in the course of our inventory of the organization of the social world.

This short analysis shows that we cannot speak of an *isolated* rational act, if we mean by this an act resulting from deliberated choice, but only of *a system* of rational acts.[2] But where is this system of rational action to be found? We have already noted that the concept of rationality has its native place not at the level of the everyday conception of the social world but at the theoretical level of the scientific observation of it, and it is here that it finds its field of methodological application. Therefore, we have to proceed to the problem of the social sciences and to the scientific methods of its interpretation.

VII

Our analysis of the social world in which we live has shown that each of us considers himself as the center of this world, which he groups around himself according to his own interests. The observer's attitude towards the social world is quite different. This world is not the theatre of his activities, but the object of his contemplation on which he looks with detached equanimity. As a scientist (not as a human being dealing with science) the observer is essentially solitary. He has no companion, and we can say that he has placed himself outside the social world with its manifold relations and its system of interests. Everyone, to become a social scientist, must make up his mind to put somebody else instead of himself as the center of this world, namely, the observed person. But with the shift in the central point, the whole system has been transformed, and, if I may use this metaphor, all the equations proved as valid in the former system now have to be expressed in terms of the new one. If the social system in question had reached an ideal perfection, it would be possible to establish a universal transformation formula such as Einstein has succeeded in establishing for translating propositions in terms of the Newtonian System of Mechanics into those of the theory of Relativity.

The first and fundamental consequence of this shift in the point of view is that the scientist replaces the human beings he observes as actors on the social stage by puppets created by himself and manipulated by himself. What I call "puppets" corresponds to the technical term "ideal types" which Weber has introduced into social science.

Our analysis of our common social world has shown us the origin of typification. We typify, in daily life, human activities which interest us only as appropriate means for bringing about intended effects, but not as emanations of the personality of our fellow-men. The procedure of the scientific observer is on the whole the

[2]See the excellent study which Professor Parsons has devoted to this problem under the heading "Systems of Action and their Units," at the end of his *Structure of Social Action*.

same. He observes certain events as caused by human activity and he begins to establish a type of such proceedings. Afterwards he co-ordinates with these typical acts typical actors as their performers. He thus ends up by constructing personal ideal types which he imagines as having consciousness. This fictitious consciousness is constructed in such a way that the fictitious actor, if he were not a dummy but a human being of flesh and blood, would have the same stream of thought as a living man acting in the same manner, but with the important modification that the artificial consciousness is not subjected to the ontological conditions of human existence. The puppet is not born, he does not grow up, and he will not die. He has no hopes and no fears; he does not know anxiety as a chief motive of all his deeds. He is not free in the sense that his acting could transgress the limits his creator, the social scientist, has fixed. He cannot, therefore, have other conflicts of interest and motives than those the social scientist has implanted in him. The personal ideal type cannot err if to err is not its typical destiny. It cannot perform an act which is outside the typical motives, the typical means-ends relations, and outside the typical situation provided for by the scientist. In short, the ideal type is but a model of a conscious mind without the faculty of spontaneity and without a will of its own. In typical situations of our daily life we all, too, assume certain typical roles. By isolating one of our activities from its interrelations with all the other manifestations of our personality, we disguise ourselves as consumers or tax-payers, citizens, members of a church or of a club, clients, smokers, bystanders, etc. The traveler, for instance, has to behave in the specific way he believes the type "railway agent" to expect from a typical passenger. For us in our daily lives these attitudes are but roles which we voluntarily assume as expedients and which we may drop whenever we want to do so. But assuming this role does not change our general attitude toward the social world or toward our own life. Our knowledge remains incoherent, our propositions occasional, our future uncertain, our general situation unstable. The next moment may bring the great cataclysm which will affect our choice, modify all our plans, perhaps destroy the value of all our experience. And we keep – even in the role – the liberty of choice, as far as such liberty exists at all within the scope of our human and social conditions. This liberty embraces the possibility of taking off our disguise, of dropping the role, of recommencing our orientation in the social world. We continue to be subjects, centers of spontaneous activities, actors.

The puppet called "personal ideal type" is on the contrary, never a subject or a center of spontaneous activity. He does not have the task of mastering the world, and, strictly speaking, he has no world at all. His destiny is regulated and determined beforehand by his creator, the social scientist, and with such a perfect pre-established harmony as Leibniz imagined the world created by God. By the grace of its constructor, he is endowed with just that kind of knowledge he needs to perform the job for the sake of which he was brought into the scientific world. The scientist distributes his own store of experience, and that means of scientific experience in clear and distinct terms, among the puppets with which he peoples the social world. But this social world, too, is organized in quite another way; it is not centered in the ideal type; it lacks the categories of intimacy and anonymity, of familiarity and strangeness: in short, it lacks the basic character of perspective appearance. What counts is the point of view from which the *scientist* envisages the social world. This point of view defines the general perspective framework in which the chosen sector of the social world presents itself to the scientific observer as well as to the fictitious consciousness of the puppet type. This central point of view of the scientist is called his "scientific problem under examination."

In a scientific system the problem has exactly the same significance for the scientific activity as the practical interests have for activities in everyday work. The scientific problem as formulated has a two-fold function:

(a) It determines the limits within which possible propositions become relevant to the inquiry. It thus creates the realm of the scientific subject matter within which all concepts must be compatible.
(b) The simple fact that a problem is raised creates a scheme of reference for the construction of all ideal types which may be utilized as relevant.

For the better understanding of the last remark we have to consider that the concept "type" is not an independent one but always needs a supplement. We cannot speak simply of an "ideal type" as such; we must indicate the reference scheme within which this ideal type may be utilized, that is, the problem for the sake of which the type has been constructed. To borrow a mathematical term we may say that the ideal type always needs a subscript referring to the problem which determines the formation of all the types to be used. In this sense, the problem under scrutiny is the locus of all possible types which may pertain to the system investigated.

I cannot go further here into the logical foundations of this thesis which I call the *principle of relevance*. But we can interpret it as an application of James's theory concerning the fringes of concepts. The ideal type, too, like all other concepts, has fringes referring to the main topic about which all the members of the thought revolve. It is easy to understand that a shift in the main topic – that is, in the problem – automatically involves a modification in the fringes of each concept revolving about it. And, as a shift in the problem means a modification in the scope of relevance too, we can explain, for the same reason, why new facts emerge with the shift in the point of view, whereas others that were formerly in the center of our question disappear. But this statement is nothing else than the original definition we have given of the passing from one level to another. To be sure, it must be admitted that the term "level" applies strictly only to whole systems of problems; nevertheless, the consequences are, in principle, the same. It seems important to me that the scientist keep in mind that each shift in the problem involves a thorough modification of all the concepts and of all the types with which he is dealing. A great many misunderstandings and controversies in the social sciences have their root in the unmodified application of concepts and types at a level other than that where they have their natural place.

But why form personal ideal types at all? Why not simply collect empirical facts? Or, if the technique of typological interpretation may be applied successfully, why not restrict oneself to forming types of impersonal events, or types of the behavior of groups? Do we not have modern economics as an example of a social science which does not deal with personal ideal types, but with curves, with mathematical functions, with the movement of prices, or with such institutions as bank systems or currency? Statistics has performed the great work of collecting information about the behavior of groups. Why go back to the scheme of social action and to the individual actor?

The answer is this: It is true that a very great part of social science can be performed and has been performed at a level which legitimately abstracts from all that happens in the individual actor. But this operating with generalizations and idealizations on a high level of abstraction is in any case nothing but a kind of intellectual shorthand. Whenever the problem under inquiry makes it necessary, the social scientist must have the possibility of shifting the level of his research to that of individual human activity, and where real scientific work is done this shift will always become possible.

The real reason for this is that we cannot deal with phenomena in the social world as we do with phenomena belonging to the natural sphere. In the latter, we collect facts and regularities which are not understandable to us, but which we can refer only to certain fundamental assumptions about the world. We shall never understand why the mercury in the thermometer rises if the sun shines on it. We can only interpret this phenomenon as compatible with the laws we have deduced from some basic assumption about the physical world. We want, on the contrary, to understand social phenomena, and we cannot understand them apart from their placement within the scheme of human motives, human means and ends, human planning – in short – within the categories of human action.

The social scientist must therefore ask, or he must, at least, always be in a position to ask, what happens in the mind of an individual actor whose act has led to the phenomenon in question. We can formulate this *postulate of the subjective interpretation* more correctly as follows: The scientist has to ask what type of individual mind can be constructed and what typical thoughts must be attributed to it to explain the fact in question as the result of its activity within an understandable relation.

This postulate finds its complement in another which I propose to call, borrowing a term of Max Weber, the *postulate of adequacy*. It may be formulated as follows: Each term used in a scientific system referring to human action must be so constructed that a human act performed within the life-world by an individual actor in the way indicated by the typical construction would be reasonable and understandable for the actor himself, as well as for his fellow-men. This postulate is of extreme importance for the methodology of social science. What makes it possible for a social science to refer at all to events in the life-world is the fact that the interpretation of any human act by the social scientist might be the same as that by the actor or by his partner.

The principle of relevance, the postulate of the subjective interpretation, and that of adequacy, are applicable at each level of social study. For instance, all the historical sciences are governed by them. The next step would be to circumscribe within the social sciences the category of those we call the theoretical ones. The outstanding feature of these theoretical sciences is the interpretation of the social world in terms of a system of determinate logical structure (Parsons, *op. cit.*, p. 7). This system of means-ends relations is also an ideal typical one, but as Professor Parsons had pointed out, it is an analytical one and not a system dealing with concrete actions as he calls it. I once formulated the same idea in the statement that the personal ideal-types of action constructed by the so-called theoretical sciences are of a maximum anonymity, that means, what is typified is the behavior of "people as such" or of "every-man." Whatever formula we may use to describe the peculiarity of the theoretical realm, it is clear that a logically interrelated system presupposes that the means-end relations together with the system of constant motives and the system of life-plans must be constructed in such a way that:

(a) it remains in full compatibility with the principles of formal logic;
(b) all its elements are conceived in full clearness and distinctness;
(c) it contains only scientifically verifiable assumptions, which have to be in full compatibility with the whole of our scientific knowledge.

These three requirements may be condensed into another *postulate* for the building up of the ideal types, that of *rationality*. It may be formulated as follows: The ideal type of social action must be constructed in such a way that the actor in the living world would perform the typified act if he had a clear and distinct scientific knowledge of all the elements relevant to his choice and the constant tendency to choose the most appropriate means for the realization of the most appropriate end. Indeed, as we had anticipated in the beginning, only by the introduction of the key concept of rationality can all the elements be provided for constitution of the level called "pure theory." The postulate of rationality implies, furthermore, that all other behavior has to be interpreted as derivative from the basic scheme of rational acting. The reason for this is that only action within the framework of rational categories can be scientifically discussed. Science does not have at its disposal other methods than rational ones and it cannot, therefore, verify or falsify purely occasional propositions.

As we stated before, each type formed by the scientist has its subscript referring to the main problem. In a theoretical system, therefore, only pure rational types are admitted. But where can the scientist find the guarantee that he is establishing a real unified system? Where are the scientific tools to perform that difficult task? The answer is that in every branch of the social sciences which has arrived at the theoretical stage of its development there is a fundamental hypothesis which both defines the fields of research and gives the regulative principle for building up the system of ideal types. Such a fundamental hypothesis, for instance, is in classical economics the utilitarian principle, and in modern economics the marginal principle. The sense of this postulate is the following: Build your ideal types as if all actors had oriented their life-plan and, therefore, all their activities to the chief end of realizing the greatest utility with the minimum of costs; human activity which is oriented in such a way (and only this kind of human activity) is the subject matter of your science.

But hidden within these statements is a very disturbing question. If the social world as object of our scientific research is but a typical construction, why bother with this intellectual game? Our scientific activity and, particularly, that which deals with the social world, is also performed within a certain means-ends relation, namely, in order to acquire knowledge for mastering the world, the real world, not the one created by the grace of the scientist. We want to find out what happens in the real world and not in the fantasies of a few sophisticated eccentrics.

There are a few arguments for quieting such an interlocutor. First of all, the construction of the scientific world is not an arbitrary act of the scientist which he can perform at his own discretion:

1. There are the historical boundaries of the realm of his science which each scientist has inherited from his ancestors as a stock of approved propositions.
2. The postulate of adequacy requires that the typical construction be compatible with the totality of both our daily life and our scientific experience.

But to one who is not satisfied with such guarantees and asks for greater reality, I want to say that I am afraid I do not exactly know what reality is, and my only comfort in this unpleasant situation is that I share my ignorance with the greatest philosophers of all time. Again, I want to quote William James and his profound theory of the different realities in which we live at the same time. It is a misunderstanding of the essential character of science to think that it deals with reality if we consider as the pattern of reality the world of daily life. The world of both the natural and the social scientist is neither more nor less real than the world of thought in general can be. It is not the world within which we act and within which we are born and die. But it is the real home of those important events and achievements which humanity at all times calls culture.

The social scientist, therefore, may continue his work in full confidence. His clarified methods, governed by the postulates mentioned, give him the assurance that he will never lose contact with the world of daily life. And as long as he uses with success methods which have stood this test and still do so, he is quite right in continuing without worrying about methodological problems. Methodology is not the preceptor or the tutor of the scientist. It is always his pupil, and there is no great master in his scientific field who could not teach the methodologists how to proceed. But the really great teacher always has to learn from his pupils. Arnold Schoenberg, the famous composer, starts the preface to his masterly book on the theory of harmony with the sentence: "This book I have learned from my pupils." In this role, the methodologist has to ask intelligent questions about the technique of his teacher. And if those questions help others to think over what they really do, and perhaps to eliminate certain intrinsic difficulties hidden in the foundation of the scientific edifice where the scientists never set foot, methodology has performed its task.

Part II
Current Perspectives

Bounded Rationality and Emotions and How Sociology May Take Profit: Towards an Interdisciplinary Opening

Dieter Bögenhold

Rationality and Max Weber and Joseph Schumpeter

Human action differs from processes in the physical world insofar as action in the social world is driven by motivation. Motivation is embedded in a social framework of social goals and related preferences. Phenomenology especially describes very clearly that social action is led by a cognitive structure of sense and relevance, which guides people through their biographies. Such cognitive structures of sense and relevance serve as a kind of normative compass indicating which aims are positive, neutral, or negative and how specific courses of social actions are related to those aims. Rationality has its origin in the Latin ratio, which is considered as another term for pure reason. Statements of reason can differ according to different social logics within a single society and across societies, in recent as well as in historical times (Swedberg 2014).

Trying to understand the meaning of social action is one of the central fields of academic activity in social sciences (for a broader discussion see Gordon 1993, Hollis 2002). However, this enterprise is also the starting point of many debates on so-called objectivity of interpretation. How can intersubjectively controlled hermeneutics be realized? Which are the parameters to measure human action? Which are, in short, the key questions asking why people do what they do and how social scientists can answer that question? Asking about rationality is closely interrelated to the question about appropriate structures of relevance, which is the domain highlighted by phenomenology. "Relevance is not inherent in nature as such, it is the result of the selective and interpretative activity of man within nature or observing nature. The facts, data, and events with which the natural scientist has to deal are just facts, data, and events within his observational field but this field

D. Bögenhold (✉)
Department of Sociology, Alpen-Adria-University Klagenfurt, Klagenfurt, Austria
e-mail: dieter@boegenhold.com

H. Staubmann, V. Lidz (eds.), *Rationality in the Social Sciences*,
DOI 10.1007/978-3-319-62377-1_9

does not 'mean' anything to the molecules, atoms, and electrons therein. But the facts, events, and data before the social scientist are of an entirely different structure. His observational field, the social world, is not essentially structureless. It has a particular meaning and relevance structure for the human beings living, thinking, and acting therein. They have preselected and preinterpreted this world by a series of common-sense constructs of the reality of daily life, and it is these thought objects which determine their behavior, define the goal of their action, the means available for attaining them" (Schutz 1982: 5–6).

Dealing with these sorts of questions is the domain of sociology, since sociology is by definition the science that—as Max Weber (1972) explained in his sociological categories—seeks to understand social action by interpretation in order to find explanations for the procedures and results (Lachmann 1979). Max Weber said that it is not necessary to be Caesar in order to understand the doings of Caesar (Weber 1972). Weber was one of the first authors who conceptualized different sources providing sense to social action. While Karl Marx, and especially Marxist thinking, idealized thought and consciousness as a kind of reflex of material conditions in society determined in one-to-one fit with the relations of production, Max Weber (1972) was led by the idea that consciousness is never right or wrong, but it always has a (relative) autonomy from the status signaled by the regime of the material world. Cultural factors including religion and related dispositions are factors influencing the rationality of social behavior according to Max Weber (see Collins 1985, Swedberg 1998). He came up with a typology of social action based upon different sources of legitimation, which are traditional social action (actions carried out on the basis of tradition and cultural norms), affective social action (actions ultimately based upon emotions), instrumental and purposeful social action ("Zweckrationalität"), and value-rational action ("Wertrationalität"), where the end justifies the means. According to that typology, there is no single type of rationality, but four different types can each be separated as an *idealtypus*; practically they overlap each other, and behavior has different compositions of elements of rationality. Weber pointed out that broad parts of economics used a nonrealistic view of human nature that reduced people by analogy to a "mathematical ideal figure" (Weber 1990: 30).

Joseph A. Schumpeter (1908) explicitly took these questions up again when he discussed assumptions and consequences of methodological individualism.[1] It was in his first book (Schumpeter 1908) that he orchestrated a broad discussion on the need to argue atomistically or think in terms of social determinism. Especially one chapter, entitled "The Methodological Individualism" (1908: Part I, Chap. 6), explained different concepts of human action and motivation. Here, Schumpeter already explicitly the term *homo oeconomicus* (Schumpeter 1908: 85), which he used as a tool for working in the domain of "pure economics" (Schumpeter 1954). Hodgson (2012: Chap. 2) describes different meanings of methodological individualism in contrast to

[1]The Schumpeter-Parsons-seminars are part of intensive discussion. See Swedberg (2015) for the relationship of Schumpeter and Parsons.

"sociological individualism." Economics primarily used a narrow interpretation of the human agent in the concept of utility maximizer.

Schumpeter's later paper on the use of rationality in social sciences (Schumpeter 1991) dealt with the question of the rationality of people and the problem of interpreting this rationality (see Bögenhold 2014 for a discussion of the interdisciplinarity of Schumpeter), which had already been raised by Max Weber. Schumpeter explicitly discussed the split between rationality as a question of the internal coherence and structure of social action and the so-called observer's rationality, the sphere of interpretation and hermeneutics on the part of academians as "third parties." "We will emphasize at once that this observer's rationality has in itself nothing whatever to do with the presence or absence of rationality in the human types or human actions reserved, or even with the applicability of the concept of rationality to the subject matter under investigation" (Schumpeter, see Part I).

Despite debates about methodological premises of rationality, economics had started to choose a way of operating that mostly adopted a concept of human behavior as egoistic utility maximizing, which corresponded exactly to the type of mathematical ideal figure already criticized by Max Weber. This type of human action was based on the idea of a *homo oeconomicus* as a rational agent motivated purely by economic rewards; being totally egoistic; having no biography, gender, or specific education; or other cultural attributes. *Homo oeconomicus* became textbook knowledge for decades until doubts about it were expressed increasingly, especially in the field of economics.

Bounded Rationality and Social Scientification of Economics

The concept of *homo oeconomicus* became so firmly integrated into education in economics and public reasoning on economic affairs that early discussions of its methodological underpinnings, such as those by Max Weber or Joseph A. Schumpeter, were forgotten. The rational agent served as the conception of social agents in economics. However, slowly but constantly, pioneering positions in economics started to change. Hodgson (2012: 46) has verified that six Nobel laureates in economics have been recognized since the 1970s for being very critical of the concept of the rational egoistic man, among other topics.

The present paper refers just to five of these figures, namely, Herbert Simon, Douglass North, Amartya Sen, Daniel Kahneman, and George Akerlof, each of whom clearly rejected the idea of rational behavior as followed for decades before. The very interesting point here is that these names stand for a new trend in economics, which can be described as a greater turn toward a social scientification of economics (Bögenhold 2010).

Herbert Simon coined the famous formulation, bounded rationality. The term has evolved to become a kind of program for diverse arguments against the neoclassical conception of *homo oeconomicus* (Larkey 2002; Sent 2005). Simon conducted theoretical studies as well as produced empirical works, and he was one of the firsts to use large data sets with the aid of computer simulations. Simon gained the distinction of Nobel laureate in economics in 1978 for his work, which has contributed widely to decision theory. He is regarded as an important author from the academic purviews of philosophy, psychology, organization theory, and economics. His principle matter of investigation may be described by the following question: "How do human beings reason when the conditions for rationality postulated by neoclassical economics are not met?" (Simon 1989: 377). Simon criticized the neoclassic model of decision processes based upon the assumption of *homo oeconomicus*. By contrast, the term, bounded rationality, takes into account that (I) agents often act in ways which could be characterized as nonrational behavior driven by emotions; (II) the use of bounded rationality emphasizes that access to information is limited, since people do not share the same bits of information necessary for deciding among the alternatives in order to achieve the optimal result; (III) even in a situation of equally shared information, human beings are characterized by cognitive diversity and by limited skills in evaluating the single best solution in any given situation with the information provided. According to that scenario, optimal solutions are vague and not easy to calculate. Thus, Simon talks about people trying to satisfice, a portmanteau of "satisfy" and "suffice" (Simon 1972: 176), because not all aspects related to concrete decisions can be analyzed adequately by human beings. Although human agents seek to come up with rational decisions, they are limited in their capabilities to find and to execute decisions, so bounded rationalities take place (Simon 1971). The processes of decision-making are governed by psychological issues among which such factors as risk, uncertainty, and complexity play parts (Simon 1972). Lastly, a major source of the phenomenon of bounded rationality is the limited information capacity with limited speed of information processing. The environment contains so many bits of information that people must reduce complexity and related uncertainties in order to arrive at a final decision at all, given their limited time to come up with responses (Simon 1962).

In a nutshell, Simon reflects upon traditional economic theory, which deals with conceptions of the "economic man," who was "economically engaged" and in the same sense also "rational." Simon is also guided by the idea that the same is true for the brother of the "economic man," the "administrative man," the conception of whom should also be revised and reformulated (Simon 1955: 99). The evolution of organizations is a necessary effect of complex environments, which present individuals with overloading quantities of information. Within organizational settings, issues such as specialization, standardization, authority, identification, and communication are among the factors that limit the "administrative man" (Simon 1971: 102–103) and also affect the ways he is portrayed. Simon argues in favor of a more appropriate understanding of learning processes but also of the evolution of processes of behavior.

Simon has become so popular as an author, because, very often, the implications of his writings are treated as their core messages: economics is too often based on ideas of rational behavior, which is an oversimplification. Instead, the restrictions of simple "clean" economic models should be examined in contexts of complexity. According to Simon, "the task is to replace the global rationality of economic man with a kind of rational behavior that is compatible with the access to information and the computational capacities that are actually processed by organisms, including man, in the kinds of environments in which such organisms exist" (Simon 1955: 99).

Discussing Simon and his famous formulation of a bounded rationality establishes him as a milestone in the history of economic theory. However, even the emergence of the term, bounded rationality, shows that the authenticity of terms and the evolution of concepts are separate matters, which should each be an object of scientific reflection and research. The success of new combinations of things is an innovation (in ideas) in a Schumpeterian understanding (Schumpeter [1911] 1963: 100–102). We can reconstruct the survival of Simon's ideas as due to placing a spotlight on specific academic questions within a larger landscape in which a number of key questions were on the agenda of economics. However, even before Simon entered the scene, other economists had puzzled over fragments of his understanding, without creating the recognized "brand" of so-called bounded rationality. And what is true for economics is also valid for other domains of the social sciences. Thinking about rationality and so-called bounded rationality as an essence of motivation raises a plea for more integrated research involving a number of academic fields including economics and, among others, management and organization theory, neurology, psychology, sociology, and history. Hodgson (2012) has formulated the problem in the same vein: "We need an economics that builds on scientific disciplines, including psychology, neuroscience, and anthropology. These studies have recently made huge strides by incorporating insights from evolutionary theory. In the light of these studies, the critique of economic man has become irresistible" (Hodgson 2012: 23).

Although Simon was awarded a Nobel Prize in the 1970s, several years passed until some of his essential messages became a kind of common knowledge. His suggestion "to turn to the literature of psychology" (Simon 1955: 99–100) was not really taken up on a greater scale until Douglass C. North, Nobel Prize recipient in economics in 1993[2], came up with nearly the same pragmatic formulations:

> "Although I know of very few economists who really believe that the behavioral assumptions of economics accurately reflect human behavior, they do (mostly) believe that such assumptions are useful for building models of market behavior in economics and, though less useful, are still the best game in town for studying politics and the other social sciences. I believe that these traditional behavioral assumptions have prevented economists from coming to grips with some very fundamental issues and that a modification of these assumptions is essential to further progress in the social sciences. The motivation of these actors is more complicated (and their preferences less stable) than assumed in received theory. More controversial (and less understood) among the behavioral assumptions, usually, is the implicit one that the actors possess cognitive systems that provide true models of the worlds about which they make choices ..." (North 1990: 17)

[2]For a history of Nobel laureates and their programs, see Vane and Mulhearn (2005).

Although North was recognized for his works on institutional economics, one clearly sees in the above quotation how much he dissented from simple and crude models that use a very narrow concept of the human being as crude economic maximizer. The same can be said regarding Amartya Sen, who highlights crucial issues that go along with individual capabilities, agency, and choice. Sen developed a kind of social relativity theory with which he explained that happiness and well-being are highly connected to individual path dependencies, comparisons, and individual choices in given situations (Sen 1999). "Sen's notion of capabilities and functionings provides us with a better and complete understanding of the quality of life of people. Functionings refer to the current or actual life conditions of people. The levels of health, happiness, income, and nourishment are some examples of functionings a person can achieve. However, the functionings of an individual or family are the result of choices made. The standard of living reflects the amount of choices a person can make for different life achievements" (Naz 2016: 4).

Kahneman is another Nobel laureate in economics, one who also has an academic background as a psychologist. Kahneman explains that social action must be interpreted as a kind of choice between alternatives (Kahneman 2003). The word "rational" stands for reasonable in everyday speech, but for economists and decision theorists, rational has a different meaning. "The only test of rationality is not whether a person's beliefs and preferences are reasonable, but whether they are internally consistent. A rational person can believe in ghosts so long as all her other beliefs are consistent with the existence of ghosts. A rational person can prefer being hated or being loved, so long as his preferences are consistent. Rationality is logical coherence—reasonable or not" (Kahneman 2012: 411).

Human beings have motives, which may be viewed as rational or irrational by observers (Lauterbach 1962; Rabin 1998). And people have emotions by which they are governed positively or negatively (Elster 1998; Scherer 2011; for historical observations, see Plamber 2015). Love, hate, and envy are expressions of human activity that are real. Human beings love human beings, yet they kill people on occasion, they take part in lotteries, and they present gifts but cheat elsewhere.

Finally, we may refer to Akerlof, the 2001 Nobel laureate in economics, who took up again the notion of motivation to discuss the topic in a framework of macroeconomics. Akerlof works at the level of macroeconomics and discusses motivation in a broad framework related to Keynesian ideas. The rationality of human beings and policy stakeholders, stable systems of preferences and consumption affairs, unintended consequences of social action, and the evolution of behavior are all topics discussed in Akerlof's works. Programmatically, Akerlof (2007) claimed that economics should provide an increased acknowledgment of motivation as a key to the question of why people do what they do. Keynes (1936) referred widely to issues of psychology and social psychology in order to explain economic life in a more sound and appropriate way and discussed expectations, uncertainties, and spirits as crucial social dimensions with impact, while Akerlof also took up questions about norm regulations and other forms of commitments. In this context, Akerlof explicitly recognized a strong impact of sociology in highlighting those thematic areas: "Sociology has a further concept that gives an easy and natural way to add those norms to the utility function. Sociologists say that people have an ideal for how they should or should not behave. Furthermore, that ideal is often conceptualized in terms of the behavior of someone they know or some exemplar who they do not know" (Akerlof 2007: 9).

It has been argued that economics, as presented by top scholars in the academic community, has opened itself to integration with behavioral and cognitive elements (Akerlof 2007; Akerlof and Kranton 2000; Akerlof and Shiller 2009) in order to assist the movement of economics from the world of abstract modeling to real-world phenomena. These voices have evolved into a credo for a new economics. In short, Akerlof referred to cultural contexts providing different norms. Religion and religious identity provide good examples of such norms (Akerlof 2007: 10) and link the discussion to issues of culture more broadly. Cultures within related times and spaces differ in the calculus of individual rationality (Gonzáles 2012). Including culture as an analytic variable indicates a need to examine different settings of norms and related behavior (North 2005; Jones 2006). Culture serves as a framework of rational behavior and is a factor that points to real societies as opposed to abstract models. Historian David Landes put it concisely when he said: "Culture makes almost all the difference" (Landes 2000: 2).

Following that line of thought, modern economics—and especially the economics that stays in the spotlight with famous Nobel laureates as key drivers—has moved considerably. The former breakthrough of Simon and his "bounded rationality" has been pushed forward by several recent authors toward a new interpretation and application of economics. One of the crucial questions to emerge has been the question of rationality and the motivation of social agents and the steps that should be taken in the direction of psychology, sociology, and cultural studies. However, time and energy are increasingly being invested academically in the direction of neurological research as well, inquiring about the functioning of the working brain, since the inner functioning processes have for decades been treated as a black box (Gazzaniga 2011; Gazzaniga et al. 2008). In recent times we have learned that cognitive processes very often depend on physiological foundations.

Evolution of the Division Among the Social Sciences

Philosophy has long dealt with the question of rationality. Karl Popper, in particular, discussed the relativity of rationality in great depth in his so-called critical rationalism (Popper 1959). Insofar as philosophy can be considered a reasonable contributor to many of the substantial questions of recent economics, integrating philosophical perspectives could possibly foster an appropriate understanding of the functioning processes of norms and conventions (Letsas 2014). Grandori (2010) discusses various competing semantic concepts with respect to their similarities and divergences.

If economics changes its self-portrait so significantly, one may ask if it is still the form of economics that many people have learned through the study of textbooks.

Where is economics coming from and where is it going to? What is the domain of economics and to what extent do different approaches in economics coexist? The question of what is the matter of economics has a long tradition. The oft-quoted statement by Jacob Viner that "economics is what economists do" (quoted in Barber 1997: 87) was long ago completed by Frank Knight, when he added "and economists are those who do economics" (quoted in Buchanan 1964: 213). Looking at the activities of economists shows that the domain of economics is always in transition. Since no clear borders exist to provide rational boundaries to the domain of economics, even a current understanding is not much further than one was at the time of Viner or Knight.

The divisional order of economics is characterized by a practice that mirrors the multiplicity of productive processes in academia, including the somehow accidental developments, rather than systematic reasoning, about the design of an academic subject. With respect to the definition of what economics is and how it is organized into different subfolders, two trends overlap. (I) We have a long-term trend in the development of economics by which the discipline increasingly gained firm ground and recognition and by which a process of differentiation began to evolve. This trend took part within the last one and a half centuries. (II) The field of economics also started to become a professional system with clear curricula, degrees, academic societies, and university departments along with an increasing number of publications and related journals. (III) Parallel to the consolidation process of economics, the subject formed border relations to neighboring fields that were formerly extended parts of economics. Looking over the course of the last 100 years, topics in economics have both modified and multiplied.

Bringing a complex development to a very brief denominator, much of the twentieth century development in economics involved the establishment of neoclassic thought, which has been taught as textbook knowledge to undergraduate students and which has dominated wide parts of the non-university public and public policy. "Pure economics" proved to be a program of abstractness, which had problems when confronted with competing empirical materials. Pure economics was related to the concept of an economy operating in a vacuum. This type of thought emerged and became a predominant paradigm during the twentieth century. In its nucleus, it served as a kind of academic religion (Nelson 2001).

Simultaneously, a variety of new special fields, which had not existed in the decades before, were founded within economics. Among them were, for example, industrial economics, labor economics, small business economics, household economics, and the economics of aging. Many additional areas evolved as well and also became impressive fields within the general trend of academic specialization and differentiation. The more complex economics proved to be, the smaller the real terrain of neoclassic theory remained, even though the general image of economics, especially when seen from outside the field, remains neoclassic orthodoxy. How scientific change and progress occur is a topic we find carefully described in the philosophy of science as case studies of how different principles and styles of work form into competing camps of thought (Kuhn 1962; Collins 2002; with special reference to economics, see Wible 1998).

If culture makes differences, capitalism does not exist in a vacuum but in a context with specific social regimes of living, producing, and exchange. Institutionalist approaches have no other aim than to highlight the respects in which different social organizations and institutions (including religion, language, law, family structures and networks, systems of education, and industrial relations) establish differences that must be considered when trying to establish statements of general principles regarding capitalist societies and economies. As we know, capitalism in Singapore differs from capitalism in Zimbabwe, which differs from capitalism in Switzerland. Accepting the idea that economies and societies are filled not by abstract but by real entities, one has to refer to concrete coordinates of time and space (Ostrom 2005). If economics rediscovers history, the recent history of economic thought breaks with the recent mainstream and goes beyond abstractivism.

Complexity, Bounded Rationality, and Converging Economics

As far as Simon's "bounded rationality" seems to be on the right track, progress can only be measured through comparison between old and new contributions to the discussion. Simon's notion of different types of social action and related rationality points to diverse areas of earlier careful discussion that now appear neglected. Whoever talks about bounded rationality nowadays (e.g., Lovallo and Kahneman 2000) does so on ground prepared by classic authors. In this way, reformulations sometimes come to be celebrated as new inventions. "Animal Spirits" (Akerlof and Shiller 2009) takes up several questions first raised by J. M. Keynes.

Simon is one of the first authors of contemporary economics who merged economics with psychology, but discussion of the social psychological dimensions of rationality can also be traced back to earlier sources in phenomenology, which described very clearly that social action is led by a cognitive structure of sense and relevance that guides people through their biographies. Such cognitive structures of sense and relevance serve as a kind of normative compass, indicating which aims are positive, neutral, or negative and how specific social actions are related to those aims.

The growing convergence between economics and psychology should not hinder an acknowledgment of the relevance of sociology and history. In sociology, Max Weber was one of the first authors who conceptualized different sources providing sense to social action. While Karl Marx and especially Marxist thinking idealized thought and consciousness in a kind of reflex to material conditions in society that determined as a one-to-one fit with the relations of production, Max Weber (1972) was led by the idea that consciousness is never right or wrong but it always has a (relative) autonomy from the status signaled by the regime of the material world.

Cultural factors, including religion and related dispositions, are factors influencing the rationality of social behavior according to Max Weber.

Thinking of rationality as a driver of social action does not imply that people can always decipher the individual elements of the forces by which they are driven. Sociology uses the term habituation to refer to deeply internalized routines of action that help to economize everyday life by avoiding the repetitious asking for the argumentative legitimation of one's own doing. In that way, habituation acts as an economy measure, since people do not have to newly seek instructions every time in order to come up with decisions (Berger and Luckmann 1966). In contrast to sociology, psychology refers to the subconscious as a separate sphere that influences people's behavior without giving full control to actors' decisions, as Sigmund Freud first explained (Freud 1995). With respect to preferences in combination with lifestyles, needs, and behavior, Maslow (1954), as a social psychologist, developed a scheme of different steps in the setting of goals for human behavior, which he ranked in the form of a pyramid. According to Maslow, people try to meet the satisfaction of basic needs first. One way out of the dilemma was taken by Gary Becker when he considered that "behavior is driven by a much richer set of values and preferences" (Becker 1995: 385), but—according to Becker—ultimately all decisions, even seemingly nonrational ones, are based upon rational decisions of selfishness. Becker put a lot of effort into explaining his idea through many examples, including choices of marriage, sports, restaurant visits, or decisions regarding family and career. But at the end, an understanding of rationality seems to become somehow self-referential, since all actions prove to be outcomes of a rational decision. If all emotion can be seen as part of rationality, the term tends to make itself obsolete, and the traditional meaning of *ratio* could be replaced by behavior (Rosenberg 2012, 89–116).

A different way to foster an understanding of rationality is through the explicit addressing of emotions as a field of research (Elster 1999; Hochschild 2013). This method of analysis merges different disciplines and has gained considerable attention during the past two decades (Scherer 2011). However, talking about rationality (or nonrationality) always implies that we practically know how people think. In that way of academic practice, the brain usually serves as a black box. Sociology, psychology, or economics is increasingly moving in new directions and also toward different integrations with neurosciences. Divergent issues, such as happiness or trust capacity, can also be analyzed in relation to the workings of the brain. Cognitive neuroscience can deal with memory, speed of thinking, creativity, attention, and flexibility much more adequately than traditional thinking could, as it did not try to merge different insights. Future discussion should acknowledge further developments in these fields in order to avoid discussion on the basis of "as if" assumptions. It is also very important to arrive at a better understanding about the degree to which behavior is socially learned and embedded in specific social contexts (Lagueux 2010) and the degree to which it is governed by neurotransmitters and neuromodulators. Given the fact that human behavior has proven to be more complex than what can be expressed in monocausal and linear assumptions of rational man who has no social context and who lives without being captured by institutions and related norms, constraints, and opportunities, without having social attributes such as age, biography and life history, family, gender, occupation, and education and without belonging to a specific concrete time or space, the rationality concept remains a vague and empty term.

Further Research Grounds of Universal Social Sciences

Scientific progress is often contingent and never rational in a sense that it follows arithmetic rules of combinations. The "market" for ideas is not precisely an efficient or perfect market. Academic progress is also related to a series of mistakes by which intellectual resources are wasted. As a consequence, there are, indeed, intellectual gems lying unexploited and waiting for someone to grasp (Boettke 2000).

Newest economics once again takes up academic perspectives that were provided by (old or new) institutional thought, asking about concrete economies in concrete societies. Of course, many new thematic arenas have opened up during the last hundred years (among them game theory, transaction cost theory, principal agent theory, public choice theory, welfare economics, and many others), so that comparisons between up-to-date economics and earlier forms suffer from a lack of integrity in many respects. If students start to get into a new academic discipline, such as medicine, biology, or economics, they usually want to learn the current state of thought. A majority of people do not want to find out which discussions were on the agenda 50 or 100 years ago but are interested instead in the predominant portraits of recent debates. What is uncontested terrain, which are the competing theories, and where can there be academic profit in future engagement? The difficult matter is that academic progress and its change must be conceptualized as a series of processes of shortcomings, which retrospectively appear as a never-ending story of failures or mistakes, to express it starkly. Since it should be an integral part of the identity of a profession (and a profession's member) to be familiar with the tradition of its own discipline, further investment in the history of economic thought should be a unifying issue for the future of economics. Since we need to know the intellectual history in order to find innovative academic concepts for the future, dealing with the history of economic thought is also a tool to undertake economics of the future.

A manual on how to treat the issues academically is still provided by Joseph A. Schumpeter's *History of Economic Analysis* (Schumpeter 1954). The preface of the book gives a thorough discussion of why histories of science are necessary for systematic reasons, not only in economics but also in other academic fields. In his substantial introduction to his study, Schumpeter explicitly raised the question, "Why do we study the history of economics?" He continued to add his own answer, which was concerned with the issue why we study the history of any science in general and of economics specifically. Just as evolutionary economists take as their credo the look at the inner dynamics of change to arrive at an understanding of principles, theoretical economists should treat their subject analogously. One has to gain a careful understanding of the history of one's own discipline to see the larger and smaller lines that have led to recent discussion and to the current state of the art. In this light, recent discussion gains much more color, and our current knowledge comes up in a historically transcendent way as a snapshot within a series of new intellectual positions, be they failures or innovations. Economic theories evolve in specific contexts of social life and societal organization. In some way, they mirror the times of their origins and serve as a diagnosis of related systems of thought.

Economics is seen as a box of tools, and it always contains "theory" (always written with quotation marks by Schumpeter 1954), economic history, sociology, political economy, statistics, and some additional fields. Finally, Schumpeter explained that "psychology is really the basis from which any social science must start and in terms of which all fundamental explanation must run" (Schumpeter 1954: 27).

Bounded Rationality and Social Networks

Discussing the seminal ideas by Simon, we should acknowledge more explicitly the obvious links to social network analysis, which has a strong anchor in the field of sociology and which has diffused and evolved increasingly toward many neighboring fields. Bounded rationality is very much to be understood in relation to asymmetric information and complexity. Bounded rationality mirrors the fact that societies, organizations, and economies are fragmented; they are organized along different lines and zones of contact, familiarity, and information exchange. In our view, modern economics could benefit significantly by integrating recent network concepts, which are fantastic tools for bridging micro- and macro-perspectives. "Network models of advantage use structure as an indicator of how information is distributed in a system of people" (Burt et al. 2013: 529). Social network analysis also continues to develop many themes enunciated by pioneering social psychologists. "At its best, social network analysis draws from traditions of research and theory in psychology, sociology, and other areas to describe how patterns of interpersonal relations are associated with diverse behavioral, cognitive, and emotional outcomes. Looking to the future, we are deepening interest in the psychological underpinnings of why some people more than others engage and benefit from the networks of contacts within which they are embedded" (Burt et al. 2013: 543). On the other hand, discussion that refers to psychological differences of human natures also urgently requires an understanding of social facts and vice versa (Walker and Lynn 2013), a point celebrated by E. Durkheim's analysis of suicide (Durkheim 1951) long ago.

Markets are always in transition, they come up, they go down, and they change. Markets are carried out by actors who know and trust sets of people while perhaps also regarding other people as hostile competitors. However concrete markets may look, they always have social traits, and economics would fall short if it did not ask about such issues. Processes of competition must also be analyzed and understood as ongoing social processes involved in social structures and permanently in processes of reorganization (Burt 1995; Bögenhold 2013) and closely linked to different formations of habits (Hodgson and Knudsen 2004). The presently existing, largely categorical descriptions of social structure have no solid theoretical grounding, but network concepts may provide the only way to construct a theory of social structure (White et al. 1976: 732). In many respects, network analysis is an excellent exemplification of what the term of social embeddedness can deliver. Network analysis furnishes the popular formulations that have become "economic sociology's most celebrated metaphor" (Guillén et al. 2002: 4).

Different capital structures correspond to different network designs and vice versa. Divergent network arrangements provide different opportunities to communicate, to receive information, and to create different structures of cultural capital. Network analysis explores modes and contents of exchanges between different agents when symbols, emotions, or goods and services are exchanged. An initial point of discussion was that up-to-date economics is increasingly willing to open up to topics of cognitive structure and motivation. Economic sociology and economic psychology share many of the same motives behind these trends, since the arguments in favor of the trends form the foundations of their own academic identity. But one should be curious as well as careful when meeting these new tendencies. Nothing should be taken for granted; one should always try to see whether pieces of the puzzle fit.

Conclusion

The title of the paper is "Bounded Rationality and Emotions and How Sociology May Take Profit." "Bounded rationality" stands for the work of Herbert Simon, but we have seen that Simon had several followers who have pushed the academic discussion much further forward. Of course, many questions were raised, but many definite answers have not been given. Rationality is the social grammar that provides the sense for social action. It is a driver that has sources in different domains.

Social sense is learned and depends upon biographies and life courses with social embeddedness in terms of culture, space, and time. The social context of judgment and decision serves as a framework. It oscillates with modes of social action, so that beginning and end are intertwined. Even the workings of the brain, as viewed in the domain of neuroscience, must be studied with a linkage to society (Pickersgill 2013). Asymmetric information and social capital, asymmetric social support through diverse social ties, and asymmetric distribution of aspiration are among the social premises of diverse behavior. Taken together, all these factors contribute to an understanding stating that economics alone "can't explain the modern world" (McCloskey 2011). These topics suggest that diverse branches of research and knowledge may benefit from further cooperation. Reasoning about rationality and her sister irrationality indicates that—besides economics and social psychology—

sociology matters. The observed social scientification of economics helps to highlight several strengths that sociology commands by nature of its domain: societies in contexts.

References

Akerlof, George A. 2007. The Missing Motivation in Macroeconomics. *American Economic Review* 97 (1): 5–36.

Akerlof, George A., and Rachel E. Kranton. 2000. Economics and Identity. *The Quarterly Journal of Economics* 115: 715–753.

Akerlof, George A., and Robert J. Shiller. 2009. *Animal Spirits: How Human Psychology Drives the Economy, and Why it Matters for Global Capitalism*. Princeton: Princeton University Press.

Barber, William J. 1997. Reconfigurations in American Academic Economics. A General Practitioner's Perspective. *Daedalus* 126: 87–103.

Becker, Gary. 1995. The Economic Way of Looking at Behavior. *Journal of Political Economy* 101 (3): 385–409.

Berger, Peter L., and Thomas Luckmann. 1966. *The Social Construction of Reality*. Garden City/New York: Anchor Books/Doubleday.

Boettke, Peter J. 2000. *Why Read the Classics in Economics?* George Mason University, Unpublished Paper.

Bögenhold, Dieter. 2010. From Heterodoxy to Orthodoxy and Vice Versa: Economics and Social Sciences in the Division of Academic Work. *The American Journal of Economics and Sociology* 69 (5): 1566–1590.

———. 2013. Social Network Analysis and the Sociology of Economics: Filling a Blind Spot with the Idea of Social Embeddedness. *The American Journal of Economics and Sociology* 72 (2): 293–318.

———. 2014. Schumpeter as a Universal Social Theorist. *The Atlantic Economic Journal* 42: 205–215.

Buchanan, James M. 1964. What should Economists Do? *Southern Economic Journal* 30 (3): 213–228.

Burt, Ronald S. 1995. *Structural Holes: The Social Structure of Competition*. Cambridge: Harvard University Press.

Burt, Ronald S., Martin Kilduff, and Stefano Tasselli. 2013. Social Network Analysis: Foundations and Frontiers on Advantage. *Annual Review of Psychology* 64: 527–547.

Collins, Randall. 1985. *Max Weber: A Skeleton Key*. London: Sage.

———. 2002. *The Sociology of Philosophers*. Cambridge: Harvard University Press.

Durkheim, Emile. 1951. *Suicide: A Study in Sociology*. New York: The Free Press.

Elster, Jon. 1998. Emotions and Economic Theory. *Journal of Economic Literature* 36: 47–74.

———. 1999. *Alchemies of the Human Mind: Rationality and the Emotions*. Cambridge: Cambridge University Press.

Freud, Sigmund. 1995. *The Basic Writings of Sigmund Freud*. New York: Random House.

Gazzaniga, Michael S. 2011. *Who's in Charge? Free Will and the Science of the Brain*. New York: Harper Collins.

Gazzaniga, Michael S., Richard B. Ivry, and George R. Mangun. 2008. *Cognitive Neuroscience. The Biology of the Mind*. New York: Norton.

Gonzáles, Ana M. 2012. Emotional Culture and the Role of Emotions in Cultural Analysis. In *The Emotions and Cultural Analysis*, ed. A.M. Gonzáles, 1–15. Surrey: Ashgate.

Gordon, Scott. 1993. *The History and Philosophy of Social Science*. London and New York: Routledge.

Grandori, Anna. 2010. A Rational Heuristic Model of Economic Decision Making. *Rationality and Society* 22 (4): 477–504.

Guillén, Mauro F., Randall Collins, Paula England, and Marshall Meyer. 2002. The Revival of Economic Sociology. In *The New Economic Sociology: Developments in an Emerging Field*, ed. Mauro F. Guillén, Randall Collins, Paula England, and Marshall Meyer, 1–32. New York: Russell Sage.

Hochschild, Arlie. 2013. *So How is the Family?* Berkeley: University of California Press.

Hodgson, Geoffrey M. 2012. *From Pleasure Machines to Moral Communities. An Evolutionary Economics Without Homo Oeconomicus*. Chicago: Chicago University Press.

Hodgson, Geoffrey M., and Thorbjørn Knudsen. 2004. The Complex Evolution of a Simple Traffic Convention: The Functions and Implications of Habit. *Journal of Economic Behavior & Organization* 54: 19–47.

Hollis, Martin. 2002. *The Philosophy of Social Science: An Introduction*. Cambridge: Cambridge University Press.

Jones, Eric L. 2006. *Cultures Merging. A Historical and Economic Critique of Culture*. Princeton: PUP.

Kahneman, Daniel. 2003. A Perspective on Judgment and Choice: Mapping Bounded Rationality. *The American Psychologist* 58: 697–720.

———. 2012. *Thinking, Fast and Slow*. London: Penguin.

Keynes, John M. 1936. *The General Theory of Employment, Interest and Money*. New York: Macmillan.

Kuhn, Thomas S. 1962. *The Structure of Scientific Revolutions*. Chicago: University of Chicago Press.

Lachmann, Ludwig M. 1979. The Method of Interpretation. In *The Legacy of Max Weber*, ed. Ludwig M. Lachmann, 17–48. Berkeley: The Glendessary Press.

Lagueux, Maurice. 2010. *Rationality and Explanation in Economics*. London: Routledge.

Landes, David. 2000. Culture Makes Almost all the Difference. In *Culture Matters. How Values Shape Human Progress*, ed. Lawrence E. Harrison and Samual P. Huntington, 2–13. New York: Basic Books.

Larkey, Patrick D. 2002. Ask a Simple Question. A Retrospective on Herbert Alexander Simon. *Policy Science* 35 (3): 239–268.

Lauterbach, Albert. 1962. *Psychologie des Wirtschaftslebens*. Reinbeck: Rowoldt.

Letsas, George. 2014. The DNA of Conventions. *Law and Philosophy* 33 (5): 535–571.

Lovallo, Dan, and Daniel Kahneman. 2000. Living with Uncertainty: Attractiveness and Resolution Timing. *Journal of Behavioral Decision Making* 13: 179–190.

Maslow, Abraham H. 1954. *Motivation and Personality*. New York: Harper & Row.

McCloskey, Deirdre N. 2011. *Bourgeois Dignity: Why Economics can't Explain the Modern World*. Chicago: Chicago University Press.

Naz, Farah. 2016. Understanding Human Well-being: How could Sen's Capability Approach Contribute? *Forum for Social Economics* 45: 1–16.

Nelson, Robert H. 2001. *Economics as Religion: From Samuelson to Chicago and beyond*. Pennsylvania: Pennsylvania State University Press.

North, Douglass C. 1990. *Institutions, Institutional Change and Economic Performance*. Cambridge: Cambridge University Press.

———. 2005. *Understanding the Process of Economic Change*. Princeton: Princeton University Press.

Ostrom, Elinor. 2005. *Understanding Institutional Diversity*. Princeton: Princeton University Press.

Pickersgill, Martyn. 2013. The Social Life of the Brain: Neuroscience in Society. *Current Sociology* 61 (3): 322–340.

Plamber, Jan. 2015. *The History of Emotions*. Oxford: Oxford University Press.

Popper, Karl. 1959. *The Logic of Scientific Discovery*. New York: Routledge.

Rabin, Matthew. 1998. Psychology and Economics. *Journal of Economic Literature* 36: 11–46.

Rosenberg, Alexander. 2012. *Philosophy of Social Science*. Boulder: Westview Press.

Scherer, Klaus R. 2011. On the Rationality of Emotions: Or, When are Emotions Rational? *Social Science Information* 50 (3–4): 330–350.
Schumpeter, Joseph A. 1908. *Das Wesen und der Haptinhalt der theoretischen Nationalökonomie*. Leipzig: Duncker & Humblot.
———. 1954. *History of Economic Analysis*. Oxford: Oxford University Press.
———. 1963. *The Theory of Economic Development*. Oxford: Oxford University Press.
———. 1991. The Meaning of Rationality in the Social Sciences. In *The Economics and Sociology of Capitalism*, ed. Richard Swedberg, 316–318. Princeton University Press: Princeton.
Schutz, Alfred. 1982. *Collected Papers, Vol. I, The Problem of Social Reality, (1961 firstly)*. The Hague: Martinus Nijhoff.
Sen, Amartya. 1999. The Possibility of Social Choice. *American Economic Review* 89 (3): 349–378.
Sent, Esther-Mirjam. 2005. Simplifying Herbert Simon. *History of Political Economy* 37 (2): 227–232.
Simon, Herbert A. 1955. A Behavioral Model of Rational Choice. *Quarterly Journal of Economics* 69: 99–118.
———. 1962. The Architecture of Complexity. *Proceedings of the American Philosophical Society* 106 (6): 467–482.
———. 1971. *Administrative Behavior. A Study of the Decision-Making Process in Administrative Organization*. New York: Macmillan.
———. 1972. Theories of Bounded Rationality. In *Decision and Organization. A Volume in Honor of Jacob Marschak*, ed. C.B. McGuire and Roy Radner, 161–176. Amsterdam: North Holland Publishing.
———. 1989. The Scientist as a Problem Solver. In *Complex Information Processing. How do Human Beings Reason*, ed. David Klahr and Kenneth Kotowsky, 375–398. Hillsdale: Erlbaum.
Swedberg, Richard. 1998. *Max Weber and the Idea of Social Science*. Princeton: Princeton University Press.
———. 2014. *The Art of Social Theory*. Princeton: Princeton University Press.
———. 2015. Schumpeter and Talcott Parsons. *Journal of Evolutionary Economics* 25 (1): 215–222.
Vane, Howard R., and Chris Mulhearn. 2005. *The Nobel Memorial Laureates in Economics. An Introduction to Their Careers and Main Published Works*. Cheltenham: Edward Elgar.
Walker, Marc H., and Freda B. Lynn. 2013. The Embedded Self: A Social Network Approach to Identity Theory. *Social Psychology Quarterly* 76 (2): 151–179.
Weber, Max. 1972. *Wirtschaft und Gesellschaft*. Tübingen: J.C.B. Mohr.
———. 1990. *Grundriß zu den Vorlesungen über Allgemeine (theoretische) Nationalökonomie*. Tübingen: J.C.B. Mohr.
White, Harrison C., S.A. Boorman, and R.L. Breiger. 1976. Social Structures from Multiple Networks I: Blockmodells of Roles and Positions. *The American Journal of Sociology* 81: 730–780.
Wible, James R. 1998. *The Economics of Science. Methodology and Epistemology as if Economics Really Mattered*. London and New York: Routledge.

The Concept of Rationality in Modern Social Sciences: A Critical Appraisal of Joseph A. Schumpeter's Essay on "The Meaning of Rationality"

Andreas Diekmann

Schumpeter's work has inspired modern economic thought, particularly evolutionary economics (Metcalfe 2012; Dopfer 2016). The ideas, essays, theories, and predictions—although some of them failed—of this grandmaster of creative thinking in social science also touch the realm of sociologists. Moreover, for social scientists generally, his methodological perspectives are still today instructive and worthy of being discussed. His essay on "The Meaning of Rationality in the Social Sciences" encompasses many issues relevant to the methodological debates of modern social sciences. Besides the discussion of the virtues and pitfalls of rationality models, there are the problems of "Wertfreiheit" and ultimate goals, the issue of macro-"laws," and the important idea that classes do not act, but agents do, and that the interest of agents may deviate from "class interests" (a view similar to Olson's *Logic of Collective Action*; Olson 1965). Schumpeter also mentions the problem that rational actions may have irrational consequences and other issues that are at the center of the methodology of the social sciences.

Here, I will confine myself to Schumpeter's discussion of rationality (see Part I) and will confront his results with today's discourse on the conception of rationality in decision theory and behavioral game theory. In part two, I will briefly broach the issue of rationality in strategic interactions. In part three, I will stress some limitations of the strict rationality principle. Nevertheless, even if actors do make decisions in accord with principles of rationality, it may happen that rational solutions will be generated by an evolutionary process. Rationality by evolution is certainly in the spirit of Schumpeter's (1912, 1942) evolutionary theory.

A. Diekmann (✉)
Department of Humanities, Social and Political Sciences, ETH Zürich, Zürich, Switzerland

Fellow of Institute for Advanced Studies, Berlin, Germany
e-mail: andreas.diekmann@soz.gess.ethz.ch

H. Staubmann, V. Lidz (eds.), *Rationality in the Social Sciences*,
DOI 10.1007/978-3-319-62377-1_10

Three Types of Rationality

Observer Rationality

There is no controversy that the natural as well as the social sciences follow rational principles in order to gain scientific knowledge. Schumpeter claims that a rational scientific procedure has to fulfill the following criteria: (1) A chosen degree of accuracy in description, (2) parsimonious assumptions, (3) the model or theory enables predictions, (4) all propositions of a theory must comply with the rules of logic, and (5) the theory allows for unobserved entities. Schumpeter is well aware that there may be a conflict or a tradeoff between the principles of accuracy and parsimony. A description of phenomena should be "most economical with reference to the assigned degree of accuracy" (for this and the following quotes, see Part I in this volume). There may also be conflict between the goal of parsimonious descriptions and the use of unobservable concepts in scientific theories. However, if unobservable terms facilitate parsimonious descriptions, such terms should not be excluded from scientific theories. In Schumpeter's words: "If the hypothesis that planets are moved by angels, opened the shortest way to describing their motions, there could be no objection to it on grounds of scientific rationality." The rationality of scientific procedures is what he called "the observer's rationality."

Objective Rationality

A different kind of rationality is "objective rationality." This is the rationality of "objects" under study, such as firms, households, or individuals. Scientific models that make assumptions about actor's rationality presuppose "an objective rationality (rationality in the object) seen through the rationality of the observer." Schumpeter's assumption of objective rationality is a controversial issue in the social science debate about theory construction.

Schumpeter does not provide an explicit definition of "objective rationality." At first glance, one is tempted to interpret the concept as the *homo oeconomicus* assumption. However, further reading clarifies that the meaning is broader. *Homo oeconomicus* is a simplified model (parsimonious but often not accurate) of human behavior. It assumes both strictly rational decisions and material goals or preferences, such as profit maximizing. While objective rationality keeps the first assumption, it dispenses with the second of material preferences.

Objective rationality is very similar to the rational choice model. Of course, many definitions of "rational choice" have been put forward. I prefer the following definition: Rational choice means consistency with the axioms of a rationality theory, i.e., the axioms proposed by Neumann and Morgenstern (1947) or Savage

(1954). A weaker version of rational choice (I call it "ordinal rationality") only claims that actors have ordinal preferences, i.e., actors choose in accordance with the axiom of transitivity: if a is preferred to b, and b is preferred to c, actors are expected to prefer a to c. Note that the transitivity axiom is testable by empirical methods. Ordinal rationality is sufficient for many explanations. However, further axioms proposed by Neumann and Morgenstern (1947) and extended by Savage (1954) are needed for rational decisions under risk and the maximization of expected utility.

As I mentioned above, Schumpeter was not explicit on the definition of the rationality of "objects." The example of a profit-maximizing firm indicates that preferences are at least ordinal. Schumpeter writes: "To be sure it is quite sufficient that what firms want is to make money and that they would rather make more than less of it." In this case, Schumpeter's reasoning is based on a *homo oeconomicus* having ordinal and material preferences.

Notice that neither rational choice theory nor Schumpeter's concept of objective rationality is restricted to *homo oeconomicus* preferences. A *homo oeconomicus* model is parsimonious and sometimes accurate. Yet, often, the predictions of the *homo oeconomicus* model fail because the model is too simple and actors pursue nonmaterial interests.

Subjective Rationality

While rational choice theory does not care about mental processes, Schumpeter does. He insists that, under certain circumstances, there would be a different result if actors made decisions consciously or not. For example, a monopolist who consciously computes an optimal path of reaction to a changing environment will react more speedily compared to the management of sluggish firms. In contrast, rational choice theory treats mental processes as a black box. The typical argument is that it docs not matter whether a decision has been made consciously or not. A cyclist reacts automatically and will keep balance without solving the differential equations of dynamic movements.

An actor's subjective rationality may also include preferences not captured by the observer's assumptions about objective rationality. To continue Schumpeter's example: "Our model may not fit a given firm also for another class of reason. The technology of its productive process may rouse the contempt of the consulting engineer, and yet the setup as a whole be quite rational because it may not pay the leading man to bother about technology: he may have such a flair for fashions for instance and be so excellent a salesman (...) that it would be sheer waste of effort for him to worry about whether or not his plant is economical (...)" Here, rational choice theory conforms to Schumpeter's thoughts. Rational choice theory based on the axiomatic approach does not exclude any preferences so long as the preferences obey the axiomatic requirements. Neither Neumann and Morgenstern's axiomatic theory nor the axioms proposed by Savage prescribe the content of preferences. Altruistic preferences do not necessarily contradict the principle of rationality. And, indeed, Andreoni and Miller (2002) demonstrated by experimental methods that altruistic probands were able to make consistently rational decisions.

Schumpeter suggests that the observer try to understand the subjective rationality of the objects under study. Understanding subjective rationality by the rational observer has another advantage. A scientist may obtain information why his model failed. Different kinds of reasoning or hidden and yet unknown preferences may be revealed. With this information at hand, the rational observer may be able to construct a revised model that better fits the actor's subjective rationality. In the words of Schumpeter: "(. . .) investigation of subjective rationality may put us on to the track of other reasons and even help us to identify the right 'objectively rational model.'" Finally, there might be the possibility that rational explanations fail. "The greatest of all the services that research into the facts of subjective rationality can render is the—possibly—melancholy one of showing up the narrow limits of its range."

Today, behavioral decision and game theory pursue research programs that incorporate nonmaterial and "other regarding" preferences in models of objective rationality. Rabin (1993) developed a model taking into account "fairness intentions," while the models by Bolton and Ockenfels (2000) and Fehr and Schmidt (1999) include, besides material preferences, a so-called preference of "inequality aversion." Other models focus on actors' inclination to reciprocate a positive action by a positive reaction (positive reciprocity) and a negative one by retaliation (negative reciprocity). Costly reciprocation might be an altruistic act. For example, costly and self-damaging punishment may stabilize social norms of cooperation. In a highly cited paper, Fehr and Gächter (2002) show experimentally that probands punish free riders even if punishment is costly. So-called altruistic punishment (Fehr and Gächter 2002) enhances the level of cooperation in a good collective situation. Models that include "other regarding preferences" are able to explain many phenomena that cannot be explained by the restrictive *homo oeconomicus*. Note that these models do not skip the principle of rationality but instead relax the assumption of material preferences.

However, it may happen that axioms of rationality are systematically violated. The Allais paradox and the Ellsberg paradox are points in case, and experimental findings for many decision problems (Tversky and Kahneman 1981; Gigerenzer and Todd 1999; Gigerenzer 2000) indicate the limits of descriptive rationality theories. Bounded rationality models with less restrictive assumptions of learning and adaptation may help to explain actor's behavior if strict rationality models fail. We will come back to this issue.

Strategic Interaction

"For many obvious reasons it is very important to distinguish between rational behavior and rational results (...). This may best be illustrated by all those cases in which the mass effect of actions, each of which may be described by a strictly rational model, spells chaos and produces results most irrational from the standpoint of the ends of the actors." More than a decade before, Robert K. Merton (1936) wrote his famous essay about the "Unanticipated Consequences of Social Action," and more recently Barry and Hardin (1982) edited a book titled *Rational Man and Irrational Society?*. Raymond Boudon (1977, 1982) used the term "effets pervers" or "paradox effects." These ideas touch a core theme of the social sciences. Social actions are interdependent; the outcome of ego's action is dependent on the alter's decision. The outcome sometimes enhances welfare, as in Adam Smith's thesis that the sum of individual egoisms furthers the collective welfare, but often does not. What Schumpeter had in mind is a so-called social dilemma as it is labeled today in social psychology, economics, and behavioral game theory. Climate change, a Hobbesian world in the many failed states, armament races, and less harmful situations of mutual distrust in daily transactions may serve as examples. The prisoner's dilemma, the trust game, and the commons dilemma are different types of models of social dilemma situations. In a social dilemma, individual rational actions lead to a collective outcome that is worse than a possible alternative outcome. However, the alternative outcome is only attainable if there was the opportunity to agree on an enforceable contract. Rational actors in a prisoner's dilemma will certainly cooperate, provided they are able to make an enforceable contract and violations of the contract are strongly enough punished.

It is worth noticing that many sociologists, even rational choice sociologists, have largely ignored the problems of strategic interaction. Game theory, the mathematics of social interaction, was until the 1980s largely unknown to economists, and even today most sociologists are unfamiliar with the basics of game theory.

Oskar Morgenstern, another Austrian, described, as early as 1928, in his book *Wirtschaftsprognose* (Economic Forecast), the importance of strategic interaction for economic predictions and behavior (Morgenstern 1928).

As is well known, the Hungarian mathematician, John von Neumann, and Morgenstern have laid the foundation of game theory (Neumann and Morgenstern 1947). With the extension of the "Nash equilibrium" and further refinements, definitions of rationality in a strategic context became feasible. Indeed, I do not believe that it is possible to provide a precise definition of rationality in situations of strategic interaction without the help of game theory. Employing an axiomatic approach, Harsanyi and Selten (1988) proposed a normative theory of rationality. The Harsanyi-Selten theory (and alternative concepts) is still discussed today, and some issues like the axiom of "payoff dominance" or "risk dominance" are still controversial. Nevertheless, most game theorists would agree that "rational behavior" should not only fulfill criteria for the assignment of cardinal utilities. In addition, individual rational behavior is expected to follow a Nash equilibrium strategy that is subgame perfect. Under incomplete information, beliefs are updated by the Bayesian rule. Admittedly, these are very restrictive criteria for rationality. Empirical research shows that actors violate the principles of rational behavior in a wide range of more or less complex situations of strategic interaction.

Rationality by Evolution[1]

Rational choice sociologists using game models assume that actors decide "rationally" about alternatives and are aware of the consequences of potential actions. There are many examples of successful explanations using the rational actor model. On the other hand, there are problems of strategic interaction that cannot easily be explained by rational actor models alone. Often foresight and knowledge of the consequences of decisions are very limited. People learn by trial and error, imitate successful modes of behavior, and adapt new strategies. Customs, conventions, social norms, and institutions are usually not results of rational design but the outcome of evolutionary forces with cultural mutations, variations, and a selection mechanism. Rational choice theory lays too much emphasis on "intelligent design" by purpose-oriented actors, whereas many social phenomena are in fact generated by processes of cultural evolution.

In economics, Schumpeter is one of the pioneers of evolutionary economics (Metcalfe 2012; Dopfer 2016). Chapter 7 of *Capitalism, Socialism and Democracy* is about the famous "process of creative destruction," whereby the inventive entrepreneur employs innovative technologies to generate new products and economic growth. This evolutionary process is driven by "industrial mutation" that brings about a new economic structure or might destroy an old one (Schumpeter 1942).

On a small scale, the process of adaption and the evolution of a new structure can even be studied in the lab. The study by Gürerk et al. (2006) is an instructive example. Their study builds on Fehr and Gächter's (2002) public good experiment with altruistic sanctions. As was mentioned above, Fehr and Gächter were able to show that participants in a public good experiment refrained from free riding if actors had the opportunity to sanction their co-players. Note that the sanctions were costly for both actors. The punished person had to pay a fine, and the person who imposed the sanction had to pay for punishment. A *homo oeconomicus* would not punish, and cooperation would be predicted to break down. However, the experiment demonstrated that subjects punish norm violators at their own cost (i.e.,

[1]The following parts are based on Diekmann (2009).

altruistic punishment occurs), thereby increasing the rate of cooperation. Altruistic punishment may be due to a tendency toward "strong reciprocity" either because of fairness considerations or because of the inclination to reciprocate the unkind actions of co-players (Charness and Rabin 2002; Fehr and Gächter 2002; McCabe et al. 2003). Now, let us imagine that actors have a choice between two different regimes or institutions. The first regime is a public good game with sanctioning opportunities ("sanctioning institution or SI") as described above. Under the second regime, sanctioning opportunities are absent ("sanction-free institution or SFI"). In an experiment conducted by Gürerk et al. (2006), subjects played over 30 rounds, and in any round, they had the choice of changing to the other type of institution. All subjects were informed about the gains of other players in both institutions. At the beginning of the experiment, most subjects exhibited a preference for the public good game without sanctions. Yet, a minority was successful in the sanctioning regime in enhancing and sustaining cooperation, while free riding became a common mode of conduct where sanctions were absent. Payoffs of free riders in the SFI groups surpassed the earnings of cooperators in the SI groups in rounds 1–3, but thereafter the gains of cooperation increased steadily. When learning of the success of the SI regime, more and more subjects changed the type of institution. Migrating individuals also changed their behavior. Former free riders in a SFI group rapidly adapted to the norm of cooperation under the sanctioning regime. This process led to extreme polarization in the society. In the end, in round 30, the researchers observed a small number of SFI groups with low payoffs, while a large majority—more than 90%—of subjects in the SI groups showed almost full cooperation.

Gürerk et al. (2006) comment that "the findings demonstrate the competitive advantage of sanctioning institutions and exemplify the emergence and manifestation of social order driven by institutional selection." Full cooperation and the predominance of sanctioning institutions were not the result of a rational choice by purpose-oriented actors with a talent for foreseeing the consequences of their actions. On the contrary, most subjects were attracted by the sanction-free regime in the beginning. But, in an evolutionary process, actors adapted step by step to more successful strategies, leading to the unintended result observed in the experiment. One might argue that step-by-step adaptation or myopic behavior does not necessarily contradict the doctrines of rational choice theory. Even if we concede that this argument might be justified, the Gürerk et al. (2006) experiment and many other examples of cultural evolution demonstrate that assumptions on globally optimizing behavior in rational choice models are often too restrictive. To achieve a better understanding, if evolutionary forces are present, these assumptions should be replaced by principles of learning, imitation, and adaptation of successful strategies and selection by cultural evolution.

The Beauty Contest Game

In the Gürerk et al. (2006) experiment on the competition between two institutional regimes, rational subjects with foresight would join the group with a sanctioning institution early. The more actors are blessed with foresight, the faster is the evolutionary process. In a beauty-contest game, even actors who are fully aware of the rational strategy would not adopt the strategy at the beginning that finally emerges by evolution.

The beauty-contest game is a metaphor for the behavior of actors with different degrees of foresight on financial markets. In a "beauty contest," N players choose a number in the interval [0, 100]. The winner is the player who chooses the number closest to $p\mu$ with mean μ and $p \geq 0$. The value of p is known to the players, i.e., p is common knowledge (Nagel 1995). The prize is shared equally if there is more than one winner. In a more general version of the game, a player's strategy set is the interval $[a, b]$, x_i $(i = 1,2, \ldots N)$ is a number chosen by player i, θ is a function of the x_i, and $|x_i - p\theta| =$ Min! is the winning number.

For $N = 2$ and $p < 1$, a beauty-contest game with $\theta = \mu$ has a special feature. In this case the lower number always wins, and picking the number zero is a weakly dominating strategy[2]. "Zero" is the unique Nash equilibrium strategy and also "an evolutionarily stable strategy" (ESS, Maynard Smith and Price 1973). For larger N, a dominating strategy does not exist. The game is more interesting if $N > 2$.

What is the best choice in a beauty contest when, for example, $p = 2/3$ and $\theta = \mu$ and $N > 2$? Assume that other players will pick a number randomly. Therefore, the expected mean is 50, and a best choice is 2/3 of 50 or 33.33. Yet, other players are expected to think strategically as well. If one believes that co-players are about to pick 33.33, second-degree reasoning leads to the choice of 22.22. Third-degree reasoning results in choosing 14.81 and so on. Actually, experimental investigations show that the numbers 33, 22, and 15 are chosen more frequently (Nagel 1995; Selten and Nagel 1998). A bounded rational strategy is to form a belief about the degree n of reasoning of the co-players and then to go one step further to $n + 1$ and to pick the respective number. We call this an "$n + 1$ strategy" for short[3].

Stock market brokers may employ this strategy. Even if an investor is afraid of a stock market bubble and even if he is convinced that stocks are overpriced, he nevertheless may decide to "buy," because of his assumption about other actors' expectations of rising prices. John Maynard Keynes describes this reasoning in *The General Theory of Interest, Employment and Money*. The following citation (Keynes 1936: 156) also makes clear why the game earned its name "beauty contest":

---

[2]For an experimental study of the two-person game, see Grosskopf and Nagel (2008).

[3]Called "iteration step n" by Nagel, "A person is strategic of degree n if he chooses the number $50p^n$" (Nagel 1995: 1315).

> "Or, to change the metaphor slightly, professional investment may be linked to those newspaper competitions in which the competitors have to pick out the six prettiest faces from a hundred photographs, the prize being awarded to the competitor whose choice most nearly corresponds to the average preferences of the competitors as a whole; so that each competitor has to pick, not those faces which he himself finds prettiest, but those which he thinks likeliest to catch the fancy of the other competitors, all of whom are looking at the problem from the same point of view. It is not a case of choosing those which, to the best of one's judgment, are really the prettiest, nor even those which average opinion genuinely thinks the prettiest. We have reached the third degree where we devote our intelligences to anticipating what average opinion expects the average opinion to be. And there are some, I believe, who practise the fourth, fifth and higher degrees. (Keynes 1936: 156)"

Of course, in general, an $n + 1$ strategy is not the rational choice in a strict sense. One strong premise of rationality theories is the symmetry principle. An actor has to assume that all other actors are guided by the same principles of rationality. However, an $n + 1$ strategy violates the symmetry principle because an actor expects co-players' strategies to be of degree n, while he or she tries to outsmart the co-players by reasoning one step ahead. Moreover, an $n + 1$ strategy is not an equilibrium strategy. With $p = 2/3$ and θ the mean, there is only one strict subgame perfect Nash equilibrium strategy: the choice of zero. If all actors decide on zero, there is no incentive to deviate from the equilibrium strategy unilaterally. Also, the Nash equilibrium strategy is Pareto-optimal, and in equilibrium all players of the symmetric game receive an equal share of the prize. In a beauty contest, no coordination problem arises as with a chicken- or battle-of-sex-type dilemma, and there is no "efficiency problem," i.e., a discrepancy between the Nash equilibrium payoff and the Pareto-optimal payoff as in a prisoner's dilemma-type game. All desirable requirements of a rational strategy are met. There is no doubt that rationality theories (i.e., Harsanyi and Selten 1988) would recommend picking the number 0 as the unique solution of the game. However, is it rational to choose the rational strategy if one is sure to lose? Assume you have full knowledge of the game and you are fully aware of the Nash equilibrium strategy, would you really choose it? You know for sure that most players won't employ the rational strategy—maybe for the same reasons that you won't. In this case, you are probably going to form an expectation of other players' "irrational" behavior, and then you will try to adapt your strategy to your expectations. In many situations of strategic interaction, individuals do not employ the rational strategy because they have not enough insight into the subtleties of the strategic situation. One example of this is the Gürerk et al. (2006) experiment regarding competition between different institutional regimes discussed above. However, in a beauty contest, actors do not employ the rational strategy even if they know the rational choice!

Experiments show that only a small minority chooses zero in a beauty contest (Nagel 1995; Selten and Nagel 1998). A student project at my chair explored the behavior of students enrolled at the ETH Zurich with an online experiment using a

Table 1 Results of an online beauty-contest game: arithmetic means of chosen number [Figures are from the data set of Kamm and Dahinden. See also Kamm and Dahinden (2008)]

	Group 1	Group 2	Group 3	Group 4	Group 5	Group 6
Group size in round 1	16	15	61	61	225	222
Group size in round 5	14	13	50	53	188	178
Information	Full	Limited	Full	Limited	Full	Limited
Round 1	35.3	27.4	35.7	32.6	30.0	31.5
Round 2	21.5	22.8	25.1	25.6	21.9	23.2
Round 3	17.1	16.9	15.9	20.7	15.7	16.1
Round 4	14.0	15.3	12.2	17.1	13.6	9.6
Round 5	13.4	14.8	12.9	11.4	10.8	6.9

repeated beauty-contest game[4]. In accordance with previous studies (e.g., Nagel 1995), the online experiment runs over five rounds. With a 3×2 design, group size and information feedback were varied. The group size factor had three categories: small, medium, and large groups. In the limited information treatment, participants were informed about the mean and the target value (2/3 of the mean) of the previous round. In the full information condition, subjects also received a graph of the distribution of numbers. The winning number in each round and treatment earned a reward of 20 CHF (about 13 €). The table contains the means for all rounds and conditions (Table 1).

Here, there are no consistent differences in means of group size categories and information feedback. However, in accordance with former studies, a pattern of change is apparent in the distributions over the five rounds in all six treatments. In the first round, with no feedback subjects, frequent choices are about 50, 33, and 22 resulting in an average in the range of 29.7–35.5 as shown in the table. With increasing round numbers, the distributions and the mean move further to the "left." The figure shows the distributions of rounds 1–5 in the largest group. Subjects adapt step by step to the information feedback of the previous round. Moreover, in thc first round, the heterogeneity of decisions is rather large; the heterogeneity or variance of the distribution then declines with the round number.

The Nash equilibrium strategy was chosen very rarely. All in all, 602 subjects made 2703 decisions in 5 rounds. A "0" was delivered in only 7 out of 2703 choices. 497 subjects participated in all 5 rounds (Fig. 1).

[4]The author initiated this project which was conducted by Dominik Kamm and Stefan Dahinden. The project was supervised by Stefan Wehrli. For a description of results, see Kamm and Dahinden (2008).

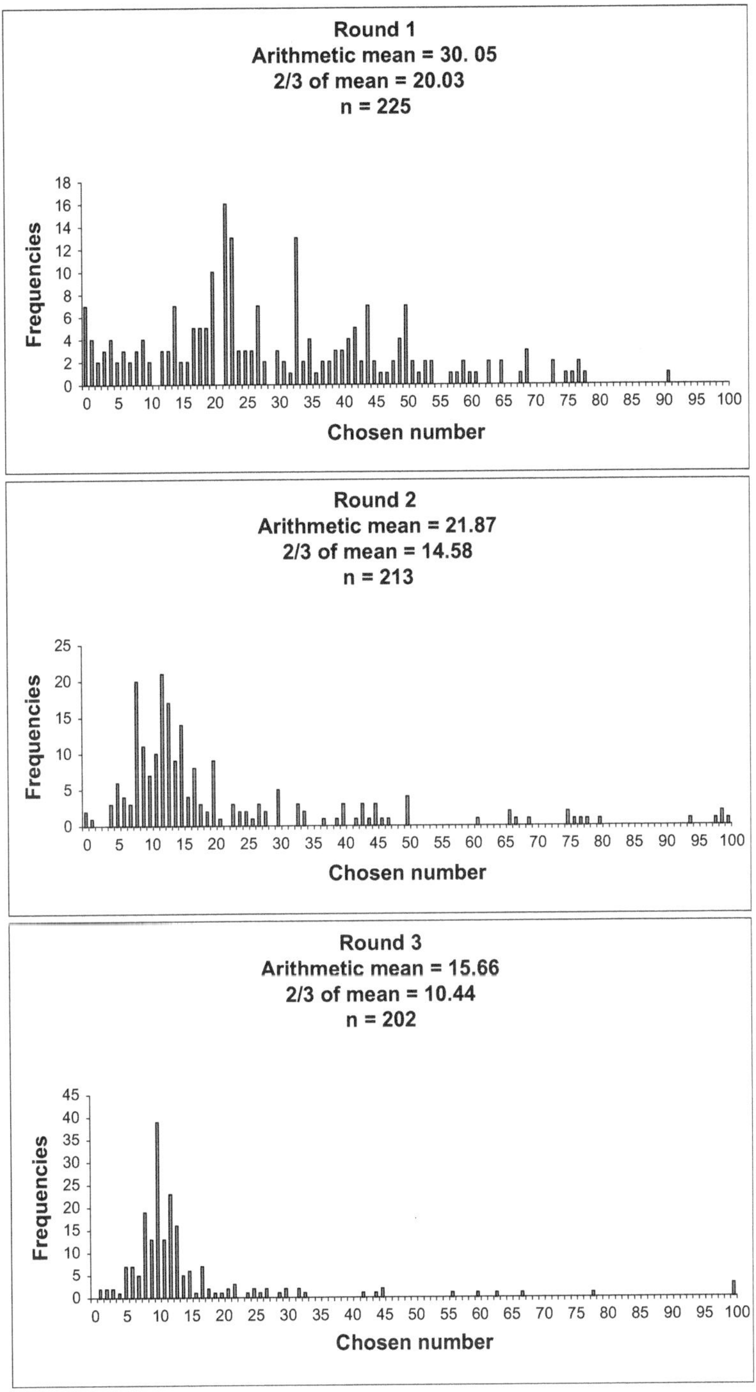

Fig. 1 Distribution of chosen numbers in rounds one to five (largest group #5) [Computed from the data set of Dahinden and Kamm. See also Kamm and Dahinden (2008)]

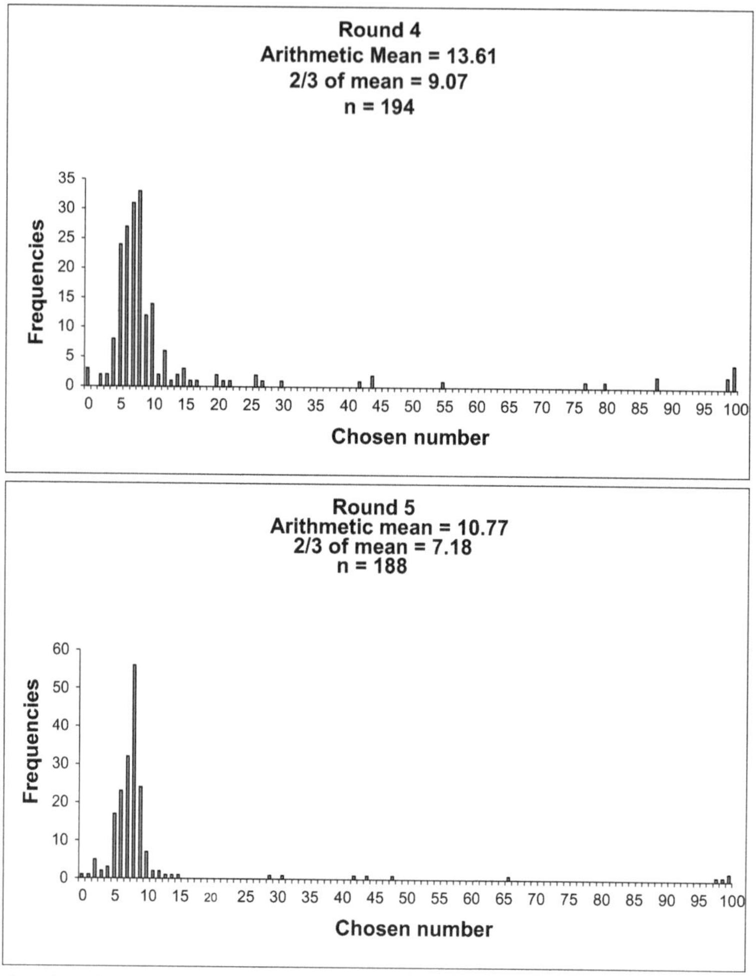

Fig. 1 (continued)

Conclusion

Binmore (1992) argues that three requirements have to be fulfilled in order to predict subjects' behavior in rationality models of game theory: (1) the structure of the game has to be simple, (2) actors should have experience of the game, and (3) incentives have to be high enough to motivate serious decision-making. A beauty-contest game is simple, and, in experiments, payoffs are probably high enough to motivate subjects. There are good reasons to assume that experienced subjects who frequently participate in the game nevertheless have a low probability of choosing the rational or Nash equilibrium strategy in the first round of a beauty contest. On the other hand, learning and adaptation to the strategies of co-players in successive rounds at least approach the Nash equilibrium. And one may hypothesize that an increase in the number of rounds to, for example, 100 will result in the mutual choice of the equilibrium strategy.

The evolutionary path may be described by the equations of replicator dynamics or by other formal models of adaptation and learning (Maynard Smith 1982; Young 1998). For example, players are myopic, begin with $\mu_0 = 50$, and simply imitate the successful strategies of round n in round $n + 1$. Thus, they choose $x_{n+1} = (2/3)\,\mu_n$. By this process, eventually the Nash equilibrium will be approached. The rational choice comes about among myopic players by means of a simple adaptation mechanism.

This does not mean that an evolutionary process always results in an optimal state. As is well known, evolutionary processes often do not lead to a global optimum. Path dependence and "lock in" are the common terms to describe the suboptimal results of evolutionary processes. Many examples of path dependence, lock-in situations, and unintended consequences are found in the history of technological inventions, particularly the evolution of railway networks. For example, railways in Europe, the USA, and many other countries use a track gauge of 1435 mm. The standard gauge goes back to a decision of George and Robert Stephenson, the engineers and inventors who constructed the first railroads in Britain. The decision for 1435 mm is probably not the optimal track gauge for today's railways after so much technological change and almost 200 years later. Yet there is no chance of switching to an optimal solution because the costs of changing existing networks are prohibitive. Local interactions may feed the evolutionary process, and, dependent on initial conditions, one of many Nash equilibria will be approached in the end. The historical process of the evolution of "left" or "right" driving rules is a good example, analyzed extensively by Young (1998). Also, actors' rational choices in situations of strategic interaction do not necessarily imply an optimal outcome in the aggregate, and the evolutionarily stable strategy or ESS does not necessarily lead to an optimal outcome on the group level (Maynard Smith 1982). Moreover, there is no guarantee that an evolutionary process approaches equilibrium if environmental conditions change rapidly (Rohde 1995).

Rational design and cultural evolution by learning and adaptation are not contradictions. Technological change may serve as an example of the interplay between rationality and evolution. An engineer who designs new machinery usually builds on existing machinery developed by forerunners. For technical devices with a history, such as steam engines or automobiles, there is a long sequence of technological evolution analogical to the sequence of changing organisms in biological evolution. Another example is the emergence of, and change in, institutions. The various institutions in western democracies developed over centuries. And there are different types, such as the Presidential system, the British "Westminster model," and the federal democracy found in Switzerland. John Locke, Charles de Montesquieu, and Thomas Jefferson were "institutional engineers" and rational designers of democratic institutions. Yet, rational designs were not developed from scratch but represent steps in a long-lasting evolutionary process.

Evolutionary models have an important advantage when explaining social patterns and institutions. No unrealistic assumptions of foresight or knowledge of the consequences of actions are necessary. In the extreme, there is no purposive action at all, and rational choice is merely a result of the process, not a prerequisite. Of course, if actors are less myopic or "more rational," the speed of the process is often increased. From this perspective, rationality is nothing more and nothing less than a shortcut in the evolutionary process. The cultural evolution of social patterns, technologies, laws, and institutions is accelerated by rational—and sometimes ingenious—design and invention.

References

Andreoni, James, and John Miller. 2002. Giving According to GARP: An Experimental Test of the Consistency of Preferences for Altruism. *Econometrica* 70: 737–753.

Barry, Brian M., and Russell Hardin, eds. 1982. *Rational Man and Irrational Society? An Introduction and Sourcebook*. Beverly Hills: Sage.

Binmore, Kenneth. 1992. *Fun and Games. A Text on Game Theory*. Lexington, MA: Heath.

Bolton, Gary E., and Axel Ockenfels. 2000. ERC: A Theory of Equity, Reciprocity, and Competition. *American Economic Review* 90: 166–193.

Boudon, Raymond. 1977. *Effets pervers et ordre social*. Paris: Presses Universitaire de France.

———. 1982. *The Unintended Consequences of Social Action*. New York: St. Martin's Press.

Charness, Gary, and Matthew Rabin. 2002. Understanding Social Preferences with Simple Tests. *The Quarterly Journal of Economics*: 817–869.

Diekmann, Andreas. 2009. Rational Choice, Evolution and the Beauty Contest. In *Raymond Boudon - a Life in Sociology. Essays in Honour of Raymond Boudon, eds.* Mohamed Cherkaoui and Peter Hamilton, Vol. II.

Dopfer, Kurt. 2016. Evolutionary Economics. In *Handbook of the History of Economic Analysis, Volume II, Schools of Thought in Economics*, ed. Gilbert Faccarello and Heinz D. Kurz. Cheltenham: Edward Elgar.

Fehr, Ernst, and Simon Gächter. 2002. Altruistic Punishment in Humans. *Nature* 415: 137–140.

Fehr, Ernst, and Klaus M. Schmidt. 1999. A Theory of Fairness, Competition, and Cooperation. *The Quarterly Journal of Economics*: 817–868.

Gigerenzer, Gerd. 2000. *Adaptive Thinking. Rationality in the Real World*. Oxford: Oxford University Press.

Gigerenzer, Gerd, and Peter M. Todd. 1999. *Simple Heuristics that Make us Smart*. Oxford: Oxford University Press.

Grosskopf, Brit, and Rosemarie Nagel. 2008. The Two-Person Beauty Contest. *Games and Economic Behavior* 62: 93–99.

Gürerk, Özgür, Bernd Irlenbusch, and Bettina Rockenbach. 2006. The Competitive Advantage of Sanctioning Institutions. *Science* 312: 108–111.

Harsanyi, John C., and Reinhard Selten. 1988. *A General Theory of Equilibrium Selection in Games*. Cambridge, MA: MIT-Press.

Kamm, Dominik, and Stefan Dahinden. 2008. *P-Beauty Contest mit unterschiedlich grossen Teilnahmefeldern*. ETH-Zurich: MTU-Gruppenarbeit.

Keynes, John M. 1936. *The General Theory of Employment, Interest and Money*. London: Macmillan.

Maynard Smith, John. 1982. *Evolution and the Theory of Games*. Cambridge: Cambridge University Press.

Maynard Smith, John, and George R. Price. 1973. The Logic of Animal Conflict. *Nature* 246: 15–18.

McCabe, Kevin A., Mary L. Rigdon, and Vernon L. Smith. 2003. Positive Reciprocity and Intentions in Trust Games. *Journal of Economic Behavior and Organization* 52: 267–275.

Merton, Robert K. 1936. The Unanticipated Consequences of Purposive Social Action. *American Sociological Review* 1: 894–904.

Metcalfe, Stan. 2012. *J.A. Schumpeter and the Theory of Economic Evolution (One Hundred Years beyond the Theory of Economic Development)*. Jena: Evolutionary Economics Group, Max Planck Institute of Economics.

Morgenstern, Oskar. 1928. *Wirtschaftsprognose: Eine Untersuchung ihrer Voraussetzungen und Möglichkeiten*. Wien: Julius Springer.

Nagel, Rosemarie C. 1995. Unraveling in Guessing Games: An Experimental Study. *American Economic Review* 85: 1313–1326.

Olson, Mancur. 1965. *The Logic of Collective Action*. Cambridge, MA: Harvard University Press.

Rabin, Matthew. 1993. Incorporating Fairness into Game Theory and Economics. *American Economic Review* 83: 1281–1302.

Rohde, Klaus. 1995. *Nonequilibrium Ecology*. Cambridge: Cambridge University Press.

Savage, Leonard J. 1954. *The Foundations of Statistics*. New York: Wiley.

Schumpeter, Josef A. 1912. *Theorie der wirtschaftlichen Entwicklung*. Berlin: Duncker und Humblot (The Theory of Economic Development. Cambridge, MA: Harvard University Press, 1934).

Schumpeter, Joseph A. 1942. *Capitalism, Socialism and Democracy*. New York: Harper.

Selten, Reinhard, and Rosemarie C. Nagel. 1998. Das Zahlenwahlspiel. Hintergründe und Ergebnisse. *Spektrum der Wissenschaft* 2: 16–22.

Tversky, Amos, and Daniel Kahneman. 1981. The Framing of Decisions and the Psychology of Choice. *Science* 211: 453–458.

Von Neumann, John, and Oskar Morgenstern. 1947. *Theory of Games and Economic Behavior*. 2nd ed. Princeton, NJ: Princeton University Press.

Young, H. Peyton. 1998. *Individual Strategy and Social Structure. An Evolutionary Theory of Institutions*. Princeton, NJ: Princeton University Press.

Schütz on Rationality

Martin Endress

The Overall Constellation

Schütz's lecture on "The Problem of Rationality", given at the Harvard Faculty Club in April 1940 on the invitation of Joseph Schumpeter and Talcott Parsons, was his first substantial academic paper in this new field of the United States. Schütz's lecture was influenced by Parsons' study of European social theorists in *The Structure of Social Action* (Parsons 1937). The journal *Politica* asked Schütz to prepare a review of this monumental study. Due to reasons that are observable in the short correspondence between Schütz and Parsons after the lecture in question, Schütz never published this review. On November 15, 1940, Schütz sent Parsons his long review-essay entitled "Parsons' Theory of Social Action" (Schütz 1978). They never ended up meeting again. Parsons' written reactions to this manuscript in early 1941 (see Schütz and Parsons 1977, 79–107, 119–122; 1978, 63–70, 72–93, 107–109) made Schütz feel uncomfortable to publish his analysis of *The Structure of Social Action*. As he wrote to Parsons on March 17, 1941: "Of course it never had been my intention to publish a paper on your work with whose whole basic concept you no less disagree than with all its particulars. My respect for the author and the book is far too great and my polemical temper far too small that I should wish to present to the scientific public an essay on your work which you, unfortunately, consider as inadequate and irrelevant" (Schütz and Parsons 1977, 119; 1978, 106).

Helmut Wagner, the biographer of Alfred Schütz, said what has to be said about the exchange between Schütz and Parsons. In his intellectual biography of Schütz, he writes (1983: 77): "Aside from differences in the personality of both, which certainly played their part, ... each of them moved in a fundamentally different direction. ... Strictly speaking, their apparently common starting point did not

M. Endress (✉)
Department of Sociology, University of Trier, Trier, Germany
e-mail: endress@uni-trier.de

H. Staubmann, V. Lidz (eds.), *Rationality in the Social Sciences*,
DOI 10.1007/978-3-319-62377-1_11

exist". Wagner concludes (1983: 78): "the Parsons-Schütz exchange of 1940–1941 shows that each was looking in the opposite direction". This is, I believe, exactly what happened. Nevertheless, in his contribution to Marvin Farber's *Philosophical Essays in Memory of Edmund Husserl*, published in 1940, Schütz wrote: "An excellent presentation of his (i.e. Weber's) theory is to be found in English in Talcott Parsons' *The Structure of Social Action*, New York 1937" (1962d: 138n).

Even though it seems problematic to consider the exchange between Schütz and Parsons as "a dialogue of the deaf", as Coser (1979) did, there are several reasons for arguing that Parsons did not understand that Schütz made considerable efforts to show him the way in which the theory of the structure of social action should develop. It is obvious that Parsons did not understand the methodological argument as well as the systematic impact of Schütz's analysis of his theoretical framework. This is clearly documented when Parsons wrote to Richard Grathoff in 1979 (see this volume Part III) that to him, Schütz's "'everyday life' stress ... is another version of what I like to call 'Gemeinschaft romanticism'" (see, as well, Parsons' retrospective perspective 1974).

It was in the midst of these failed exchanges that the Harvard seminar on rationality took place. We do not know whether Schumpeter and Schütz ever came to meet in their Vienna years or in the years after the Harvard seminar in America. We know that Schütz's reference to Schumpeter's paper on rationality, at the beginning of his original lecture (which is not included in the printed version of 1943), seems to be the only one that he ever included in his work. As Schütz said (1996b: 7) in his lecture when referring to "the many and heterogeneous concepts labelled 'rationality'", Schumpeter, with his own contribution, offered him a proper starting point for his own analysis. Comparing the contributions of Schumpeter and Schütz to the Schumpeter-Parsons Seminar, the authors seemed to face the problem at hand from different ends: while Schumpeter wrote about "The Problem of Rationality in the Social Sciences", Schütz entitled his contribution "The Problem of Rationality in the Social World". Social sciences, on the one side, and the social world, on the other, are the twofold problems Schütz examined. To be more precise, he was exploring this fundamental methodological problem on two analytical levels: the first level aimed to clarify the difference and similarity between Schütz's and Parsons' notions of rationality, while the second level identified the structural analogies between social science and the social world. As Schütz said: "I want to defend the following thesis: In its strict meaning, rationality is a category of the scientific observation of the social world and not a category of the mind of the actor within the social world. Therefore, in its primary denotation, the conceptual scheme of rationality is valid only on the level of theoretical observation; its application to other levels of our experience of the social world is possible only in a modified and restricted sense" (1996b: 7).

The version of Schütz's paper on rationality, included in this volume, is the one published in *Economica* in 1943 (see Schütz 1964: 64–88). It is a slightly abridged version of the original paper that Schütz submitted during the Parsons-Schumpeter Seminar (Schütz 1996a: 6–24; here Parts I and II on pp. 7–9). For Schütz, Parsons' invitation to the Harvard seminar was a unique opportunity to introduce and discuss his thoughts with one of the leading sociologists of the time. Due to this constellation, Schütz wrote a long, very detailed, and sophisticated paper on the problem of rationality. Schütz, himself, seemed to consider that the exposition of his arguments in the 1940 paper presented his views and his systematic position on the matter in a most appropriate way. Schütz referred to his own clarifications again, more than 10 years later, in his seminal essay on *Common-Sense and Scientific Interpretation*, systematically explaining his understanding of "rational action" and of the "scientific model of the social world" (see 1962b: 27ff., 40ff.). This final statement on the topic of rationality reflects most of what he had already prepared for his Harvard lecture.

Schütz as a Reader and a Critic of Parsons

Shortly after emigrating from Europe, Schütz made strong efforts to familiarize himself with North American sociological and philosophical debates. Even though Parsons had already become central to these discussions, Schütz only had a selective and quite unique reading of his work. For example, his annotations on Parsons' 1937 study, *The Structure of Social Action*, although extensive, are restricted to the main parts of the introductory Chap. 1 (pp. 16–41) and to a few pages of Chap. 2 (pp. 43–51), a section on *The Unit of Action Systems*. In addition, more annotations are found on selected pages from Parsons' discussion of Pareto (pp. 238–261); on some pages from the last chapter on Durkheim, entitled "Religion and Epistemology" (Chap. 11, pp. 439ff.); and in the final Chap. 12 of volume I (pp. 451ff.). Finally, Schütz made annotations to "Part IV: Conclusion", the closing chapter of volume II (pp. 697–775).[1]

There are already several published papers commenting on the so-called Schütz-Parsons exchange, primarily focusing on Schütz's unpublished review of Parsons' classic *The Structure of Social Action* and on their following correspondence (Schütz and Parsons 1977, 1978).[2] This exchange received widespread attention after its publication in 1977 (German edition) and 1978 (English edition). Walter Sprondel in 1977 was able to shed light on the origins of this correspondence (see

[1]Having this very selective reading of *The Structure of Social Action* by Schütz in mind, it is not likely that the copy of this book, which is now part of the Schütz library at the Alfred Schütz Memorial Archives at the University of Konstanz (Germany), is the original one Schütz read in 1938 and 1939, i.e. during his stay in Paris.

[2]These are, in alphabetical order, Amann (1988), Butts (1975), Coser (1979), Eberle (1984), Eberle and Srubar (2004), Embree (1980), Endress (2009, 2012), Fitzhenry (1986), Garfinkel (1952), Giddens (1979), Grathoff (1978a, 1978b), Hama (1989), Honolka (1978), Jules-Rosette (1980), Kassab (1991), Natanson (1978), Nasu (1991), Procter (1980), Psathas (2004), Rehorick (1980), Rehorick and Buxton (1988), Schwinn (1993), Sprondel (1977), Tibbetts (1980), Tyrell (1996), Valone (1980), Wagner (1979, 1980), Wilson (2005) and Zaret (1980).

Sprondel 1977: 138 f., n.1). Sprondel analysed what Parsons wrote in his first letter to Schütz on October 30, 1940, a letter not included in the German edition of 1977, saying: "I had wondered a little why I had not heard from you with regard to the manuscript I sent to you" (Schütz and Parsons 1978: 3). Sprondel identified this manuscript as Parsons' essay *Actor, Situation, and Normative Pattern*, which he seemed to have finished in late 1939 (see Parsons 1986, 2010).

On the one hand, this information is of considerable importance, because Schütz, in his reply to Parsons from November 15, 1940 (originally written in German), argues that he, in his paper (i.e. "Parsons' Theory of Social Action"), has "tried to present [Parsons'] ideas [of *The Structure of Social Action*] with reference to this as yet unpublished manuscript". Schütz continues: "The further development of your ideas to be found there has contributed a great deal to my clearer understanding of your published work" (Schütz and Parsons 1977, 22; 1978, 5). On the other hand, it is quite important as well to keep in mind that Schütz did not receive Parsons' essay *Actor, Situation, and Normative Pattern* before his lecture on the "Interdepartmental Conference of Harvard University" on April 13, 1940. Parsons wrote to Schütz, on January 10, 1940, that he had sent it to Raymond H. Williams, asking him to send it to Schütz after he had read it (see Part III in this volume). Unfortunately, the copy of Parsons' essay is not in the Schütz papers anymore, because Parsons also asked Schütz in his letter of October 30, 1940, "to send it to Dr. Voegelin at the University of Alabama" (Schütz and Parsons 1978: 3). We can only find six pages of notes (excerpts) in Schütz's literary estate, notes he drew from this manuscript (microfilm 1, 561–566).

This leads to another question concerning the preconditions of Schütz's preparation for his Harvard lecture. As Grathoff (1978a: xxxiv) wrote in his introductory essay about the Schütz-Parsons exchange, Parsons, in his letter to Schütz from January 24, 1940, mentioned his "little discussion of rationality" (Schütz and Parsons 1978: 133n11), a copy of which could not be found in the Schütz papers. We do not know whether Schütz knew about this paper while preparing his lecture of April 13 of the same year, but one can assume that Parsons referred to his seven-page-long contribution included in the current volume under the title "An Approach to the Role of Rationality in Social Action". The only thing we currently know is that on November 15, 1940, Schütz wrote to Parsons: "As far as your manuscript on rationality is concerned, I have read it thoroughly three times and made myself a list of comments" (see Schütz and Parsons 1978: 5). Be that as it may, as a participant at Schütz's lecture,[3] Parsons probably commented on Schütz's presentation during the discussion that followed. Thus, Parsons's interventions as well as his paper, mentioned above, helped Schütz prepare his lecture for publication. It is especially Schütz's criticism of Parsons's misunderstanding of the subjective point of view

[3]See Schütz's letter to Fritz Machlup of April 16, 1940 (Alfred Schütz Memorial Archives, University of Konstanz, Germany) (Schütz 1940).

and his overstretching of the term "choice", which form the core of his critique of Parsons' theory as pure methodology.[4]

Schütz' Analysis of the Relevance of the Concept of Rationality

It is helpful to first summarize the central points of Parsons' short statement on the "role of rationality in the social sciences" before looking at Schütz's main points of criticism. The central notions of Parsons' short statement on the concept and role of rationality seem to be the following (see Part I in this volume):

1. The "concept of rationality as . . . part of a generalized conceptual scheme".
2. This concept is useful for both "description and analysis".
3. The "central point of departure" for treating the role of rationality in social action "is the conception of choice".
4. The concept of choice "implies" that "probable consequences of two or more alternative courses of action are foreseen or predicted".
5. Hence, "knowledge" is involved, and its "core" consists of "statements of observable facts", which are "subject to empirical verification" and which underlie criteria of "logical reasoning".
6. Moreover, "one of the important criteria of logical adequacy of knowledge is the . . . lack of ambiguity of concepts or propositions".
7. If "knowledge consists of more than one proposition", it "is rational only insofar as the various propositions . . . are logically consistent".
8. Finally, according to Parsons, there are "three criteria of verifiability": "observation, precision and consistency", which serve as "the primary criteria of the rationality of knowledge".

These seem to be the central statements Parsons explores in the beginning of his paper. As I will try to show, Schütz did not oppose the scientific reasoning of these eight theses or their methodology. However, he did not think that they provided an adequate basis for a theory of social action aiming to understand acting and actions in everyday life.

Schütz, in his 1940 lecture on rationality, directly addresses the concept of rationality underlying Parsons' statements. He begins by contrasting "different attitudes toward the social world", i.e. "the actor within this world", on the one hand, and "the scientific observer of it", on the other hand (1943: 64 (93)[5]).

[4]For an analysis of the Schütz-Parsons exchange focusing on Schütz's criticism of Parsons' misunderstanding of the subjective point of view, his shortenings or reductions in the theory of intersubjective motivation as well as his overstretching of the term "choice", see Endress (2009, 2012).

[5]This second reference here (and in the following) refers to the reprint of Schütz's paper in the current volume.

Differentiating these social positions, Schütz agrees with Parsons "in so far as it [his understanding of rational action] refers to the level of social theory" (1943: 65 (94)). Thus, central to Schütz's position right from the beginning is the argument that one has to distinguish "different levels in observing the social world" (ibid.). He continues, therefore, "with the shift from one level to another all the conceptual schemes and all the terms of interpretation must be modified" (1943: 65 (95)). Because of "the simple fact that new problems and aspects of facts emerge with the shift in the point of view, while others that were formerly in the centre of our question disappear", a "thorough modification of the meaning of all the terms correctly used at the former level" is needed (1943: 67f. (97)). According to Schütz, it follows from this indispensable phenomenon of perspectivity that the meaning of key concepts such as "rationality" within the social sciences "does not depend on the level of the actual research, but, on the contrary, the level on which the research may be done depends upon the meaning attributed to the key concepts" (1943: 69 (98)). Bearing this in mind, it is Schütz's central conviction that "in 'just living along,' ... we are guided neither by methodological considerations nor by any conceptual scheme of means-end relations, nor by any idea of values we have to realize" (1943: 72 (102)).

To Schütz, it is because of this dominant practical interest that in everyday life "we are satisfied if we have a fair chance for realizing our purposes". Insofar as "the ideal of everyday knowledge is not certainty, nor even probability in a mathematical sense, but just likelihood. ... The consistency of this system of knowledge is not that of natural laws, but that of typical sequences and relations" (1943: 73 (103f.)). This remarkable conclusion obviously reflects Max Weber's eminent distinction between rules and regularities, which he introduces in his early paper, entitled *Critique of Stammler* (see Weber 1977: 98ff.). With regard to this typical character of everyday knowledge, it follows, for Schütz, that in everyday life, it is characteristic for routine actions that "the problem of choice between different possibilities does not enter into the consciousness of the actor" (1943: 75 (105)).

In line with this clarification, he also turns to the problem of logic, to which Parsons referred. Schütz states: "On the level of everyday experience, logic in its traditional form cannot render the services we need and expect. ... Our everyday thoughts are less interested in the antithesis 'true-false' than in the sliding transition 'likely-unlikely'" (1943: 76 (107)). Schütz here refers to Husserl's notion of "occasional propositions" (1943: 76 (107)), indicating the overall situational character of everyday thinking. We might call this the occasionality of everyday reasoning. Once again, Schütz here accentuates the difference in modes of thinking in reference to different realms of reality. He makes the same argument to distinguish the modes of being aware of choices: Because "it is a prerequisite of all choices that the actor has clearly in mind that alternative ways of applying different means or even alternative ends do actually exist. It is erroneous to assume that consciousness of such alternatives and therefore choice is necessarily given before every human action and that in consequence all acting involves deliberation and preference" (1943: 78 (108f.)). Thus, according to Schütz, the typical style of thinking is not the same in the sphere of logic as it is in the "sphere of everyday life" (1943: 79 (110)). Due to these differences, Schütz concludes: "What I wish to emphasize is only that the ideal of rationality is not and cannot be a peculiar feature of everyday thought, nor can it, therefore, be a methodological principle of the interpretation of human acts in daily life" (ibid.). To understand Schütz's general line of argument and his implicit critique of Parsons' idea of general theory in sociology, one must have in mind some of his previous clarifications. Already in his so-called personality manuscript, Schütz claims to have developed a "systematic theory of social action" in his study, *Der sinnhafte Aufbau der sozialen Welt*, by identifying the variations in the mechanism of the constitution of social reality due to its different typicality and different structures of relevance. He systematically develops this analysis in his so-called theory of multiple realities (see Schütz 1962e). Thus, because Parsons supposed a very specific level of reflexivity as a precondition for analysing social action, he was unable to understand Schütz's approach, due to its conceptualization of multiple realities. In respect to this analysis, it is Schütz's assumption that a general theory of action cannot restrict itself to the realm of scientific reasoning, unlike Schumpeter—as the title of his contribution to the Harvard seminar suggested—and Parsons. It has to reflect the social world and its manifold perspectives and relevancies.

According to Schütz, any institutionally mediated action or interaction has to be analysed differently than the analysis of the world of everyday life. This is due to changes in the "tension of consciousness . . ., a specific epoché . . ., a prevalent form of spontaneity . . ., a specific form of experiencing one's self . . ., a specific form of sociality . . ., [and] a specific time-perspective", as he developed in his analysis "on multiple realities" (Schütz 1962e: 230). This analytical frame for distinguishing the cognitive style of multiple realities is one of his major contributions to the methodology of the social sciences, going back to his late Vienna manuscripts (see Schütz 1936, 1937). We can refer to this theory as a theory of cognitive differentiation. It is due to these differentiations that Schütz, in his Harvard lecture as well as in some of his later publications, paid special attention to what he called "postulates" in order to examine the "principles governing the construction of scientific models of human action in general" (1962b: 43).

These "postulates" form the other core of Schütz's contribution to the methodology of social sciences. Beginning with his explication of these postulates in the Harvard lecture (Schütz 1996b, 1943: 84ff. (117ff.)), he extended and clarified his position in several of his contributions to the field (see Schütz and Parsons 1978, 49f., 59f.; Schütz 1962e, 249ff.; 1962b, 34ff., 43f.; 1962c, 62ff.; also, Schütz and Parsons 1977: 65, 75). Besides the "postulate of relevance", indicating the principal of perspectivity of social scientific observations, and the "postulate of subjective interpretation", pointing to the specific level of observation and its "occasionality", Schütz's "postulate of adequacy" demands that "the interpretation of any human act by the social scientist might be the same as that by the actor or by his partner" (1943: 86 (117); see Schütz 1962a, 44). It is these postulates, which, according to Schütz, entail social sciences to understand and explain the rationality embedded in everyday actions as well as to identify its sense.

While it is Parsons overall problem to understand the chances for the institutionalization of a complex societal order, he was unable to understand Schütz's interest in reconstructing an actor's natural attitude and the everyday processes of constituting the social world. Therefore, to analyse the world of everyday life as a social scientist, according to the postulates just mentioned, one has to be aware of three aspects: (1) "a shift in the problem means a modification in the scope of relevance too", i.e. "that each shift in the problem involves a thorough modification of all the concepts and of all the types with which [one] is dealing" (1962a: 84 (115f.)), (2) that one "has to ask what typical thoughts must be attributed to [the individual mind] to explain the fact in question as the result of its activity within an understandable relation" (1962a: 85 (117)) and (3) that "each term . . . must be so constructed that a human act performed within the life-world by an individual actor in the way indicated by the typical construction would be reasonable and understandable for the actor himself, as well as for his fellow-men" (1962a: 85 (117)).

These three postulates serve, for Schütz, as requirements for the construction of ideal types in order to understand the social world. Therefore, they constitute what he calls "the postulate of rationality": "The ideal type of social action must be constructed in such a way that the actor in the living world would perform the typified act if he had a clear and distinct scientific knowledge of all the elements relevant to his choice and the constant tendency to choose the most appropriate means for the realization of the most appropriate end" (1962a: 86 (118)).

Concluding Remarks

The correspondence between Schütz and Parsons took place at a critical moment in Parsons' intellectual development. Schütz was in a continual process of developing a systematic theory, while Parsons, to a certain degree, stood at the beginning of his systematic thinking, finding himself in an ongoing flux of ideas and conceptual revisions. Schütz was able to consolidate the systematic alignment and orientation of his approach after *Der sinnhafte Aufbau der sozialen Welt* (1932, 1967) and during the years he worked on personality manuscript (1936, 1937), following his prior analysis of the attitude of the scientific observer. In contrast, Parsons was in a highly dynamic period of his intellectual development, still seeking a general direction for continuing the elaboration of his early idea of a general theory of action, as presented in his *The Structure of Social Action*.

Schütz's overall position is that Parsons failed to understand the rationality of action in everyday actions and interactions. According to Schütz, it is a methodological mistake to confound a theory of the constitution of scientific rationality with an analysis of the constitution of rationality in everyday actions and interactions. One always has to take into account this "shift in the central point" (1962a: 81 (112)). Due to this fundamental difference, Schütz, in his lecture on rationality given at Harvard, emphasizes perspectivity (1962a: 71, 83 (101, 114)), typicality

(1962a: 72, 81f. (102, 113)) and occasionality (1962a: 76, 87 (107, 119)) as the core principles for analysing everyday life. Therefore, his lecture provides an application of his overall theory of relevance. The latter urges social scientists to take into account the reflexivity of any scientific procedure: "It seems important to me that the scientist keeps in mind that each shift in the problem involves a thorough modification of all the concepts and of all the types with which he is dealing. A great many misunderstandings and controversies in the social sciences have their root in the unmodified application of concepts and types at a level other than that where they have their natural place" (1962a: 84 (116)).

Parsons places alternatives, choices, criteria of logical reasoning, a lack of ambiguity and logical consistency at the heart of social scientific methodology, understood as a set of principles for a theory of action. Schütz, on the contrary, emphasizes that regularities, routine actions, fair chances and "the sliding transition 'likely-unlikely'" are at the heart of social scientific observation, the aim of which is to understand everyday human acting and actions. Schütz thus denies that Parsons was able to present either a theory of social action or an adequate approach to understanding rationality in social action.

References

Amann, Anton. 1988. Alfred Schütz und Talcott Parsons – Zur scheinbaren Folgenlosigkeit eines Briefwechsels. In *Vertriebene Vernunft II*, ed. Friedrich Stadler, 333–344. Wien: Jugend und Volk.

Butts, Steven. 1975. Parsons, Weber and the Subjective Point of View. *Sociological Analysis and Theory* 5: 185–217.

Coser, Lewis A. 1979. A Dialogue of the Deaf. *Contemporary Sociology* 8: 680–682.

Eberle, Thomas S. 1984. Die Schütz-Parsons-Debatte. In *Sinnkonstitution in Alltag und Wissenschaft. Der Beitrag der Phänomenologie an die Methodologie der Sozialwissenschaften*, ed. Thomas S. Eberle, 260–303. Bern: Haupt.

Eberle, Thomas S., and Ilja Srubar. 2004. Einleitung. In *Schütz, Alfred Schütz Werkausgabe Vol. IV: Zur Methodologie der Sozialwissenschaften*, ed. Thomas Eberle, Jochen Dreher, and Gerd Sebald, 9–44. Konstanz: UVK.

Embree, Lester. 1980. Methodology is Where Human Scientists and Philosophers Can Meet: Reflections on the Schutz-Parsons Exchange. *Human Studies* 3: 367–373.

Endress, Martin. 2009. Two directions of continuing the Weberian project: Alfred Schutz and Talcott Parsons. In *Alfred Schutz and His Intellectual Partners*, ed. Hisashi Nasu, Lester Embree, George Psathas, and Ilja Srubar, 377–400. Konstanz: UVK.

———. 2012. Theorie sozialen Handelns – Zur Kontroverse zwischen Alfred Schütz und Talcott Parsons. *Zeitschrift für Theoretische Soziologie* 1 (1): 47–60.

Fitzhenry, Roy. 1986. Parsons, Schutz and the problem of Verstehen. In *Talcott Parsons on Economy and Society*, ed. Robert J. Holton and Bryan S. Turner, 143–178. London: Routledge.

Garfinkel, Harold. 1952. The Perception of the Other: A Study in Social Order (PhD Thesis, Harvard University, June 1952), Chap. 5: *A Comparison of the Decisions of Parsons and Schütz*, 90–151.

Giddens, Anthony. 1979. Schutz and Parsons: Problems of Meaning and Subjectivity. *Contemporary Sociology* 8: 682–685.

Grathoff, Richard. 1978a. Introduction. In *The Theory of Social Action*, ed. Richard Grathoff, xvii–xxvi. Bloomington: Indiana University Press.

———. 1978b. How long a Schütz-Parsons divide? In *The Theory of Social Action*, 125–130. Bloomington: Indiana University Press.

Hama, Hideo. 1989. Schutz-Parsons-Controversy. *Tsukuba Journal of Sociology (Japanese)* 14: 47–56.

Honolka, Harro. 1978. Review of Alfred Schütz/Talcott Parsons: Zur Theorie sozialen Handelns. Ein Briefwechsel. *Soziologische Revue* 1: 382–384.

Jules-Rosette, Bennetta. 1980. Talcott Parsons and the Phenomenological Tradition in Sociology: An Unresolved Debate. *Human Studies* 3: 311–330.

Kassab, Elisabeth. 1991. *The Theory of Social Action in the Schutz-Parsons Debate: Social Action, Social Personality and Social Reality in the Early Works of Schutz and Parsons. A Critical Study of the Schutz-Parsons Correspondence*. Fribourg: Editions Universitaires Fribourg.

Nasu, Hisashi. 1991. On the 'Schutz-Parsons Dispute'. *The Annuals of Sociology (Japanese)* 32: 17–43.

Natanson, Maurice. 1978. Foreword. In *The Theory of Social Action*, ed. Richard Gratoff, ix–xvi. Bloomington: Indiana University Press.

Parsons, Talcott. 1937. *The Structure of Social Action*. New York: The Free Press.

———. 1974. A 1974 retrospective perspective. In *The Theory of Social Action*, 115–124. Bloomington: Indiana University Press.

———. 1986. *Aktor, Situation und normative Muster. Ein Essay zur Theorie sozialen Handelns*. ed. and with an Introduction by Harald Wenzel. Frankfurt/M: Suhrkamp.

———. 2010. *Actor, Situation and Normative Pattern. An Essay in the Theory of Social Action*. ed. and with an Introduction by Victor Lidz and Helmut Staubmann. Vienna: Lit Verlag.

Procter, Ian. 1980. Voluntarism and Structural-Functionalism in Parsons' Early Work. *Human Studies* 3: 331–346.

Psathas, George. 2004. Alfred Schutz's Influence on American Sociologists and Sociology. *Human Studies* 27: 1–35.

Rehorick, David Allan. 1980. Schutz and Parsons: Debate or Dialogue. *Human Studies* 3: 347–355.

Rehorick, David, and William Buxton. 1988. Recasting the Parsons-Schutz dialogue: The hidden participation of Eric Voegelin. In *Wordly Phenomenology: The Continuing Influence of Alfred Schutz on North American Human Science*, ed. Lester Embree, 151–169. Washington: CARP and University Press of America.

Schütz, Alfred. 1932. *Der sinnhafte Aufbau der sozialen Welt. Eine Einleitung in die verstehende Soziologie*. Vienna: Springer.

———. 1936. Das Problem der Personalität in der sozialen Welt. In *Alfred Schütz Werkausgabe Vol. V.1: Theorie der Lebenswelt 1: Die pragmatische Schichtung der Lebenswelt*, ed. Martin Endress and Ilja Srubar, 33–90. Konstanz: UVK.

———. 1937. Das Problem der Personalität in der sozialen Welt. Bruchstücke. In *Alfred Schütz Werkausgabe Vol. V.1: Theorie der Lebenswelt 1: Die pragmatische Schichtung der Lebenswelt*, ed. Martin Endress and Ilja Srubar, 91–176. Konstanz: UVK.

———. 1940. Letter to Fritz Machlup, April 16. In Schütz Papers, Alfred Schütz Memorial Archives: University of Konstanz.

———. 1943. The Problem of Rationality in the Social World. *Economica* X: 130–149.

———. 1962a. In *Collected Papers I*, ed. Maurice Natanson. The Hague: Nijhoff.

———. 1962b. Common-sense and scientific interpretation of human action. In *Alfred Schütz, Collected Papers I*, 3–47. The Hague: Nijhoff.

———. 1962c. Concept and theory formation in the social sciences. In *Alfred Schütz, Collected Papers I*, 48–66. The Hague: Nijhoff.

———. 1962d. Phenomenology and the social sciences. In *Alfred Schütz, Collected Papers I*, ed. Maurice Natanson, 118–139. The Hague: Nijhoff.

———. 1962e. On multiple realities. In *Alfred Schütz, Collected Papers I*, ed. Maurice Natanson, 207–259. The Hague: Nijhoff.
———. 1964. In *Collected Papers II*, ed. Arvid Brodersen. The Hague: Nijhoff.
———. 1967. *The Phenomenology of the Social World*. Evanston, IL: Northwestern University Press.
———. 1978. Parsons' theory of social action. In *The Theory of Social Action*, 8–60. Bloomington: Indiana University Press.
———. 1996a. In *Collected Papers IV*, ed. Helmut Wagner and George Psathas. Dordrecht: Kluwer.
———. 1996b. The problem of rationality in the social world. In *Alfred Schütz, Collected Papers IV*, ed. Helmut Wagner and George Psathas, 6–24. Dordrecht: Kluwer.
Schütz, Alfred and Talcott Parsons. 1977. *Zur Theorie sozialen Handelns. Ein Briefwechsel*. ed. and with an Introduction by Walter M. Sprondel. Frankfurt/M.: Suhrkamp.
———. 1978. *The Theory of Social Action*. ed. Richard Grathoff with a Foreword by Maurice Natanson. Bloomington: Indiana University Press.
Schwinn, Thomas. 1993. *Jenseits von Subjektivismus und Objektivismus. Max Weber, Alfred Schütz und Talcott Parsons*. Berlin: Duncker & Humblot.
Sprondel, Walter M. 1977. Einleitung. In *Schütz/Parsons, Zur Theorie sozialen Handelns. Ein Briefwechsel*, 10–18.
Tibbetts, Paul. 1980. The Issue of Human Subjectivity in Sociological Explanation: The Schütz-Parsons Controversy. *Human Studies* 3: 357–366.
Tyrell, Hartmut. 1996. Review of Thomas Schwinn: Jenseits von Subjektivismus und Objektivismus. Max Weber, Alfred Schütz und Talcott Parsons. *Kölner Zeitschrift für Soziologie und Sozialpsychologie* 48: 195–199.
Valone, James J. 1980. Parsons' Contributions to Sociological Theory: Reflections on the Schutz-Parsons Correspondence. *Human Studies* 3: 375–386.
Wagner, Helmut R. 1979. Theory of Action and Sociology of the Life-World. *Contemporary Sociology* 8: 685–687.
———. 1980. Reflections on Parsons' '1974 Retrospective Perspective' on Alfred Schütz. *Human Studies* 3: 387–402.
———. 1983. *Alfred Schutz. An Intellectual Biography*. Chicago: University of Chicago Press.
Weber, Max. 1977. *Critique of Stammler*. Trans. with an Introductory essay by Guy Oakes. New York: Free Press.
Wilson, Thomas P. 2005. The problem of subjectivity in Schütz and Parsons. In *Explorations of the Life World*, ed. Martin Endress, George Psathas, and Hisashi Nasu, 19–49. Dordrecht: Springer.
Zaret, David. 1980. From Weber to Parsons and Schutz: The Eclipse of History in Modern Social Theory. *American Journal of Sociology* 85 (5): 1180–1201.

Rationality, Norms, and the Sociological Reconstruction of Economic Theory

Mark Gould

This paper provides a contemporary sociological perspective on the Schumpeter-Parsons rationality seminar. I characterize the interface of economic and sociological theory, focusing on Parsons' analysis of the "problem of order" and on Weber's and Marx' analyses of the emergence of machine capitalism. I demonstrate the consistency of both perfect-information, Arrow-Debreu models and models of competitive markets under machine capitalism with the assumptions of neoclassical theory, most especially the contention that all actors at all times act rationally and maximize (arguments in their utility functions) against (situational) constraints. I also demonstrate that imperfect-information models and models of capitalist production that are not competitive generate anomalies that manifest certain fallacies within neoclassical theory, most especially the contention that we can explain social action successfully if we assume that all actors are instrumentally rational all of the time.

I argue that Parsons misunderstood the reasons why there was a problem of order in economic (utilitarian, neoclassical) theory and that this misunderstanding precluded him from understanding both when and why the conceptualization of social norms was crucial. Parsons missed the importance of the (sometimes implicit) assumptions used in the construction of then contemporary economic models, and this precluded him from understanding the importance of uncertainty[1] as the reason for the emergence of the problem of order and as the crucial condition for the emergence and importance of social norms. In addition, he failed to emphasize sufficiently that "rationality" was an assumption about individual actors in

[1]Parsons had, if only tacitly, discussed uncertainty under the rubrics of error and ignorance in *The Structure of Social Action* (TSSA) (Parsons 1949 [1937]), and uncertainty was crucial in his analyses of professionalism.

M. Gould (✉)
Haverford College, Haverford, PA, USA
e-mail: mgould@haverford.edu

H. Staubmann, V. Lidz (eds.), *Rationality in the Social Sciences*,
DOI 10.1007/978-3-319-62377-1_12

economic theory, one present for every actor in every situation, while it was something in need of explanation within a sociological theory.

Crucial in the logic of utilitarian, neoclassical theory is the fact that there is a single, positively stated normative orientation for all actors at all times. At least within the context of this theory, endless discussions about how to characterize the norm of rationality are beside the point; what is crucial for the logic of the theory is that there is only one positively stated normative orientation, not how it is characterized. This amounts, as Boudon put it, to the postulation of an a priori psychology (Boudon 1986 [1984]: 38), one that remains the same across both time and space. While both Parsons and analytical Marxists attributed this point of view to Marx, it is easy to show that they generalized falsely from Marx' analysis of machine capitalism, ignoring Marx' analysis of why actors in this system had to act rationally if they were to remain incumbents in certain social roles (Träger) and ignoring Marx' analysis of the first stage of manufacture (a form of capitalism), where rationality needs to be explained.[2]

There is no problem of order in perfect-information Arrow-Debreu general equilibrium models. In equilibrium, these Walrasian models result in a "Pareto optimum," where every actor is as well off as she/he could be given her/his starting endowment of alienable and inalienable assets. Here, as Koopmans demonstrated, increases in profitability are always congruent with increases in efficiency (Koopmans 1957), and in consequence, actors may be postulated to act rationally. "Equilibrium" means that no actor has any incentive to change her/his economic position. These happy conditions dissolve if the assumption of perfect information is relaxed. Even when all actors are assumed to maximize against constraints (act rationally), if imperfect information is assumed, disorder will be manifested (there may not be a Pareto optimum in equilibrium), and in the world the theory attempts to model, social norms will emerge to (at least partially) resolve it (Luhmann 1985 [1972]). I discuss this process in an examination of principal-agent relationships.

While the assumption that all actors act rationally at all times is consistent with the constraints that emerge within competitive markets, at least consistent for those actors who continue to occupy crucial economic roles, it results in a presumption of the rationality of actors, a rationality that may not be present and, if present in the absence of competitive markets, needs to be explained. The presumption of rationality may lead to errors in the analysis of monopolistic relationships [as in Schumpeter's discussion, p. 22, above; cf. (Friedman 1953)], where, by definition, competitive, objective, constraints are absent. I focus on what we may refer to as the first stage of manufacture, what Marx calls the formal subsumption of labor under capital, where the valorization process is capitalist, but the production process is precapitalist. Here, increases in production manifest constant returns to scale; there is

---

[2]I have discussed Parsons' misunderstanding of Marx in (Gould 1981). Analytical Marxists characterized Marx as a neoclassical theorist and attempted to reconstruct his analysis of capitalism within models isomorphic with Arrow-Debreu general equilibrium analyses. The crucial texts are (Elster 1985, 1986; Roemer 1981, 1982, 1986a, 1986b [1982]).

no increase in productivity, there is no reduction in per unit costs with increases in production, and there are no competitive constraints to force actors to produce efficiently or profitably (rationally). This is the situation analyzed by Weber, where he demonstrated that rationality (in the form of the spirit of capitalism), manifested as capital accumulation, need not be present (traditional orientations and actions may be sustained) and thus needed to be explained if we were to understand the conditions that led to the genesis of machine capitalism. His explanation was, of course, that the Protestant ethic generated an inner-worldly asceticism; when the value commitments that characterized innerworldly asceticism interpenetrated a manufacturing economy, they generated the spirit of capitalism and the subsequent systematic rationalization of economic activity (Gould 2016a; Weber 1958 [1904–1905]).

While perfect-information Arrow-Debreu models solve the problem of order theoretically, they are empirically, nearly vacuous. Imperfect-information models, while empirically much more fruitful, reintroduce the problem of order, a set of anomalies, into neoclassical, utilitarian, theory. These anomalies cannot be resolved from within neoclassical theory, in part because we cannot introduce multiple, positively stated normative orientations within this theory (and thus cannot characterize normative obligations). Further, while neoclassical theorists can conceptualize competitive markets consistently within the logic of their theory, in the absence of competition, the presumption that actors are instrumentally rational (except in cases of error and ignorance due to imperfect information[3]) results in an inability to explain systematic deviations from rationality that may be due to the institutionalization of nonrational social values and norms. If we are to address the anomalies that emerge in imperfect-information models and noncompetitive markets satisfactorily, we must sociologically reconstruct economic theory (Gould 1990a, 2001b; Kuhn 1970 [1962]).

Methodologically, I show that my analyses have consequences for an evaluation of Milton Friedman's contention that the empirical veracity of the assumption of rationality is irrelevant because the predictions that derive from models where rationality is assumed are empirically warranted. We will see that these empirical predictions presume other attributes of the "real world," like competitive constraints, that are not always present and thus that the predictions are often false. In consequence, we will conclude that the veracity of the assumptions in our models is often crucial to the model's empirical warrantability. Even when the assumption of rationality is justified, it should not be taken a priori; it requires explanation. Since actors may conform to a variety of normative orientations (other than the norm of rationality), and since the conceptualization of these alternative, positively stated normative orientations is impossible within utilitarian theory, this suggests that neoclassical theory must be reconstructed sociologically.

[3]Actors are intendedly rational, but they might fail to act rationally due to complexity (bounded rationality) or to uncertainty. For Parsons, "error" characterized the first, the attempt and failure to act rationally, while "ignorance" is the situation where an actor thinks she/he understands what is instrumentally rational and the most efficient way to attain her/his end, but she/he is wrong.

The Structure of Social Action

Parsons' goal in *The Structure of Social Action* was to differentiate between theories of social action that necessarily generate error and theories where such errors were not a necessary consequence of a theory's logic. He created a conceptual framework, the unit act, within which social action theories might be characterized, enabling him to create a pile of "bad" and another pile of "good" theories. Even though Parsons' language characterizing the unit act was ambiguous, the unit act was not intended as a conceptual tool within the type of voluntaristic theory Parsons favored. Instead, his analysis led to the conclusion that autonomous unit acts were characterizable only within atomistic theories, theories that fell into the "bad" pile.

Some papers for the Schumpeter-Parsons volume are grounded in a misunderstanding of the nature and function of the unit act. This misunderstanding was exemplified by Parsons, himself, in a paper that he never published (Parsons 2010 [1939]), where he used the unit act as a tool of analysis in his own theory of social action. This is a clear indication that we should not rely on innovators to explicate their own intellectual creations.

Paradoxically, this self-misunderstanding suggested the viability of a form of theory, utilitarianism, and neoclassical economics, which Parsons endeavored to demolish in the text of his great book.[4] A central argument of the book is that utilitarian theories (more generally, positivist theories, especially in their atomistic forms) generate errors when analyzing noncoerced social action.

In the most famous discussion in the book, Parsons argues that a consistent utilitarian theory, for example, Hobbes' theory, must explain social order through situational constraints.[5] Actors conform to social norms only when it is in their interest to do so[6]; from within utilitarian theory, multiple, positively stated social norms are reduced to either the situational constraints that may support them or the

---

[4]Utilitarian theories may be characterized through four attributes: they are atomistic (methodological individualism), and only one positively stated normative orientation may be conceptualized within these theories. While the normative orientation is usually characterized as the norm of instrumental rationality, the nature of the characterization is unimportant. The ends of action are exogenous, and the theory is empiricist, introducing concepts only when they can be related directly to observables. See Parsons (1949 [1937]) and, for some emendations to Parsons' analysis (Gould 1989, 1991a, 1991c).

[5]This is not quite correct. There are three operative mechanisms explaining action in utilitarianism, the end, the situation, and the single, positively stated normative orientation. Actors are understood to maximize (arguments in their utility functions) against (situational) constraints. If autonomous ends (for Hobbes, passions) are eliminated, as in the two forms of radical positivism Parsons discusses, there are two mechanisms left, the situation and the single, positively stated normative orientation (Parsons 1949 [1937]).

[6]Post hoc, we may characterize any social action in a way that is consistent with utilitarian theory. The action, itself, reveals the goal the actor was seeking to maximize. Any action may be conceptualized as an attempt to rationally attain that revealed preference. Thus, the theory is tautologous.

ends of discrete actors. Hobbes' state, the Leviathan, seeks to order situational constraints to make it in the interest of actors to conform to "social norms," thereby creating social order; from within the analysis of a utilitarian theory, if it is not in an actor's interest, if it does not result in the maximization of her/his goals, an actor will not conform to social norms.[7] In contrast, Parsons argues that Locke characterized social order in a way that was correct empirically when he recognized, in his analysis of the state of nature, that noncoerced social order was possible, but Locke's explanation for noncoerced order was theoretically inconsistent, appealing to what Halévy called a "natural identity of interests" (Halévy 1966 [1928, 1901]), thereby introducing a second, positively stated normative orientation into an otherwise consistent utilitarian theory.[8]

Parsons contends that the development of economic theory relied on this assumption, enabling its elaboration into the best articulated theory in the social sciences, but leaving it open to the criticism Parsons mounts in the book that economic theory could not consistently explain noncoerced social order.[9] This set of contentions is erroneous. Economists are able to explain noncoerced social order. They do so not by introducing multiple normative orientations into their theory, contradicting its logic, but by assuming perfect information (for all actors, at all times), constructing theoretically consistent models that solve the problem of order. It is only when the assumption of perfect information is relaxed that the problem of order emerges. Further, as we will see, it is easy to show that, when uncertainty is assumed, the problem of order is irresolvable from within a consistent utilitarian theory.

Perfect-Information General Equilibrium Models

The first fundamental theorem of welfare economics tells us that, in equilibrium, all factors of production receive the value of their marginal product as a price. Prices depend only on the attributes of the individual unit of production. This seems counterintuitive to many sociologists, who see both production and productivity

[7]The theory of deviance articulated within contemporary economic theory might be summarized by the contention that actors will violate legal norms when it is in their interest to do so (see Becker 1976).

[8]The "natural identity of interests" is a form of "right reason" enabling actors to see that their short-term interest may not coincide with their long-term interests. To work theoretically, it requires the resolution of a collective action problem, the regulation of the pursuit of attainable short-term interests that might harm the social order in a way that harms the long-term interest of the individual actor. There is, of course, an extensive literature dealing with these problems.

[9]Noncoerced social order refers both to situations where order is manifest solely not only because of social norms but also to situations where order is inexplicable without the characterization of social norms, even if situational sanctions contribute to its development and sustenance (see Gould 2001a and Hart 1997 [1961]).

as a factor of a combinatorial process, of, for example, the attributes of an individual worker and the technology (and organizational attributes) of her/his firm.

For example, if we imagine two workers producing commodities, one using a great deal of capital (to produce widgets) and one only a small amount of capital (to produce doodads), we would presume that the first worker would be more productive than the second and that the value of her/his marginal product would be greater than that of the second (Granovetter 1981). This is, no doubt, correct, but our economist friends remind us that in a model presuming perfect information and no transaction costs, the second worker will offer to work for the first employer for a wage below the wage the first worker receives. As she/he changes her/his employer costlessly and as the number of persons working for the widget producer increases, the value of the marginal product of employees producing widgets will decline, and as the number of employees producing doodads declines, the value of their marginal product will increase. Equilibrium comes when the values of their marginal products are equivalent. No employer will pay a worker more than the value of her/his marginal product because the employer would lose money in doing so; but an employer will pay workers more than the current wage if the new wage is below, or equal to, the value of their marginal products and if the employer makes a profit in doing so. The same analysis holds for any factor of production.[10]

For economists, an economy is in equilibrium when no actor has an incentive to alter her/his position. Firms are constrained to produce efficiently, and consequently this outcome is both best for each individual participant and also for all participants together; production is maximized and, it can be argued, allocated in terms of the contribution each factor of production (including workers) makes. This Pareto optimum is a measure of economic efficiency (each firm is compelled to produce efficiently), and this analysis constitutes a critical theory, delimiting an ideal to which, we might argue, economies ought to aspire.

All of this presumes, for all actors, satisfaction with their starting positions, with the alienable and inalienable capital each possesses at the beginning of the analysis. As has been pointed out frequently, such an analysis thus depends on mechanisms to protect the property and person. I leave those aside here because it is easy to demonstrate that if we can show the inadequacy of economic theory's analysis of

[10]In a perfect-information model, the analysis is the same for all factors of production. This is because from within perfect-information models, there is a determinate relationship between labor-power, the capacity to work, and labor, the work undertaken. Thus, labor-power may be treated as a commodity (like any other commodity). This neat equivalence breaks down in imperfect-information models, where, as Marx tells us, labor must be extracted from labor-power and workers must be motivated to work both effectively and hard [as Williamson puts it, consummately, instead of perfunctorily (Williamson 1975, 1985)] and where the relationship between labor-power and labor is not known costlessly. We may conclude from this that Marx has constructed an imperfect-information model, where the key insight is that labor-power is different from any other factor of production. We may also conclude that any attempt to assimilate Marx's analysis into a perfect-information Arrow-Debreu model is doomed to failure. Roemer acknowledges, and then ignores, this insight (Roemer 1986b [1982]: 94).

principal agent problems, we can show its inadequacy when analyzing law and the state.

Thus, if we are willing to stipulate individual starting positions, each actor is, in equilibrium, without a motivation to alter her/his position. This equilibrium constitutes social order because each actor is as well off as possible, and no actor has an incentive to alter her/his position in it. This analysis does not require that we violate the logic of utilitarian theory; it requires, instead, that we presume perfect information.[11]

Imperfect-Information Models and the Recreation of the Hobbesian Dilemma

Does the fact that order is created in perfect-information, Arrow-Debreu models mean that we have to rethink our understanding of Parsons' argument in Chap. 3 of *The Structure of Social Action*? It depends; it depends on why we are asking the question. If our concern is whether we can, from within a neoclassical (utilitarian) theory, and contrary to what Parsons argues, resolve the problem of order successfully, then, yes, we have to conclude that Parsons' argument was erroneous. If, however, we are concerned with the development of a viable social theory, it turns out, for reasons I will explicate, that Parsons was correct in his condemnation of utilitarian theory.

Two generations ago economists began to realize that while Arrow-Debreu models were logically coherent and the greatest theoretical edifice constructed by social scientists, these models were largely, empirically vacuous. In consequence, they began constructing models grounded in a different set of assumptions, most importantly, assuming imperfect or asymmetrical information and uncertainty.[12] They discovered that when the assumption of perfect information was relaxed, many of the most important conclusions they had drawn from perfect-information models were not robust. For example, in imperfect information models, supply might not equal demand, i.e., markets might not clear in equilibrium, and there might not be a single price for economically homogeneous commodities. Further, markets conceptualized within imperfect-information models are unlikely to be constrained Pareto efficient. This means that we cannot separate out issues of efficiency from issues of equity; not only is an equilibrium unlikely to be a Pareto optimum, but we might enhance total production, through government intervention, without reaching a Pareto optimum because some actors might be harmed in the process (Shapiro and Stiglitz 1985; Stiglitz 1987, 1991).

[11]Above, I mentioned transaction costs; in this paper the assumption of perfect information means that there are no transaction costs.

[12]In Frank Knight's sense, we can insure against risk, but not against uncertainty (Knight 1965 [1921]).

It should be obvious that the problem of order is not resolved in imperfect information neoclassical models. As Bowles argues, these imperfect-information models are Hobbesian (Bowles 1985); they recreate the problem of order in exactly the way Parsons characterized it. Further, it is easy to demonstrate the importance of the mechanisms, shared social values and norms, Parsons uses to resolve the problem of order, and it is easy to demonstrate that this resolution is inconsistent with the logic of utilitarian, neoclassical theory.

The simplest way to see all of this is through a discussion of principal-agent problems. From within a utilitarian, neoclassical theory, when a principal wants to motivate an agent to act in the principal's interest, the principal is understood to attempt to align her/his own and the agent's interest through the manipulation of situational sanctions. She/he rewards conformity if the agent fulfills her/his expectations, and she/he punishes deviance and violations of those expectations. For example, within an employer-worker relationship, the employer might pay the worker for each widget she/he produces, and she/he might fire him if she/he produces insufficient widgets. As Parsons recognized in his characterization of voluntarist theories and in his critique of idealist theories, these situational sanctions are crucial in understanding social action (Parsons 1949 [1937]). Even so, focusing on them alone is insufficient.

Neoclassical principal-agent models fall short because of their failure to recognize what every manager knows, that employees may enhance the quantity and quality of their effort when they are committed to their firms and/or to the tasks they undertake.[13] Ceteris paribus (e.g., at the same wages, the same working conditions, and the same probability of getting fired if one shirks), in situations where employers cannot monitor their workers both effectively and costlessly, committed workers will be more productive than those who calculate cost versus benefit.

In a situation of perfect information, both employer and employee know the value of the worker's marginal product costlessly. As we saw above, the employer cannot pay the worker less than this value because the worker is protected by the willingness of other capitalists to pay her/his a higher wage approaching this value. In contrast, in a situation of imperfect information, where it is costly or impossible to determine the value of a worker's marginal product, workers may shirk. In situations of imperfect information, workers will act opportunistically, strategically, with self-seeking guile (Williamson 1985).

There are many examples where economists have recognized that in this situation of imperfect information and significant monitoring costs, value commitments, positively conceptualized normative orientations other than the norm of instrumental rationality, are relevant in understanding the motivation of individual actors and in the solidarity of groups of actors. For example, Kenneth Arrow, when analyzing doctor-patient relationships, found it necessary to introduce into his model a

[13](Gould et al. 1996) This is, of course, too simple a way to put it. The due process justification of orders in terms of legitimate procedures is just as important as the legitimacy of those orders and their consistency with shared social values (see Gould 1993).

collectivity orientation shared by physicians, a set of ethical, professional commitments, which lead physicians to act as fiduciaries for their patients. The physicians conform to a set of social norms, which results in their not acting with self-seeking guile even when doing so would be instrumentally rational.[14]

These insights are real, but they are not sustainable from within a neoclassical theory. There multiple positively stated normative orientations must be reduced to arguments within actors' utility functions or to situational sanctions that support the normative orientations. In the first case, the theory becomes indeterminate whenever this reduction results in ill-ordered (non-transitive) arguments in the utility function. In the latter instance, the anomalies in the theory that gave rise to the conceptualization of normative orientations reappear because the reduction of normative orders to situational sanctions returns us to the starting point, where the anomalies appeared originally in imperfect-information models.

We might conclude that while the a priori assumption that all actors at all times and in all places maximize against constraints appears consistent with successful perfect-information neoclassical models, this assumption disables us from being able to explain social order in imperfect-information models, for example, to explain empirically when and why workers will work either consummately or perfunctorily (Williamson 1975, 1985). To do so successfully, we must introduce multiple, positively stated normative orientations into our theory; we must reconstruct economic theory sociologically.

Rational Actors in the First Stage of Manufacture and in Machine Capitalism

Marx distinguishes between two stages of capitalism; they share the capitalist valorization process but have different labor processes. When labor is formally subsumed under capital, during what I call the first stage of manufacture, the labor process is precapitalist; the labor process replicates the one present before the development of capitalism. During the first stage of manufacture, workers use raw materials and/or means of production owned by capitalists, the capitalists own the commodities they produce, workers are paid a wage, and capitalists garner surplus value.[15] Because the actual process of production has not changed, increases in production occur with constant returns to scale, through the replication of the precapitalist processes of production. This means that there are no increasing returns to scale and, crucially, it means that there are no reductions in per unit costs when capital is accumulated within a firm. Thus, as both Weber and Marx

[14]For a more extensive discussion of Arrow's and Parsons' characterizations of doctor-patient relationships, with the relevant citations, see Gould (2015).

[15]This discussion draws on previous work, where the characterization of the two stages of manufacture and machine capitalism is much more comprehensive (Gould 1987, 2016a).

recognized, producers could have continued to produce traditionally without fear of being driven from the market.

Marx contrasted between subjective and objective motivations for accumulating capital. In the first stage of manufacture, the motivation was subjective. During the first stage of manufacture, capital accumulation cannot be explained because of objective competitive constraints (that were not in play) (Marx 1976). Weber had the same insight, and he set about to explain the nature of the subjectivity that resulted in capital accumulation (Weber 1958 [1904–1905]). The Protestant ethic was not a consequence of the emergence of capitalism (during the first stage of manufacture). Its origins were in the form of religious commitment that emerged out of Calvinism (Gould 1986, 2005, 2016b). This inner-worldly asceticism, when it interpenetrated with an economy characterized by the first stage of manufacture, gave rise to the spirit of capitalism and to a systematic process of capital accumulation.

This capitalist accumulation, during the first stage of manufacture (characterized by simple cooperation), resulted in the development of the second stage of manufacture (characterized by complex cooperation), represented in Adam Smith's characterization of the production of pins (Smith 1937 [1776]). The second stage of manufacture narrowed each segment of the productive process in a way that enabled the development of machines and the development of machine capitalism and the correlative increasing returns to scale. Here competitive constraints were objective. Machine capitalism was characterized by the real subsumption of labor under capital, where the process of production is revolutionized continuously and where capitalists who continued to produce traditionally were driven out of business.

In a structural analysis of machine capitalism, capitalists may be assumed to maximize against constraints. While it is not the case that all will do so, it is the case that those who fail to do so may be assumed to cease functioning as capitalists. In this situation, it seems reasonable (as in analytical Marxism) to assume instrumental rationality as the sole, positively stated normative orientation for all actors. However, when we reflect back on the first stage of manufacture, it is clear that this a priori assumption is bogus. It presumes what must be explained.

If all actors, at all times, maximized against constraints, there would always be capital accumulation during the first stage of manufacture, and machine capitalism would have emerged with the first development of the formal subsumption of labor under capital. Given the numerous cases where the first stage of manufacture did not generate machine capitalism,[16] it should be obvious that "rationality" requires an explanation, and Marx recognized the need for an explanation, while Weber provided us with that explanation.

[16]It is, of course, the case that there are other conditions for this transformation from the first stage of manufacture to machine capitalism. I both discuss some of those conditions and explain why they do not problematize my argument in (Gould 1986, 1987, 1997, 2005, 2016b).

In machine capitalism, while it appears that we may presume what Weber explained, that actors maximize against constraints, in a careful reading of both Marx and Weber, we see that this is wrong. Marx suggests that in machine capitalism, actors face objective constraints. In neoclassical terms, this means that the constraints they face are so confining that they must act rationally because rational action is the only effective choice they have (they must maximize profits to attain their constrained ends).[17] This sounds very much like Parsons' analysis of Marx (Parsons 1949 [1937]), but Marx recognized that individual actors might conform to alternative normative orientations and fail to reproduce themselves as capitalists. One might counter that for Marx, this failure was due only to error and ignorance (in situations of uncertainty); rather than argue this point, we may shift to Weber, where it is clear that such individual actors may be understood to conform to "traditional" values. While Marx creates the space for such an analysis, Weber provides us with a model manifesting it.[18]

In the previous discussion, I showed that the a priori assumption that actors maximize against constraints appeared to be tenable within perfect-information Arrow-Debreu models. We saw, however, that when the assumption of perfect information was relaxed, it was easy to show that imperfect-information models created theoretical anomalies that were impossible to resolve from within a neoclassical theory. The resolution of such anomalies, the explanation of noncoerced social order within these models, requires the conceptualization of normative expectations, of several positively stated normative orientations, which violates the logic of neoclassical theory (Gould 1990b, 2013). Thus, the assumption that all actors, at all times, are instrumentally rational (aside from error and ignorance) is theoretically untenable.

In this section, we have discussed two structural models of capitalist economies. In the model of machine capitalism, where increases in production manifest increases in productivity and result in reduced per unit costs, competitive constraints force actors to act instrumentally rationally (efficiently). It thus seems as if the assumption that all actors act rationally makes sense. We saw, however, that when we looked at models of the first stage of manufacture, the formal subsumption of labor under capital, that increases in production simply replicated existing labor processes (constant returns to scale); they did not result in the reduction of per unit costs and thus did not constrain capitalists to give up their traditional mode of

[17]In neoclassical models, only attainable ends will be selected.

[18]Another way to put this argument is to note that Marx did not reduce individual actors to the social positions they occupy. Marx did not contend that all machine capitalists acted instrumentally rationally; he contended that if they failed to do so, they would be driven out of business. This point is sometimes obscured because his analysis in *Capital* is of a social structural model, where individuals are present only as the bearers (*Träger*) of social positions. Weber provides us with the tools to understand why some actors may fail, even in machine capitalism, to maximize against constraints; they may be committed to alternative social values. He also understood that while these capitalists might survive during the first stage of manufacture and that those machine capitalists who failed to accumulate capital would be driven out of business.

production. Here, in the absence of objective constraints, actors had to be motivated to accumulate capital; for this motivation to be systemic, it had to be regulated by shared social values. Once again, this manifests that the a priori assumption of instrumentally rational actors is fallacious; that rationality needs to be explained.

The Assumption of Rationality and the Methods of Theory Construction

Much of Milton Friedman's argument in "The Methodology of Positive Economics" is a defense of abstraction.[19] He is correct when he claims that theory is never literally descriptive, but this is very different from the commonplace lesson learned from his article that while the assumption of instrumental rationality may not describe how people act, theories presuming it yield empirically correct predictions, and thus the lack of descriptive accuracy of the assumption is unimportant. This contention is not the same as Newton's abstraction that reduces planets to points in a model of the solar system, where the fact that planets are much more than points is irrelevant to the veracity of his contentions. Friedman's is an essential theoretical claim (one partially constitutive of neoclassical economic theory) that we may assume a single, positively stated normative orientation to which all action conforms (perhaps with the exception of error and ignorance). As such, while we may, as Friedman suggests, construct ideal types that make this assumption (e.g., perfect-information, Arrow-Debreu models), it is a false characterization of social action, one that we have shown to generate erroneous predictions.

Friedman suggests that our confidence that capitalists maximize returns "is justified by evidence. . .unless the behavior of businessmen in some way or other approximated behavior consistent with the maximization of returns, it seems unlikely that they would remain in business for long.. .. The process of 'natural selection' thus helps to validate the hypothesis—or, rather given natural selection, acceptance of the hypothesis can be based largely on the judgment that it summarizes appropriately the conditions for survival" (Friedman 1953: 22). As we have seen, this contention is valid within the context of machine capitalism, but not during the first stage of manufacture, a situation of the formal subsumption of labor under capital. We can see that this distinction between systems controlled subjectively versus those controlled objectively matters by turning to a brief discussion of monopoly.[20]

Friedman assumes "entrepreneurs seek to maximize their returns by any means including acquiring or extending monopoly power. . ." (Friedman 1953: 27). Further, he presumes that while "this hypothesis can, as usual, be stated without specifying

[19]This section is inspired by, but not a direct critique of, Friedman's essay (Friedman 1953: Part I). For example, I do not discuss the "as if" arguments Friedman characterizes (see Vaihinger 1952 [1924, 1911]).

[20]Cf., what follows with Schumpeter's discussion in this volume, at p. 22

any 'assumptions[,]'" we may "suppose it can be shown that it is equivalent to a set of assumptions including the assumption that man seeks his own interest. The hypothesis then gains indirect plausibility from the success for other classes of phenomena of hypotheses that can also be said to make this assumption..." (Friedman 1953: 29). His test case for this contention is a discussion of labor market discrimination.

Friedman contends that "the hypothesis that the extent of racial or religious discrimination in employment in a particular area or industry is closely related to the degree of monopoly in the industry or area in question and that if the industry is competitive, discrimination will be significant only if the race or religion of employees affects either the willingness of other employees to work with them or the acceptability of the product to customers and will be uncorrelated with the prejudices of employers. This hypothesis is far more likely to appeal to an economist than to a sociologist. It can be said to 'assume' single-minded pursuit of pecuniary self-interest by employers in Competitive industries.... On the other hand, the hypotheses to which the sociologist is accustomed have a very different kind of model or ideal world, in which single-minded pursuit of pecuniary self-interest plays a much less important role (Friedman 1953: 29)".

This amounts to the contention that discrimination is a form of inefficiency that will be driven out of a competitive model.[21] When, however, there is an absence of competition, for example, in cases of monopoly, discrimination may persist. What is missing here is the "because"; discrimination may persist in cases of monopoly because of the absence of competitive constraints. In Gary Becker's terms, employers may act out their taste for discrimination (Becker 1971 [1957]), a taste that would be driven out of competitive markets.

While Friedman appears to see the cases of the emergence of monopolies and of increased levels of discrimination in monopolies (as against competitive markets) as analytically the same, in fact, they are opposites (at least with regard to my argument). He explains the emergence of monopolies by presuming that actors always maximize economic gains against constraints and act rationally. In contrast, he recognizes, contrary to this presumption, that actors might not choose to maximize economic gains against constraints in monopolies.

We might suggest that in the case of competitive markets, the assumption that actors will maximize their returns against constraints is isomorphic to the explanation of competition, and thus of the natural selection within a competitive situation of those who maximize and the "termination" of those who fail to do so. The fallacy of this contention may be seen when we look at the situation of monopoly, where there is something that we are unable to explain within the context of a neoclassical theory. Why will some capitalists maximize economic returns, while other capitalists, with monopoly power, chose to discriminate and act irrationally (at least in regard to economic returns)? While this difference may be described by suggesting that some have a taste for discrimination, this characterization is arbitrary,

[21]If a capitalist pays higher wages to white than to equally productive black workers, this is inefficient.

appealing to a variable inexplicable within neoclassical theory (where tastes are exogenous). To explain it adequately, we need to create a sociological theory that lets us characterize the consistency of this taste with a set of social values that legitimate discrimination.[22]

To be clear about this contention, we must distinguish between the assumptions that constitute neoclassical theories (e.g., the "assumption" that there is a single, positively stated normative orientation that actors maximize against constraints) and the assumptions that characterize particular models constructed within these theories (e.g., the assumption of perfect information). Our simple discussion of discrimination shows that an assumption integral to neoclassical theory, the a priori assumption of instrumental rationality, makes it impossible to explain social action when that action is not constrained situationally to mimic the assumptions that characterize the theory. Relatedly, this theoretical assumption disables our ability to construct redeemable predictions in models that do not assume perfect information.

Conclusion

Parsons' analysis of the problem of order was fallacious. Order is explicable within a neoclassical theory when models constructed within that theory assume perfect information. Economists did not have to presume a natural identity of interests to explain social order. Given the equilibrium conditions specified in the first theorem of welfare economics, a Pareto optimum, where given her/his starting conditions of alienable and inalienable capital, each actor is as well off as possible, and therefore no actor has any reason to endeavor to alter her/his position (equilibrium); social order will be manifested.

This theoretical outcome, which provides a critical standard by which to evaluate actual economic performance, is often vacuous empirically. To make the theory more tractable empirically, economists developed a variety of imperfect-information models. We have shown that these imperfect-information models generate anomalies because actors will often act in ways that are inexplicable if

[22]"Tastes" are exogenous in economic models; they are given, parameters of the models, and thus inexplicable within them. The only exception is when constraints narrow the possible goals to the degree that only one goal may be implemented successfully. This is the case in competitive but not in noncompetitive models. Thus, Becker's argument fails in competitive markets, where inefficiencies, like discrimination, are driven from the market.

I have attempted to explain the persistence of labor market discrimination in competitive labor markets (Gould 1991b, 1992a). I do this by constructing a sociological model that presumes imperfect information; in such a model, capitalists may have power over workers (Gould 1995). It is possible to show that in this model, discrimination may be both inefficient *and* profitable because it may increase the power of capitalists over workers and that employers are constrained to maximize profitability and not efficiency. I explain the "new racism" that legitimates discrimination in the contemporary United States in (Gould 1992b), and I discuss some of its other consequences in (Gould 1999, 2011).

we assume that, a priori, all actors maximize against constraints. In such models, it is necessary to conceptualize alternative, positively stated normative orientations to which actors may conform (both out of commitment and because the expectations are supported by situational sanctions). This set of conceptualizations violates the assumption of instrumentally rational action as the single, positively stated normative orientation.

The assumption that actors always maximize against constraints is also justified in structural models of competitive markets. However, in structural models where competition is absent (e.g., where monopolies are present or during the first stage of manufacture), the assumption of instrumental rationality can be shown to result in erroneous analyses. This insight leads to the conclusion that even where the assumption is justified, it should not be taken a priori; it requires explanation. The nature of actors is not miraculously transformed in cases of monopoly, where it must be explained when and why they will or will not maximize. The internalized normative orientations that actors adopt must be characterized sociologically in terms of the institutionalized normative orientations that regulate social action. It is only then that we will be able to explain why and when discrimination increases in situations of imperfect competition. Since the conceptualization of these alternative, positively stated normative orientations is impossible within a neoclassical model, even those that assume imperfect information, this suggests that that neoclassical theory must be reconstructed sociologically.

References

Becker, Gary S. 1971 [1957]. *The Economics of Discrimination*. Chicago: University of Chicago Press.

———. 1976. *The Economic Approach to Human Behavior*. Chicago: University of Chicago Press.

Boudon, Raymond. 1986 [1984]. *Theories of Social Change: A Critical Appraisal*. Trans. J.C. Whitehouse. Berkeley: University of California Press.

Bowles, Samuel. 1985. The Production Process in a Competitive Economy: Walrasian, Neo-Hobbesian and Marxian Models. *American Economic Review* 75: 16–36.

Elster, Jon. 1985. *Making Sense of Marx*. Cambridge: Cambridge University Press.

———. 1986. *An Introduction to Karl Marx*. Cambridge: Cambridge University Press.

Friedman, Milton. 1953. *Essays in Positive Economics*. Chicago: University of Chicago Press.

Gould, Mark. 1981. Parsons versus Marx: 'An earnest warning…'. *Sociological Inquiry* 51: 197–218.

———. 1986. *Puritanism and the English Revolution*. Presented at a Princeton University Mellon Colloquium. New Jersey: Princeton.

———. 1987. *Revolution in the Development of Capitalism: The Coming of the English Revolution*. Berkeley: University of California Press.

———. 1989. Voluntarism versus Utilitarianism: A Critique of Camic's History of Ideas. *Theory, Culture and Society* 6: 637–654.

———. 1990a. The interplay of general sociological theory and empirical research. In *Robert K. Merton: Consensus and Controversy*, ed. J. Clark, C. Modgil, and S. Modgil, 499–516. London: Falmer.

———. 1990b. *The Problem of Order in Perfect and Imperfect Information Theories*. Presented at the Annual Meeting of the American Economic Association, Washington, DC.
———. 1991a. Parsons' Economic Sociology: A Failure of Will. *Sociological Inquiry* 61: 89–101.
———. 1991b. The reproduction of labour market discrimination in competitive capitalism. In *Exploitation and Exclusion: Race and Class in Contemporary US Society*, ed. A. Zegeye, L. Harris, and J. Maxted, 102–129. London: Hans Zell.
———. 1991c. The structure of social action: At least sixty years ahead of its time. In *Talcott Parsons: Theorist of Modernity*, ed. R. Robertson and B.S. Turner, 85–107. London: Sage.
———. 1992a. Law and Sociology: Some Consequences for the Law of Employment Discrimination Deriving From the Sociological Reconstruction of Economic Theory. *Cardozo Law Review* 13: 1517–1578.
———. 1992b. The new racism in United States society. In *The Dynamics of Social Systems*, ed. P. Colomy, 154–174. London: Sage.
———. 1993. Legitimation and justification: The logic of moral and contractual solidarity in Weber and Durkheim. In *Current Perspectives in Social Theory*, ed. B. Agger, vol. 13, 205–225. Greenwich, CT: JAI Press.
———. 1995. *Unconscionability, Free Contract and the Law Against Employment Discrimination: Richard Epstein On and Against the Government's Fiduciary Responsibility for Contract Regulation*. Presented at the Annual Meeting of the Law and Society Association, Toronto, Canada.
———. 1997. *Puritanism and the English Revolution: The Role of Social Values in the Constitution of the Economic Tendencies Leading to a Political Revolution*. Presented at the Annual Meeting of the American Sociological Association, Toronto, Canada.
———. 1999. Race and Theory: The Culture of Poverty and Adaptation to Discrimination in Wilson and Ogbu. *Sociological Theory* 17: 171–200.
———. 2001a. *Social Norms: A Critique of Law and Economics Formulations and a Guide to their Correct Conceptualization*. Presented at the Joint Meeting of the Law and Society Association and the Research Committee on the Sociology of Law, International Sociological Association.
———. 2001b. *A Theory of 'Scientific Revolutions'*. Presented at the Annual Meeting of the American Sociological Association, Anaheim, CA.
———. 2005. Understanding Jihad. *Policy Review* 129: 15–32.
———. 2011. More Than Just Social Structure: The Poverty of Cultur(al) Analysis. *The Du Bois Review* 8: 476–488.
———. 2013. God and the Problem of Order: the Role of Perfect Information and Absolute Power in Economics, Religion and Law. *RIMCIS - International and Multidisciplinary Journal of Social Sciences* 2: 257–272.
———. 2015. *Professional Autonomy: The Reconciliation of Principal Agent Conflicts in Professional Relationships*. Presented at the Bi-Annual Meeting of the European Sociological Association.
———. 2016a. Marx and Weber and the Logic of Historical Explanation: The Rise of Machine Capitalism. *Journal of Classical Sociology* 16: 321–348.
———. 2016b. *Natural Law, Human Fallibility and the Transcendence of God: Islam, Christianity (Confucianism, Judaism) and Democracy/Human Rights*. Presented at an International Conference on the Legacies of Shmuel Noah Eisenstadt, Paris.
Gould, Mark, Charles Heckscher, and Frank Domurad. 1996. *Loyalty, Professionalism, and Rationality in Corporate Downsizing*. Presented at the Annual Meeting of the American Sociological Association, New York, NY.
Granovetter, Mark. 1981. Toward a sociological theory of income difference. In *Sociological Perspectives on Labor Markets*, ed. I. Berg, 11–47. New York: Academic Press.
Halévy, Elie. 1966 [1928, 1901]. *The Growth of Philosophical Radicalism*. Trans. M. Morris. Boston: Beacon.
Hart, Herbert L. A. 1997 [1961]. *The Concept of Law*. Oxford: Oxford University Press.

Knight, Frank. 1965 [1921]. *Risk, Uncertainty and Profit*. New York: Harper Torchbooks.
Koopmans, Tjalling C. 1957. *Three Essays on the State of Economic Science*. New York: McGraw-Hill.
Kuhn, Thomas. 1970 [1962]. *The Structure of Scientific Revolutions*. Chicago: University of Chicago Press.
Luhmann, Niklas. 1985 [1972]. *A Sociological Theory of Law*. Trans. E. King and M. Albrow. London: Routledge & Kegan Paul.
Marx, Karl. 1976. *Capital*, Vol. 1. Trans. B. Fowkes. Harmondsworth: Penguin.
Parsons, Talcott. 1949 [1937]. *The Structure of Social Action*. New York: Free Press.
———. 2010 [1939]. *Actor, Situation and Normative Pattern: An Essay in the Theory of Social Action*. Berlin: LIT Verlag.
Roemer, John. 1981. *Analytical Foundations of Marxian Economic Theory*. Cambridge: Cambridge University Press.
———. 1982. *A General Theory of Exploitation and Class*. Cambridge: Harvard University Press.
———. 1986a. 'Rational choice' Marxism: Some issues of method and substance. In *Analytical Marxism*, ed. J. Roemer, 191–201. Cambridge: Cambridge University Press.
———. 1986b [1982]. New directions in the Marxian theory of exploitation and class. In *Analytical Marxism*, ed. J. Roemer, 81–113. Cambridge: Cambridge University Press.
Shapiro, Carl, and Joseph E. Stiglitz. 1985. Equilibrium Unemployment as a Worker Discipline Device: Reply. *American Economic Review* 75: 892–893.
Smith, Adam. 1937 [1776]. *The Wealth of Nations*. New York: Modern Library.
Stiglitz, Joseph. 1987. The Causes and Consequences of the Dependence of Quality on Price. *Journal of Economic Literature* 25: 1–48.
Stiglitz, Joseph E. 1991. *The Invisible Hand and Modern Welfare Economics*. NBER Working Paper #3541.
Vaihinger, Hans. 1952 [1924, 1911]. *The Philosophy of 'As If': A System of the Theoretical, Practical and Religious Fictions of Mankind*. Trans. C. K. Ogden. London: Routledge.
Weber, Max. 1958 [1904–1905]. *The Protestant Ethic and the Spirit of Capitalism*. Trans. T. Parsons. New York: Scribner's.
Williamson, Oliver. 1975. *Markets and Hierarchies*. New York: Free Press.
———. 1985. *The Economic Institutions of Capitalism*. New York: The Free Press.

Conceptualizing Rational Social Action

Victor Lidz

My point of departure is the faculty seminar on the topic of Rationality that the great Austrian economist, Joseph A. Schumpeter, then a professor at Harvard University, convened together with his younger colleague, the sociologist Talcott Parsons, in the academic year of 1939–1940. Parsons and Schumpeter had arrived at Harvard University in the Economics Department in successive years, Parsons in 1927 as a young instructor with a growing knowledge of German historical economics, Schumpeter in 1928 as a figure with a long-established international reputation. Parsons knew that he did not have adequate mastery of neoclassical, marginal utility theory in economics and audited Schumpeter's seminar, among others given by the senior faculty, including Frank Taussig. Apparently something of a colleagueship developed between Parsons and Schumpeter, one that was sufficient to survive Parsons' transfer to the new Sociology Department in 1930. For Parsons, it persisted even after Schumpeter's retirement and death: as late as the 1960s, Parsons assigned Schumpeter's *Theory of Economic Development* (1987a) of 1911 to his students. Many also knew *Capitalism, Socialism and Democracy* (1987b), still widely read at the time among undergraduates in the social sciences at Harvard. The seminar on Rationality apparently eventuated from Schumpeter's reading of Parsons' *The Structure of Social Action*, published in 1937, which addressed issues related to rationality in a number of ways.

We do not have complete records of presentations to the seminar, but we do have copies of the contributions by Schumpeter, Parsons, and Alfred Schütz, the already distinguished Austrian social phenomenologist then living in New York City. Presumably, Schumpeter as well as Haberler had known Schütz from Vienna and invited him to present to the seminar, the event that also initiated a series of

V. Lidz (✉)
Department of Psychiatry, Drexel University College of Medicine, Philadelphia, PA, USA
e-mail: lidzvic@gmail.com

H. Staubmann, V. Lidz (eds.), *Rationality in the Social Sciences*,
DOI 10.1007/978-3-319-62377-1_13

exchanges marred by misunderstandings between Parsons and Schütz (Grathoff 1978).[1] The materials collected by Professor Staubmann from the seminar include as well papers of lesser importance by the sociologist Wilbert Moore, a student of Parsons, and the agricultural economist, Rainer Schickele, and notes from a few other sessions.[2] Participants in the seminar discussions who apparently did not make independent presentations included John Dunlop, later the chief labor economist at Harvard and briefly federal Secretary of Labor; Paul Sweezy, who applied marginal utility analysis to socialist economics but withdrew from academic life early in his career; Abram Bergson, later the leading Western economist of the Soviet Union and of the adaptive difficulties in supplanting market systems with central planning; Alexander Gerschenkron, a leading economist and economic historian of Russia; and Wassily Leontief, developer of input-output analysis and an early Nobel laureate in economics. All of the latter economists aside from Sweezy later became full professors at Harvard and were among the colleagues with whom Parsons maintained friendships for decades.

I

The seminar talks by Parsons, Schumpeter, and Schütz presented three rather different conceptions of rationality or, at least, conceptions of three different aspects of rationality. Parsons repeated the definition of rationality given in *The Structure of Social Action* with just slight variation in wording. Rationality in this conception is a mode of organization of the elements of the general schema of action: a unit act involves an actor voluntaristically making choices or decisions regarding the ends of a course of action, the means to be used, whether and how appropriate norms will be observed, how given conditions may be managed, and the effort to be allocated to the process. Thus, rational action involves "statements of observable fact subject to verification" and logical reasoning in the planning of a course of action. It also involves use of "empirical knowledge to the clarification of alternative courses of action and their consequences..." to yield "the most favorable utility/cost balance." Parsons emphasized the voluntarism of choice of ends and means and also rationality or truth as a guiding normative element. The pure type of rational action is scientific research and creation of knowledge, but the general type extends to appropriately formed economic action, perhaps political action as well. Rational action contrasts with irrational, traditional, and what Pareto

[1]The difficulty in the relationship between Schütz and Parsons started when Schütz stated in his letter of November 15, 1940, that he would publish his critical commentary of some 20,000 words on Parsons' *The Structure of Social Action* if Parsons agreed "in principle" with it. Parsons could not agree, so Schütz's position, an unusual one in terms of American academic customs, put Parsons in the awkward position of seeming to suppress publication of a major critique of his work.

[2]All of these materials are included in the present volume. Quotations in the following section are from the papers of Parsons, Schumpeter, and Schütz, respectively.

termed nonlogical or Weber termed nonrational action. Parsons seems in this specific account to have left out the Weberian type of emotional or affective action. He noted that the domains of metaphysics, ontology, the nonempirical realm, problems of meaning, problems of evil, and so forth may be handled with logical consistency and precision but are nonempirical, hence nonrational—although not in principle irrational. That is, the standards that determine rationality or irrationality do not apply to nonempirical statements or beliefs even if they are logically conceptualized. A limitation of Parsons' conception is that in its strict terms, authentic rational action probably occurs relatively rarely.

Schumpeter focused on the "observer's rationality" in the social sciences, which, he emphasized, does not differ in principle from the observer's rationality in the natural sciences. He then noted that the aggregate economic measures used by economists in their models do not reflect the concepts of the unit act presented by Parsons. Yet, he later suggested that *understanding* (in the sense of Weber's usage of *Verstehen*) of actual economic processes (or other forms of everyday action) does require attention to ends, means, and the outlook of the economic actor. Thus, models of the rationality of everyday actors are needed.

Schumpeter goes on to acknowledge that models of the entrepreneur developed by economists and using concepts of marginal utility and marginal costs do not reflect the actual mental processes and economic planning of businesspersons. The businessperson probably follows previously established practices with modifications as conditions change, thus relying on rules of thumb and other types of informal reasoning. Nevertheless, economists' models have value; they may be viewed as analogous to frictionless models in mechanics. Yet, they differ from mechanics insofar as they also set up a norm or ethical standard for the conduct of business.

Schumpeter emphasized that it is difficult to capture the actual mental processes of any individual or collective actor, whether acting rationally or deviating from norms of rationality. The difficulty is even greater for actors who are remote in history or culture from the observer. Economists tend to speak of "preferences" instead of "utility" to address some of the problem of understanding actors' decision-making, but this does not alter the basic problem. In sum, Schumpeter's general theme was that rational models tend to work heuristically even if an actor is following general rules of thumb, not the mental processes hypothesized in formal models, because they often lead to similar outcomes. In this respect, he concluded that Parsons' definition of rational action is not helpful to the economist, even one who posits that economic actors proceed rationally in their conduct.

Schütz presented by far the best-developed argument and most complete paper. He announced his topic as exploring "the underlying and concealed meanings" of rationality and rational action in the social world. Examining the actor in his engagement with the everyday world, he suggested, will lead to different concepts than Parsons' elements of rational action.

He compares the "naïve" resident of the city who knows how to get where he needs to go with the cartographer attempting to map the city. They hold and use quite different models of rational knowledge. So, too, does the scientist in his research and in his everyday relations with colleagues, family members, and others. In everyday life, we rely upon various types and typifications of other people, various situations, and various activities.

In Weber's sense, we disenchant the everyday world through the typifications our personal life experiences enable us to employ in familiarizing ourselves with its many aspects. Such typifications and the following of practical interests facilitate action that may not involve discrete ends, means, or values. The intermingling of typifications, vague conjectures, presuppositions and prejudices, habits, and rules of thumb in everyday life involves motives, means and ends, and causes and effects, conjoined in various ways. The jumble of elements enables us to master our lives without formal rationality. We use anticipations rather than predictions, typifications and typical sequences rather than hypotheses or laws. We face everyday life with a cookbook or recipe knowledge, not formally rational knowledge.

Everyday action is not deliberative in a methodical way, although it may be planned in various degrees. An actor can anticipate the chain of means-ends relations for getting to his or her place of work: buying a ticket to take the subway, leaving the train at the correct stop, walking to the familiar building, taking the elevator to the right floor, etc. But such action is neither logical in Pareto's sense nor rational in Parsons' terms. Thinking of alternative courses of action, as in Parsons' model of rational action, involves thinking in the future perfect tense—what will have happened. Everyday life can follow this rational form on occasion, but it generally does not. Parsons' model cannot provide a principle for understanding everyday life.[3] Rational action is an ideal type in the sense that Weber cited as contrasting to traditional or habitual action.

Schütz then turns to the task of the social scientific observer seeking to understand the "everyday" actor. He must use ideal types of individual persons or "puppets" to understand the features of social action under investigation. The puppet "is not born, he does not grow up, and he will not die." He lacks hopes, fears, anxieties, and conflicts of interest. He is a model only of the conscious mind of an actor engaged in a specific form of action. He is a consumer, taxpayer, member of a club, and so forth, but engages only in the form of action that figures in the particular "reference scheme" of the social scientist.

The typical actor or puppet should also meet two postulates: the postulate of subjective interpretation and the postulate of adequacy. Together, they require that the model of the puppet's action represents the actual mental processes of the observed actor and should seem "reasonable and understandable" to the observed actor and his or her "fellow men." Such an explanation of an actor may demonstrate his or her rationality, but this would be in a sense different from Parsons'.

[3]We may agree with Schütz on this important point, but we should also note that Parsons did not present his model of rational action as explaining the mental processes of actors in their everyday courses of conduct.

Schütz emphasizes that the explanation itself should be developed on the basis of logic and rationality, as should all scientific knowledge. He cites the marginal principle of economics as an example but does not address Schumpeter's point that marginal theories in economics do not generally model the thought processes or mentality of businesspeople.

The key respect in which Schütz's analysis of the rationality of everyday social action differs from Parsons' analysis of the elements of the rational unit act involves the claim that there is a kind of rationality that does not meet the standard of "statements of observable fact subject to verification." I do not think this is a refutation of Parsons' analysis. Parsons would likely have responded that everyday social action and relationships generally fall under the type of habitual/traditional social action. Parsons might also have insisted that the terminology of typifications and related elements of thought embed means, ends, and norms far more than Schütz, with his different terminology, acknowledged.

Together, Parsons, Schumpeter, and Schütz essayed different aspects of the phenomena of rational social action and rational analysis of social action. Their modes of analysis differ primarily in apprehending the ways in which elements of rationality are—or are not—embedded in everyday conduct. However, aside from Parsons' references to scientific knowledge and Schumpeter's defense of scientific modeling of human decision-making, they do not address the ways in which *cultural* emphases on rationality and, in particular, rationally developed *institutions* promote social patterns of rational action or conduct. Yet, this was a major concern of Max Weber's, a crucial figure in the background of the theoretical work of all three: Schumpeter, Schütz, and Parsons. By reverting to a Weberian perspective, I hope now to amplify our understanding of the prominence of rationality in modern civilization. I will begin by following Weber's methodology and examining some specific historical formations.

II

It is not unusual for commentators on Max Weber's *The Protestant Ethic and the Spirit of Capitalism* (1930) to regard the Protestant ethic and the spirit of capitalism as basically the same thing. However, Weber clearly distinguishes between them. The spirit of capitalism is an intermediate variable in his study, standing between the Protestant ethic that gave rise to it and the dependent variable of modern capitalism with its complexes of rationalized economic institutions. Weber discusses the spirit of capitalism before his more intensive analysis of the Protestant ethic as a key, but not the only, cause of its historical emergence. He introduces the spirit of capitalism by turning "to a document of that spirit. . .in almost classical purity," which, he highlights, stands "free from all direct relationship to religion. . ." (1930: 48). Weber quotes extensively from it, emphasizing at the outset that it displays an economic ethic that is quite independent of any particular religious orientation (1930: 48).

Over two-and-a-half pages, Weber's quotations illustrate the following themes: Time is money, and wasted time means that money that might have been earned is lost. Money produces money; owning and using money enables one to gain more money, whether through interest on loans or through its use as capital in direct processes of production. Wasted money loses all the income it might have produced in the future. Paying bills or debts promptly and fully earns one credit and thus the use of borrowed capital. Industry, frugality, and timeliness in payment create credit. Showing that one works hard, is firmly disciplined, and maintains a frugal lifestyle enables one to gain credit from others in the community. One should keep an "exact account" of both income and expenditures to prevent even small losses of funds. "For six pounds a year" a person of good credit "may have the use of one hundred pounds," so avoiding even small unnecessary expenditures every day can gain the use of a significant capital. If a young man saves even "five shillings" for use in his business dealings, he can realize through investments "a considerable sum" for his old age (1930: 48–50). For Weber (1930: 53), these points show a clear ethic of methodical use of capital as investment for renewed or future enterprise. Money is not regarded for its "eudaemonistic" or "hedonistic" value but as capital for economic productivity. Moreover, it is a duty to treat money in this matter. And that duty is an aspect of a secular calling or vocation.

Only after quoting it extensively does Weber identify the work as the *Autobiography* of Benjamin Franklin.[4] Franklin served Weber's argument neatly: he was a transitional figure of special importance.[5] He had been raised in a religiously disciplined Presbyterian (that is, Calvinist) family in Boston, approximately two generations after the founding of the colony. His father had left England as a dissenter seeking greater religious freedom and had raised his many children with a strictly Calvinist ethic and regimen. Franklin recalled his father's strict ethics in respectful, indeed, thankful terms throughout his life. Yet, he had become a Deist in his early adult, if not his adolescent, years and had absorbed at least substantial elements of the thought of the Enlightenment. Weber knew that Franklin had before middle age developed a successful printing, newspaper, and almanac publishing business in predominantly Quaker Philadelphia. His business was that of an artisan

[4]See *A Benjamin Franklin Reader*, edited by Nathan G. Goodman (New York: Thomas Y. Crowell Company, 1945 and 1971), pp. 47–201 for *Autobiography*. The volume includes a useful brief biography of Franklin, although it is not accurate on all details.

[5]Facts of Franklin's life in the present account are drawn from Carl Van Doren, *Benjamin Franklin* (New York: Viking Press, 1938); Edmund S. Morgan, *Benjamin Franklin* (New Haven: Yale University Press, 2002); Walter Isaacson, *Benjamin Franklin; An American Life* (New York: Simon and Schuster, 2003); and Gordon S. Wood, *The Americanization of Benjamin Franklin* (New York: Penguin, 2004). The Van Doren volume has the virtue of quoting extensively from Franklin's own writings. The Morgan volume presents a more up-to-date analysis of Franklin's developing thought during his stays in London as an agent of American colonies and then as representative of the United States in Paris during the Revolutionary War. Isaacson's work is the most recent full-length biography. Wood's book emphasizes the life change in Franklin's career between his years as an increasingly successful printer and entrepreneur and his assumption of gentlemanly status devoted to public service.

in a small shop, aided by a few or several journeymen and apprentices working on a press operated by hand, hardly a modern capitalist or industrial enterprise. His sense of a *calling* as a printer, who held himself to stringent standards of hard, disciplined work, frugality in living standards, saving, development of creditworthiness, methodical use of capital, and reinvestment of profits, demonstrated the emergence of a spirit of capitalism "before the capitalism order" existed (Weber 1930: 55).

With his upbringing, Franklin stood for Weber as proof that the disciplined sense of a calling promoted by the ascetic or Calvinist-influenced Protestant sects gave rise to the spirit of capitalism that then promoted the development of modern capitalism. We may add that as nonrational as the premises of the ascetic calling may have been, they advanced a definitely rational methodology of work, personal discipline, and use of capital. What we now call economic rationality has been a historical outcome of the early spirit of capitalism that, over time, has been ever more thoroughly institutionalized in modern enterprises, industrial and "postindustrial."

We should note that the *Autobiography* had a specific moralizing purpose: Franklin said that he wrote the first section, not long before the rupture between the American colonies and the British Empire, to use his own successful life as an example to persuade his son William to change his career. Indeed, the first words of the *Autobiography* are "Dear Son." William was at the time Governor of the Colony of New Jersey, appointed several years earlier by the British crown largely through Franklin's own influence. As relations between the colonies and the Empire frayed, Franklin wanted William to give up office-holding with its implicit dependence on unreliable political sponsorship and ethically compromising connections within the British power structure. He hoped that William would follow his own path of working at a skilled craft or trade or otherwise take up farming on the western frontier of Pennsylvania. He believed that an independent craft or trade, or farming, would be a proper calling, while dependence on distant political powers was ethically tainting.

Weber quoted from the *Autobiography* as published in the 1882 edition of Franklin's *Collected Works* prepared by the American historian, Jared Sparks.[6] The *Collected Works* also enabled Weber to quote from pamphlets in which Franklin published compilations of epigrams of advice to young artisans and shopkeepers, mainly ones drawn from *Poor Richard's Almanac*. Citing extracts from these writings, Weber created the model of the spirit of capitalism as an "historical individual," which he held to be a source of modern capitalism, treated as an ideal type. Yet, Weber did not quote from Franklin's more generally moralizing essays or from his extensive political writings.[7] For example, he took no note

[6]Jared Sparks, *The Works of Benjamin Franklin, with notes and a life of the author by Jared Sparks*, ten volumes (Chicago: T. MacCoun, 1882). I do not know whether Weber examined all ten volumes.

[7]Franklin's selections from Poor Richard's Almanac designed as guidance for citizens of modest means, but hopeful futures are still in print in brief but popular volumes, for example, *The Way to Wealth; Advice, Hints, and Tips on Business, Money, and Finance* (New York: Skyhorse

of Franklin's satirical essays, many of them political in nature and some of them written as early as his adolescent years. The most important ones appeared during his years in London as sharp attempts at intervention in the relations between the United Kingdom and its American colonies. Perhaps the most brilliant essay, written when the American colonies were disputing Britain's right to tax them, presented itself as the king of Prussia's claim to tax the British Isles because they had been colonized centuries earlier by ancestors of his Saxon subjects (Goodman 1971).[8] It seemed real enough to have briefly caused political consternation in London before the clever hoax was recognized. By focusing on Franklin's expression of the spirit of capitalism while leaving aside a wealth of his other writings, Weber presents a truncated account of Franklin's thought and its importance in early American political and intellectual history, however valid the analysis he does present.

To be sure, Weber knew enough about Franklin's business career to justify his characterization of it as exemplary in the early development of rational capitalism. All his adult life, and on his tombstone, Franklin identified himself as "Benjamin Franklin, printer" and viewed the business of printing as the core of his career and personal success. He sustained this identity even after he had achieved much greater recognition as a philanthropist, scientist, philosopher, statesman, and diplomat. As late as his time in Paris during the Revolutionary War, Franklin set up a press in his personal residence and continued on occasion to print his own new writings. In his later political activities, he favored the class of "leather apron" artisans, shopkeepers, and freehold farmers of which he had been a part rather than the class of public officials, professionals, and merchants to which he later notably belonged.

Yet, Franklin's career in business was more ramified and more successful than Weber appears to have known. After setting up his print shop with a partner—on the basis of funds lent by his partner's father—his success enabled him to buy out the partner (who had been contributing little to the enterprise); purchase the failing *Pennsylvania Gazette* from a competitor and make it a successful newspaper; publish the annual *Poor Richard's Almanac*, which eventually had a circulation of 10,000 per issue; and obtain the printing contracts, first, of the colony of Pennsylvania and, later, the colonies of Delaware and then Maryland as well. He became the postmaster for Pennsylvania, then assistant postmaster for the 13 British colonies, and later postmaster of the 13 original states, positions that aided his newspaper by collecting news from Europe and the various colonies/states ahead of competing publishers. He also gained the position of clerk of the Pennsylvania

---

Publishing, 2012) and *The Art of Virtue; Ben Franklin's Formula for Successful Living* (New York: Skyhorse Publishing, 2012). See also *Wit and Wisdom from Poor Richard's Almanac* (New York: Dover Thrift Editions, 1999), a selection of quotations from the almanac published between 1733 and 1758. See also the materials in Ralph Ketcham, editor, *The Political Thought of Benjamin Franklin* (Indianapolis: Hackett Publishing, 2003).

[8]Printed in *A Benjamin Franklin Reader* as "A Clever Hoax. An Edict by the King of Prussia," pp. 624–627.

Assembly, the colony's unicameral legislature, again giving him access to political information that improved the competitive position of his newspaper. It was in *Poor Richard's Almanac*, a major source of his wealth, that he first published the epigrams and mottos that, for Weber, exemplified the spirit of capitalism.

With the capital earned in his early printing and publishing business, Franklin set several of his former journeymen up in their own printing and newspaper publishing businesses in other colonies, ranging from Rhode Island to South Carolina. He purchased the printing presses, sets of types, and other equipment and then retained 40% of the profits for himself. Franklin invested fairly extensively in Philadelphia real estate, drawing income from rents. He later invested in real estate in other towns and, with coinvestors, speculated in land on the frontier. He developed paper mills on a substantial scale and, as Gordon Wood's biography notes, "may have been the largest paper dealer in the English speaking world" (2004: 54). He made money from the sale of his invention, the Pennsylvania stove (now called the Franklin stove), which greatly improved the efficiency of indoor heating and was soon adopted internationally. He lent funds to other businessmen on a scale that amounted, in the standards of the time, to operating a small bank.

Wood reports that his annual income eventually amounted to around 2000 pounds per year at a time when successful manufacturers in England earned 40 pounds per year and successful lawyers perhaps 200 pounds per year. At Mount Vernon, George Washington, among the wealthiest of Virginia planters, was earning 300 pounds per year in the 1770s (Wood 2004: 54). Thus, Franklin was a more diverse and more successful entrepreneur than Weber knew and, by the standards of his time, became very wealthy. His wealth subsidized his public service as colonial agent in London and later, with greater luxury, as American representative in Paris during the Revolutionary War.[9]

Franklin's business was "rationalized on the basis of rigorous calculation" as Weber says of the capitalist spirit (1930: 76). Given the expansion and use of credit relations, it amounted to a closer approximation to modern entrepreneurship than Weber knew, although, to be sure, its technology remained on a craft basis and the scale of business remained small by later standards.

In the decades that Franklin was building his businesses, he, his wife, and his two children lived in part of a small rented house with minimal-to-modest furnishings. For years, his wife complemented the family income by managing a small shop selling stationery, soaps, and sundries next door to the print shop. Only after he had gained considerable wealth did Franklin build the complex of shops and houses around a courtyard on Market Street that are now parts of a museum. And only then did he purchase the furnishings of a genteel home and the library of a wealthy intellectual. Thus, he exemplified in his early adulthood the personal frugality that complemented the disciplined manner of work, the protection of creditworthiness,

[9]Franklin's style of life in Paris offended the other American representatives, especially the ascetic New Englander, John Adams, but Franklin correctly believed it important for sustaining influence in the political and intellectual circles of the French aristocracy with whom he had to deal.

the saving and reinvesting of profits, and the expansion of enterprise that were bases of his economic ethic.

Weber only notes in passing that Franklin had been engaged in "civic improvements" in Philadelphia. They started with the "Junto," a group of a dozen or so craftsmen and shopkeepers who shared an ambition for self-improvement and economic advancement that Franklin organized around the same time as he established his printing business. The Junto met weekly for many years to discuss ways in which the members could advance themselves, one another, and their community through exchanges of helpful ideas and plans. It was out of Junto members' sharing of books that Franklin developed a plan for the Philadelphia Library Company, the city's first lending library, which still exists. Plans for the city's first fire company, first hospital, first "academy" of higher learning, and the American Philosophical Society, followed over the years. Although Franklin originally envisioned the academy as focusing on preparing young men for practical trades, it gradually morphed into the University of Pennsylvania, a large, complex, and thoroughly modern institution. As early as the late eighteenth century, it became the first American university to include a School of Medicine. Difficulties in establishing these institutions taught Franklin that, as craftsman and shopkeeper, he could be more effective in presenting his ideas for civic improvements by enlisting more influential figures in the city to assume public leadership in the undertakings.

Franklin's devotion to solving civic problems by creating new practical institutions fits Weber's analysis of a figure who complemented a religiously learned inner-worldly asceticism with an Enlightenment expectation of progress. However, a crucial change in Franklin's career departs from aspects of the economic ethic that Weber attributes to him. After he had gained considerable wealth, Franklin "retired" from active participation in his printing and related businesses to assume the status and lifestyle of a "gentleman."[10] His partners managed the printing businesses, while he received his shares of the profits, collected rents, received interest payments, and oversaw other investments. But rather than devoting the long daily hours to entrepreneurship as required by the capitalist ethic, he reserved the preponderance of his time for public affairs and "philosophy," which included science. His famous experiments with electricity followed, along with such inventions as the lightening rod, the Pennsylvania stove, bifocal glasses, the rocking chair, and many others. He continued to write and publish occasional pieces on civic improvements or public affairs in his newspaper and, later, in the London press, where "The Edict of the King of Prussia" first appeared. With his changed social status, he and his family began to live in a more comfortable manner. He built new houses, purchased new furnishings, set aside his "leather apron" style of clothing and dressed in a gentlemanly manner. In sum, he began to present himself differently to his fellow citizens and assume new roles in the community.

---

[10]Wood's biography makes an original contribution in highlighting not only Franklin's wealth but also his assuming the more prestigious social status of "gentleman" in midlife.

As a gentleman, Franklin shifted from being clerk to the Pennsylvania Assembly to accepting election as a representative of Philadelphia in it. He was soon elected to be its president. He then served for many years as the agent of Pennsylvania and other colonies in London, again becoming President of the Assembly on his return to Philadelphia. As representative of Pennsylvania to the Continental Congress, he helped draft the Declaration of Independence, became the new nation's key representative to France, obtained substantial support in arms and finances for the Revolution from the French court, negotiated the treaty that brought a French army into the American Revolution, and became America's principal negotiator of the peace treaty with Great Britain, thereby securing the independence of the new nation. He then returned to Philadelphia, at over 80 years of age, to participate in the Constitutional Convention. Although his own constitutional ideas, such as a unicameral legislature, were not adopted, and he said little in the convention's formal meetings, he played an important role as a mediator among the different interests and outlooks of other members, sometimes hosting crucial informal discussions in the courtyard of his home.

It is clear that his many and diverse achievements were animated by a much broader ethic, set of ethics, or ideology than the spirit of capitalism alone.

III

Weber cautions that the spirit of capitalism should not be understood "as part of the development of rationalism as a whole," because "the history of rationalism shows a development which by no means follows parallel lines in the various departments of life" (1930: 76–77). While it is clear that the rationalized institutions of modern societies have not emerged in lockstep with one another, but with various advances or lags among them, it is nevertheless also true that they have shared cultural-ideological foundations. In Franklin's case, the elements of the spirit of capitalism that he espoused were linked with a number of other ideological or ethical themes, including a Deism separated from sectarian thought and organization, community improvement and progress, and republican ideals of political constitution.

I have not been able to learn in any comprehensive terms what Franklin read and knew. In the *Autobiography*, he says that he read a great deal from his early years and sustained his reading throughout his life. He encouraged members of the Junto to share books and he established the Library Company of Philadelphia in part because their sharing proved insufficient for his appetite for new books. We know that he reserved Sundays not for church but for reading and study. Late in life he had a library of some 4000 books, perhaps as large a personal library as Thomas Jefferson's and certainly one of the largest in the United States at the time. But I have neither seen a listing of the books nor a reference to one.

We know that Franklin was influenced by *The Spectator* as early as his adolescent years when apprenticed to his older brother James, who had in London been the apprentice of Addison and Steele. The satire that became a major form of Franklin's writings was largely in imitation of *The Spectator* and *Cato's Letters*.

Franklin in the *Autobiography* mentions that he read and was deeply impressed by Locke's *Essay Concerning Human Understanding* already in his youth. He likely knew works of Hutcheson, Ferguson, and other writers of the Scottish moralist school from early on. When he later met Hume and Smith in Scotland, he seems to have been familiar with their writings. He was friendly enough with Hume to have visited with him for a few weeks and apparently the two engaged in extensive intellectual discussions. Later, it was his editing of Jefferson's draft of the Declaration of Independence that inserted "self-evident" to the key pronouncement, "We hold these truths to be self-evident," giving them the status of analytical truths in Hume's philosophy (Isaacson 2003: 321). He knew Adam Smith's *Theory of Moral Sentiments* and on a visit to Edinburgh in the early 1770s was shown parts of the manuscript of *The Wealth of Nations* by Smith himself. In London, Franklin associated and lobbied as colonial agent with members of the "real Whig" political faction, heirs to the Commonwealth tradition and ardent philosophic rationalists in British politics (Morgan 2002).

In France, Franklin met an elderly and ailing Voltaire and appeared to appreciate the importance of his works. Franklin developed friendships with Condorcet, Holbach, and Madame Helvetius that must have been based on knowledge of key works of the French Enlightenment as well as his own fame for his experiments with electricity. Thus, in London, visits to Scotland, and in Paris, his exchanges with major figures of the Enlightenment seem to have entailed knowledgeable sympathy for their views as well as recognition on their part of his attachment to principles consistent with theirs. It is thus with good reason that one biographer has characterized Franklin, who was decades older than Thomas Jefferson and James Madison, as "the first great American exemplar of the Enlightenment" (Isaacson 2003: 95).

Despite ambiguities about what he read and knew in ethical and ideological terms, several principles of Franklin's social and political thought are very clear. First, he maintained a principled toleration of religious sects and ideological movements. Franklin was a Deist who repeatedly affirmed his belief in God but held that it should be works in service to one's fellow men that brought earthly recognition and heavenly salvation, not a Calvinist conception of grace or Lutheran conception of faith. Aside from one brief period, he did not attend church with any regularity, although he apparently expected his wife and children to attend church to preserve family respectability. Yet, he believed that churches were good institutions that benefit the community and he contributed to churches of various denominations as well as to the building fund for Philadelphia's first synagogue. From early in his life, Franklin championed the civil liberties of free speech, free association, and, especially, free press, practically without qualification or limitation. Although he proudly assumed the role of gentleman in his mature years and, like many others of his era, worried about the "mob rule" that might follow from thorough democracy, Franklin opposed privileges and social elites, thus affirming a central element of what Tocqueville (1941) was later to call the "social condition of democracy" in the United States. He believed that public policy should favor the "mediocre" class of artisans, farmers, and shopkeepers—the leather apron class—and their productivity, which was crucial to a thriving economy and the common well-being. He dissented from the views of the Virginia statesmen, including Jefferson, most of them wealthy and educated plantation owners, who hoped that the new American political order would promote an "aristocracy of talent and virtue," living in easy economic circumstances to enable the advantaged, although not in the European sense privileged, elite to devote themselves to public affairs. His skepticism about popular democracy was offset by a strong commitment to representation of the people of every community in legislative processes, and thus belief in a franchise extended to citizens of middling or common circumstances.

In London, he argued that American Englishmen should have political equality with subjects in the United Kingdom and, hence, that the colonies should have representation in Parliament. When he saw that stance gaining no traction in London, he proposed that the colonial legislatures should supplant Parliament in creating laws, under the British King, for their respective territories and populations. In the newly independent United States, he held that high public officials should serve without salary in order to assure that they did not seek office out of self-interest.

Franklin was an American "nationalist" before there was a nation, possibly the first to envision, as early as the 1750s, unification of the American colonies. He believed that the government should have modest powers, that each form of power should always be limited, checked, or counterbalanced by other powers, and that the political order should encourage private associations to promote the welfare of the community. He held that society should be open to social mobility, especially to the possibility that members of the leather apron class might advance to wealth through expansion of their businesses. This commitment to a society in which individuals could advance materially and in social status seems to have been part of a generalized Enlightenment optimism about progress. Late in life, Franklin became active in opposition to slavery. Earlier he had opposed the importation of slaves and the expansion of slavery, but, until past middle age, he had himself owned a pair of houschold slaves, even taking them to London when he began his service as agent of Pennsylvania.

Although he was not a philosopher in our contemporary sense and did not write philosophic treatises, his scientific work and inventions were seen in his own time as philosophic in the sense of being founded on reason, observation, and experimentation and undertaken to create new knowledge and practical human betterment. It was in this sense that his work made him, as a philosopher, the most famous American of his lifetime in Europe.

IV

Franklin, being older, was on the cutting edge of the American Enlightenment, but he was followed in attachment to Enlightenment principles by nearly all of the political and intellectual leaders of the American Revolution and in the writing of state constitutions and the federal constitution. The doctrine of common sense in the Commonwealth literature and the affirmation of a universal human reason in the major works of the Scottish Enlightenment were being taught as moral philosophy in the American colleges from around 1750, even at the colleges, including Harvard, Yale, and Princeton, whose curricula continued to emphasize Calvinist thought and the preparation of educated clergy. Lawyers both in New England and Virginia put forward ideas about the need for rational reforms of the British Common Law. In the 1760s and 1770s, Jefferson and some others, especially in Virginia, were importing works of the French *philosophes*, with Montesquieu's conception of a "mixed constitution" especially affecting the design of the federal constitution (Wood 2004).[11]

The Enlightenment, as received in the American colonies, established the legitimacy of the ideal that the institutions of secular society should be worked out on the basis of reason. It also established the principle that ordinary human individuals were endowed with the common sense that enabled them to judge the legitimacy of secular institutions, a principle that became a foundation of American conceptions of citizenship. The American reception of the Enlightenment also maintained that ordinary members of society, as individuals, were entitled to certain basic or natural rights—the rights of freedom of conscience or belief, association, speech, and publication—that are *antecedent* to the organization of society itself. As such, they must be recognized and protected by the institutions of society or the latter must be regarded as illegitimate (Commager 1977).[12] The 20 years or so of conflict between the American colonies and the British king and Parliament resulted fundamentally from colonists' growing insistence upon their natural rights and their standing to assert them while British authorities, overlooking these matters, persisted in asserting the legitimacy of the Empire and its institutions of authority, including the right of Parliament to tax colonies not represented in it (Bailyn 1967).

As they claimed independence, the former American colonies revised or wrote new constitutions to establish their political and legal orders on rational bascs. The culminating event of the constitution writing occurred in 1787 when, meeting in Philadelphia, a new convention, superseding an ineffective Congress formed under the wartime Articles of Confederation, wrote the federal constitution. The writing required a long summer of deliberation and debate to find terms that would satisfy both small states and large states, the more commercial and urban, the more rural- and farming-based economies, the slave-holding states, and the states moving toward prohibition of slavery. However, there was near unanimity on the principles that a new secular order could be designed for the nation, that the component

---

[11]See also Bernard Bailyn, *The Ideological Origins of the American Revolution* (Cambridge: Harvard University Press, 1967).

[12]Also, Henry F. May, *The American Enlightenment* (New York: Oxford University Press, 1976), which attends closely to the tensions between the Calvinist and Enlightenment traditions of the eighteenth-century American culture.

measures had to be justified by reason, and that the natural rights of citizens had to be secured. The design encompassed a mixed constitution in terms derived from Montesquieu: the presidency representing a monarchical principle, the Senate, with members to be chosen by the state legislatures, representing the aristocratic principle, and the House of Representatives, based on popular election, representing the democratic principle. The ideal of equality before the law and a specific prohibition of aristocratic titles established what Tocqueville later termed the "social condition of democracy": a society without legal and political privileges, hence no aristocracy, and thus a *formal* equality of citizens, regardless of differences in wealth. The independence of the judiciary, and hence the protection of the law from entanglement in politics, was secured by life tenure of federal judges. Despite the many controversies that needed resolution to arrive at the design of the constitution, it conformed closely to models instituted in many of the state constitutions adopted in the previous decade.

V

The Enlightenment was an intellectual movement that originated and remained centered in Europe (Commager 1977). Major European nations all participated in various degrees in the Enlightenment. Scottish, English, French, Dutch, and German intellectuals all made major scientific and philosophic contributions. By comparison, the American colonies and early states were a backwater to the movement. Only several figures, including Franklin, made important contributions to fundamental science. Only a handful of Americans, including the second and third presidents, John Adams and Thomas Jefferson, wrote notable works of Enlightenment thought, and only *The Federalist Papers*[13] written by James Madison, Alexander Hamilton, and John Jay to promote the acceptance of the constitution by the various states, made a substantial American contribution to political philosophy. Yet, the Enlightenment was genuinely international with thinkers in the various nations importantly oriented to and engaged with one another's ideas. Franklin himself, friendly with both Hume and Condorcet, apparently accommodated the differences between their philosophies. Franklin's enthusiastic reception in England, Scotland, the Low Countries, and France, originally due to the fame of his experiments with electricity, but then encompassing his broad engagement with Enlightenment philosophies, is one indication that Americans participated in a genuinely international cultural movement.

The crux of Enlightenment thought was the establishment of a new degree of dignity for secular thought and ethics. We may identify four key elements of

[13]James Madison, Alexander Hamilton, and John Jay, *The Federalist* (New York: Modern Library, edition not dated; originally published as 84 brief essays in the popular press, October, 1787 to May, 1878).

Enlightenment ideology. First, reason was elevated to transcendental status and brought to focus on secular affairs and the design of secular institutions. A result was that a culture, in which Christian theology had previously absorbed philosophic concerns with reason, became differentiated, so that secular moral thought, the arts, and the sciences gained new levels of autonomy as spheres of culture. Second was the conception of natural or human rights as antecedent to social order and requiring protection within the institutions of any society in order for its social order to stand as legitimate. Together with the transcendental reason, the doctrine of natural rights promoted principles of universalism as a kind of solvent to the particular claims of traditional social orders. Third was the concept of progress as a generalized hope that reason would guide overall improvement in human affairs. It grounded an expectation that any society as a whole and its citizens in their various circumstances should expect betterment in actual life experience.[14] Fourth, in every domain of culture, new and rational methodologies emerged to guide the development of ethics, the arts, and the specific sciences and intellectual disciplines. The new methodological foundations over time promoted the accumulation of complex specialized cultures of thought, experience, and knowledge, generally universalistic and international in their makeup.

In varying degrees across the societies of Western civilization, Enlightened reason undermined the traditional religious legitimation of social institutions. Ideals of rational design of social orders took hold as independent of previous religious frameworks, whether Catholic or Protestant. In England, economic rationalization progressed rapidly with the enclosures; the emergence of a mobile, largely urban, labor force; and the growth of industrial enterprises, often led by Dissenters. In France, economic transformation was more limited, but the Revolution precipitated a diffuse attack on aristocracy and its privileges. For nearly a century, down to the consolidation of the institutions of the Third Republic, political life and its ties to the broader social order oscillated between Revolutionary ideals and reestablishment of religious and hierarchical traditions. In Germany, Enlightened reason undermined small-state particularism and fostered rationalization of the law and administrative institutions and, later, investment in science and large-scale

[14]Talcott Parsons identified failure to experience progress or improvement in one's personal circumstances, especially in terms of relative social status in comparison with different but symbolically or culturally salient groups and categories of individuals, as a source of right wing ideologies. This analytic theme was first suggested in his essays on the rise of Nazism in Germany and, later, within a different empirical setting in his famous essay on the Joseph McCarthy movement in the United States in the 1950s. As I write, one can observe a similar pattern in the followers of Donald Trump's campaign for President of the United States. See Talcott Parsons, *Politics and Social Structure* (New York: Free Press, 1969), Chapters 3, 4, and 5 addressing the Nazi movement in Germany and Chapter 7, "Social Strains in America," on the Joseph McCarthy movement. Of present concern is the cultural strength of the underlying belief in the importance of personal and collective experience of progress in life circumstances in Western rationalistic secular culture.

industrial enterprise, but long accommodated itself to aristocracy and monarchy.[15] Spain largely contained rationalizing change to the domain of the arts for many decades. The Austrian-Hungarian Empire, its continuing particularism evident in the Emperor's coats of arms for over 50 formally independent domains, largely contained rationalization to the means of rule—law, administration, the military, politically controlled industry—although Vienna became a major center of music and the arts, including urban planning and architecture. By comparison, the United States, where aristocracy and monarchy had never been institutionalized, experienced an easier, more comprehensive, and more peaceful rationalization of its social order (Hartz 1955)—except for the confrontation over slavery in its Civil War and the continuing discord over race and ethnic relations.

The different experiences in implementing Enlightenment ideals across Europe and North America, to say nothing of elsewhere in the world, underscore Weber's point that rationalism is not implemented in lockstep, whether across societies or across the different spheres of institutions.

VI

What I hope the foregoing story has made clear is that rational action is not simply a matter of the voluntaristic conduct of individuals, as Parsons' and Schütz's essays emphasize, nor even a result of aggregate actions of individual actors as Schumpeter's vindication of economic modeling implies. It is, of course, true that individuals can act rationally without being oriented by a rationalistic culture. Wilbert Moore made that point in his contribution to the Rationality seminar, noting that Trobriand Islanders as studied by Malinowski acted rationally in making their dugout canoes with their axes, even though they resorted to "magical" means to secure success in their fishing. We should also note Weber's point that in non-Western civilizations, there have been thoroughly rationalized religio-philosophic belief systems that have not favored the progressive rationalization of social institutions but firmly legitimated traditionalisms. Weber's examples included the other-worldly frames of Hinduism and early Buddhism and the worldly mysticism of Confucian thought. The latter, for example, promoted worldly rationalization, but only of very specific institutions, especially the mandarin examination system. However, the examination system required thorough training in such traditional cultural forms as the eight-legged essay, which, despite its elegance, imposed profound limitations on the capacity of mandarins, when in

---

[15]On the different trajectories of economic development and institutional change in the United Kingdom, France, and Germany, see Jerrold Siegel, *Modernity and Bourgeois Life; Society and Politics in England, France, and Germany since 1750* (Cambridge: Cambridge University Press, 2012). Also Joel Mokyr, *The Enlightened Economy: An Economic History of Britain 1700–1850* (New Haven: Yale University Press, 2009).

office, to engage difficult conditions in practical and empirical ways.[16] By contrast with these cases of limited rationality, the modern tendency to advance rational designs for social institutions in increasingly comprehensive ways derives, as I have argued, from the Enlightenment's transcendental anchoring of reason.

To be sure, other comprehensive intellectual movements, such as Romanticism in the nineteenth century and relativism in the twentieth century, have succeeded the Enlightenment. But the cultural themes of rationality, natural rights, expectation of progress, and validity of intellectually rationalized methodologies persisted through these later movements. They remain with us today, central elements of contemporary Western civilization, even despite the critiques of some "postmodern" philosophies. Indeed, I believe they define what we mean by modern civilization.

It remains to highlight that the implementation of culturally grounded rationality has resulted in a plurality of specialized rationalisms. The clearest example is the specialization of rationality in the many sciences that have emerged since the eighteenth century, e.g., physics, chemistry, biology, and the various psychological and social sciences, each with its characteristic methodologies. In recent decades, the picture has been made still more complex by the many interconnections among the sciences, as in biochemistry, biophysics, biopsychology, evolutionary sociology, and so forth, again with each "interdisciplinary" field developing its own methodological foundations.

We can follow this model of specialized rationalities into the sphere of social institutions. In his late work, Talcott Parsons sought to clarify differences in the *modes* of rationality across the major institutional spheres of modern societies, an effort he saw as following up on a key aspect of Weber's *Wirtschaft und Gesellschaft* (1968) with its distinctions between economic rationality, legal rationality, and bureaucratic rationality. In the economic case, Parsons emphasized, with a great deal of economics, that competitive markets facilitate rational allocation of resources among various economic goals. He cited Abram Bergson's research on the economy of the Soviet Union (1964) as having demonstrated the intrinsic impossibility of achieving rational allocations of resources in a centrally planned economy. Parsons also highlighted the importance of money as both store and measure of value in enabling individual actors to make rational decisions regarding purchases or sales of goods and services. We may note that in times of high inflation or deflation, the capacity of money to facilitate rational decision-making—to enable actors to calculate the worth of goods and services over extended periods—is reduced.

In one of his boldest papers, Parsons (1969) argued that institutions of authority and uses of power are political analogues of the markets and money complex in the

[16]See Max Weber, *The Religion of India* (New York: Free Press, 1958) and *The Religion of China* (New York: Free Press, 1951). Both volumes emphasize the high degree of rationalization of major religious cultures in Oriental societies but in directions that restricted the valuation of thought about thorough rationalization of secular institutions.

economy.[17] Power in his conception is both a measure and store of capacity to implement policies that bind collectivities or organizations, especially the typecase of politically organized sovereign states. Political actors can make rational calculations of the power they expend in promulgating policy decisions that bind citizens, public agencies, and various private organizations, so that they can balance such expenditures against the prospects of gaining future incomes of power if their policies prove successful. To be sure, such calculations have a rather approximate nature as compared with economic investments made in monetary units measured on continuous scales in the manner of euros, dollars, or pounds. Yet, political actors can recognize having or expending greater or lesser power and to a degree the contingencies that may increase or decrease their power as consequences of new policies. Parsons also held that similar possibilities of power calculations are obtained in nongovernmental, private organizations, especially formally organized corporations. The rationality that power mechanisms make possible in planning and implementing policies both constrains and opens opportunities for the executive of a private organization as well as the politician. To the best of my knowledge, Parsons never discussed in more than perfunctory terms budgetary processes that entail both economic-monetary and political-power forms of rationality.[18]

In his writings on influence, Parsons (1937) suggested, although in less clear terms, that actors have rational means of persuasion of others.[19] He drew a distinction between intrinsic persuaders, such as clear facts of a situation, and the symbolically mediated persuasion involved in the use of influence. I have argued that influence is more satisfactorily viewed as a symbolic means of invoking solidary relations with others in order to gain their collaboration in some undertaking, including persuading them to change views, opinions, or associations with others.[20] The complex pattern of association creation and network formation and the cross-linking of relationships among independently formed associations or networks provide the organization of solidary ties that uses of influence can activate

[17] Talcott Parsons, "On the Concept of Political Power," Chapter 14 in his *Politics and Social Structure*.

[18] As a so-called principal investigator of federally funded research and service grants, I have exercised power over numbers of researchers whose contributions in various roles were needed to implement the projects. Much of that power involved establishing project-long and then annual revisions of project budgets. Federal regulations made it the obligation of principal investigators to develop and certify such budgets within government and university guidelines. The budgets specified who would be employed on the projects, what their qualifications were, what duties they would assume in the work of the projects, and what salaries and benefits they would receive. Of course, the project budgets also had to dovetail with departmental budgets that were the responsibility of the department chair.

[19] Talcott Parsons, "On the Concept of Influence," Chapter 15 in *Politics and Social Structure*.

[20] Victor Lidz, "Influence and Solidarity; Defining a Conceptual Core for Sociology" in Roland Robertson and Bryan S. Turner, editors, *Talcott Parsons; Theorist of Modernity* (Newbury Park, CA: Sage Publications, 1991) and "Language and the 'Family' of Generalized Symbolic Media" in A. Javier Trevino, editor, *Talcott Parsons Today; His Theory and Legacy in Contemporary Sociology* (Oxford: Rowman and Littlefield, 2001).

within local, occupational, political, scientific, or society-wide communities. Again, actors can make judgments of which solidary relationships they will invoke and how much influence they will expend or withhold as they plan to participate in a specific undertaking. Uses of influence are intrinsically quantitative in this respect, and thus actors can make rational judgments in expending influence, even if they have no specific units of influence to measure their expenditures or anticipated incomes of influence with precision.

Parsons (1969) identified one additional symbolic medium that plays an important part in social relationships and institutions, namely, value-commitments or, more simply, commitments.[21] They consist of the promises of actors, single or collective, to perform valued services or participate in valued relationships at future times. Vows of marriage are commitments. Assuming the responsibility to raise children represents commitment. Acceptance of employment in a particular role is a commitment. Commitments enable others in relationships to count upon an actor's future conduct of a specific type. Commitments again have a quantitative aspect: they involve promises of future conduct that may require greater or lesser effort, be more or less difficult to fulfill, or may extend over shorter or longer periods. Actors weigh this quantitative aspect as they make commitments; they may decline to make certain commitments due to a calculation that they are already "overcommitted." In the highly pluralistic pattern of role relationships in which we engage in modern societies, the manifold of commitments we make are often complex. I suggest that typically they are rather thoroughly rationalized by the actors involved.

Finally, each of the four complexes of institutions and symbolic media that we have noted is associated with a distinctive mode of rationality in judgments that actors make in their social relationships. Moreover, each complex has developed only through elaborate rationalization of underlying institutions over extended periods. If we think of the modern economic corporation as an example, it is clear that its emergence has depended on (1) value-commitments made by workers, executives, board members, and so forth to fulfill a very large number of specialized roles. Most of these roles require specialized education and training in the backgrounds of individuals involved and, often, extensive prior experience, or they would not be able to make the required commitments. (2) Influence relations extend throughout the corporation to facilitate organized communication among its staff members in their many roles. Capacities to exercise influence vary by rank, specialty, and experience in the organization and by the types of issue under consideration. Influence may also vary with the quality of personal relationships, for example, qualities of trust among particular individuals in different departments of the organization. The influence also extends from the corporation into the wider community in various ways, for example, to advertise and market products, for professional staff to participate in professional associations, to affect legislation that may harm or advantage the business, to maintain overall prestige to attract

[21]Talcott Parsons, "On the Concept of Value-Commitments," Chapter 16 in his *Politics and Social Structure*.

highly qualified employees, and so forth. (3) The formal bureaucratic organization of the corporation involves lines of hierarchy and also differentiation into separate departments, each with its own lines of authority. Modern corporations have departments of production, marketing, human resources, accounting, law, overall management or leadership, and so forth. The formal organization is also highly dependent on the society-wide legal order with the law of property, incorporation, contract, employment, accounting regulations, taxation, environmental protection, and so forth. For corporations engaged in international business, the dependence upon legal orders may extend to several nations, each with its own laws. (4) The corporation also depends on regularly active market institutions that enable it to hire employees; obtain raw materials, equipment, and other supplies; and to market the goods and services it produces. Often the reliance on markets extends nearly worldwide. The variety of goods and services on which many corporations depend may run to many thousands of physical objects and hundreds of separate roles that must be fulfilled through relations of employment.

Conclusion

None of the complexes of institutions and symbolic media just discussed are static. They undergo continual adjustment and frequent rationalization. While the modalities of rationalization are highly ramified and over time have grown increasingly differentiated and complex, the general process of continuing rationalization, typically progressive rationalization, has its historical foundation in the secularity of the Enlightenment. To understand not only the rational actor, whether in the dimensions explored by Parsons, Schumpeter, or Schütz, but also more comprehensively the institutional settings that undergo their own specific rationalization processes, we must, following Weber, examine the cultural frames of reference that provide the animating patterns of meaning for rationalization.

References

Bailyn, Bernard. 1967. *The Ideological Origins of the American Revolution*. Cambridge: Harvard University Press.

Bergson, Abram. 1964. *Economics of Soviet Planning*. New Haven: Yale University Press.

Commager, Henry Steele. 1977. *The Empire of Reason. How Europe Imagined and America Realized the Enlightenment*. Garden City, NY: Doubleday.

Goodman, Nathan G. 1945 and 1971. *A Benjamin Franklin Reader*. New York: Thomas Y. Crowell Company.

Grathoff, Richard, ed. 1978. *The Theory of Social Action. The Correspondence of Alfred Schutz and Talcott Parsons*. Bloomington: The Indiana University Press.

Hartz, Louis. 1955. *The Liberal Tradition in America. An Interpretation of American Political Thought Since the Revolution*. New York: Harcourt/Brace.

Isaacson, Walter. 2003. *Benjamin Franklin. An American Life*. New York: Simon and Schuster.

May, Henry F. 1976. *The Enlightenment in America*. New York: Oxford University Press.
Morgan, Edmund S. 2002. *Benjamin Franklin*. New Haven: Yale University Press.
Parsons, Talcott. 1937. *The Structure of Social Action*. New York: McGraw-Hill.
———. 1969. *Politics and Social Structure*. New York: Free Press.
Schumpeter, Joseph A. 1987a. *Theory of Economic Development*, recent ed. New Brunswick, NJ: Transaction Press.
———. 1987b. *Capitalism, Socialism, and Democracy*. 6th ed. Boston: Unwin Paperbacks.
Sparks, Jared. 1882. *The Works of Benjamin Franklin*, with notes and a life of the author by Jared Sparks, 10 Vols. Chicago: T. MacCoun.
Tocqueville, Alexis de. 1941 (originally published in French in 1835 and 1840). *Democracy in America*, 2 Vols. New York: Knopf.
Weber, Max. 1930 (originally published 1903–1904). *The Protestant Ethic and the Spirit of Capitalism*. Trans. T. Parsons. New York: Scribner's.
———. 1968. *Economy and Society*, 3 Vols. New York: Bedminster Press.
Wood, Gordon S. 2004. *The Americanization of Benjamin Franklin*. New York: Penguin.

Ordinary Beauty, Ordinary Ugliness, and the Problem of Rationality

Antonio Strati

The essays that composed the Parsons-Schumpeter seminar held at Harvard at the end of the 1930s explored the subject of rationality in the social sciences from different standpoints that highlighted diverse aspects of this topic. In fact, Joseph Schumpeter's essay treated the "meaning" of rationality in action and in the social sciences, while that by Talcott Parsons analyzed the "role" of rationality in social action. To meaning and role, the essay by Alfred Schütz added the issue of the "problem" of rationality in the social world. Moreover, Wilbert Moore's paper explored the "extension and limitation" of rationality, while Rainer Schickele's conducted critical reflection on the rational means-end schema, investigating it in terms of a "tool" to be utilized in empirical research on social action. Lastly, Donald McGranahan's contribution consisted in an attempt to formulate a discussion protocol relative to rationality in action.

The importance, still today, of the Parsons-Schumpeter seminar is therefore evident. Rationality in social sciences was analyzed, illustrated, and discussed along several important dimensions, that is, by exploring its meaning, role, and both extension and limitation, by investigating its abilities to produce tools for research and protocols to frame its study, and by discussing it as a sociological and philosophical problem. Both Schumpeter's and Schütz's essays were published separately, but the essays that composed the debate stimulated by the Parsons-Schumpeter seminar at Harvard were not published all together. They therefore did not all together have a strong influence on the interdisciplinary debate regarding rationality and the social sciences. Can we therefore ask ourselves what followed in sociological thought after the debate conducted in those essays? Probably not.

A. Strati (✉)
Research Unit on Communication, Organizational Learning and Aesthetics, Università di Trento, Trento, Italy

i3-CRG, École polytechnique, CNRS, University Paris-Saclay, Paris, France
e-mail: antonio.strati@unitn.it

H. Staubmann, V. Lidz (eds.), *Rationality in the Social Sciences*,
DOI 10.1007/978-3-319-62377-1_14

But we can imagine ourselves as scholars participating, mind and body, in the Parsons-Schumpeter seminar: how would we contribute to it?

This is the question that inspires this chapter, and the sociological study of organizations constitutes the setting of the arguments raised and discussed in it. This is because I am a sociologist of work, innovation, and organizations and also because of the incredible growth and spread of the organization in modern and contemporary society that has brought with it a strong belief in rationality. Luciano Gallino, a recently deceased Italian sociologist, remarked on this phenomenon and stressed that organizations are the principal social structures in which rationality "has become itself a value and a norm" (1978: 553). On the other hand, the belief that contemporary society cannot be grounded and cemented in irrationality is largely plausible. Who, for instance, needing a surgical operation, would imagine being benefited by the irrational organization of the hospital where she/he is to undergo the operation? Or who, while waiting to board a plane, would feel secure and imagine benefiting from the irrational organization of air traffic control? "The fact that all would benefit if all acted irrationally is neither here nor there," Jon Elster (1989: 29) declared in concluding his chapter devoted to the theme of rational choice.

However, all this stress on the rationality of social action, on rationality in social sciences, and on the rationality of social worlds is excessive, while a large number of other aspects and dimensions of human action are neglected, despite their importance in society and in organizational life. Toward the end of the 1980s—that is, four decades after the Parsons-Schumpeter seminar—the "grand image" of rationality was much debated and argued among sociologists and social scientists. Alberto Izzo (1995: 197), another Italian sociologist, expressed the matter aptly in the conclusions to his book on the different paths of reason: why rationality is preferable to irrationality is not a problem that can be solved rationally.

In this chapter, I shall further explore the problem of rationality in social sciences as illustrated in Schütz's contribution to the seminar published separately in vol. II—*Studies in Social Theory*—of his *Collected Papers* (1964). I will begin by discussing the crucial features of rationality in organization theory and decision making. I will then introduce the main aspects of the study of the aesthetic side of organization: that is, analysis of an organizational dimension that problematizes the dominance of rationality in organizational contexts. I shall conclude by discussing the relation between aesthetics and rationality by illustrating the philosophy and the epistemological background of approaches that study the aesthetic dimension of organizations.

Once Upon a Time, Rationality Was "The Grand Concept"

Rationality and the "rational quality" have received close consideration as theoretical issues to be debated in organization theory and the sociology of organizations, and as a style of performance in management. Edward Gross and Amitai Etzioni stated in the first pages of their influential handbook *Organizations in Society* (1985) that "to a degree, *organizational rationality and human happiness go hand in hand*" (1985: 4) and that without organizations that are efficient and well managed "our standard of living, our level of culture, and our democratic life could not be maintained" (1985: 3–4). The "rational quality" denotes one of the three principal approaches—rational models, interactionist models, and structuralist models—in terms of which Gross and Etzioni organized their handbook. A similar feature is apparent in another highly influential handbook, Richard Scott's *Organizations: Rational, Natural, and Open Systems* (1981). The rational models proposed by Gross and Etzioni did not refer to the same organization theories that Scott had included a few years previously in his perspective on organizations as rational systems. But some important organization theories, such as Taylor's scientific management, Fayol's administrative theory, or Simon's theory of administrative behavior, are present in both rational models and the rational system perspective. Other theories, by contrast, are more difficult to label "rational." This is the case, for example, of Max Weber's theory of bureaucracy, which is considered to be part of the rational system perspective, but not of rational models. In this case the two criteria—model and system perspective—differ crucially as regards the definition of "rational quality."

I shall not discuss this difference further. Instead, I shall underline two important issues regarding rationality in organization theories and management studies. The first is that organizational rationality and human happiness support each other only to a degree, since not "all work can be well paid or gratifying, and not all regulations and orders can be made acceptable," and this represents "a true dilemma" (Gross and Etzioni 1985: 4). The second issue is that rationality is "not only used with different meanings—and this sometimes in the writings of the same author as, for instance, Max Weber," but also that this term represents "only very inadequately the underlying conceptual scheme" (Schütz 1964: 64). There are various equivocal understandings of rationality, Alfred Schütz (1964: 74–77) continues, primarily in the fact that in our everyday experience rational may (a) be used as a synonymous with reasonable, (b) mean logical, (c) imply acting deliberately as in planned or predictable action, and (d) denote making a choice between alternatives. Moreover, Schütz writes (1964: 79):

> 'rational acts' together with their antithesis, defined by Max Weber as 'traditional' or 'habitual' acts, represent rather ideal types which will be found very seldom in their pure form in everyday action. What I wish to emphasize is only that the ideal of rationality is not and cannot be a peculiar feature of everyday thought, nor can it, therefore, be a methodological principle of the interpretation of human acts in daily life.

The ideal of rationality is, on the contrary, a feature of social sciences, since "the concept of rationality has its native place" and "finds its field of methodological application" not in the conception of everyday life in social worlds, "but at the theoretical level of the scientific observation of it" (1964: 80). The problem of rationality, in other words, is for Schütz not the problem of the social world in its quotidian experience, but a problem of the social sciences and of scientific methods.

This is apparent in the study of organizations, where rationality once constituted the crucial dilemma for the sociological, economic, and psychological approaches, while more recently, during the "cultural turn" that occurred in organization studies during the 1980s, the stress on rationality has lost its strength. I shall illustrate this first by outlining the diverse forms that configured the critical subject of organizational decision making, and then by describing how my aesthetic approach to organization studies originated during empirical research on the organizational culture of an Italian mathematics department.

Organizational Decision Making: From Rational to Casual

The organizational subject of decision making is particularly interesting because it constitutes a "thematic continuity" (Strati 2000: 105) in the history of organization studies research, despite being continuously revised and profoundly rethought.

If we go back to the terms that Talcott Parsons used to define rational action in his book, *The Structure of Social Action*, and which Alfred Schütz (1964: 64) cites at the very beginning of his essay, rationality was conceived in the following way:

> Action is rational in so far as it pursues ends possible within the conditions of the situation, and by the means which, among those available to the actor, are intrinsically best adapted to the end for reasons understandable and verifiable by positive empirical science. (Parsons 1937: 58)

These notions of rationality and rational action did not coincide with the classic instrumental rationality of economics that insists on maximization of profits and minimization of costs. Values, intentionality, and voluntariness are important features for Parsons' conception, probably because of his attention to European sociology—in particular to Weber's, Durkheim's, and Pareto's writings—and to European psychoanalysis, such as Freud's work. At the time when *The Structure of Social Action* was published, World War II was just beginning and society was less a society of organizations than it became a couple of decades later. Put differently, organizations were increasingly widespread in society, but society was not yet a network of organizations to the degree it would become in the late 1960s. One has to imagine what profound change was then produced by the pervasiveness of organizations in society to fully comprehend the impact on society of the view of organizations "as the primary vehicle" of rationality in people's lives, which are therefore rationally "planned, articulated, scientized, made more efficient and orderly, and managed" by the "experts," as Richard Scott remarked (1981: 5).

The Organizational Condition of Certainty

Decision making in organizations has been a crucial theme since the beginnings of sociology of organization, organization theory, and management studies. How is an organizational decision taken? What theory could help to describe and explain but also to inspire, prescribe, and plan how to take decisions? "By far," James March wrote (1994: 1), "the most common portrayal of decision making is one that interprets action as rational choice." The theory of rational choice presupposed that (a) goals and values are identified and hierarchized, (b) all the possible means to achieve them are known, (c) the outcomes are thoroughly analyzed, and (d) the rational choice is intended to maximize the organizational result. This was how organizational decisions ought to happen according to the rational choice theory debated in organization studies at the time of the Parsons-Schumpeter seminar. What is striking in this definition is the scant influence of the specific characteristics of the subjects of decision making and the fact that the theory anticipated that the decision makers, a range of managers, supervisors, and experts act all together as a single organizational decision maker.

The Organizational Condition of Uncertainty

A crucial change to this frame of reference for taking decisions was introduced by Herbert Simon with his notion of "bounded rationality" (1947). This notion, which was highly debated and frequently criticized at the beginning, constitutes a milestone in the study of organizational decision making. Bounded rationality is the rationality that characterizes an organizational decision taken amid uncertainty due to a number of diverse factors, that is, in a condition profoundly different from the certainty foreseen by the theory of rational choice and one that renders the choice of the most profitable alternative unambiguous. When the condition of a decision involves uncertainties about risks, the characteristics of the decision makers are critical for the choices made. Some fifteen years later, however, this notion was at the basis of a very important decisional model: that of bounded rationality. Something of great importance for organization studies had therefore happened, given that in *Organizations*, the book coauthored by March and Simon, they observed that in the case of uncertainty, "the definition of rationality becomes problematic" (1958: 138).

The Organizational Condition of Ambiguity

The condition of uncertainty thereafter characterized the most influential models of organizational decisions, such as the behaviorist model, the disjointed incrementalism model, and the political-bureaucratic model. Then another model gave novel shape to the decision-making process: the "garbage can" model proposed by Michael Cohen, James March, and Johan Olsen (1972). Here the condition of the decisional model changed again: it was neither certainty nor uncertainty; it was ambiguity, that is, the condition when:

> a decision maker is less confident that any one thing is true, or that the world can be partitioned into mutually exhaustive and exclusive states, or that information will resolve the lack of clarity. Ambiguity refers to features of decision making in which alternative states are hazily defined or in which they have multiple meanings, simultaneously opposing interpretations. Students of ambiguity argue that information may not resolve misunderstandings of the world; that the «real» world may itself be a product of social construction, thus not so much discovered as invented; that interpretations of experience and desires may be fundamentally ambivalent rather than simply uncertain; and that ambiguity may be used to augment understanding through imagination. (March 1994: 178–179)

Improvisation, randomness, time dependency, and contingency constitute key determinants of an organizational decision-making process, which consists more in random action than rational action. The condition of ambiguity does not characterize all the decision-making processes that occur in organizational life; it characterizes decisions to be taken in organizations in consideration of the ambiguity condition. In these cases, rationality is not only problematic, as noted with regard to the model of bounded rationality, but entirely absent; and the connection that links a solution to a problem is casual rather than causal. Moreover, the decision does not prove to be instrumental to a purpose.

Crisis of the Overly Rational Image of Organization

Almost in the same years, between 1973 and 1976, rationality and rational action were defined in a revised way when Talcott Parsons included the cognitive dimension. Giuseppe Sciortino (2007: 424) noted that Parsons was "satisfied with the result and thought" of his new analysis. This is important since these writings were published posthumously. "Let us venture a statement," Parsons wrote (2007: 444):

> a pattern or type of action may be said to be rational insofar as in varying components of its structure it may be considered to be normatively 'bound by'— and thereby its success legitimately evaluated in terms of adherence to— relevant *cognitive* standards of meaning, namely of validity and significance. The bearing of cognitive standards in this sense is of course inherently relational.

In this statement of rational action, the connection is constituted by cognitive congruence among the items invoked. What Parsons means by referring to the components of what is "most generally called rationality" is closely related—"most intimately related"—to the "primary aspects of the cognitive complex" (Parsons 2007: 444). Standards of logical coherence, logical relatedness, and empirical validity are crucial; and for the "the cognitive focus of the problem of rationality" (ibid.), the concept of economic rationality continues to be of particular importance. Also non-cognitive factors, such as existential orientations or political ones, "should be fully integrated with the cognitive, with the latter clearly in control, in the cybernetic sense" (2007: 444–445), in accordance with the awareness that cognitive investigation is not just purely rational (2007: 496).

Parsons' cognitive focus on rational action, as well as that of March, Simon, and colleagues, on the uncertainty and ambiguity inherent to organizational decision-making processes, shows the general awareness in the social sciences that rationality is a theoretical and methodological problem—as Alfred Schütz pointed out during the Parsons-Schumpeter seminar held at Harvard. The principal criticisms echoed his observation that rationality cannot be the distinctive aspect of human action in quotidian life nor can it be the inspiring principle of the methodologies used by the social sciences to interpret it. Organization theories, Mary Zey-Ferrel (1981) wrote concerning the general sense of inadequacy in understanding organizations, yield an image of organizational processes, dynamics, and structures that are overly rational. Research well represents "the prototype of rational action," as Parsons (2007: 444) noted, but its rationality was the principal obstacle to comprehending, studying, and communicating organizational life. In this problematic condition for studying organizational contexts, "the social scientist must have the possibility of shifting the level of his research to that of individual human activity, and where real scientific work is done this shift will always become possible" (Schütz 1964: 85).

This was the intellectual context when I introduced the notion of the aesthetic understanding of organizational life into the sociology of organizations and organization theory, as I shall illustrate in the next section. At that time, several other approaches—from organizational cognitivism to organizational learning, from the neo-institutionalist school to the dramaturgical school, and from the organizational symbolism to the narrative approach—were flourishing (Strati 2000: 61–62), and the emphasis on rationality and rational action appeared to be in profound crisis.

A Problem of Rationality? The Mathematics Department!

Seen from afar, the work of mathematicians is generally associated with the social imagery of rationality and scientific logic, as generally happens also with the notions of decision making and the organization. Even the architectural style of the building that housed the mathematics department—where the research reported here on the introduction of the departmental structure into the organization of the Italian university system (Gherardi and Strati 1990) was conducted—expressed rationality, functionalism, efficiency, and modernity. The building had been specially commissioned to a leading Italian architect and was erected in the late 1960s. However, its style did not represent how mathematicians in the department worked. On the contrary, they expressed incomprehension or indifference toward the architecture in the interviews conducted with them. In fact, it emerged during the empirical research that the mathematicians saw themselves as artists of mathematics rather than as being inspired only by rationality and science.

Aesthetics and Organizational Cultures

The mathematician as an artist was a discovery that emerged from the research. The discovery, to be precise, concerned not only the relation between aesthetics and mathematics, but also the pervasiveness of aesthetics in the daily work and organization of the mathematicians (Strati 1990). The aesthetics of sciences, in fact, has been theoretically treated, for instance, from the philosopher Francis Hutcheson, who asserted, in 1725, that mathematics has a certain aesthetic value, to the mathematician, Henri Poincaré, who, in 1908, maintained that mathematics has an aesthetic value, a philosophical value, and a physic-instrumental value. The novelty, in the mathematics department studied, was that the aesthetics referred (a) to the mathematician's action, (b) to the mathematics created, (c) to the relationship between the mathematician-artist and his/her colleagues, and (d) to the relationship with the architectural style of the organizing space.

This "discovery" did not emerge all at once, but in a rather circular way. In the course of the empirical research, reference was occasionally, but repeatedly, made to aesthetic categories such as the beautiful, the gracious, the sublime, the sacred, and the ugly. I was sensitive to these phenomena both on the basis of personal taste and because of my involvement in organizational research on the symbolic construction of the organizational culture by actors within the organization. In the organizational symbolism research, there was a certain attention given to the study of the organizational image, to the pathos of organizational artifacts, to the relation between art and organization, and to the aesthetic dimension of organizational life. In brief, the organizations were seen in terms of organizational cultures *tout court*. I thus decided to enrich the research by adding a specific inquiry into aesthetics where they appeared as an organizational dimension: that is, when aesthetics influenced the dynamics of the work of the mathematicians, and the values and beliefs at the basis of their organization.

I made this research choice aware that the aesthetic dimension of the mathematics department constituted a rather mysterious subject of study and that I could not "draw upon clear-cut definitions of the aesthetic feeling, nor on any personal conviction on the matter" (Strati 1990: 207). I thus began to ask the mathematicians whenever possible: "Do you do beautiful things?" This question marked a shift from the inquiry into rationality and rational action and constituted a methodological turn in my sociological study of human action in organizational settings (Gherardi and Strati 2012: 234–235).

The research on the organizational culture of the university department included two other Italian departments, education and visual arts, of the same highly prestigious Italian university. Each of the three departments showed a peculiar relation between aesthetics and organization, but only in the mathematics department did aesthetics emerge as influencing the work practices, organizational culture, and academic communities of practice. Apparent at the education department was the aesthetic appreciation of teaching and managing the university, but the emphasis was on an ethic of the social utility of teaching, running the university, and doing social and educational research. As a well-known professor pointed out—beautifully!—in that department, aesthetics was considered to be an "organizational sin." Also the organizational and work cultures of the visual arts department were informed by an emphasis on an ethical dimension that concealed organizational aesthetics. This was a surprising research finding for a department in which even the librarian was a connoisseur of art, and the visual appreciation of beauty was a fundamental factor in the career choices of the researchers and lecturers. Apparent in this department was a conflictual coexistence between the professional skills of appreciating the artworks studied in aesthetic terms and the professional deontology of being an academic who performs useful work and does so with abnegation and, occasionally, with stylistic elegance.

The Mathematics Department's Aesthetics

In the mathematics department, by contrast, aesthetics and aesthetic action were found principally in the creative act that formulates mathematical concepts and relations. This aesthetic sense configured a distinctive separation between the beauty of everyday work dedicated to pure mathematics theory and the ugliness of doing mathematics through heavy calculation. The image of the mathematical creation supported by just a pencil and a sheet of blank paper was opposed in aesthetic terms to that of working with a computer. Only the mathematicians who resorted to their own personal, and frequently geometric, intuitions, using a technology that was elementary and essential—pencil and a sheet of paper—were doing beautiful mathematics. This was the organizational aesthetic of the department, and it influenced the division of labor, the reputational hierarchy, and power relations. Second, the importance of aesthetics and aesthetic action was evident in the organizational communication among mathematicians. A beautiful result in mathematics is often one in which the mathematician gives only the idea of its demonstration, without proofs, so that it cannot work by itself. But giving an idea to colleagues, inventing a problem to be studied, and making it available to the other mathematicians constituted what, in the department, was termed a mathematician's "beautiful" gesture. This brings to light a third aspect: the importance of the tacit dimension of knowledge (Polanyi 1962) in mathematics, rather than its explicit, scientific, and formal dimension, since, as stressed by an internationally well-known "master" working in the department, a beautiful result in mathematics "is often one in which the author demonstrates more than he says" (Gherardi and Strati 2012: 136).

We may conclude this section by observing that rationality did not constitute "the grand concept" in the work and organization of the mathematics department. "Yet if we then hear that," Georg Simmel (1918: 104–105) wrote in his last publication during his lifetime:

we should always keep to the golden mean, or that we should always be able to imagine our actions as a universal law, or that we should judge ourselves according to the greatest good for the greatest number, or that one should in every instant overcome the nature in himself by reason, then perhaps we sense that indeed deep and content-rich ethical experiences have developed these formulations in some measure as their silhouettes—now, though, they stand as fixed structures and attempt by force to assimilate a life that is endlessly dynamic, endlessly differentiated, endlessly obligated, and which nonetheless sometimes overflows these structures and sometimes leaves them unfilled. (Simmel 1918: 104–105)

In fact, if one considers rationality to be separate from everyday life, and rational action to be "a universal law," one might assume that mathematical logic and absolute rationality are the main features of a mathematics department. One would then fail to see how influential aesthetics is in the creation of mathematical logic and rationality. If, on the contrary, one takes due account of everyday life, routine work, skill practices, and organizational communication, then one will understand the importance of the fact that rationality and rational action obstruct the understanding of organizational life and also that other features of human action operate in organizations. This understanding has generated new intellectual currents in organizational research like the aesthetic approach (Smircich et al. 1992: 610–611), as I shall further illustrate in the next section.

From Rational Interpretation to Aesthetic Understanding

The achievements of human action, Simmel (1916; Eng. trans. 2005: 155) wrote in the conclusions to his book on Rembrandt, are the outcome of simultaneous fashioning and creating. Moreover, the "achievements of intellectual history are shot through with a contrast that can be characterized as that between the capacity to create [*Schöpfertum*] and the capacity to fashion [*Gestaltertum*]."

Humans, precisely because they do not merely repeat but create something new, cannot start anew each time. Rather, they need a given material, a given antecedence on which, or on the basis of which, they accomplish their achievements as a reshaping [of the material]. We would not, however, be historical beings were we absolutely creative; were our work to create the new as such. We would then be, so to speak, transhistorical. Nor would we be historical beings without creativity, holding on absolutely to that which is given and its mechanical rearrangement, its reforming in a narrow sense. (Simmel 1916; Eng. trans. 2005: 155)

The human capacity to create—that is, to bring into being something that does not yet exist—is interwoven with the capacity to fashion and to give form to material elements that can also be intellectual, as in the case of the configuration of new approaches in the study of organization. Simmel's thought, as underscored by Helmut Staubmann (1997: 603), highlights that social reality "cannot exist independently of its form," and both form and matter constitute "fundamental categories in Simmel's writings, playing an important role in his early works on moral sciences, in his writing on aesthetics and the philosophy of money, and continuing as such up to his later philosophy of life, and upon which he relied in defining his pure sociology." However, Luigi Pareyson (1954: 188; Eng. trans. 2009: 112), the existentialist and hermeneutic Italian philosopher who had Umberto Eco and Gianni Vattimo among his pupils, observed in his work on aesthetics as a theory of formativeness that "the process of interpretation is endless, because as long as there is knowledge, there is no interpretation that is definitive, and that is not subject to a perpetual process of revision that aims at an ever greater adjustment." Invention and organization are interwoven, and formativeness leads to realizations where, in the doing, the human action invents its own way of doing through attempts and improvisations, through corrections and redoings, through the formative operations by which an object, a work of art, or an event acquires its distinctive form.

In the next section, I shall illustrate the distinctive form acquired by the aesthetic discourse on organization by means of some fundamental concepts that constitute its theoretical bases and its relation to rationality and rational action: the tacit dimension of knowledge, sensible knowing, empathic understanding, and the philosophical sensibilities of the aesthetic understanding.

The Interweaving Between Aesthetics and Tacit Knowledge

In the mathematics department, organizational beauty was also seen, among other aspects, in the mathematical result that demonstrates more than the mathematician explicitly says. This represents the tacit aspect of the mathematician's organizational action: that is, the tacit dimension of knowledge that cannot satisfy the rationality requirements of scientific knowledge. The distinction between knowledge that is tacit, because it is just indicated and vaguely described, and knowledge that is explicit, because it is formalized according to rational analysis and scientific thought, derives from work published by the philosopher, Michael Polanyi, immediately after World War II and during the 1960s. What explicit relations can be established among sensory data? And even when these explicit relations are established, will they be executed? Polanyi discussed these issues on the basis of his study of the ability to ride a bicycle. When he interrogated engineers and bicycle manufacturers, he came to the conclusion "that the principle by which the cyclist keeps his balance is not generally known" (Polanyi 1962: 49). In fact, the analysis "shows that for a given angle of unbalance the curvature of each winding is inversely proportional to the square of the speed at which the cyclist is proceeding" (1962: 50). But, he continued:

> does this tell us exactly how to ride a bicycle? No. You obviously cannot adjust the curvature of your bicycle's path in proportion to the ratio of your unbalance over the square of your speed; and if you could you would fall off the machine, for there are a number of other factors to be taken into account in practice which are left out in the formulation of this rule. (1962: 50)

Rules are useful; they can provide guidance. But the practice of an organizational skill is often more like an art, rather than being the execution of rational knowledge. The case of riding a bicycle may seem peculiar, but it is not so if one considers the industry manufacturing bicycles, the large number of people using them, or the expert cyclists riding them in sport competitions. Indeed, it shows how closely aesthetics interweaves with the tacit dimension of knowledge, and the importance of researching aesthetics and aesthetic action for the sociology of organization and organization theory. This is also because the aesthetics discussed in organization studies emphasizes the act of perceiving as evidenced by the etymology of the word "aesthetics," which is rooted in terms like *aisthánomai*, *aisthetikós*, *aisthánesthai*, or *aisthetes* in ancient Greek. It was to these terms that Alexander Gottlieb Baumgarten (1750–1758) referred coining a name for this new branch of philosophy. The perceptive-sensorial capacities and their faculty of sensitive-aesthetic judgment constituted the bases of Baumgarten's philosophical aesthetics: the *ars analogi rationis*, which comprises the science of sensible knowledge as well as the art of beautiful thought, and which is not subjugated to rationality and intellectual knowledge.

Sociological Significance of Sensible Knowledge

"The social question is not only an ethical one, but also a nasal question," Georg Simmel observed (1908; Eng. trans. 2009: 577). By this he meant that sensory perception is closely involved in shaping social issues, and it is important for the sociological study of human action.

> The personal contact between cultivated people and workers, so often enthusiastically advocated for the social development of the present, which is also recognized by the cultivated as the ethical ideal of closing the gap between two worlds "of which one does not know how the other lives", simply fails before the insurmountable nature of the olfactory sense impressions. (1908; Eng. trans. 2009: 577)

As the philosopher John Dewey pointed out, "sense," like rationality, denotes a variety of contents, from the sensory perception of an experience to its meaning. Moreover, each sensorial organ has a distinct sociological accomplishment that is interwoven with the specific characteristics of the other senses that compose the human perceptive-sensorial capacities, as well as with their faculty to make sensitive-aesthetic judgments. Put differently, the sense organs of vision or hearing, or those of smell, touch, and taste, do not operate individually and autonomously. Nor do these external perceptive-sensorial faculties operate without being in perceptual relation with the internal human senses that are at the basis of proprioception and kinaesthetic feelings (Shustermann 2008). Rather, each sense creates a specific fundamental sociological significance.

> If the other senses build a thousand bridges among people, if they can soothe over with attractions the repulsions that they repeatedly cause, if weaving together the positive and negative values of their feelings gives the total concrete relationships among people their coloration, one can note, by way of contrast, that the sense of smell is the dissociating sense. Not only because it communicates many more repulsions than attractions, not only because its judgments have something of the radical and unappealing that lets it be overcome only with difficulty by the judgements of the other senses or minds, but also precisely because the bringing together of the many never grants it any such attractions as that situation can unfold them for the other senses [...]. (Simmel 1908; Eng. trans. 2009: 578–579)

If smell is the dissociating sense, sight represents the purest, most immediate interaction of individuals. In eye-to-eye contact, one "cannot take with the eye without at the same time giving," and in the "look that takes in the other one reveals oneself; with the same act, in which the subject seeks to know its object, it surrenders itself to the object" (Simmel 1908; Eng. trans. 2009: 571). By contrast, the sense of the ear has a very different sociological significance. While the eye cannot receive without giving, "the ear is the quintessentially egoistic organ that only takes but does not give" (Simmel 1908; Eng. trans. 2009: 575). But we cannot prevent ourselves from hearing as we can prevent ourselves from seeing merely by closing our eyes, even when this may prompt conflicting organizational issues (Strati 1999: 1–3). While the eye has sociological significance for activating the individual's interaction, the sense of hearing has sociological importance because the supra-individualistic nature of this perceptual faculty makes it able to create a sentiment of sharing and a sense of communality in social relationships.

> One may compare a museum audience with a concert audience; for the determination of the hearing impression to communicate itself uniformly and in the same way to a crowd of people—a determination by no means simply external-quantitative but bound up deeply with its innermost nature—sociologically brings together a concert audience in an incomparably closer union and collective feeling than occurs with the visitors to a museum. (Simmel 1908; Eng. trans. 2009: 576)

Sensitive-perceptual capabilities and the sensitive-aesthetic judgment engender social microprocesses that constitute the "actual *activity*" of human action (Simmel 1908; Eng. trans. 2009: 33), bringing to light the significance of aesthetics for sociological study and theory.

Rationality, Empathy, and *Logica Poetica*

Rationality is a problem for the aesthetic understanding. But the concept of meaningful social action that Max Weber discussed remains fundamental for the aesthetic interpretation of organizational life. Thus, in my book, *Organization and Aesthetics* (Strati 1999), I returned to an important methodological debate over the cultural sciences that at the beginning of the last century preceded the Parsons-Schumpeter seminar: the Methodenstreit. I wanted to examine the relation between rational interpretation and the empathic comprehension of intentional action with particular reference to Max Weber's sociology. Weber, in fact, as Parsons observes (2007: 356), "was perhaps the most eminent theorist" of the past century who dealt "with the problems of 'rationality,' its potentials and its dangers, in the field of human action." He considered that, frequently, the understandable components of a process are interwoven with its non-understandable components that the rationalist methodological device "does not involve a belief in the actual predominance of rational elements in human life" (Weber 1922; Eng. trans. 1978: 7) and that rationality does not provide the only way to interpret meaningful and intentional social action.

> The basis for certainty in understanding can be either rational, which can be further subdivided into logical and mathematical, or it can be of an emotionally empathic or artistically appreciative quality. Action is rationally evident chiefly when we attain a completely clear intellectual grasp of the action-elements in their intended context of meaning. Empathic or appreciative accuracy is attained when, through sympathetic participation, we can adequately grasp the emotional context in which the action took place. (Weber 1922; Eng. trans. 1978: 5)

Weber certainly preferred the rational analysis of meaningful action to its empathic comprehension, in part to oppose the psychologistic vitalism circulating at the time in various areas of European culture. But one can observe an aesthetic side in his choice, influenced—notes the philosopher Remo Bodei (1997: 52–53)—by a pathos of objectivization. In fact,

> aesthetic considerations can be seen in the close connection established by Weber between the individual and the moment when she/he is "objectified" in a social fact by his/her action. And they are also apparent in the *pathos* that Weber imputed to objectivity and to fecund operativeness, without thereby reducing the weight of subjectivity, or of individual responsibility, or of ethics. The individual is anchored in action that produces ascertainable effects. (Strati 1999: 50)

Weber's choice is a paradigmatic one, and aesthetic features and aesthetic considerations—"fortunately," we may say with Thomas Kuhn (1962: 155)—are influential and can be observed. My preference for empathic understanding is again a paradigmatic choice influenced by aesthetic considerations and in particular by the fascination of the ability to imagine oneself within the specific situation in which a meaningful social action is taking place. Empathic understanding is deeply rooted in the origins of philosophical aesthetics thanks to Giambattista Vico's *logica poetica* (1725). The Neapolitan philosopher envisaged the empathic understanding of civil society rather than the rational one, "a sort of *Einfühlung ante litteram*" (Dorfles 1967: 19), arguing that:

> as rational metaphysics teaches that man becomes all things by understanding them (*homo intelligendo fit omnia*), this imaginative metaphysics shows that man becomes all things by not understanding them (*homo non intelligendo fit omnia*); and perhaps the latter proposition is truer than the former, for when man understands he extends his mind and takes in the things, but when he does not understand he makes the things out of himself and becomes them by transforming himself into them. (Vico 1725; Eng. trans. 1968: 130)

Philosophical Sensibilities of Aesthetic Understanding

There are three philosophical and epistemological sensibilities that have been fundamental in the configuration of organizational aesthetics research: (1) hermeneutic sensibility, which relates the study of the aesthetics of organization to the organizational culture of an organization; (2) aesthetic sensibility, which gives definitive form to the aesthetic understanding of human action in organizational life through an epistemological shift from the study of aesthetics to aesthetic study; and (3) performative sensibility, which enhances artistic intervention, management as art, and the analysis of micro-practices in organizational contexts (Strati 2016).

Hermeneutics is important for refining the aesthetic interpretation of "organizational signs," which are shaped by a complex set of operations due to different organizational cultures and different stages in an organization's history. The authors and users of such operations are of equal importance. Aesthetic philosophy is relevant for highlighting the sensory world of human action in organizations and the material creation of forms of sensory experience through the negotiation of aesthetic feelings, judgments, and values. Performative sensibility has influences the depicting of interaction within an organization as artistic performance, artifacts in an organization as vehicles of aesthetic feelings that may contribute to the exercise of organizational control, the tacit dimension of knowing in organizational life, and the aesthetics of micro-organizational practices in an organization.

These three philosophical sensibilities receive a different emphasis in each of the four approaches—archaeological (Berg and Kreiner 1990), empathic-logical (Gagliardi 2006), aesthetic (Strati 1999), and artistic (Guillet de Monthoux 2004)—into which organizational aesthetics research is articulated (Gherardi and Strati 2012: 196–202). But all together these philosophical sensibilities shape a specific position of the aesthetic discourse on organization among Gibson Burrell and Gareth Morgan's (1979) four sociological paradigms of organization studies, depicted in Fig. 1, radical humanist, interpretative, radical structuralist, and functionalist.

Organizational aesthetics research extends across the two paradigms of radical humanist and interpretative sociology, the two sociological paradigms that stress organizational interaction and the collective construction of the organization as a social form that cannot exist in itself as an objective reality independent of the

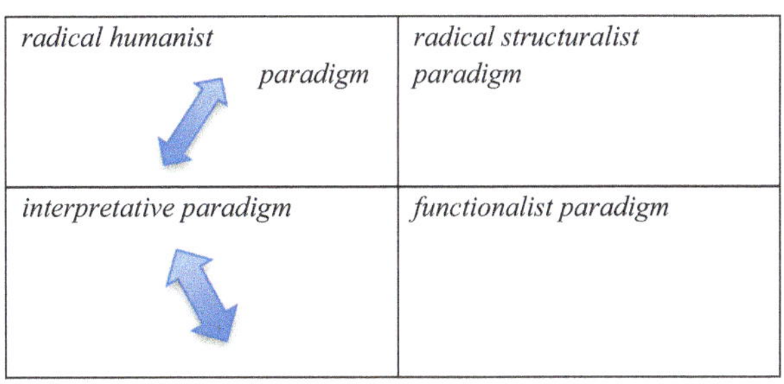

Fig. 1 Organizational aesthetics research and Burrell and Morgan's sociological paradigms

continuous interaction of human and nonhuman elements. The radical humanist paradigm, in particular, favors intuition and knowledge-evoking processes, and, together with the interpretative paradigm, it opposes positivism and the dominance of rationality in the social sciences.

Conclusion

In this chapter, rationality has been considered in its purity and objective reality. The ambiguity between rationality and reason (Elster 2009) or motivation (Boudon 1992) has been deliberately avoided, as well as the sociological debate that Vilfredo Pareto (1916) prompted on logical and nonlogical action. The crucial organizational feature of the decision-making process was thus chosen in order to discuss rationality and rational action, since organizational decision making is a classic subject treated in the light of rational choice theory. As an empirical case, the discussion of the organizational culture of an Italian university department of mathematics brought to light the inner problems of the relation between mathematical logic and the aesthetics of the everyday work and organizational life of mathematicians. Rationality was then discussed in relation to the tacit dimension of knowledge, sensible knowledge, empathy, *logica poetica*, and the philosophical and epistemological background of the aesthetic understanding of organizations.

In fact, the aesthetic dimension of organizational action in everyday work in organizations (King and Vickery 2013), in management and entrepreneurship (Hjorth and Steyaert 2009; Meisiek and Barry 2014), as well as in the society at large (Murphy and de La Fuente 2014), together with its problematic feature of also being responsible for an-aestheticizing human action, precisely through its aestheticization (Marquard 1989; Welsch 1996), highlights the critique of the dominance of rationality in understanding human action, organizational settings, and the social world. This critique shows, on the one hand, the variety of different aspects that rationality neglects, as stressed by Alfred Schütz during the Parsons-Schumpeter seminar. On the other hand, it reveals the status of rationality as just one quality among several others with which to comprehend meaningful social action.

Stated differently: is the subject of rationality and rational action less relevant to the contemporary sociology of organization and the social sciences in general than it was at the time of the Parsons-Schumpeter seminar? My answer to this question is that it is less relevant because the "cultural turn" that occurred during the 1980s has been decisive in circumscribing the influence of rationality in everyday human action.

References

Baumgarten, Alexander Gottliebe. 1750–1758. *Aesthetica*, Vol. I–II. Frankfurt a.d. Oder: Kleyb (Photostat: Olms, Hildesheim, 1986).

Berg, Per Olof, and Kristian Kreiner. 1990. Corporate architecture: Turning physical settings into symbolic resources. In *Symbols and Artifacts: Views of the Corporate Landscape*, ed. P. Gagliardi, 41–67. New York: Berlin de Gruyter.
Bodei, Remo. 1997. *La filosofia del novecento*. Roma: Donzelli.
Boudon, Raymond. 1992. *Traité de sociologie*. Paris: Presses Universitaires de France.
Burrell, Gibson, and Gareth Morgan. 1979. *Sociological Paradigms and Organizational Analysis*. Aldershot: Gower.
Cohen, Michael D., James G. March, and Johan P. Olsen. 1972. A Garbage Can Model of Organizational Choice. *Administrative Science Quarterly* 17 (1): 1–25.
Dorfles, Gillo. 1967. *L'estetica del mito. Da Vico a Wittgenstein*. Milano: Mursia.
Elster, Jon. 1989. *Nuts and Bolts for the Social Sciences*. Cambridge: Cambridge University Press.
———. 2009. *Reason and Rationality*. Princeton: Princeton University Press.
Gagliardi, Pasquale. 2006. Exploring the aesthetic side of organizational life. In *The Sage Handbook of Organization Studies*, 2nd ed., eds. S. R. Clegg, C. Hardy, T. B. Lawrence and W. R. Nord, 701–724. London: Sage.
Gallino, Luciano. 1978. *Dizionario di Sociologia*. Torino: Utet.
Gherardi, Silvia, and Antonio Strati. 1990. The "Texture" of Organizing in an Italian University Department. *Journal of Management Studies* 27 (6): 605–618.
———. 2012. *Learning and Knowing in Practice-Based Studies*. Cheltenham: Edward Elgar.
Gross, Edward, and Amitai Etzioni. 1985. *Organizations in Society*. Englewood Cliffs, NJ: Prentice-Hall.
Guillet de Monthoux, Pierre. 2004. *The Art Firm: Aesthetic Management and Metaphysical Marketing from Wagner to Wilson*. Stanford: Stanford Business Books.
Hjorth, Daniel, and Chris Steyaert, eds. 2009. *The Politics and Aesthetics of Entrepreneurship*. Cheltenham: Edward Elgar.
Izzo, Alberto. 1995. *I percorsi della ragione: il tema della razionalità nella storia del pensiero sociologico*. Roma: La Nuova Italia Scientifica.
King, Ian W., and Jonathan Vickery, eds. 2013. *Experiencing Organisations: New Aesthetic Perspectives*. Faringdon: Libri Publishing.
Kuhn, Thomas. 1962. *The Structure of Scientific Revolutions*. Chicago: University of Chicago Press.
March, James G. 1994. *A Primer on Decision Making. How Decisions Happen*. New York: Free Press.
March, James G., and Herbert A. Simon. 1958. *Organizations*. New York: Wiley.
Marquard, Odo. 1989. *Aesthetica und Anaesthetica. Philosophische Überlegungen*. Paderborn: Schoningh.
Meisiek, Stefan, and Daved Barry. 2014. The Science of Making Management an Art. *Scandinavian Journal of Management* 30 (1): 134–141.
Murphy, Peter, and Eduardo de La Fuente, eds. 2014. *Aesthetic Capitalism*. Leiden: Brill.
Pareto, Vilfredo. 1916. *Trattato di sociologia generale* (Eng. Trans.: The Mind and Society. Ed. A. Livingston. Cambridge, MA: Harvard University Press, 1935).
Pareyson, Luigi. 1954. *Estetica: Teoria della Formatività*, Torino: Edizioni di "Filosofia", 4th ed., 1988. Milano: Bompiani (Partial Eng. Trans.: Existence, interpretation, freedom. selected writings. Ed. P. D. Bubbio. Aurora, Colorado: The Davies Group, 2009).
Parsons, Talcott. 1937. *The Structure of Social Action*. New York: McGraw-Hill.
———. 2007. In *American Society. A Theory of the Societal Community*, ed. G. Sciortino. Boulder, CO: Paradigm Publishers.
Polanyi, Michael. 1962. *Personal Knowledge. Towards a Post-Critical Philosophy*. London: Routledge & Kegan Paul (1st ed., 1958).
Schütz, Alfred. 1964. The problem of rationality in the social world. In *Collected Papers II. Studies in Social Theory*, ed. A. Brodersen, 64–88. The Hague: Nijhoff.
Sciortino, Giuseppe. 2007. Preface to Chapter 10. In *American Society. A Theory of the Societal Community*, ed. T. Parsons, 424. Boulder, CO: Paradigm Publishers.

Scott, Richard W. 1981. *Organizations: Rational, Natural, and Open Systems*. Englewood Cliffs, NJ: Prentice-Hall.

Shustermann, Richard. 2008. *Body Consciousness. A Philosophy of Mindfulness and Somaesthetics*. Cambridge: Cambridge University Press.

Simmel, Georg. 1908. *Soziologie. Untersuchungen über die Formen der Vergesellschaftung*. Leipzig: Dunker & Humblot (Eng. trans.: Sociology. Inquiries into the construction of social forms, Vol. I–II. Ed. A. J. Blasi, A. K. Jacobs & M. Kanjireathinkal, Leiden: Brill, 2009).

———. 1916. *Rembrandt. Ein kunstphilosophischer Versuch*. Leipzig: Verlag (Eng. trans.: Rembrandt. An essay in the philosophy of art. Trans. & Ed.: A. Scott, H. Staubmann, London: Routledge, 2005).

———. 1918. *Lebensanschauung: Vier Metaphysische Kapitel*. Leipzig: Dunker & Humblot (Eng. trans.: The view of life. Four metaphysical essays with journal aphorisms. Trans.: J. A. Y. Andrews, D. N. Levine, Chicago: University of Chicago Press, 2010).

Simon, Herbert A. 1947. *Administrative Behavior*. 2nd ed., 1957. New York: Macmillan.

Smircich, Linda, Marta Calás, and Gareth Morgan. 1992. Afterward/After Words: Open(ing?) Spaces. *Academy of Management Review* 17 (3): 607–611.

Staubmann, Helmut M. 1997. The Ornamental Form of the Iron Cage: An Aesthetic Representation of Modern Society? *International Journal of Politics, Culture and Society* 10 (4): 591–607.

Strati, Antonio. 1990. Aesthetics and organizational skill. In *Organizational Symbolism*, ed. B.A. Turner, 207–222. Berlin: de Gruyter.

———. 1999. *Organization and Aesthetics*. London: Sage.

———. 2000. *Theory and Method in Organization Studies: Paradigms and Choices*. London: Sage.

———. 2016. Aesthetics and design: An epistemology of the unseen. In *The Routledge Companion to Philosophy in Organization Studies*, ed. R. Mir, H. Willmott, and M. Greenwood, 251–259. London: Routledge.

Vico, Giambattista. 1725. *Principi di una scienza nuova*. Naples: Mosca, 3rd ed., 1744. (Eng. trans.: The New Science of Giambattista Vico, ed. T.G. Bergin and M.H. Fisch. Ithaca, NY: Cornell University Press, 1968).

Weber, Max. 1922. *Wirtschaft und Gesellschaft. Grundriss der verstehenden Soziologie*. Tübingen: Mohr. (Eng. trans.: Economy and society: An outline of interpretive sociology. I–II. Berkeley: University of California Press, 1978).

Welsch, Wolfgang. 1996. Aestheticization Processes. *Theory, Culture & Society* 13 (1): 1–24.

Zey-Ferrel, Mary. 1981. Criticisms of the Dominant Perspective on Organizations. *Sociological Quarterly* 22 (Spring): 181–205.

Continuity and Change in Parsons' Understanding of Rationality

Raf Vanderstraeten

The chapter that Talcott Parsons prepared for the Parsons-Schumpeter Seminar on Rationality in the Social Sciences consists of not more than five and a half pages. It gives the impression of being a hastily drafted, somewhat incoherent text, which mainly reiterates arguments presented in the chapters on Vilfredo Pareto in *The Structure of Social Action* (Parsons 1937, 1968a). In the period around 1940, when the Seminar on Rationality took place at Harvard University, Parsons seemed to have lost much of his original interest in discussing, revisiting, and complementing economic approaches to the nature of rationality and the rational pursuit of self-interest.

In the autobiographical essay "On Building Social System Theory: A Personal History," Parsons shed some light on his own intellectual trajectory and academic career—including the period after the completion of *The Structure of Social Action*. In the late 1920s, he had entered Harvard University through the Economics Department. But in the course of the following decade, he transferred, both intellectually and institutionally, from economics to sociology. Relatively late, in 1939, he received tenure in Harvard's Department of Sociology. "In spite of the friendliness of [the economists] Taussig, Gay, and Schumpeter, I am quite sure I could not have counted on a future in economics at Harvard. But basically I did not want to do so... Though I wanted to keep my contact with economic theory, and in fact have done so in various ways, I saw clearly that I did not want to be primarily an economist, any more than Weber turned out to be" (Parsons [1970] 1977: 32).

Parsons, however, also explicitly referred to the Seminar on Rationality in the Social Sciences: "There was one interesting episode which might, at a relatively late time, have turned me at last farther in the direction of economics. After my

R. Vanderstraeten (✉)
Center for Social Theory, Ghent University, Ghent, Belgium

Department of Sociology, University of Chicago, Chicago, IL, USA
e-mail: Raf.Vanderstraeten@UGent.be

H. Staubmann, V. Lidz (eds.), *Rationality in the Social Sciences*,
DOI 10.1007/978-3-319-62377-1_15

formal transfer to sociology, Schumpeter organized a small discussion group with younger people, mostly graduate students, on problems of the nature of rationality. After a few meetings he proposed to me that the group should aim at producing a volume, of which he and I should be at least coeditors, if not coauthors. Though not specifically rejecting the proposal, at least immediately, I remember having reacted rather coolly, and in fact I let it die. I am not wholly clear about my motives, but I think they had to do with the feeling that I needed a relatively complete formal break with economics." ([1970] 1977: 32–33).

Despite his career change, Parsons' decision to "let it die" is a remarkable one. Parsons was some 20 years younger than Schumpeter. While he was in the late 1930s in an early stage of his career, Schumpeter was a well-established economist and an ex-minister of finance, who had also expressed his willingness to support Parsons' career within the Harvard setting. Parsons described Schumpeter's proposal as "flattering ... for a young and still insecure scholar" ([1970], 1977: 35).[1] Moreover, problems of rationality remained central to Parsons' sociological theory throughout most of his career. Some commentators have even argued that Parsons' sociological project can be defined as an ongoing reflection on the meaning and limits of rationality (see Stichweh 1980; Hein 2009). It therefore seems relevant to pay attention to transitions in Parsons' understanding of rationality. Next to Parsons' formal transfer from the Economics to the Sociology Department at Harvard, such transitions might also have affected his collaboration with Schumpeter.

I will now proceed to highlight some lines of continuity and change in Parsons' understanding of rationality in order to shed light on his decision to "let it die." I will, more particularly, point to a basic transition in Parsons' understanding of rationality in society—from an individualized, actor-oriented conception of rationality to one which deals with rationality as value pattern at the level of social systems. The first indications of this transition can already be observed in work on the professions, on which Parsons embarked shortly after the publication of *The Structure of Social Action* (e.g., Parsons [1939] 1954). But *The American University* (Parsons and Platt 1973), which is the last monograph that Parsons saw into print, also contains elaborate discussions of the problem of rationality. Perhaps Parsons' chapter on cognitive rationality in that monograph might be read as his full chapter for the Seminar on Rationality, which took place more than three decades earlier.

On the following pages, I argue that the tensions which accompanied the transitions in Parsons' understanding of rationality account for Parsons' ambivalent attitude toward the publication project with Schumpeter and others in the period

[1]Schumpeter had been one of the supportive reviewers of the manuscript of *The Structure of Social Action* for the Committee on Research in the Social Sciences (which had financed Parsons' research). At the same time, however, Schumpeter was in this report one of the first to comment on Parsons' cumbersome prose: "The author has in fact so deeply penetrated into the German thicket as to lose in some place the faculty of writing clearly in English about it, and some turns of phrase become more fully understandable only if translated into German" (cited by Swedberg in Schumpeter 1991: 97). For more background information on the relation between Schumpeter and Parsons, see also Allen (1991: 98) and Swedberg (2015).

around 1940. By focusing on the shifting architecture of his theoretical account of rationality and modern society, I intend to discuss this transition—or this process of "continuity and change," as Parsons typically liked to put it—in somewhat more detail. Although facing the risk of oversimplification, I hope to show some lines of transition in the large body of scholarly work that Parsons produced in the course of about half a century.

The Structure of Action

In his early writings, Parsons advocated using an "analytical realism" to build a coherent theoretical or conceptual framework for sociology. In *The Structure of Social Action*, he stated that this theoretical framework had to consist of a limited number of important concepts that "adequately 'grasp' aspects of the objective external world... These concepts do correspond, not to concrete phenomena, but to elements in them which are analytically separable from other elements" ([1937] 1968a: 730). Much like Max Weber, Parsons argued that theory had to involve the development of concepts that grasp the systemic features of the universe without being overwhelmed by empirical details. Social theory, more particularly, had to reflect significant features in the organization of social phenomena. For Parsons, the "voluntaristic theory of action," presented in a number of early essays and in *The Structure of Social Action*, constituted an important step in this direction.

Critically building on the writings of classical economists, such as Marshall and Pareto, Parsons took the "problem of the rationality of action" as starting point for his reflections on the nature of modern capitalism. In *The Structure of Social Action*, he maintained that there was "obviously a very solid common-sense foundation for attributing a large importance to rationality in action. We are all engaged in multifarious practical activities where a great deal depends on the 'right' selection of appropriate means to our ends, and where the selection, within the limits of knowledge current at the time and place, is based on a sound empirical knowledge... [T]here can be no question of the pervasiveness of the rational case in all systems of human action" ([1937], 1968a: 57).

Parsons not only linked rationality with the use of empirically sound knowledge. He also connected the concept of rationality with what economists called the process of want satisfaction. The model of the individual *homo economicus*, who strived to satisfy his wants to obtain his goals in the most efficient way, constituted the paradigmatic example of rationality: "the process of want satisfaction is itself the most general and obvious meaning of rationality of action" ([1937], 1968a: 133). In many ways, the analyses Parsons presented in his early work departed from such an economic, utilitarian conception of rationality at the individual level ("Crusoe economics"). So also did Parsons' emphasis on the "unit act" and its basic constituents in *The Structure of Social Action*. The point of departure of

Parsons' "analytical realism" was a critique of the writings of classical economists. He did not reject the basic assumptions of this approach but aimed to modify and complement them.[2]

In a discussion of Pareto's logical norm of rational action, for example, Parsons put emphasis on the "theoretical significance" of Pareto's approach. Pareto had been able to "define rigorously one of the principal types of norm governing the means-end relationship" (1937, 1968a: 191). At the same time, however, he also put stress on the limitations of Pareto's approach. He proposed a "slightly different use" of the norm. In this light, he defined the aim and program of *The Structure of Social Action* in the following terms: "The most important questions for further inquiry will be, what is the rest of the structure of acts and systems of action of which a norm of this character can form a part and at what point does the 'logical' norm fit into this structure?" (1937, 1968a: 191). Stated somewhat differently, Parsons' aim was to situate the concept of rationality in action within a broader framework, within which the nonrational conditions and components of action could also be taken into account.

To arrive at this framework, Parsons proposed several modifications to the existing conception of rationality. Already in his early essays, in which the relation between economics and sociology was an explicit topic of discussion, he stated that rationality, defined in terms of economizing or exploiting means in order to achieve ends, is not "a descriptive generalization ... [but] a *norm* of rational action" (1934: 520, orig. emphasis). Economic "laws" were very different from "Newtonian or Einsteinian formulae." The empirical relevance of rationality "rests on the circumstance that men do in fact *try* (not merely 'tend') ... to 'exploit' the conditions of their lives rationally in order to satisfy their wants. This idea of a norm which men can be conceived as striving to attain by *effort* is something entirely foreign to the 'positive' physical sciences" (1934: 520, orig. emphases). For Parsons, a sociologically adequate theory of action thus had to be based on a "voluntaristic" foundation. "Effort," as he put it in *The Structure of Social Action*, "is a name for the relating factor between the normative and the conditional elements of action. It is necessitated by the fact that norms do not realize themselves automatically but only through action, so far as they are realized at all" ([1937], 1968a: 719).

Parsons tried to develop this "voluntaristic" theory of action in two different directions. On the one hand, he aimed to include the nonrational components or conditions of action. A theory of action not only had to account for rational action, for the rational pursuit of self-interest. He also looked for ways to distinguish this

---

[2]In an article on utilitarianism, written for the *International Encyclopedia of the Social Sciences*, Parsons later also wrote: "The primary focus of utilitarianism was on the process of action designed to satisfy given wants of individuals—that is, on goal-attainment, or want-satisfaction, whichever way it was put. The process was understood to be one of choosing means that would effectively gain the end. Since this conception was inherently 'teleological', ... it required some normative reference beyond the mere desirability of being satisfied. This was the origin of the famous concept of rationality in the restricted sense of choosing those means and concrete behaviors that are 'best adapted' to attainment of the end" (1968b: 229).

form of action from other forms of irrational or nonrational action. For the individual, action could also be *symbolically* meaningful, as in the case of religious rituals in which the means are symbolically but not rationally related to the religious goals (see also Parsons 1939, 2010). At the end of his short contribution to the Seminar on Rationality, Parsons equally pointed to the cultural determinants of rationality in the system of action: "there is a great deal of evidence that rationality is only one of the modes in which systems of action are integrated. The attempt to fit action in such fields as religion, magic, art and perhaps various others entirely into the conceptual scheme of rationality, results in severe distortion of the facts and gross misinterpretations" (p. 40 of this volume). Next to the norm of rationality, other social norms could also motivate individuals to act meaningfully in particular situations or circumstances.

On the other hand, he questioned the instrumentalist assumption underlying economic accounts of rationality. For Parsons, existing economic theories exclusively discussed rationality in terms of the relation between means and ends. These theories did not include the ends or goals in the interest of which such "instrumental rationality" was brought to bear within their frame of reference. Parsons also spoke of the assumption of the "randomness of ends." In his autobiographical essay "On Building Social System Theory: A Personal History," he later wrote: "The utilitarians, and still for the most part, economists, treated consumption 'wants' as given, that is, as *not* constituting the locus of intellectual problems for their purposes" ([1970], 1977: 72). For Parsons, the status of these ends also needed to be specified theoretically. Ends often were embedded within systems of ends—and therefore anything but random or irrational. The implication was that "the 'universe of values' is not devoid of rational organization and that decisions of 'commitment to' values ... have a rational component which is independent of instrumentality" ([1970], 1977: 73).

To elucidate his point of view, Parsons distinguished between three realms: ultimate means, ultimate ends, and an intermediate chain of means-end relations in which ends are always also means to achieve other ends. He claimed, for example, that most actions are "both means and ends—means to more ultimate ends, but also ends of the actions leading up to them. In this intermediate sector of the means-end chain will belong all elements of action other than the ultimate ends, except the 'ultimate means' at the other end of the chain, the fundamental 'positivistic' factors of 'environment' and 'human nature'" (1934: 529). In "The Place of Ultimate Values in Sociological Theory," he also stated that action in "pursuit of immediate non-ultimate ends" was subjected "to normative rules which regulate that action in conformity with the common ultimate value-system of the community" (1935: 299). In this sense, Parsons extended the reach of rationality. He argued that rationality could not only pertain to means-ends relationships; rational action not just took place in an environment of "random ends." The normative organization of the chain of "unit acts," of intermediate means-ends relationships, had itself to be addressed within the action theoretical framework.

Parsons' rejection of the utilitarian assumption of the randomness of ends thus led him to focus on the normative organization of action. In his view, actors typically relied on an *integrated* system of ends. He also believed that such integrated system of ends had to exist at the social level. Without coherent system of ends, no social order could exist. Without a broad range of social institutions that could specify and concretize the ultimate values and thereby provide structure to social action, no conformity with the ultimate ends of the total society could be ensured. Parsons thus expressed a concern with the institutionalization of ultimate ends or values, with the ways in which these values could circumscribe systems of social action. From this point of view, he maintained that sociology "would become the science of the rôle of ultimate common ends and the attitudes associated with and underlying them, considered in their various modes of expression in human social life" (1934: 529). Like Durkheim, Parsons believed that ultimate common ends or values "constrained" human action. By focusing upon the relation between social institutions and common values, Parsons believed that sociology would be able to legitimize itself as one of the behavioral sciences.

While Parsons sketched the outlines of what he thought to be sociology's mission in his early work, it has also often been remarked that he was hardly able to provide detailed hints of how this mission was to be carried out (e.g., Turner 1988). Near the end of *The Structure of Social Action*, Parsons also recognized that "any atomistic system that deals only with properties identifiable in the unit act ...will of necessity fail to treat these latter elements adequately and be indeterminate as applied to complex systems" (1937: 738–739). It is evident that his focus on the atomistic unit act ensued from his orientation toward individual action—and the ways it had been conceived in the economic, utilitarian tradition. For our purposes, it is also instructive to point to some underlying ambiguities in the voluntaristic theory of action, which might account for its limitations.

It is particularly instructive to pay attention to the distinction that Parsons drew between two types of norms organizing and controlling human action: efficiency norms and institutionalized moral norms. In "The Place of Ultimate Values in Sociological Theory," he used the example of religious rituals to contrast "two types of authority in norms—efficiency and moral obligation... Our attitude to [religious] ritual hence tends to be that kind of respect which we give to moral rules rather than the utilitarian attitude which predominates in attempts to realize a norm of efficiency" (1935: 303–304). Elsewhere, he discussed in a similar way the modes in which economic institutions could exercise control in order to "govern the whole complex of economic activities of a society. This control operates essentially in the form of a set of normative rules, obligatory on the participants (quite different from norms of 'efficiency') and governing the whole complex of economic activities of a society" (1934: 533). As these examples show, Parsons' concern was with the institutionalized moral norms or obligations, not with "the utilitarian attitude" or the "norm of efficiency." Despite his focus on voluntarism and normative constraints, he tended to treat rationality as a "natural" phenomenon that did not need sociological explanation.

Another illustration can be found in Parsons' discussion of "rationalization." The concept of rationalization is introduced at the end of *The Structure of Social Action*. Parsons proposed, more particularly, an "analytical law" of "increasing rationality": "a process of action can proceed only in the direction of increase in the value of the property rationality" ([1937], 1968a: 751). This law was compared to the second law of thermodynamics (entropy)—with the purpose of highlighting the irreversibility or directionality of rationalization processes. "Rationality occupies a logical position in respect to action systems analogous to that of entropy in physical systems... Effort energy is, in the processes of action, converted into realization of ends, or conformity with norms. Rationality is one, at least, of the properties in terms of which the extent of this change is to be measured for any *given* system at any given point in the process of change" ([1937], 1968a: 752, orig. emphasis). Rationalization thus referred to the realization or implementation of ultimate ends or values. While Parsons stressed that ultimate ends could vary and that different "value spheres" (Weber) existed, he again adhered to a universalist conception of rationality. While he stressed cultural relativity at the level of the ultimate ends, he also believed that some kind of "value pressure," oriented toward the rational and efficient implementation of these values, was intrinsic to human action systems.

Again, we may assume that these tensions and ambiguities are a result of Parsons' starting point. Parsons departed from an instrumental and individualized conception of rationality. He built on the utilitarian assumption that individual action was rational in as far as the available means were used in the most efficient way for attaining the goals. In *The Structure of Social Action*, he wrote: "the procedure throughout has been one of cautious advance from well-known and clearly formulable 'islands' of theoretical knowledge—above all the conception of science in relation to the rationality of action—bit by bit into the unknown" ([1937], 1968a: 627). But his starting point and cumulative "procedure" led him to accept a natural inclination to act rationally or efficiently. Both stood in the way of a sociological understanding of rationality. He did not yet offer an account of the problem of *social* rationality. In his early work, rationality seemed exempted from social determination. Parsons rather seemed inclined to define sociology as the science of the nonrational.

The Professions

After the completion of *The Structure of Social Action*, Parsons embarked on a large and ultimately lifelong study of the professions. This project closely built upon the analyses presented in *The Structure of Social Action*. His interest remained in the development of a theoretical account of the conditions of modern capitalism. He again questioned the reach and adequacy of existing utilitarian theories, in which the modern world is paradigmatically understood as a more or less integrated collective of individual actors, who are rationally pursuing their self-interests.

The starting point of Parsons' writings on the professions was the question whether professional activity could be adequately understood as a special form of economic activity as conceived in the utilitarian tradition. He particularly questioned whether the relationship between professionals and clients could be understood as a special form of economic relationship. For Parsons, professional activity could not be driven by self-interest alone, because clients could not be treated as means toward ends. But he also believed that professional activity was a (if not *the*) form of rational activity. As no other type of work, professional work depended on the application of scientifically sound knowledge (e.g., Parsons 1937, [1939] 1954). The extensive scientific and humanistic training which professionals had to undergo at the university level made it in his view clear that professions had to be dealt with as applied sciences, as distinctly rational institutions.

From this point of view, Parsons again touched upon the meaning of the concept of rationality. One of the main assumptions of the utilitarian paradigm, viz., that the rationality of action follows from the pursuit of self-interest, made it difficult to understand the rationality of professional work. For Parsons, the question was how the orientation to one's own interests could be combined with the "disinterestedness" of the professions. In his early sociology of the professions, Parsons thus already introduced one of the pattern variables he would later develop more systematically, viz., self- vs. disinterestedness or self- vs. collectivity-orientation (e.g., Parsons and Shils 1951: 90–91).

In these writings, one can also observe how his understanding of rationality started to shift. For Parsons, rationality no longer was a kind of "natural" implication of the pursuit of self-interest. He put more emphasis on the institutional and normative framework within which professional activities had to be carried out. He defined rationality as a value pattern that was characteristic of modern society. In different contexts, this overarching value pattern could be specified in different ways. Depending on the situation, rational orientations could call for "self-interest" or "disinterestedness." Seen in this light, one may also understand why Parsons was hesitant to collaborate with economists, such as Schumpeter, in order to develop another, sociological conception of rationality.

In the essay "The Professions and Social Structure," which was originally published in 1939, Parsons explicitly questioned the naturalness or universality of rationality. He described the context within which the business man, the foreman of labor, and the professional man had to define "the 'best' thing to do" or to find "the most 'efficient' way of carrying on his function" in the following way: "rationality in this sense is institutional, a part of a normative pattern: it is not a mode of orientation which is simply 'natural' to men. On the contrary comparative study indicates that the present degree of valuation of rationality as opposed to traditionalism is rather 'unnatural' in the sense that it is a highly exceptional state. The fact is that we are under continual and subtle social pressure to be rationally critical, particularly of ways and means" ([1939] 1954: 37). The shift in meaning of the concept of rationality is evident. Parsons did not hold onto the universality of rationality but instead drew attention to what he considered to be characteristic of modern, Western rationality.

It might be added that Parsons afterward also started to explore micro-sociological phenomena in his sociology of the professions. Best known perhaps are Parsons' analyses of the "sick role," of the institutionalization of the social role of being sick, and of the socialization of individuals into this role. His concern with psychosomatic problems, and eventually those of mental illness, led him to discuss the accessibility of non- and irrational forces to rational understanding. It also led him to consider the compatibility between social rationality and individual nonrationality (or irrationality). In this sense, his micro-sociological analyses of professional activities led him to distinguish more systematically between different levels or dimensions. His understanding of rationality clearly started to shift: from an emphasis on individual rationality to one on the social system and its major institutions. As he later would put it, next to the distinction and relation between the social and the cultural system, he now also started to consider the distinction and relation between the social and the personality system (e.g., Parsons 1951: 428–479, 1968c, 1969; Parsons and Platt 1973: 225–266).

In the period around 1940, when the Seminar on Rationality took place, the problem of rationality was not yet formulated in these terms. Only after the introduction of the AGIL scheme (see below), these distinctions were more systematically addressed. Parsons' early sociology of the professions was driven by a scholarly interest in the conditions of modern capitalism and modern society. Parsons looked for structural anomalies, i.e., structural phenomena that did not fit into the dominant utilitarian paradigm. His understanding of rationality started to shift as a consequence of his attempts to deal with the many complexities of professional work. In his autobiographical essay "On Building Social System Theory," he referred to this "shifting ground" in the following way:

> "I used the economic paradigm of the 'rational pursuit of self-interest' as the major point of reference, but in this case negatively, to throw light on the *differences* between the classical economic model of market orientation and the professional case with which I was concerned... The most important theoretical implications concerned the problem of the nature of rationality, the very question with which I had been involved, not only in my own work, but also in my work with Schumpeter. What opened up was a distinction, not only between economic and noneconomic aspects of rationality, but also, within the latter category, between two different modes or directions of considering the rationality problem. The first concerned a very old problem, even for me, namely the relation between rational (mainly scientific) knowledge and action in the sense of 'application'... The concern with psychosomatic problems, and eventually those of mental illness, noted above, raised a different set of questions... I suspect that concern with this complex of problems had a good deal to do with my coolness toward Schumpeter's overture, flattering as that was for a young and still insecure scholar." ([1970], 1977: 34–35, orig. emphasis; see also Parsons [1973] 2006: 8–14)

Multiple Rationalities

As we have seen, Parsons' half-hearted attempt to support the book project with Schumpeter concealed underlying transitions in his approach to the rationality problem. In the decades after the publication of *The Structure of Social Action*, however, Parsons did not lose sight of this problem. Quite to the contrary, it reappeared repeatedly in his writings. After the development of the AGIL scheme, the first version of which was presented in the *Working Papers in the Theory of*

Action (Parsons et al. 1953: 180–269), Parsons also started to address the problem of rationality through the construction of analytical schemes or models satisfying the AGIL requirements.[3]

In *Economy and Society: A Study in the Integration of Economic and Social Theory*, published in 1956 and coauthored by Neil J. Smelser, Parsons returned to the relation between sociology and economic theory (see also Smelser 1981). It should therefore not come as a surprise that Parsons also returned to the problem of rationality and rationalization. In *Economy and Society*, he particularly highlighted the relationship with the adaptive requirements of social systems: "we would like to reformulate the process of rationalization as the tendency of social systems to develop progressively higher levels of structural differentiation under the pressure of adaptive exigencies. Adaptive exigencies are not ... given only in the external situation, but involve the *relation* between the system and the situation. One aspect of this adaptive relation in every social system is a certain pressure to actualize the value system which is institutionalized in the system" (Parsons and Smelser 1956: 292, orig. emphasis). For Parsons, processes of rationalization thus now referred to processes of adaptation of social systems to the environment, which were elicited by cultural pressures ensuing from the value system of these social systems. Rationalization also referred to subsequent processes of structural differentiation, which facilitated the implementation of these cultural value systems.

Referring to Weber, Parsons also discussed the existence of "a plurality of possible value systems." Parsons and Smelser wrote: "Given tension between system and situation, ... economic production itself is a mechanism which helps to meet the adaptive exigencies of the system. This is the basis on which we have treated the economy as differentiated relative to the society's adaptive function. Mobilization of societal resources for adaptive functions, however, occurs on more than one level" (1956: 292). Structural differentiation thus allowed for the genesis of different rationalities. These rationalities were now seen as value patterns of differentiated subsystems, which defined "ideal types of action" (Weber). The form of "economic rationality," which dominated in the economic subsystem, constituted a straightforward expression of this societal rationality.

In *Economy and Society*, it is argued that "in the American case ... there is good reason to believe that economic functions are ranked highest" (1956: 176). But Parsons and Smelser did not specify why this adaptive function had gained primacy within the value system of "the total society." Neither did they address the question of the coherence of the plurality of systemic rationalities (or value systems) and thus the question of value integration in Western and especially American society. In later works, however, Parsons addressed several aspects of these questions. In a range of publications, he described the fundamental patterns of orientation in

---

[3]As is probably well known, AGIL is an acronym composed of the initials of what Parsons claimed were the four analytic dimensions of any system of action: adaptation, goal attainment, integration, and latent pattern maintenance. For an instructive history of the elaboration of this scheme, see Sciortino (2015).

modern Western society in terms of "instrumental activism" or "worldly instrumental activism" (e.g., Parsons 1973, 1991, 2007: 144–147). In this characterization, *instrumental* indicates that human action does not find its ultimate aim in itself but is treated as instrumental to some interest or task imposed from outside its own sphere of interest. In modern society, Parsons maintained, the emphasis on transcendental religious goals has been replaced by a strong emphasis on individuals as final reference point (hence *worldly* instrumental activism). Accordingly, modern society is seen to exist for the benefit of independent individuals. It tends to be judged in terms of its effectiveness in satisfying the independently given wants of individuals. By contrast, the *activistic* component refers to the system/environment relations of society and its subsystems and points to the formation of value preferences that stimulate social systems to engage in an internal transformation of, and control over, objects in their environment. Modern society is not concerned with adaptation to the world but with adaptation of the world to society's needs. It is concerned with mastery or control over the world (see also Weber [1920] 1988: 17–206; Parsons 1966).

In short, Parsons introduced a multidimensional concept of rationality in the 1950s. But he also believed in the existence of an overarching value system that could guide and control the different rationalities. The value system of instrumental activism gave preference to the different adaptive functions, to the adaptive upgrading of action, while "value generalization" defined the relation between different rationalities. These rationalities ensued from specifications of the same overall value system. Against this background, Parsons' emphasis also gradually shifted from the economy as the adaptive subsystem of the social system to education and the rationality system as the adaptive subsystem of the fiduciary system (see also Luhmann [1968] 1973: 14–17; Baum 1976).

Cognitive Rationality

In his late work, Parsons argued that the value pattern of "instrumental activism" found its most clear-cut expression in two recent phases in the evolution of Western society (e.g., Parsons 1971: 86–121). He pointed, on the one hand, to the industrial revolution of the eighteenth century with its emphasis on economic production, instead of on the extraction of natural resources. On the other hand, the interest in scientific knowledge, which became dominant in the second part of the twentieth century, also expressed this value pattern. For Parsons, both the industrial and the "postindustrial" types of society were exponents of a similar value pattern. Both the industrial revolution and the educational revolution (i.e., the realization of mass higher education) were manifestations of adaptive value patterns. The adaptive stress that gave primacy to economic production also legitimized the concern with the "cognitive complex" within modern society, i.e., the development and dissemination of scientific knowledge. Both the forms of economic production and knowledge acquisition were (or had) to be subsumed under a more generally conceived valuation of enhanced adaptive capacity in the contemporary society. In this regard, the analyses and reflections presented in *The American University* (Parsons and Platt 1973) can be seen to provide a complement to those first presented in *Economy and Society* (Parsons and Smelser 1956).[4]

In *The American University*, Parsons' theoretical focus is on what he called the value component of cognitive rationality: "the term 'cognitive' has a cultural reference whereas that of the term 'rational' is primarily social. Cognitive rationality is a value-pattern linking the cultural and the social levels which are not reducible to one another" (Parsons and Platt 1973: 38). Parsons, moreover, stressed the distinction and the affinity between the value patterns of economic and cognitive rationality in the American society of his time. "As opportunities opened up, the normative pressure of the value-system worked to encourage concern with rationality, not only in the economic direction but also in the cognitive and in certain others. The link lies in the adaptive function... *The same* value-system that favored economic development also favored cognitive development" (Parsons and Platt 1973: 44–45, orig. emphasis). Interestingly, "cognitive rationality" is now also dealt with as one particular mode or type of rationality. Parsons saw the current primacy of scientific knowledge and cognitive rationality as constituting one phase in the process of rationalization. It was a consequence of the way in which the modern, American society itself had become organized.

Against this background, *The American University* concentrated on "the modern university, especially in its American version," while the university was seen as "the current culmination of the educational revolution" and "the lead component of an extensive process of change permeating modern society at many levels" (Parsons and Platt 1973: 3). Following Parsons, the "educational revolution," i.e., the swift expansion of the system of higher education in the course of the twentieth century, facilitated the implementation and actualization of the value pattern of cognitive rationality. By enhancing the capacity for rational action, the rapid expansion of the academic system had been instrumental in "upgrading" the adaptive potential of modern societies, such as the American type of society. In the course of the twentieth century, he argued that "higher education, including the research complex, had become the most critical single feature of the developing structure of modern societies" (1973: vi). Elsewhere Parsons and Platt likewise argued: "There is a more or less unconscious sense of affinity with cognitive rationality among most of those who share the instrumentally activist orientation; this sense of affinity becomes more positive and more explicit in the increasingly large proportion of the population which has itself received a higher education" (1968: 507).

---

[4]For this reason, Smelser originally also was asked to coauthor *The American University*. However, differences of opinion about various lines of analysis imperiled the renewed collaboration. Eventually, Smelser wrote a critical epilogue to the monograph. For a detailed analysis of the making of *The American University*, based upon archival material, see Vanderstraeten (2015). For an illuminative view on Parsons' account of the functions of culture in social action, see Staubmann (2005).

In the aforementioned autobiographical essay, Parsons spoke with reference to Freud, of his return to the problem of rationality in *The American University* as the "return of the repressed" ([1970], 1977: 36). Reading between the lines of his autobiographical essay, one may gain the impression that the book or at least its second chapter, which delineates the problem of cognitive rationality, constituted the chapter that he did not write some three decades earlier for the Schumpeter-Parsons Seminar on Rationality. In *The American University*, Parsons clearly opted for a constructivist approach, which focused on the consequences of the expansion of the cognitive complex at the level of the total society. He focused on the ways in which cognitive rationality penetrated and transformed other subsystems of society. But despite the prominence that, in his view, the cognitive complex had gained in modern society, Parsons also relativized its impact. Its primacy was historically contingent, because science was only one of many subsystems in society—which only at the moment occupied a relatively high position in the hierarchy of functions on behalf of the total society.

Elsewhere, Parsons also stated that the culturally sanctioned primacy of active adaptation in modern societies served to legitimate the pursuit of empirical knowledge, which could be used to master the world, and thus to increase rationality and further rationalization. In his own words, "indeed a society, the central values of which are 'activistic', is almost driven to the feeling that ... the pursuit of knowledge is essential to its prosperity and development as a society. Broadly speaking I feel that this activistic component of values has indeed been prominent in the whole of modern society, perhaps particularly the United States, and that these values have given a strong impetus to welcome rationalization in this broad sense and indeed actively to promote it" (1970: 612). On the basis of the workings of this overarching value pattern, he believed that the coherence of the heterogeneous rationalities of the different societal subsystems could be guaranteed. The basic value pattern of instrumental activism ensured the unity of the different rationalities in society as a system.

In a number of ways, much of his late work also departed from the idea that the primacy given to adaptive functions accelerated structural differentiation processes within modern societies. As a consequence, he believed, social systems were increasingly faced with problems of integration. Social differentiation would especially lead to strains and tensions within the "societal community" (see Vanderstraeten 2013). For Parsons, rationalization thus particularly had an effect on systems specializing in the functions of either adaptation (A) or integration (I). Against this background, he discussed in his later, and partly posthumously published, writings several historical "crises" that, alternately, put emphasis on either of these functional requirements. He paid ample attention to the industrial (A) and the democratic (I) revolution in the "long" nineteenth century but also to the educational (A) and the expressive (I) revolution of the twentieth century (e.g., Parsons 2007).

In *The American University*, Parsons and Platt explicitly maintained that "the net impact of the educational revolution is constructive" (1973: 3). While the student revolt of the 1960s and early 1970s put emphasis on the nonrational and expressive aspects of the human condition, Parsons did not believe that a fundamental distrust of cognitive culture was developing at that time. Parsons and Platt discussed the disturbances as consequences of the swift expansion of the university system but also thought of the "permanent institutionalization of the extreme positions prominent in the acute phase of disturbance" (1973: 345) was something very unlikely to occur. In the long run, "continuity and change" had to go hand in hand in modern society. As a consequence of his untimely death, however, most of these reflections have remained incomplete.

Conclusion

Parsons famously characterized himself as an "incurable theorist." In the course of his long and productive career, he indeed never stopped reconsidering and revisiting basic theoretical concepts. On the foregoing pages, it was not possible to deal in every necessary detail with the lines of continuity and change in his understanding of rationality. But, at the risk of oversimplifying the nuances of his analytic approach, it can be maintained that Parsons' understanding of rationality shifted from an orientation to the individual economic actor to one that emphasized the complex structure of the value system at the social level (see also Staubmann 2015). He thereby moved from a "natural" or universalist conception of rationality to a constructivist one, which particularly put emphasis on the impact of the "cognitive complex," i.e., the systems of science and university education, both in and on modern society.

In the years 1939 and 1940, when Schumpeter and Parsons co-organized the Seminar on Rationality in the Social Sciences at Harvard University, this transition had not yet taken place. Parsons seemed in these years no longer satisfied with the concept of rationality, which he had used and developed in his early writings, including *The Structure of Social Action*, and which had also attracted Schumpeter's interest. In his own autobiographical statements, Parsons referred to institutional changes, viz., his transfer from the Economics to the Sociology Department at Harvard University, to account for his reticence with regard to the Seminar on Rationality. On the foregoing pages, I have suggested that new intellectual challenges also triggered his reconsideration of his relation to economics and economic theory. These intellectual challenges continued after Parsons' formal transfer to the Sociology Department and later the interdisciplinary Department of Social Relations. I have here tried to sketch why Parsons had difficulty participating in a project that (still) took its point of departure from an economic concept of rationality. Parsons' decision "to let it die" can best be understood against the background of these shifting interests and concerns.

In the 1950s and 1960s, Parsons' micro-sociological account of rationality was gradually replaced by a macro-sociological one, in which attention was focused on the social conditions that allowed for the institutionalization of particular value orientations. In his later work, Parsons dealt with rationality as part of the shared system of social values, as the institutionalization of particular social norms and expectations—and no longer as the mode of implementation of those values. He also put stress on the functional affinity between rationality and adaptation. Hence, he emphasized connections between rationality and social subsystems specialized in "adaptive upgrading." It is perhaps too strong to contend that the second chapter of *The American University* constitutes the chapter Parsons did not complete about three decades earlier. But, in his own self-understanding, this analysis of the rise and social impact of cognitive rationality seems to come closest to the largely unwritten chapter of 1940.

References

Allen, Robert Loring. 1991. *Opening Doors: The Life and Work of Joseph Schumpeter*, Vol. 2: America. New Brunswick: Transaction Publishers.

Baum, Rainer C. 1976. Introduction to Part IV. In *Explorations in General Theory in the Social Sciences: Essays in Honor of Talcott Parsons*, ed. Jan J. Loubser, Rainer C. Baum, Andrew Effrat, and Victor M. Lidz, vol. 2, 448–469. New York: Free Press.

Hein, Stephan. 2009. *Konturen des Rationalen: Zu einem Grundmotiv im Theoriewerk von Talcott Parsons*. Konstanz: UVK.

Luhmann, Niklas. 1973. *Zweckbegriff und Systemrationalität*. Frankfurt a.M.: Suhrkamp.

Parsons, Talcott. 1934. Some Reflections on 'The Nature and Significance of Economics'. *The Quarterly Journal of Economics* 48 (3): 511–545.

———. 1935. The Place of Ultimate Values in Sociological Theory. *International Journal of Ethics* 45 (3): 282–316.

———. 1937. Remarks on Education and the Professions. *International Journal of Ethics* 47 (3): 365–369.

———. 1951. *The Social System*. New York: Free Press.

———. 1954. *Essays in Sociological Theory*. Revised ed. New York: Free Press.

———. 1966. *Societies: Evolutionary and Comparative Perspectives*. Englewood Cliffs: Prentice Hall

———. 1968a. *The Structure of Social Action*. New York: Free Press.

———. 1968b. Utilitarianism: Sociological thought. In *International Encyclopedia of the Social Sciences*, ed. David L. Sills, vol. 16, 229–236. New York: Macmillan.

———. 1968c. Professions. In *International Encyclopedia of the Social Sciences*, ed. David L. Sills, vol. 12, 536–547. New York: Macmillan.

———. 1969. Research with Human Subjects and the 'Professional Complex'. *Daedalus* 98 (2): 325–360.

———. 1970. The Impact of Technology on Culture and Emerging New Modes of Behaviour. *International Social Science Journal* 22 (4): 607–627.

———. 1971. *The System of Modern Societies*. Englewood Cliffs: Prentice-Hall.

———. 1973. Nature and extent of value systems of modern society. In *New Problems of Advanced Societies*, 137–142. Tokyo: Japan Economic Research Institute.

———. 1977. *Social Systems and the Evolution of Action Theory*. New York: Free Press.

———. 1991. A tentative outline of American values. In *Talcott Parsons: Theorist of Modernity*, ed. Roland Robertson and Bryan S. Turner, 37–65. London: Sage.

———. 2006. A Seminar with Talcott Parsons at Brown University. *American Journal of Economics and Sociology* 65 (1): 1–58.

———. 2007. In *American Society: A Theory of the Societal Community*, ed. Giuseppi Sciortino. Boulder: Paradigm.

———. 2010. Actor, situation and normative pattern. In *Actor, Situation and Normative Pattern: An Essay in the Theory of Social Action*, ed. Victor Lidz and Helmut Staubmann, 31–167. Wien: LIT Verlag.
Parsons, Talcott, Robert F. Bales, and Edward A. Shils. 1953. *Working Papers in the Theory of Action*. New York: Free Press.
Parsons, Talcott, and Gerald M. Platt. 1968. Considerations on the American Academic System. *Minerva* 6 (4): 497–523.
———. 1973. *The American University*. Cambridge: Harvard University Press.
Parsons, Talcott, and Edward A. Shils. 1951. Categories of the orientation and organization of action. In *Toward a General Theory of Action*, ed. Talcott Parsons and Edward A. Shils, 53–109. Cambridge: Harvard University Press.
Parsons, Talcott, and Neil J. Smelser. 1956. *Economy and Society*. London: Routledge & Kegan Paul.
Schumpeter, Joseph A. 1991. In *The Economics and Sociology of Capitalism*, ed. Richard Swedberg. Princeton: Princeton University Press.
Smelser, Neil J. 1981. On Collaborating with Talcott Parsons: Some Intellectual and Personal Notes. *Sociological Inquiry* 51 (3–4): 143–153.
Staubmann, Helmut. 2005. Culture as a subsystem of action: Autonomous and heteronomous functions. In *After Parsons: A Theory of Social Action for the Twenty-First Century*, ed. René Fox, Victor M. Lidz, and Harold Bershady, 169–178. New York: Russel Sage.
———. 2015. Rise and Decline of Functionalism and Current Problems of Methodology in the Social Sciences. *Sartoniana* 28: 145–159.
Stichweh, Rudolf. 1980. Rationalität bei Parsons. *Zeitschrift für Soziologie* 9 (1): 54–78.
Swedberg, Richard. 2015. Schumpeter and Talcott Parsons. *Journal of Evolutionary Economics* 25 (1): 215–222.
Turner, Jonathan H. 1988. *A Theory of Social Interaction*. Stanford: Stanford University Press.
Vanderstraeten, Raf. 2013. Talcott Parsons and the Enigma of Secularization. *European Journal of Social Theory* 16 (1): 69–84.
———. 2015. The Making of Parsons's 'The American University'. *Minerva* 53 (4): 307–325.
Weber, Max. 1988. *Gesammelte Aufsätze zur Religionssoziologie I*. Tübingen: Mohr.

Inchoate Situations and Extra-Rational Behavior

Christopher Winship

"What will the situation be like in twenty years? Maybe somebody will come along with a more general and powerful theory, which includes rational choice as a special case, and that will have different behavioral implications in some of these intractable areas. I am open-minded about this." Gary Becker, Nobel Laureate in Economics in Swedberg (1990, p. 40)

Social scientists, particularly sociologists and economists, have battled for decades about whether people are rational and what it might mean for people to be rational. In this chapter, I take a different approach. Specifically, I argue that for an actor or actors there are situations where the conditions for rationality, in the strict sense meant by economists, are not met. In such situations, they cannot act rationally, even if people are capable of acting and do act rationally otherwise. Thus, it is the situation, not solely individual psychology, that determines whether individuals act rationally. It is the structure of the situation that makes rationality impossible. I term such situations inchoate. The question then is how do people act in inchoate situations. How do they act *extra-rationally*.[1]

There is a large literature under the heading of "bounded rationality" that has considered situations in which individuals are likely to not act rationally in the strict sense meant by economists—that they do not make the choice that is optimal given their preferences and the constraints they face. In adopting the phrase "bounded rationality," Herbert Simon (1956, 1957) was not pointing to any particular phenomena. Rather, his purpose was to indicate that much of human behavior was not rational in the economist's sense. To quote Simon:

I have never thought of either bounded rationality or satisficing as precisely defined technical terms but rather as signals to economists that they needed to pay attention to

[1]"Extra" is used here in the same way it is used to modify "terrestrial," as in "extraterrestrial," meaning beyond "terrestrial." By "extra-rational," I do not mean "superrational."

C. Winship (✉)
Department of Sociology, Harvard University, Cambridge, MA, USA
e-mail: cwinship@wjh.harvard.edu

H. Staubmann, V. Lidz (eds.), *Rationality in the Social Sciences*,
DOI 10.1007/978-3-319-62377-1_16

the reality and a suggestion of some ways in which they might. (Letter to Gerd Gigerenzer reprinted in Gigerenzer 2008, p. 91. Also see interview of Simon at: https://www.youtube.com/watch?v=ErnWbP_Wztk.)

Although the initial literature on bounded rationality considered many types of non-maximizing behavior, in recent years, bounded rationality has come to be associated with System I or fast, generally unconscious, thinking in dual processing models with rationality representing System II or slow thinking (Kahneman 2011). Kahneman did this most explicitly and influentially in his Nobel Prize lecture (Kahneman 2002, also see Kahneman 2003). In sociology, the importance of slow or similarly habitual thinking is often connected to Bourdieu's work (1977) and his analysis of habitual behavior, among others. Also see Gross (2009).[2]

A strong critic of the narrow identification of bounded rationality with System I thinking is the German psychologist Gerd Gigerenzer. In a series of books and papers (e.g., Gigerenzer 2000, 2008; Gigerenzer and Selten 1999; Gigerenzer et al. 1999, 2011), he has argued for the importance of heuristics in human decision-making. In overly simple terms, Gigerenzer contends that humans confront problems in novel situations and then develop simple rules for solving those problems that are then applied in the future in similar situations.

In this chapter, I point to a different type of behavior that I call extra-rational behavior that is also not rational in the economist's sense but is quite different from Kahneman's System I thinking or Gigerenzer's heuristics. Specifically, I focus on situations where rationality is not possible because what is optimal is not known or defined. These are situations I label inchoate. Thus, the fact that a situation is inchoate prevents individuals from being rational, not, as often argued, solely individual psychology.

It is important to appreciate that I am not claiming that rational choice theory is wrong. The chapter instead is motivated by the fact that there are manifold situations in which the conditions necessary for rational action do not hold and yet people act nonetheless. If, as sociologists, we are concerned primarily with explaining action, an alternative theory is needed to explain action where rational choice does not apply and how people act in such situations.

My position is similar to that of Whitford (2002, p. 325), who argues that "rational choice theory does not deserve paradigmatic privilege," implying that in studying any situation, one should not simply assume that rational choice theory is the appropriate model for analysis. Thus, in studying specific situations, rational choice theory may be quite useful, but this does not imply, by any means, that it is appropriate for the study of all situations (Whitford 2002).

In important respects, my argument also resembles that of Weick (2001) who is interested in situations that "lack sense." Although I consider our respective theories to be complementary, mine is more precise and more general. First, I delineate specifically why rational action is not possible in a particular situation—the failure

[2]Long before Bourdieu, Dewey examined the importance of habits as a mode of behavior (Dewey 1939). For a more extended discussion, see Gross (2009).

of one or more of Gintis's necessary conditions for rationality, what he calls his beliefs, preferences, and constraints or BPC model. Second, I examine the wide array of strategies—in addition to Weick's "sense making"—that are potentially available to individuals in such situations.

In developing my approach, I draw from pragmatist thinking, particularly that of John Dewey.[3] As Whitford (2002) discusses in detail, in a Deweyian and more generally pragmatist account, ends are situation specific, discoverable, and revisable. As such, ends are endogenous and require explanation. A theory of action is much less about simply choosing between a set of options as is fundamental to rational choice theory but is rather about understanding how ends and means (options) are discovered and acted upon in a particular situation. As such, individual behavior can be intentional without being rational in the economist's sense of the term. I discuss this in more detail below.

One goal of this chapter is to prevent Simon's notion of bounded rationality from being narrowly defined, as Kahneman's does, simply as System I thinking. Rather, I suggest that individuals can be nonrational in multiple ways. As such, I argue that there are multiple modes of individual thought, not just the economist model of rationality or the psychologist's System I and System II thinking [for a review of different dual processing models in psychology, see Evans (2008)].

To make my argument, I first consider a canonical example of extra-rational behavior—a jigsaw puzzle where neither the form nor the content of the completed puzzle is known. Besides providing an extended illustration of what I mean by extra-rationality, the example demonstrates that behavior can be intentional without being rational. I then propose a rough typology consisting of three types of behavior—rational, subrational (Kahneman's System I), and extra-rational. In a subsequent section, I consider Gintis's beliefs, preferences, and constraints (BPC) model as a way to delineate the conditions needed for rationality in the economist's sense, a second goal of the chapter. I then consider situations where one or more of his three conditions are not met. Specifically in terms of his BPC model, I consider where for the individual there is (**B**) incomprehensibility, one's **beliefs** are insufficient to understand one's options; (**P**) incommensurability, one's options are known but can't be compared, that is, one's **preferences** are ill-defined; or (**C**) unspecified attainability, one's options are known but the **constraints** on choosing or acting upon them are unknown. Failure of one or more of Gintis's conditions in his BPC model leads to what I call an **inchoate situation**, inchoate in the sense that the situation is not fully formed or structured. As stated above, my question then is how do individuals behave in inchoate situations, that is, what is the nature of extra-rational behavior?

The central portion of the chapter follows and addresses two questions: (1) What are common examples of inchoate situations? (2) What strategies do people use to deal with such situations? Having discussed examples of inchoate situations and

[3]Muller and Winship (2010) discuss Dewey's theory of action in more detail. Joas' *The Creativity of Action* (1996) provides the most thorough analysis (see also Whitford 2002; Stark 2009).

strategies used to navigate them, I discuss another canonical example, that of work and the transition to adulthood pointing out that for some individuals, the transition is automatic, e.g., one does what one's parents did; for others, it is highly strategic, e.g., one enters an apprenticeship in order to enter a guild; and finally for still others, it is a process of discovering what one wants to do and what options one has.

Arguing from a pragmatist perspective, I conclude that what we need is not a single theory of action as advocated by Gintis and others but rather a comprehensive set of *theories* of action. My classification of action into the rational, subrational, and extra-rational constitutes a preliminary effort to do this.

Intentionality Without Rationality: The Jigsaw Puzzle

To establish what I mean by extra-rational behavior and demonstrate when behavior can be intentional without being rational, consider a jigsaw puzzle (also see Winship 2006).

The picture (Fig. 1) depicts what appears to be a very difficult jigsaw puzzle. Make it even harder. First, assume that we have lost the box cover for the puzzle so that we don't have any idea what the picture will look like when it is fully assembled. In fact, we have no reason to even know what shape the final form

Fig. 1 Jigsaw puzzle (Photograph by Kim Piotrowski; http://www.kimpiotrowski.net/)

will be: a rectangle, a circle, a trapezoid, or some highly irregular shape. Second, assume that it is possible that some pieces are missing and other pieces are extraneous, i.e., they come from other puzzles. Finally, assume that it may be the case that pieces do not uniquely go together and in fact there may be more than one way to complete subcomponents of the puzzle and perhaps the whole puzzle itself.

What I want to suggest is that human action, at least some if not much of the time, is similar to putting a jigsaw puzzle like that above together. In his 2009 book, *The Sense of Dissonance*, David Stark quotes a web designer who describes his work in exactly this way.

> No matter how many new changes come across, for every new change, you can tie up and get your arms around, get a resolution to, and get it implemented; then that actually serves to be a greater step toward the realization than just figuring out how the two pieces you had in the beginning fit together the way that you thought they would, because it's now more like you're getting these undefined pieces and you're able to define them, and that sort of leapfrogs you toward that realization. At some point when you get all of those changes done and a good portion of the rest of it done and at that point, that's usually when I have that realization that Yes! I see what it is that we're doing now. I have a good understanding of the whole thing and what it's going to end up looking like. For me, it usually happens toward the end (Web-designer. Quoted in David Stark, *The Sense of Dissonance*, 2009. p. 100).

Our jigsaw puzzle and situations analogous to it have three important properties. First, the goal is highly general. There is intentional behavior. We want to put the puzzle together. We are not sure what it will look like when finished; we may or may not know when it is complete. Second, there is no obvious (optimal) best strategy. We could hypothesize that the final puzzle forms a rectangle and sort out all the straight pieces. Of course, if the final picture is a circle, this would be a highly unproductive strategy. We might assume that the puzzle contains a picture of the sky and sort all the blue pieces together. Of course, if the puzzle does not have a sky, as is true of the puzzle above, which is a Jackson Pollock painting, this would also be very nonproductive. A third strategy might be to pick a piece at random and see what other pieces fit it. However, if this piece doesn't actually belong to the puzzle, this strategy will be fruitless. There are certainly other possible strategies.[4]

The problem is that because we do not understand *specifically* what we are trying to do, it is impossible to know what strategies are likely to be effective, much less optimal. Finally, because pieces may not uniquely fit together, two different things may happen. First, we may hit a dead end. After assembling pieces in a way that seems to be working, we may find that we can go no further. We may have to undo what we have done. This is common with another type of puzzle, the Rubik's cube. Second, it may be the case that there is more than one solution to the puzzle. This is true of Scrabble.

[4]The use of multiple strategies relates to John Dewey's theory of holism. Richardson (1997) describes Dewey's theory as the recognition and commitment to a strategy that seeks coherence through analysis and evaluation at multiple levels.

What the puzzle metaphor demonstrates is that we can have intentionality without knowing what specifically we are trying to accomplish, without having an idea of what strategies might be effective, much less optimal, or without being confident that the action we have chosen will turn out to be feasible. We can have intentionality in a situation that is inchoate.

An important class of inchoate situations involves actors who have generic as opposed to specific goals. By a generic goal, I mean an end that is insufficiently specified that it is not possible to evaluate what would be the best strategy for achieving it. The discussion above of a difficult jigsaw puzzle constitutes one such example. Other examples of generic goals are easy to come by: "to live a full life," "to have a well-functioning organization," and "to have a good marriage." In each of these cases, it is not precisely clear what it would mean to achieve the goal. The actors may come to know, however, upon obtaining the goal that it has been reached. Since it is not clear ex ante what it would mean to achieve the goal, it is also not possible to know the optimal way to achieve it. It may be clear that some choices almost certainly wouldn't lead to the goal, e.g., moving to the country if one hates rural life and has bad hay fever.

Modes of Rationality: The Rational, Subrational, and Extra-Rational

For the purpose of distinguishing my concept of extra-rationality from other modes of thought, I propose a rough typology consisting of three types of rationality: the traditional rationality of economics, Kahneman's System I thinking which I label subrationality, and extra-rationality. I make no claim that this typology is fully adequate for understanding different modes of behavior. Rather my goal is just to use it as a means to distinguish extra-rationality from traditional rationality and subrationality, most closely thought of as Kahneman's System I thinking. Below, I focus primarily on the contrast between traditional rationality and extra-rationality.

In my typology, traditional rationality is what economists mean by the term. This is a narrow concept of rationality that understands people as having known options, an understanding of what options are feasible, and an ability to evaluate the desirability of these options. Traditional rationality predicts that individuals will choose that option they most prefer. More generally, traditional rationality encompasses various forms of game theory as well as Gintis's BPC model, to be discussed in detail below, of beliefs (B), preferences (P), and constraints (C).[5]

Subrationality describes situations and choices where traditional rationality is potentially applicable, but individuals rely on simpler mechanisms of choice:

[5]It should be clear that this notion of rationality is quite distinct from Weber's different concepts of rationality (Brubaker 1984) or the more generic common concept of rational meaning reasonable or sensible behavior.

satisficing, heuristics, or habits. Generally, this type of action is considered to be automatic, possibly to take place unconsciously, and as such does not involve the conscious consideration found in the economist's model of rationality. As such, it is meant to include Kahneman's System I. Often these methods can lead to good or near-optimal choices (Gigerenzer et al. 1999, Gigerenzer 2000); other times, they can fail miserably. For example, the assumption that a catastrophic earthquake is highly unlikely to happen is often a very good one, though, as the experience of Japan in 2011 demonstrates, it can also be a very bad one. These methods are attractive, in part, because they often involve less effort.

Subrationality is also the world of cognitive biases—situations where individuals are consistently shown to make choices that are biased in the sense that they are not fully rational. Subrationality, therefore, in part consists of *psychological* deviations from rationality. Individuals could make the rational decision, but for a variety of possible reasons, they don't.

The world of the extra-rational is about situations where traditional rationality is not possible because the situations are inchoate: we cannot understand the situation, we understand it partially but don't know how to evaluate different options, and/or we do not know what options are feasible. An individual might prefer to act rationally (or subrationally) but cannot. To provide a fuller understanding of extra-rationality, we need first to examine the necessary conditions for standard rationality in more detail.

Conditions for Standard (Economic) Rationality: Gintis's BPC Model[6]

In his 2009 book, *The Bounds of Reason: Game Theory and the Unification of the Behavioral Sciences*, Herbert Gintis provides an elegant and at times highly technical presentation of rational choice theory in the context of game theory in its past and recent manifestations. As the subtitle of the book suggests, Gintis believes that game theory—and especially newer variations such as epistemic game theory—provides a singular theory of behavior capable of unifying the social sciences. As noted above, Gintis refers to this as the beliefs, preferences, and constraints (BPC) model of behavior.

Gintis's formulation of rational choice theory is particularly advantageous for my analysis of extra-rationality, because it precisely elaborates the conditions that must obtain if rational action in an economist's sense is to occur. Drawing from Gintis's definition, I discuss what it means within rational choice theory for there to be beliefs, preferences, and constraints. In subsequent sections, I provide various examples of situations where one, many, or all of these conditions are not met.

[6]In an old and infrequently cited paper, James March (1982) provides a very similar typology for what he terms standard theories of choice.

Beliefs In the BPC model, beliefs imply a number of conditions. First is that an individual has a well-defined set of options to choose from. In the context of game theory, this means that there are well-specified moves in the game. An actor may use a probabilistic mechanism to make different choices, but in any one play of the game, he chooses, perhaps randomly, one specific option or alternative. Second is that an individual knows the consequences of these choices. These too can be deterministic or probabilistic, but if probabilistic, the probabilities of different outcomes are known.[7] In other words, an individual can place a bet in a lottery but know what the likelihood of winning is and if they win what they will win.

Preferences Preferences imply that an individual can rank the order of desirability of different outcomes. For an individual's preferences to be consistent, they must be transitive, i.e., if A is preferred to B and B is preferred to C, then A must be preferred to C.[8] What is key about preferences is that individuals find the choices they are faced with commensurable, that is, they can compare them and are able to decide which choice is preferable.

Constraints A central question in economics is how individuals behave in the context of scarcity. All of us have a finite amount of time and money to allocate. In a famous 1962 paper in the *Journal of Political Economy*, Gary Becker showed that most of the results from consumer demand theory could be derived by simply assuming that individuals lie across an income constraint line where one then analyzed how their behavior would change as the line was moved out or rotated. Thus, key to Becker's analysis is that for individuals to choose among different options, they need to know which options are feasible, that is, the constraints that they face.[9]

Inchoate Situations

If beliefs, preferences, and specified constraints are necessary for rational choice theory, what do situations look like where one or more of these conditions are not satisfied? To convince the reader that this sort of situation is fairly common, I provide a variety of examples below.

---

[7]Or more precisely, individuals have a Bayesian prior specifying the likelihood of the different outcomes.

[8]An extensive literature in economics and political science has examined how group preferences are not necessarily consistent in the sense of being transitive. This goes back at least as far as Condorcet's paradox (1785) and is at the core of Arrow's impossibility theorem (Arrow 1951).

[9]There is an important subtlety to the rational actor model. When it is pointed out to economists that actual individual behavior often does not appear rational, they will respond that what rational choice theory requires is that individuals act in a way that is consistent with rationality, not that they actually will be rational (Friedman 1953). The argument is that if people are not rational, the market (world) will punish them and their behavior will not be sustainable as actors who act rationally are more successful. Implied in this argument is the assumption that markets are sufficiently tightly coupled that one cannot get away with irrational behavior over the long term.

Below, I first discuss situations that are incomprehensible in that an individual or group may not have an adequate set of beliefs about a situation. This is the case where Gintis's "B" component fails. Subsequently, I discuss situations where there is incommensurability, that is, preferences are not well defined. This is the case where Gintis's "P" component is absent. Finally, I discuss of unspecified attainability, that is, situations, where constraints are unknown. This is the case where Gintis's "C" component is problematic.

Incomprehensible Situations The classic discussion in economics of situations that are incomprehensible is found in Frank Knight's distinction between situations that are risky versus uncertain (Knight 1921). A risky situation is one in which outcomes are determined probabilistically and the probabilities are known or at least believed to be known. It is under these circumstances that economists' well-developed extension of rational choice theory, expected utility theory, as well as epistemic game theory applies. The basic assumption is that rather than maximizing actual utility, individuals will choose, because outcomes are probabilistic, that strategy that maximizes their expected utility (where the expected utility of any particular strategy is the probability weighted average of the utility of the different outcomes that may occur under that strategy).

In contrast, according to Knight, situations are uncertain or, as I term it, incomprehensive, when outcomes are probabilistically determined but the probabilities are unknown to the decision-maker. In this case, where there is no way to calculate the probabilistically weighted average of different outcomes under different strategies, expected utility theory fails to apply. A piece of information necessary for individuals to evaluate the desirability of different choices—the likelihood of different outcomes under alternative strategies—is missing.

Consider a quite different example of incomprehensibility from political science. In the opening chapter to his rightly famous book, *Seeing Like a State*, James Scott (1998) describes the challenge faced by the Prussian state in the eighteenth century in trying to estimate the economic value of its forests. Because these were natural forests, they were "untamed." From the state's perspective, the forests, to use Scott's felicitous term, were "illegible." The state had no way of calculating their economic value. In short, the forests are incomprehensible. We will discuss Scott's work further below.

Incommensurability[10] Some situations may be comprehensible, but still not yield to rational choice—one's options are well defined, but the values of different options are not commensurable. One of the most famous examples of incommensurability is Sartre's young man described in his book *Existentialism and Humanism* (Sartre 1960). The time is World War II. A man's older brother has been killed while fighting in the French Resistance. His mother, meanwhile, is ill and in need of care. The question the young man faces is whether to join the resistance and thereby

[10]For a detailed philosophical treatment of the problem of incommensurability, see the essays in Ruth Chang, *Incommensurability, Incomparability, and Practical Reason* (1997).

honor his brother's commitments or stay home and care for his ailing mother. Sartre's point is that there is no a priori way for the young man to decide or in economist's terms to order his preferences. His two choices are incommensurable. In deciding one way or the other, he will become a particular type of person with preferences consistent with that choice, but there is no reason prior to making the choice he should value one option over the other.

In his trade book, *The Paradox of Choice*, Barry Schwartz (2004) discusses a line of experiments in which individuals are asked to choose an item from a set of consumer goods. Typically, this takes place in a supermarket. If individuals are given either too many choices or choices varying across too many dimensions, more often than not, they will refrain from choosing altogether. The result is a straight contradiction of rational choice theory: when there are few choices, the individual prefers the good, call it A, to buying nothing; when he has more choices, he prefers nothing to A.[11] An article in *Newsweek* (Begley 2011) discusses the neurophysiology of such situations. Apparently, when an individual is faced with too many choices, or more generally with too much information, a portion of the prefrontal cortex, the area where rational calculation occurs, ceases functioning. The brain "freezes." It becomes impossible for the person to assess their preferences, and thus, their different choices are incommensurable.

More generally, if we are in any situation where there are competing and contradictory goods in the philosophical sense, incommensurability, a lack of preference ordering, is a problem. A classic example is going to dinner at one's mother and having a bad meal. How does one choose between being frank, i.e., truth telling, and protecting one's mother's feelings? In being frank, one is telling the truth but will hurt her feelings. However, in being diplomatic, one is less than truthful, but her feelings are spared.[12] There is no obvious standard by which to choose between the two options. Certainly, many more examples of incommensurability could be given. The point is that such situations are common (e.g., see Sandel 2010). When options are incommensurable, there is no rational basis for making a choice.

Unspecified Attainability (Unknown Constraints) The rational choice model assumes that in making a choice, one knows how to attain it. Examples violating this assumption abound. In the decision theory literature, there is the problem of multiple local maxima. If a function has multiple maxima, then the only way to discover the global maximum is to try a large number of starting points. With single maxima (or for that matter, various computer algorithms), we know how to find it: go uphill till one finds the top, i.e., the most preferred outcome. If multiple maxima exist, then each hill must be climbed to discover which is the highest. If there are

[11]Technically, this is a violation of the independence of irrelevant alternative assumption.

[12]Some philosophers, most notably Kant, have argued that true moral conflicts are inconceivable. See articles in Christopher Gowan, editor, *Moral Dilemmas* (1987).

many, possibly infinite maxima (hills), attaining the true maxima may well be unattainable.

A similar set of issues exist in what computer scientists call NP-hard computing problems. For this class of problems, it is relatively easy to test whether something is a solution. Finding solutions, however, can be hard. A computing problem is NP-hard if, as the size of the problem grows, the time needed to find a solution grows faster than polynomial time. Intuitively, what this means is that as the size of the problem increases the amount of computer time needed to solve it grows so fast that finding a solution becomes infeasible. Many everyday problems turn out to be NP-hard. For example, finding an overall schedule that provides a solution where all individuals who want to meet separately with each other can do so is NP-hard.[13] A second example of an NP-hard problem is any (Boolean) truth statement. As the number of terms or conditions involved grows, the amount of computing needed makes finding a solution infeasible. In general, there are entire groups of problems involving storage and retrieval, sequencing and scheduling, and games and puzzles that are NP-hard.[14] In each of the cases, the computational demands may make finding the optimal solution impossible, that is, unattainable.

The problem of unspecified attainability, that is unknown constraints, also occurs in many real-world problems. Consider a couple's decision to have children. Will they be able to conceive naturally? Will one or both of them need fertility treatments? Will it be necessary to use in vitro fertilization? Will adoption be an option? People make many decisions without knowing what constraints they will face. If the likelihood of different constraints being binding can be calculated, then the economic theory of expected utility can be used. One wonders, however, how often individuals have even the vaguest idea of the constraints that may circumscribe their behavior.[15]

More generally, any exploration involves a situation where the explorer may have no idea of what constraints he will face. In Knight's language, there is (complete) uncertainty. In attempting to find a passage to India, Columbus had no idea that his path would be constrained by a large continent and not one, but two oceans. As Zerubavel (2003) describes in detail in his book *Terra Cognita*, it took multiple trips before Columbus realized that the New World was not simply a set of islands off the coast of China. Exploration of new lands, new situations, or new times often means having no understanding of the constraints that will appear. As such, one does not even know what options are viable, much less optimal.

[13]For a discussion of scheduling problems, see Winship (2009).

[14]The classic discussion of NP-hard or in their NP-complete problems is Garey and Johnson. 2002. *Computers and Intractability: A Guide to the Theory of NP-Completeness.*

[15]L. A. Paul argues that having a child is such a transformative experience that one cannot possibly know what having a child would be like (Paul 2014). This raises the deep question of what it means to have a preference for some option when one cannot evaluate what it would be like for that option to be realized.

Extra-Rational Behavior Strategies I: Incomprehensible Situations/Unspecified Attainability

The strength of rational choice theory is that it makes specific predictions about how people's behavior will change when the constraints they face change. No such analogous theory exists for extra-rational situations. Examples of how people actually respond to inchoate situations, however, are easy to come by. In what follows, I describe a wide variety of responses, starting with incomprehensible situations and/or situations with unspecified attainability. Strategies in these situations appear to be similar. The first solutions discussed are variants on a common theme—take action even if you do not know what the consequences of the action will be. The second set of strategies involves assuming or imposing a simplifying structure on the world. A third strategy is avoidance. I then turn to situations characterized by incommensurability. In this case, the solutions apparently are more specialized.

Taking Action: Random Choice Sometimes, individuals may act randomly in a situation. Karl Weick (1979) describes the hunting strategy of the Naskapi Indians. The question the Naskapi face is in what direction to search for a game. They decide by holding a caribou shoulder over a fire. A shaman then decodes the spots that appear and points the hunters in a direction. Weick interprets this procedure as providing a randomized way of determining a direction for the hunt. As Weick understands it, the problem for the Indians was how to adjudicate between two competing principles. On the one hand, if they had found a game in one place, it would make sense to return there. On the other hand, repeatedly returning to the same place would deplete the game in that area. Weick argues that in this context, a random strategy may well be optimal and in so doing treat different alternatives as incomprehensible.

Taking Action: Being Present In his book, *The Sense of Dissonance*, David Stark (2009) describes how in the late 1990s a group of web designers working in Silicon Alley in New York had no idea what products they should be producing—their situation was incomprehensible. They realized, however, that in order to compete, they needed to be carrying out designs. As a result, they found themselves creating products the end result of which was only clear near their completion.

In a similar way, the inner-city black ministers I have observed in my research on youth violence decided "to be present" on the streets. After an attempted slaying in a church during the funeral of a gang member, the ministers were unsure about what to do. They couldn't comprehend their current situation. They decided to walk the streets from 10 PM to 2 in the morning and then to meet until dawn to discuss what they had seen and experienced. Asked to describe their decision, they simply stated that God had called on them to be present. In multiple interviews, they have been quite explicit about the fact that they had no specific goal or, perhaps more precisely, the goal was unknown to them (Winship, unpublished).

Taking Action: One Step at a Time In her fascinating book, *Impossible Engineering*, Chandra Mukerji (2009) describes the construction in the seventeenth century of the Canal du Midi in Southwestern France. Mukerji points out that the engineering knowledge required to build a canal connecting the Atlantic to the Mediterranean did not exist at that time. As in my other examples, they couldn't comprehend everything that needed to be done. Despite this, engineers and local workers led by a prominent farmer combined abstract and local knowledge and successfully completed the canal. The basic strategy was to figure out what needed to be done one piece or one step at a time.

Taking Action: Keep Trying An important argument in the literature on entrepreneurship is that success may be simply a function of how many different initiatives one tries. In colloquial language, the number of hits one is likely to get is simply a function of how many times one has gone to bat. Recent research on entrepreneurs suggests that they often do not have well-developed plans but rather simply place themselves in a context they hope will be productive (Sutton 2002). As such, they act in a situation which is not fully if at all comprehensible.

More generally, learning can take place through a process of trial and error. The business consultant Jim Manzi has pointed out that in situations where one totally lacks any knowledge, trial and error may be an effective means of acquiring that knowledge. Rather than making assumptions about how the world works, one can try out different strategies and use their success or failure to gain an understanding of one's situation (Manzi 2012).

Simplifying In contrast to strategies that put acting first, another strategy is to assume that a simpler understanding of a situation is correct. Kahneman and Shane (2002) describe this as substitution: one substitutes a simpler and inaccurate understanding of the situation for a more complicated one. Basically, one declares a situation to be comprehensible. They point out that individuals often do this unknowingly. More familiarly, any math modeler should recognize this strategy. An accurate mathematical model is simply too complicated to analyze. In order to make the analysis tractable, a modeler makes simplifying assumptions. The debate then is about whether those assumptions have sufficiently distorted the world to make the conclusions of the analysis invalid (Rodrik 2015).

More drastic than making simplifying assumptions, actors can restructure the world so that it becomes simpler. In the introduction to *Seeing Like a State*, James Scott describes in detail how the seventeenth-century Prussian government reengineered its forests so that they were legible (comprehensible). Scott uses two photos to illustrate the difference between the illegible, untamed forest, and the structured, legible, tamed forest. In one photo, the forest is untamed and chaotic. In the other, trees grow in clean, straight rows.

Of course, a moment's glance around our world of buildings, roads, and information systems reveals how humans over centuries have not only restructured the world to make it more usable but to make it, in Scott's terms, more legible. If some component of the world is not easily comprehended, then one can restructure it so that it is. Obviously, the huge advances of the last several decades in information technology are only the latest examples of this effort.

"No, Thursday's out. How about never—is never good for you?"

Fig. 2 Cartoon (printed with permission of *The New Yorker*)

Avoidance I am told by the people at *The New Yorker* that the illustration (Fig. 2) is one of their most popular cartoons of all time. It illustrates the simplest strategy in dealing with an inchoate situation: to simply give up or avoid such situations. As the cartoon indicates, sometimes finding a solution is just too hard. But underlying the cartoon's humor is a deeper point. We often seek to live our lives in worlds that are comprehensible. We may well choose a career, a spouse, or an area to live in because it is "familiar" to us. In the extreme, we choose to live in "civilization" as opposed to the "frontier" because it is "known" territory.

Strategies II: Incommensurability

As noted above, situations that lack commensurability involve different strategies. I discuss three here.

Packaging Wakeham (2012) has studied juvenile sentencing in Massachusetts. Sentencing in Massachusetts is not decided by a judge but rather by an administrative committee appointed by the court consisting of different types of professionals. In deciding on a juvenile's sentence, many different criteria could be used: state guidelines, therapeutic interests, the safety and rights of the community, and/or the abstract idea of what would be "just." Wakeham finds that these committees rarely argue about what the appropriate criteria should be. Instead, they work hard to understand the situation and in doing so find a sentence that is simultaneously consistent with all of the above criteria. In contrast to Walzer's (1983) work in *Spheres of Justice* or that of Boltanski and Thévenot (2006) in *On Justification*, the question is not one of deciding which sphere or logic is appropriate but rather of finding an understanding that makes them all appropriate.

Patience In any situation where one is faced with two incommensurable options, most of us would simply like to have both. We would, according to the popular idiom, like to "have our cake and eat it too." In *The Struggle for Water: Politics, Rationality, and Identity in the American Southwest*, Wendy Espeland (1988) describes a multi-year conflict between the US Army Corps of Engineers and the Yavapai Indian Tribe in Arizona. The Corps of Engineers wanted to build a large dam that would provide water for the rapidly growing population in Arizona and Southern California. However, any dam they built would flood the Yavapai's ancestral burial grounds. Over the years, the corps' offers of more and more money for the land were met by the Yavapai's insistence that "one does not sell one's mother." Thus, there appeared to be no way to both build the needed dam and to maintain the Yavapai's burial grounds. The problem was resolved after many years, when a new generation of engineers who believed in small as opposed to large dams joined the corps. By building small dams, it proved possible to provide the water needed without flooding the Yavapai's burial grounds.

Emotions Recent psychological research has focused on the role of emotions in decision-making. An important result in this literature is that emotions may be critical to helping individuals make better decisions in complicated decision contexts. If one is currently at Harvard and trying to decide whether to move to Yale, one could create a long list of the areas in which one institution was superior to the other. Presumably, on some criteria, Harvard would be superior to Yale, and on other, Yale superior to Harvard. If not, the decision is easy. However, unless we know how to aggregate over these criteria, such a list may not be very helpful. We cannot quantitatively decide whether one choice should be preferred to another. We, however, might make the decision that feels right with research showing that making a decision emotionally is likely to result in a better decision (Bechara et al. 1997; Shiv and Fedorikhin 1999).

An Extended Example: Work and the Transition to Adulthood—Three Ideal Types for Work[16]

Above, I have offered a typology of rationality: subrationality in the sense of fast, subconscious, and habitual thinking; the traditional rationality of economists based on optimizing behavior; and the extra-rationality where either because of undefined

[16]I am grateful to Neil Gross for suggesting this example. An earlier draft of this chapter used the analogy to being on a "boat": subrationality as being on a pleasure cruise with no need

preferences, a lack of knowledge, or unknown constraints, pursuit of a specific, concrete goal is impossible. In bringing this chapter to a close, I briefly discuss the application of this typology to one particular context—the transition into adulthood and work. In doing so, my aim is to illustrate the differences in the three types of rationality within a single broad context. In addition, I demonstrate the potential importance of the typology in analyzing a social phenomenon of broad sociological interest.

For many individuals at different times and places, the available employment options open to them have been essentially fixed and often singularly. Focusing on relatively recent examples, there is the son who follows his father to the coal mines (McIntosh 2000) or the auto-plant (Milkman 1997) and a daughter who becomes a housewife or works as a seamstress as her mother did (Glenn 1991; Shaffer 1980). Conscious rational thought is typically not needed—one starts work in the "job," perhaps even as a child (McIntosh 2000), that is available and expected and in the process takes a step in the transition to adulthood. The mindless nature of this process is famously documented by Willis (1977) in his classic book *Learning to Labor*.[17] Such singular pathways often characterize the working class and the total lack of any opportunity for upward mobility. There are of course important exceptions—the child who inherits his father's business (Gersick 1997) or, in the extreme, the son who succeeds his father as King. Additional historical examples across multiple societies are ubiquitous and don't need to be rehearsed here. Here, preferences are generally irrelevant—there is no choice involved. The process is explicit—one follows in the appropriate manner through a predetermined pathway. The constraints are known and fully binding. The thought that one might do something different may never occur.

More recent times and more typically for the children of middle-class families, career choice can be a fundamental decision point in the transition to adulthood. Here, rationality in the economist's sense may be operative. The choice of college major or program is often explicitly linked to particular occupational choice with the end goal of optimal success. One goes through premed in order to go to medical school, working to get top grades so that one can get into the most selective school possible; one then goes on to an internship and residency, each time hoping to maximize one's career chances (Becker et al. 1961; Freidson 1988). Similarly, one may major in economics and specialize in finance with the hope of landing a job at a top Wall Street firm (Roose 2014). In the working class, this may involve choosing a particular vocational track in high school. In countries such as Germany and Japan, among others, where firms are tightly linked with specific high schools and have formal apprenticeship structures, what one needs to do in order to succeed in a particular career line may be quite explicit (Rosenbaum 2001; Ryan 2001). In these

---

to optimize, a racing yacht where optimality is critical, and a raft made of flotsam in the open where the hope is to find unsighted land at some point.

[17]Other relevant examples would be Halle's (1984) *America's Working Man* and Desmond's (2008) *On the Fireline*.

cases, there are multiple, distinct pathways leading to different careers that individuals choose from. In addition, within each pathway, individuals typically do their best to succeed in order to achieve an optimal outcome. Here, one's preferences guide one's choices. One knows what one has to do to realize those preferences—e.g., if one wants to become a doctor, one needs to go to medical school—finally, constraints are known or knowable, e.g., one needs to find means to pay for medical school though medical schools may or may not make different options explicit.

In contrast to the subrational situation where choice is not relevant and the rational situation where preferences, processes, and constraints are known and thus rational choice is possible, young adults may find that there are many potential pathways where they have no idea what career or occupation would suit them well, only the vaguest idea of process involved or the constraints involved in any specific choice—on the later point, for example, whether one needs to pay in order to get a Ph.D. in a liberal arts and sciences discipline.

In the current period (2016) in the USA, there has been much anguish about the number of young adults who seem to have no idea what career they should pursue. The popular movie *Failure to Launch* in which Matthew McConaughey is still living with his parents at age 40 typifies this anxiety. There have also been multiple books written describing these young adults as lost or adrift (e.g., Arum and Rosksa 2011; Smith 2011). Perhaps the most dramatic contemporary example as documented by Brinton (2010) is the situation in Japan where changing economic structures and breakdown of traditional linkages between high schools and employers have left a whole generation of noncollege-educated youth not knowing the what or the how of pursuing a career. As a result, they, particularly males, spend endless hours at home playing video games. Here, the situation is sufficiently *inchoate* that they have no idea what to do in order to make the transition into adulthood.

What the above three classes of examples illustrate is the social context that drives the nature of choice. Thus, whether behavior is subrational, rational, or extra-rational is not so much a matter of an individual's psychology but rather the properties of the social context an individual finds themselves in and their relation to it. To be blunt, it is the sociology of the situation, the context, and an individual's relation to it, not an individual's psychology, that determines what type of rationality is possible and what type is needed. At one extreme in the subrational, rational choice may not be needed—one just does what the situation defines as obvious or appropriate. In situations where multiple options are available, traditional rational choice may be operative, but this requires that individuals have defined preferences and understand a situation and the constraints they are faced with. In the absence of these later requirements, individuals may find themselves lost, randomly choosing directions, exploring different options, and making false assumptions about the situation but making decisions based on those assumptions nonetheless. This is the world of extra-rational behavior.

Conclusion

In a pragmatist spirit, this chapter suggests that social science needs multiple theories of action. Economists have long used the rational actor as their core concept for understanding human behavior. What happens, however, if the conditions needed for rationality are not present in a specific situation? I suggest that when situations are "inchoate," individual's behavior will be "extra-rational." I use Gintis's beliefs, preferences, and constraints (BPC) model to specify his three conditions for rationality. I have examined a variety of real-world situations that are inchoate, that is, situations in which one or more of these conditions do not hold. I provide a non-exhaustive list of how individuals behave in situations where rationality is not possible. In the case of situations where the conditions for rationality in terms of beliefs and/or constraints are not met, I suggest that there are a variety of possible ways people may respond.

Acknowledgments Neil Gross, Isaac Reed, Van Tran, and Josh Wakeham made useful suggestions based on an earlier version of the chapter. Jonathan Imber provided helpful information. Special thanks to Christopher Muller who provided in-depth suggestions on multiple drafts. I also particularly appreciate comments and encouragement Herb Gintis offered. Genevieve Butler provided important editorial advice. Of course, any remaining errors and flaws are the author's responsibility.

References

Arrow, Kenneth J. 1951. *Social Choice and Individual Values*. New York: Wiley.

Arum, Richard, and Josipa Roksa. 2011. *Academically Adrift: Limited Learning on College Campus*. Chicago: University of Chicago Press.

Bechara, Antoine, Hanna Damasio, Daniel Tranel, and Antonio Damiso. 1997. Deciding advantageously before knowing the advantageous strategy. *Science* 28 (February): 1293–1295.

Becker, Gary. 1962. Irrational behavior and economic theory. *Journal of Political Economy* 70 (1): 1–13.

Becker, Howard S., Blanche Geer, and Everett C. Hughes. 1961. *Boys in White: Student Culture in Medical School*. Chicago: University of Chicago Press.

Begley, Sharon. 2011. The Science of Making Decisions. *Newsweek*, February 27, 2011.

Boltanski, Luc, and Laurent Thévenot. 2006. *On Justification: Economies of Worth*. Princeton: Princeton University Press.

Bourdieu, Pierre. 1977. *Outline of a Theory of Practice*. Vol. 16. Cambridge: Cambridge University Press.

Brinton, Mary. 2010. *Lost in Transition*. Cambridge: Cambridge University Press.

Brubaker, Rogers. 1984. *The Limits of Rationality: An Essay on the Social and Moral Thought of Max Weber*. London: Allen & Unwin.

Chang, Ruth, ed. 1997. *Incommensurability, Incomparability, and Practical Reason*. Cambridge: Harvard University Press.

Condorcet, Marquis de. 1785. *Essai sur l'application de l'analyse à la probabilité des décisions rendues à la pluralité des voix* (*Essay on the Application of Analysis to the Probability of Majority Decisions*)

Desmond, Matthew. 2008. *On the Fireline: Living and Dying with Wildland Firefighters*. Chicago: University of Chicago Press.

Dewey, John. 1939. Theory of valuation. *International Encyclopedia of Unified Science*.

Espeland, Wendy N. 1988. *The Struggle for Water: Politics, Rationality, and Identity in the American Southwest*. Chicago: University of Chicago Press.

Evans, J.S.B. 2008. Dual-processing accounts of reasoning, judgment, and social cognition. *Annual Review of Psychology* 59: 255–278.

Freidson, Eliot. 1988. *Profession of Medicine: A Study of the Sociology of Applied Knowledge*. Chicago: University of Chicago Press.

Friedman, Milton. 1953. *The Methodology of Positive Economics. Essays in Positive Economics*. Chicago: University of Chicago Press.

Garey, Michael R., and David S. Johnson. 2002. *Computers and Intractability: A Guide to the Theory of NP-Completeness*. Vol. 29. New York: W. H. Freeman.

Gersick, Kelin E., ed. 1997. *Generation to Generation: Life Cycles of the Family Business*. Boston, MA: Harvard Business Press.

Gigerenzer, Gerd. 2000. *Adaptive Thinking: Rationality in the Real World*. Oxford: Oxford University Press.

———. 2008. *Rationality for Mortals: How People Cope with Uncertainty*. Oxford: Oxford University Press.

Gigerenzer, Gerd, and Reinhard Selten, eds. 1999. *Bounded Rationality: The Adaptive Toolbox*. Cambridge: MIT Press.

Gigerenzer, Gerd, Peter M. Todd, and the ABC Research Group. 1999. *Simple Heuristics That Make Us Smart*. Oxford: Oxford University Press.

Gigerenzer, Gerd, Ralph Hertwig and Thorseten Pachur (Eds.) 2011. *Heuristics: The Foundations of Adaptive Behavior*. Oxford University Press Oxford.

Gintis, Herb. 2009. *The Bounds of Reason: Game Theory and the Unification of the Behavioral Sciences*. Princeton: Princeton University Press.

Glenn, Susan A. 1991. *Daughters of the shtetl: Life and labor in the immigrant generation*. Ithaca: Cornell University Press.

Gowan, Christopher, ed. 1987. *Moral Dilemmas*. Oxford: Oxford University Press.

Gross, Neil. 2009. A pragmatist theory of social mechanisms. *American Sociological Review* 74 (3): 358–379.

Halle, David. 1984. *America's Working Man: Work, Home, and Politics Among Blue Collar Property Owners*. Chicago: University of Chicago Press.

Joas, Hans. 1996. *The Creativity of Action*. Chicago: University of Chicago Press.

Kahneman, Daniel. 2002. *Maps of Bounded Rationality: A Perspective on Intuitive Judgment and Choice*. Nobel Prize Lecture, December 8, 2002.

———. 2003. Maps of bounded rationality: Psychology for behavioral economics. *The American Economic Review* 93 (5): 1449–1475.

———. 2011. *Thinking, Fast and Slow*. New York: Macmillan.

Kahneman, Daniel, and Frederick Shane. 2002. Representativeness revisited: Attribute substitution in intuitive judgment. In *Heuristics and Biases: The Psychology of Intuitive Judgment*, ed. Thomas Gilovich, Dale Griffin, and Daniel Kahneman, 49–81. Cambridge: Cambridge University Press.

Knight, Frank H. 1921. *Risk, Uncertainty and Profit*. New York: Hart, Schaffner and Marx.

Manzi, Jim. 2012. *Uncontrolled: The Surprising Payoff of Trial-and-Error for Business, Politics, and Society*. New York: Basic Books.

March, James G. 1982. Theories of choice and making decisions. *Society* 20 (1): 29–39.

McIntosh, Robert. 2000. *Boys in the Pits: Child Labour in Coal Mines*. Montreal: McGill-Queen's Press-MQUP.

Milkman, Ruth. 1997. *Farewell to the Factory: Auto Workers in the Late Twentieth Century*. Berkeley: University of California Press.

Mukerji, Chandra. 2009. *Impossible Engineering: Technology and Territoriality on the Canal du Midi*. Princeton: Princeton University Press.
Muller, Christopher, and Christopher Winship. 2010. John Dewey: The sociology of action. In *Sociological Insights of Great Thinkers: Sociology through Literature, Philosophy, and Science*, ed. Christofer Edling and Jens Rydgren. Santa Barbara, CA: Praeger.
Paul, Laurie A. 2014. *Transformative Experience*. Oxford: Oxford University Press.
Richardson, Henry S. 1997. *Practical Reasoning About Final Ends*. Cambridge: Cambridge University Press.
Rodrik, Dani. 2015. *Economics Rules: The Rights and Wrongs of the Dismal Science*. New York: W. W. Norton.
Roose, Kevin. 2014. *Young Money: Inside the Hidden World of Wall Street's Post-Crash Recruits*. London: Hackette.
Rosenbaum, James. 2001. *Beyond College for All: Career Paths for the Forgotten Half*. New York: Russell Sage Foundation.
Ryan, Paul. 2001. The school-to-work transition: a cross-national perspective. *Journal of Economic Literature* 39: 34–92.
Sandel, Michael J. 2010. *Justice: What's the Right Thing to Do?* New York: Macmillan.
Sartre, Jean-Paul. 1960. *Existentialism and Humanism*. London: Methuen.
Schwartz, Barry. 2004. *The Paradox of Choice*. New York: Harper Collins.
Scott, James. 1998. *Seeing Like a State: How Certain Schemes to Improve the Human Condition Have Failed*. New Haven: Yale University Press.
Shaffer, John W. 1980. Family, class, and young women: Occupational expectations in nineteenth-century Paris. In *Family and Sexuality in French History*, ed. Robert Wheaton and Tamara K. Hareven, 179–200. Philadelphia: University of Pennsylvania Press.
Shiv, Baba, and Alexander Fedorikhin. 1999. Heart and Mind in Conflict: Interplay of Affect and Cognition in Consumer Decision Making. *Journal of Consumer Research* 26 (December): 278–282.
Simon, Herbert. 1956. Rational choice and the structure of the environment. *Psychological Review* 63 (2): 129–138.
Simon, Herbert A. 1957. *Models of Man: Social and Rational*. New York: Wiley.
Smith, Christian. 2011. *Lost in Transition: The Dark side of Emerging Adulthood*. Oxford: Oxford University Press.
Stark, David. 2009. *The Sense of Dissonance: Accounts of Worth in Economic Life*. Princeton: Princeton University Press.
Sutton, Robert I. 2002. *Weird Ideas That Work: 11 1/2 Practices for Promoting, Managing, and Sustaining Innovation*. New York: Simon and Schuster.
Swedberg, Richard. 1990. *Economics and Sociology: Redefining Their Boundaries: Conversations with Economists and Sociologists*. Princeton: Princeton University Press.
Wakeham, Josh. 2012. *Managing in the Face of Ambiguity and Uncertainty: The Problems of Interpretation and Coordination in Juvenile Justice Organizations*. Ph.D. Dissertation, Harvard University.
Walzer, Michael. 1983. *Spheres of Justice: A Defense of Pluralism and Justice*. New York: Basic Books.
Weick, Karl. 1979. *The Social Psychology of Organizing*. Reading, MA: Addison-Wesley.
Weick, Karl E. 2001. *Making Sense of the Organization*. Oxford: Blackwell.
Whitford, Josh. 2002. Pragmatism and the untenable dualism of means and ends: Why rational choice theory does not deserve paradigmatic privilege. *Theory and Society* 31 (3): 325–363.
Willis, Paul E. 1977. *Learning to Labor: How Working Class Kids Get Working Class Jobs*. New York: Columbia University Press.
Winship, Christopher. 2005. *Between Two Rationalities*. Cambridge: Harvard University. unpublished.

———. 2006. Policy analysis as puzzling. In *Oxford Handbook of Public Policy*, *Oxford Handbooks of Political Science*, ed. Michael Moran, Robert E. Goodin, and Martin Rein, vol. 10, 109–123. Oxford: Oxford University Press. Chapter 5.

———. 2009. Time and scheduling. In *The Oxford Handbook of Analytical Sociology*, ed. Peter Hedstrom and Peter Bearman, 498–520. Oxford: Oxford University Press.

Zerubavel, Eviatar. 2003. *Terra Cognita: The Mental Discovery of America*. New York: Transaction Publishers.

Part III
Letter Exchange on the Rationality Seminar

Letter Exchange Regarding the Seminar and Plans for Publication

Helmut Staubmann and Victor Lidz

January 10, 1940

Adams House
G 23

Dr. Alfred Schuetz,
102 West 80th Street,
New York City, N.Y.

Dear Doctor Schuetz:

I am sending a copy of my manuscript under the title *Actor, Situation and Normative Pattern*, about which we have talked, to Mr. R. H. Williams. When he has read it, I have asked him to send it on to you, and I hope it reaches you before too long.

The next meeting of our discussion group on problems of rationality, will be held on Monday afternoon, February 12, at 4 o'clock. It is not yet altogether certain what the program will be. As I told you, at the last meeting I presented a very brief outline of certain aspects of my own approach to the problem, some notes of which I enclose. This next meeting will either continue the discussion of that approach, or will be concerned with material to be presented by a member of our Department of Psychology, Dr. D. V. McGranahan. We should, of course, be delighted if you could be present, but in any case would count on your presenting some of your own ideas to a later meeting. I hope you will be able to stay long enough so that there could be an opportunity for some discussion outside the meeting. Perhaps I could assemble a small group to have dinner with you that evening and carry on the discussion afterwards.

Sincerely yours,

Talcott Parsons

H. Staubmann (✉)
Department of Sociology, University of Innsbruck, Innsbruck, Austria
e-mail: Helmut.Staubmann@uibk.ac.at

V. Lidz
Department of Psychiatry, Drexel University College of Medicine, Philadelphia, PA, USA
e-mail: lidzvic@gmail.com

H. Staubmann, V. Lidz (eds.), *Rationality in the Social Sciences*,
DOI 10.1007/978-3-319-62377-1_17

January 24, 1940

Dr. Alfred Schuetz
102 West 80th Street
New York City

Dear Dr. Schuetz:

It is entirely a question of your own convenience as to whether you can come to the meeting of our discussion group on February 12th. If you get back from California in time we would be very glad to have you. Otherwise, as far as I can see, it would be just as favorable from our point of view to have you come to the next meeting which will probably be two weeks later, that is, February 26th. There is no need to let us know very much in advance but we will be very glad indeed to have you whichever time you can come. I would hope to be able to have a group get together to meet with you privately in addition to the regular discussion group.

I will be much interested in any comment you can give me both on the little discussion of rationality and on the larger manuscript which I hope you received in good time.

Sincerely yours,

Talcott Parsons

May 15, 1940

Emerson Hall
Cambridge, Mass.

The undersigned Committee from the Seminar on Rationality has decided upon the following plan, which we hope will meet with your approval.

1. Members of the Seminar who contributed papers during the year are requested to send their papers to Professor Parsons or Dr. McGranahan as soon as possible, with June 15 as a deadline. The papers should be in manuscript form, and should take into account the points that were raised by other members of the Seminar in discussion. (Protocols of the discussions may be obtained from members of the Committee.)
2. The Committee will have all contributions multigraphed and will mail copies to the members of the Seminar on or before July 1.
3. Members of the Seminar who did not contribute papers are requested to submit by September 1 either original papers or criticisms of the contributions they will receive by mail.
4. All contributions will be reviewed in September and a decision will be made then as to the desirability of publication.

Both Professor Parsons and Dr. McGranahan may be reached by mail in Emerson Hall until the end of Summer School. If your mail address as of July 1 is different from that given in the College Catalogue, please inform a member of the Committee.

Respectfully yours,

J. A. Schumpeter
Talcott Parsons
D. V. McGranahan

June 12

Joseph A. Schumpeter
Windy Hill
Taconic, Connecticut

Dear Parsons,

I have today sent off my paper on rational schemata to be typed. It should reach you at, or not much after, the dead-line date of June 15. Though I have rewritten and amplified (also modified), I am not yet pleased with the thing. But if we ever get beyond collecting contributions, another revision will in any case be necessary for dovetailing them together. So here goes, for the time being.
I see that I have Moore's contribution still with me. Since it is a carbon however I thought that I might keep it. If you don't get another copy from him, and if you need this, please drop me a line. Schütz' paper is, I think, still with Haberler.
I feel stale and oppressed by a feeling of futility.. . . still, work to which I now return (and which someday I hope to get your reaction to) is at least a sedative.
Let me thank you for all I feel I personally owe to your contributions to, and leadership in, the discussions of our group. I am all for going on with the work of developing and coordinating the material we have so far – and for something further on too.

Best wishes
Cordially yours
Joseph Schumpeter

Original Letter Schumpeter to Parsons

JOSEPH A. SCHUMPETER - WINDY HILL - TACONIC, CONNECTICUT

June 12

Dear Parsons,

I have to-day sent off my paper on national schemata to be typed. It should reach you at, or not much after, the dead-line date of June 15. Though I have rewritten and amplified (also modified), I am not yet pleased with the thing. But if we ever get beyond collecting con-

tributions, another revision will
in any case be necessary for
dovetailing them together. So here
goes, for the time being.

I see that I have Moore's
contribution still with me. Since it
is a carbon however I thought that
I might keep it. If you don't get
another copy from him and if you need this
please drop me a line. Wirth's
paper is, I think, still with Heberle.

I feel stale and oppressed by a
feeling of futility .... still, work

to which I now return (and which some day I hope to get your reaction to) is at least a sedative.

Let me thank you for all I feel I personally owe to your contributions to and leadership in the discussions of our group. I am all for going on with the work of developing and coordinating the material we have so far — and for venturing further on too.

Best wishes

Cordially yours

[illegible]

October 9, 1940

Dr. John P. Dunlop
Lowell House M-11
Cambridge, Massachusetts

Dear Dunlop:

I have just been talking to Schumpeter about the papers from the rationality discussion group last year, and we have decided that it is well worthwhile to attempt to get them together and then consider the question of possible publication.

We have put some time about the first of December as a tentative deadline, and very much hope that you will be in a position to give us something by that time. I think your idea of tackling some phase of the uncertainty problem is excellent and will be interested in what you turn out.

Sincerely yours,

Talcott Parsons

October 9, 1940

Professor Gottfried Haberler
Littauer Center
Cambridge, Massachusetts

Dear Haberler:

Schumpeter tells me that you did not receive any request for a contribution to the bundle of manuscripts growing out of our discussion group on rationality last year. If so, it was either an error on the part of McGranahan or myself, or the one mailed to you must have gotten lost in the mail. We certainly meant to include you.

I have just been talking to Schumpeter, and even though we now have only three completed manuscripts, we agree that it would be worthwhile to try to get together as near the full complement as we can, and we would very much appreciate a contribution from you if you can possibly find the time to write it. We should like to have these available, if possible, by about the first of December, and then very likely get the group together shortly after Christmas to discuss the next step. We very much hope you can give us something.

Cordially yours,

Talcott Parsons

October 9, 1940

Dr. D. V. McGranahan
Emerson Hall
Cambridge, Massachusetts

Dear Don:

I have just been talking with Schumpeter about the papers growing out of the rationality group. We agree that it is worthwhile to get in as many contributions as we can and then consider the possibility of publication. We very much hope to have something along the line of what you presented to the group included in these manuscripts, and hope you can manage it. We have set about December 1 as the new deadline.

I am writing now to all the people concerned since the delinquency in the summer was mainly my fault and it doesn't seem fair to burden you with any responsibility except for your own contribution.

Sincerely yours,

Talcott Parsons

October 9, 1940

Professor Wilbert E. Moore
Pennsylvania State College
State College, Pennsylvania

Dear Wilbert:

Doubtless in the rush of events you have more or less forgotten the intention of our discussion group on rationality to request that contributions made by individual members should be put in pretty full written form sometime this summer. McGranahan and I have both been delinquent in the matter and only now have we pulled ourselves together to try and get something done. It is agreed with Schumpeter that we ought not to let the thing drop, but should try to get as complete a set of manuscripts as we can, and then consider the question of the possibility of publication. We would appreciate it a great deal if you could work yours up and get it to us by about the first of December. Of course you are not too closely bound to exactly what you presented to the group last year.

Congratulations on your attainment of a new status in the social system. I trust that the experience is proving satisfactory and also that “mother and child are doing nicely.” Also I hope you like your new job, and would be delighted to hear about it when you have the time to write.

Cordially yours,

Talcott Parsons

October 9, 1940

Dr. Paul M. Sweezy
Department of Economics
Harvard University
Cambridge, Massachusetts

Dear Paul:

You probably received last June a request form Schumpeter, McGranahan and myself to write up some phase of the range of problems discussed by the rationality group last year which interested you. With the usual laxity we have neglected to get much further with the project until now. I have just been talking with Schumpeter about it and we agree that it is highly desirable to get together as many manuscripts as we can and then consider the problem of whether they could be worked into a publishable volume.

We very much hope that you have something on your mind of sufficient urgency so that you could work it into a contribution. If that is the case, we should like, if possible, to have the manuscript available by about the first of December.

Sincerely yours,

Talcott Parsons

October 9, 1940

Dr. Robert Waelder
85 Lancaster Terrace
Brookline, Massachusetts

Dear Dr. Waelder:

I have just been talking to Professor Schumpeter about the status of the papers growing out of our discussion group last year. We agree that it would be highly desirable to have as full a group of papers as possible, although so far only a few have come in. We are not certain that we would have the material for a volume, but feel that we would like to consider the question seriously when we had first drafts of all the contributions before us.

With that in mind we very much hope that you will be able to submit a manuscript by about the first of December, as we would then intend to go over them all and present the problem to the group as a whole. From what you said the other day you will probably be able to do it and we very much hope that is the case.

Sincerely yours,

Talcott Parsons

October 17, 1940

Dear Talcott,

I have your note about the possibility of getting a volume out of last year's "rationality" discussion group. I think it's an excellent idea, but I am afraid I shouldn't have anything to contribute. I attended very much as an amateur in search of enlightenment; but it would still take a lot longer than from now to December, before I could have anything very intelligent to say on my own.

Sincerely,

Paul Sweezy

October 22, 1940

The Pennsylvania State College
School of the Liberal Arts
State College, Pennsylvania

Professor Talcott Parsons
Adams House G-22
Harvard University
Cambridge, Massachusetts

Dear Talcott:

I was glad to hear from you that the proposed publication of last year's papers has not been abandoned. Last spring I submitted a brief summary of my paper to McGranahan before I understood his purpose in requesting it, and have done no more on it since. I should like to supplement and document a little what I had to say in the paper, and shall get to work on it immediately. Naturally, I should like to see the thing go through, and I should like to submit a reasonably respectable essay.

Time being a notoriously scarce resource, I shall of course not be able to devote my exclusive attention to the paper, but I shall certainly get it to you by December first. I am finding very little time for my own work these days, since working up courses about consumes my time and energy. It is fortunate that I had not planned very much in the way of working up old materials or undertaking new projects, for I only have seven courses to prepare for this year. The twelve-hour teaching load does not look particularly heavy until it is broken up into eight one-semester courses, only one of which is repeated.

The quality of the undergraduate students here is not particularly impressive. I feel this has some relation to the general rah-rah spirit prevailing. However, we have several very good graduate students who contribute the necessary spice to the dissemination of the gospel.

After you have time to size them up I should like to hear how Sutton and Bales are getting along. I trust they have not been diverted from their original intention of working with you this year.

Paternity, I find, is a status which one may approach by degrees. Perhaps this is because most of the onerous obligations still devolve upon Dorothy. We consider the baby to be very well behaved and to shop promise of being a reasonably respectable citizen. We have not yet planned a career for her.

I shall be glad to hear from you about the state of affairs at Harvard and your own activities if you find time to write.

Sincerely,

Wilbert

Wilbert E. Moore

November 8, 1940

Harvard University
Department of Economics
Cambridge Massachusetts

Professor Talcott Parsons
Department of Sociology
Emerson Hall
Harvard University
Cambridge, Mass.

Dear Parsons:

Many thanks for your note. I intended to answer you, but I have been busy all the time.

I am not sure whether I shall be able to contribute anything to your volume. The only possibility I can see is to write some comments on the other contributions. Perhaps you could let me inspect the other contributions. Then I could let you know after a while whether I can do something or not.

Very sincerely yours,

G. Haberler

December 5, 1940

Dr. Wilbur[1] E. Moore
Pennsylvania State College
State College, Pennsylvania

Dear Wilbur:

Thank you very much for taking the trouble to get a manuscript in to us so promptly. I have not yet had time to read it, but wish to acknowledge it right away. Others will not be as prompt as you, but I think that by early in the year we will have enough to take up the question of what is to be done with the manuscripts seriously. I will let you know what happens as soon as I possibly can.

I am sorry my personal plans seem to work out so that I shall not get to Chicago this year. I will be sorry to miss the opportunity to see so many old friends, but hope you will be in this part of the country before too many months.

Best regards,

(Talcott Parsons)

[1]Note the error in Moore's first name. Parsons did not often misaddress a friend, student, or protégé. It is likely that the letter was dictated and that his secretary erred in hearing the name and that Parsons later signed the letter in haste, failing to note the mistake, or that the letter was sent unsigned. Eds.

March 2, 1941

Dr. Wilbur E. Moore
Department of Sociology
Pennsylvania State College
State College, Pennsylvania

Dear Wilbur:

Thank you for your information about Richard Davis. I remember meeting him in Detroit and hearing a good deal about him from Bob Merton and others. I sincerely hope we will be granted a fellowship here. As you probably know, I am not on the fellowship committee, but will have an opportunity to say something when the list comes before the Department. As you know, we can always stand good graduate students.

I am sorry that as yet nothing has come of the rationality group problem. I met Schumpeter in the Yard the other day and he asked when I was going to do something about it. I hope not to delay it too long but seem to have been very busy of late. As I suppose might have been expected, several of those asked to contribute have not come through, some asking to see what the others had done before they did so. I sincerely hope that your hard work will not have been in vain.

Sincerely yours,

(Talcott Parsons)

P.S. You have doubtless seen the current issue of *Click*? No further comment is necessary.

Later Letters Regarding the Seminar

Helmut Staubmann and Victor Lidz

December 4, 1973

Universität Konstanz
Fachbereich Soziologie
Richard Grathoff, Ph.D.
D 7777 Salem 3
Oberer Weingarten 6
Federal Republic of Germany

Dear Professor Parsons,

Mrs. Alfred Schütz has asked us to be editors of the correspondence on „The Structure of Social Action" and on Schütz's critique, which have been written between the fall of 1940 and Spring 1941. We feel highly honored by this offer. Distance does not permit us to introduce ourselves in a personal visit. Would you, please, allow us to raise some questions in writing?

We intend to draw an editorial frame for this correspondence, which – if we see the matter correctly – grew out of your and Professor Schumpeter's Harvard Seminars on Rationality in early 1940. We have asked Professor Burns to be so kind as to convey this letter to you. We had the pleasure of meeting him in Konstanz some time ago and we are confident that he would also be willing to comment on our qualifications and backgrounds.

Official editorial correspondence, we understand, is being conducted directly by Northwestern University Press who have offered to publish the American edition.

H. Staubmann (✉)
Department of Sociology, University of Innsbruck, Innsbruck, Austria
e-mail: Helmut.Staubmann@uibk.ac.at

V. Lidz
Department of Psychiatry, Drexel University College of Medicine, Philadelphia, PA, USA
e-mail: lidzvic@gmail.com

H. Staubmann, V. Lidz (eds.), *Rationality in the Social Sciences*,
DOI 10.1007/978-3-319-62377-1_18

A German edition of the correspondence and the discussions on rationality has found the interest of Suhrkamp in Frankfurt.

In preparing the manuscript we thought it advisable to clarify several points and perhaps – if we may express this hope – to include a retrospect on this very basic dispute, which in our opinion and from today's perspective displays a lesser degree of divergence than some letters suggest on first sight. But we have no right to claim your time in these matters. We would understand it perfectly, if you decided our questions should be answered only very briefly, if at all. Here they are:

1. Schütz was in Harvard, we understand, on April 13, 1940, to give his lecture on "The Problem of Rationality in the Social World", reprinted in Collected Papers II, 64-88. What was the occasion in Harvard? Was he invited by "The Faculty Club of Harvard University" as Schütz notes on p. 72 of his paper on your "Theory of Social Action?" Or did he present it at the "Interdepartmental Conference at Harvard University" as the editor of his Collected Papers II writes on p. XIII.?
2. The letters reveal Schütz was invited to give his lecture to your "Discussion Group on Problems of Rationality" (your letter of March 11, 40). Apparently, Professors Schumpeter and Haberler were members of that circle. Would you be so kind to say a word on the general composition of this group, its themes of presentation, its style of discourse? On October 30, 1940, you mentioned that the manuscripts of the group were reviewed for possible publication. Did you decide against it?
3. Could you say in a few words, how Schütz' contribution to that group was received?
4. In your letter of January 24, 40, you mention that you had mailed Schütz "the larger manuscript" – which Schütz was later to mail to Voegelin in Alabama. Which MS? Was that already a very early version of the "Social System?"

We do not wish to go further and ask for details which might seem irrelevant for the core of the conversations between you and Alfred Schütz. We have already taken too much of your time.

But may we close with a sentence you wrote on March 29, 41, to Schütz: "I remember about 1937 having a rather long conversation with Schelting about it ("Der sinnhafte Aufbau der sozialen Welt") and saying essentially that I could not see that for the purpose of my treatment of Max Weber, for instance it was necessary to go into the kind of analysis of the subjective point of view in relation to the time element which was the central theme of your analysis." More than 30 years have passed since. Would you care to comment on this point again, from your present perspective?

If you should find one or the other point of this letter significant enough to be answered shortly, we would be very grateful, indeed. Please, accept our best wishes for the Christmas Season and the coming New Year.

Sincerely yours

Walter M. Sprondel Richard Grathoff

August 9, 1974

Harvard University
Department of Sociology
William James Hall
Cambridge, Massachusetts 02138

Mr. Richard Grathoff
1107 South 3rd Street
St. Charles, Illinois 60174

Dear Professor Grathoff:

Ten days or so ago I drafted, through dictation, a rather long letter addressed to you which constituted my commentary on your edition of Dr. Schütz's article on my book *The Structure of Social Action,* and some of the correspondence between us which followed on his submitting the manuscript of that article to me. Unfortunately, I garbled the dictation process so that I now am forced to begin again. I will attempt, as best I can, to reconstruct what I had already meant to say. Fortunately, I spoke to my machine with fairly detailed notes in hand and I still have those notes.

First, I think it should be remembered that this contact with Dr. Schütz took place more than thirty years ago and, unfortunately, was broken off in the Spring of 1941. I sincerely hope that my own thinking has not ceased to develop in the long intervening period. I am therefore writing now from the point of view of the way I see some of these problems in 1974, not the way I saw them in 1940 or 1941 or in *The Structure of Social Action*, which was put on paper a few years before that. It will in the nature of the case be impossible for me to give a fully detailed commentary on all the significant points which came up. I should rather like to concentrate on two or three main considerations, which seem to me to be particularly salient from my present retrospective perspective.

Perhaps I had best start with a topic on which I remember having had rather extended, but not terribly productive, discussion with Dr. Schütz, and with respect to which subsequent intellectual developments which have impinged on me have introduced what seems to me to be a very considerable clarification. I think I would formulate these problems somewhat differently from the way Dr. Schütz did, but I think I understand very much better than I did about 1940 what is at issue.

This concerns the question of time orientations. They are not very prominent in the material you have edited, but certain are very important in the background. As I remember, Schütz was particularly insistent on the fundamental distinction between the meaning of time orientation prospectively, that is, from the point of view of an actor, in initiating and carrying out what Schütz calls a "project" of action, and secondly, the meaning of time perspective in a retrospective situation where an actor and, indeed, also an observer is conceived as thinking about what has in fact occurred, including his own agency in bringing it about and "explaining" these occurrences.

There may be various other differences, but I have become increasingly aware of one which seems to me altogether fundamental. Part of my perspective rests on my very long-standing conviction that all scientific analysis is at some level and to some degree abstract. This is a point of view I derived particularly from Max Weber and from A. N. Whitehead. The position of a human actor clearly involves limitations which necessitate such abstraction in his viewing of the situation in which he acts and particularly in the perspective of future conditions and events, including the consequences of his own intervention, which he must take account of in conceiving a project in Schütz's sense, and proceeding to implement his plan for it. I have found it convenient to refer to the limitations on possible full determination of the future as focusing in contingencies which may arise in the course of implementation of a project, but which cannot be predicted in detail in advance.

After a course of action has been completed, however, the situation is very different and a substantially higher order of determinateness becomes feasible. The basic reason for this is that at the many junctures along the way where there may have been contingently open alternatives when seen prospectively, something specific actually has occurred, and this something specific constitutes a selection among the alternatives which were previously open. Therefore, the attempt to explain how an outcome of an action process came about, whether this is done by the actor himself or some observer, can be much more determinate than can the prospective view. This, obviously, is because action, like other empirical processes, is in many fundamental respects irreversible. What has happened has, in fact, happened, and its consequences will have to be coped with.

At the time that Schütz and I were discussing these problems what is now frequently called the cybernetic point of view was scarcely on the horizon. This seems to me, however, to have served immensely to clarify this kind of consideration, essentially by introducing a component of what one might call limited reversibility. The obvious point is that when the actor encounters an unexpected contingency, he may take action which he perceives not to be in accord with his plan for his project. Negative feedback about the course the action is taking and forecasting of the probable consequences can lead him to reconsider and to take a different tack, that is, to take corrective action. It is therefore possible through retreating a short part of the way to reorient the course of action and bring the probabilities into closer accord with realization of the goal which has been fixed in the project.

It seems to me that looking at action from this point of view has a very important bearing on the problem of rationality. An older perspective often seemed to require the postulate that an action could be rational seen prospectively only if every single step in it could be accurately foreseen and decided upon at the beginning of the course of action. The cybernetic mode of coping with the unexpected contingencies, however, makes that postulate unnecessary or greatly restricts the scope which must be assumed. Indeed, it seems to me substantially to broaden the scope of the concept of rational action. One condition remains, namely, that the goal of action should not be "utopian" in the sense that it is impossible of attainment given the exigencies of the situation, including the capacities of actors. This implies that there is a sufficiently accurate estimate of the range and limits of contingencies so that the actor is not in a position of postulating too many impossibilities. Action, however, to be rational, need not have a built-in guarantee of success. The factor of contingency which I have been stressing may include the possibility and varying degrees of probability that things might happen which would make attainment of the goal impossible, though there would be sufficient probability that this would not be the case so that the investment in attempting to attain the goal could not be treated as irrational. This would be, of course, an element of risk with which we are quite familiar.

Considerations of this sort are particularly important when the type of action to which criteria of rationality are being implied involved social interaction. This is because, from the point of view of any given actor of reference, a major source of contingency is uncertainty about how his interaction partners will "react" to his actions. It seems to me that as early as the work I and my colleagues did on *Toward a General Theory of Action* and *The Social System*, I have advanced considerably beyond the level I had attained in the discussions with Schütz in appreciating the nature of social interaction. This, I think, has a bearing on certain of the problems still to be discussed. I should also point out, before going on, that the above discussion of rationality applies above all to what Weber called *Zweckrationalität*. The same order of criteria of success and feasibility are much more difficult to apply, at least they would have to be differently applied in Weber's other case of *Wertrationalität*.

I may next come to what is to me the central issue between Dr. Schütz and myself, namely, that of the status of what we have both called "the subjective point of view." The primary difference, it seems to me, is already indicated in his opening statement where he criticizes the concept of fact which I introduced in *The Structure of Social Action*, leaning in the first instance on a well-known paper of L. J. Henderson, but taking a position which I think in certain fundamentals goes back to Kant. The fundamental point here is that I defined a fact as a *statement about* one or more phenomena of the external world rather than as itself a phenomenon. Schütz takes issues with this and suggests that something like "experience" of phenomena is attainable without the mediation of what Henderson called a conceptual scheme, Kant the categories of the understanding. The problems at issue in this discussion are then applied to what has sometimes been called "the state of mind" of an actor, either an actor as observed by an external scientific observer or an actor reflecting upon his own action.

Though I think I have become considerably more sophisticated in understanding these matters, since the early 1940's, I still adhere with undiminished conviction to what from this point of view may be called a Kantian point of view. It seems to me that this connects with the importance of the Kantian influence on Weber's work and that my view is basically in accord with Weber's. This is to say that the rational understanding of human action, including especially the subjective states of minds of actors, requires the combination of the equivalent of what Kant called sense data and categorization which is to my mind ultimately a cultural entity. It seems to me that Schütz on the other hand takes the view that the subjective state of the actor is accessible to immediate experience through what Husserl called "phenomenological reduction" without the necessity of such "experience" being organized in terms of any kind of a "conceptual scheme," to use Henderson's phrase.

If this is correct, as Kant held, about knowledge of objects in the external world, it seems to me it is *mutatis mutandis* correct about the observation of the "motives" of other actors and the self-observation of acting individuals.

At one level I think it can be said that Freud brought consideration of comparable problems to a new focus. It seems to me clear that Freud's position was Kantian-Weberian and not phenomenological. He felt that the understanding of motives required cognitive ordering on the part of not merely the external observer, *vide* the psychoanalyst, but also on the part of the analysand himself in that through interpretation the analysand could come to understand his own motives. This was in my opinion the underlying meaning of Freud's famous aphorism about the psychoanalytic procedure that it could bring about a change such that "where id was there shall ego be."

This problem becomes particularly salient in connection with a phenomenon of which I was only vaguely aware at the time of writing *The Structure of Social Action*. This has come to be called rather generally, and I have followed this usage, the internalization of situational objects and cultural patterns, particularly norms, as definitely part of the structure of the personality of the individual. Weber clearly had a somewhat undeveloped version of this idea, but it was particularly developed by Freud on the one hand, Durkheim on the other, and by the group of American social psychologists who have come to be called "social interactionists," notably, Mead, Thomas, and Cooley. It seems to me that the phenomenon of internalization renders very strong support to my point of view because objects not only in the Cartesian sense, but also that of Freud, and cultural norms, especially as emphasized by Durkheim, are not devoid of categorial components. They do not constitute pure and unadulterated "experience."

In this as in a variety of other respects it seems to me that Schütz and other phenomenologists think unrealistically in terms of polar opposites, not at the level of a distinction between analytical components of a complex phenomenon such as Kant's sense data and categories, but at the level of relatively concrete objects and alternative approaches to their analysis.

This seems to me to be involved in what for long was to me a puzzling contention of the phenomenological school which is prominent in Schütz's work and has been carried on by such followers of him as Harold Garfinkel. This is the special emphasis on phenomenological access to what is called "everyday life" and the insistence that everyday life in this sense is radically distinct from any perspective of the scientific observer. This, of course, constitutes a problem which is central to the consideration of rationality. It seems to me to be an unreal dichotomy. There is not a radical break between everyday life and the behavior of scientifically trained people, but science constitutes an accentuation and special clarification of certain components which are present in all human action no matter how untutored the actor may be. Here it seems to me that the perspective of Malinowski in *Magic, Science, and Religion* is extremely instructive. To him "primitive man" acted quite rationally in certain contexts and the paradigms of rational action of a sort which Pareto worked with are quite applicable to, for example, his technology in the field of gardening.

Indeed, since Schütz and I had our discussions, there has been a notable development in the modern world in the generalization of levels of rationality which are more congruent with those exemplified in science than most of the categories of common sense.

When I argue in the above vein, I do not for a moment wish to be interpreted as a certain type of rationalist. I am exceedingly highly aware of the factors of non-rationality rather than *ir*rationality in very large sectors of human action. This constitutes one of the cardinal problems of social sciences and it will be a long time before the difficulties are finally laid to rest. The tendency of Schütz and other phenomenologists to dichotomize at the more concrete level seems to me not to be helpful in straightening out these many difficulties. I feel personally much closer to Weber and Freud than I do to Schütz in these to me centrally important respects.

It would, of course, be possible to elaborate very much further, but I hope I have already said enough to make my main critical position clear.

Addendum to letter to Richard Grathoff of August 9, 1974

I drafted the above material without the transcript of what had survived of my earlier draft available and then later I received that transcript. It has seemed to me better to turn it over to you, though there is some overlap. Should you wish to publish the material, most of the overlap could easily be edited out. I add a brief introduction to this material.

The "neoKantian" point of view which I take is to my mind closely connected with the frame of reference of the theory of action, particularly where social interaction is involved. Now, differently from the phase of *The Structure of Social Action*, I conceive a social system as constituted by a plurality of actors who interact with each other. From the point of view of any one actor, both the others and himself as objects constitute the *situation* of action. Every concrete unit in the interaction system, every "individual" is then at the same time *both* an actor, characterized, e.g., by "motives" or as Weber said, "intentions," *and* an object of the situation of action. I would then treat both actors and objects outside the boundaries of the system of reference as belonging to the environment of that system. This distinction is of paramount importance. Of course within limits the definition of a system for analysis rests on more or less free or even "arbitrary" decisions of the investigator.

The actor – situation, or object – distinction, of course, constitutes a generalization from Descartes' famous dichotomy of knowing subject and object known. In its generalization as a frame of reference for the analysis of action, of course, it ceases to be purely or even predominantly cognitive in reference and includes a variety of components not appropriate to what is only a "theory of knowledge" in the epistemological sense, such as goals, sentiments, norms, values, and various others.

I do not accord priority to either the object component of this relational conception or the knowing subject component. In extreme cases there has been the advocacy of the virtually total elimination of one of them in favor of the other. There has also been advocacy of the position that the distinction in itself is totally irrelevant. For example, it has been claimed that there are languages in which the grammatical distinction between subject and predicates does not figure at all – I happen not to believe this allegation. The phenomenological point of view, particularly in the version represented by Schütz is a relatively modest attempt to give special advantages to the subjective part of the type or if one will horn of the Cartesian dilemma. In doing so, however, as I have suggested, it seems to me to have leaned too far in the direction of attributing a quasi-metaphysical status to immediate knowledge to the subjective and a corresponding derogation of the importance and certain special roles of objectification.

It is altogether natural that this problem should have become acute with the development of technical theoretical schemes in the field of human action and especially social interaction at the human level. The situations which make this an acute problem became particularly saliently evident in the work of the generation of writers who were the subject of my *The Structure of Social Action*. In one context Durkheim posed the problems most saliently in that he tended to think of the individual actor as acting in a social environment which in its empirical aspect consisted of social facts. Unlike the natural environment of human action, however, the objects in relation to which an actor acted were historically considered "constructed" outcomes of previous human action. They were not in the usual sense natural phenomena. From one point of view they were objects the genesis of which had been determined by the subjective activity of actors. In some sense or other they were both objective and subjective in meaning at the same time.

It seems to me essential always to keep clearly in mind that the same concrete entities dealt with by a theory of action are both subjectively oriented actors and objects. This duality of status applies not only to discreet types of unit or entity, but is an analytical line which must be drawn through every concrete entity. One implication of this is amply documented in the history of thought, namely, that the self becomes object to the thinking person as formulated, for example, in Mead's distinction between the me and the I. Certain implications of this, however, must be carried farther. To me a particularly important consideration which is not covered by Dr. Schütz in his article in my work and of which I was not clearly aware at the time of writing *The Structure of Social Action* is an implication of what has generally come to be called the internalization of objects in the life history of the human individual. This is a fundamental perspective on which Freud, Durkheim, and the American social psychologists Mead, Thomas, and Cooley converged. This set of considerations seems to me to make the rigidity of the dichotomy Schütz draws specifically with reference to time untenable except at the most abstract analytical levels. This is incorporated in his distinction between in order to motives and because motives and the sharp distinction between the subjective experience in the course of carrying out an action project on the one hand and reflection on what has happened after the completion of the program on the other. This implication I have in mind is that action processes themselves are in important parts the outcome of the existence of objects, not merely the conditionally and instrumentally significant objects of the actor's situation, but also the objects internalized as part of his own personality or self. Freud in his later years went very far in this direction, not confining internalization to the superego parts of the personality, but extending it quite explicitly to the ego and inferentially to the id. If so prominent a part of the personality of the human individual is to use Freud's phrase "the precipitate of lost objects," it can hardly be true that his subjective experience is analytically totally independent of the object world. To be sure the relevant category of objects is not natural objects, but what I and others have called social objects. A phrasing which is meant to accentuate the fact that they are or have been actors in the present technical sense.

It seems to me that failure to deal with the problem of internalization is an example of a tendency which is prominent in Schütz's writings very much including the paper and correspondence now under discussion to pose unduly sharp either/or alternatives. The deepest underlying one seems to be the alternative between object status and subject status for any given entity of reference. The combinatorial aspects of actors thus seems to me to appear at many different levels. One of these is the experience of actors in the course of action. They act as well as think, in my opinion, in "terms of a conceptual scheme" to use the phrase I borrowed from L. J. Henderson's definition of fact. They also appraise or evaluate in terms of a conceptual scheme in the retrospective understanding of their own and other's action. In principle the situation is not different for the scientific observer whose treatment of the subjective point of view must also in my opinion take place in terms of a conceptual scheme, that is, some set of categories in the Kantian sense.

It seems to me that Dr. Schütz poses an altogether unrealistically sharp contrast between the point of view of the actor and the point of view of the scientific observer and analyst. Virtually dissociating them from each other. Quite the contrary it seems to me that they are closely connected and that science is an extreme type of action.

This in turn seems to me good ground on which to question the ubiquitious references in Schütz's and others phenomenological writing to the world of everyday life or everyday experience, particularly as sharply contrasted with the experience of the scientist. Of course the world of everyday life is "constructed" in the sense to which I referred above, but it seems to me that the operations of science should not be so radically dissociated from ordinary action as the Schütz point of view suggests they are. I think my point of view on this is strongly confirmed by recent developments in the philosophy of science which includes the observer as actor and the various instrumentalities he employs in their conception of the system subject to theoretical interpretation. (See, for example, recent writings of Gerald Holton on Einstein and Bohr in Holton's book *Thematic Origins of Scientific Thought.*)

It thus seems to me that the special status given by Schütz and many of his followers to the category of everyday life or experience is highly questionable so far as its special status is concerned.

This point has a particularly important bearing on the understanding in the theory of action of the problem of what constitutes the rationality of action. I have come recently (see Parsons and Platt, *The American University*, 1973) to view the phenomena of rationality of action as part of a wider complex which I have been calling the cognitive complex. This includes in addition to rationality as an ideal type of social action, knowledge as a type of cultural object, competence as a feature of the socialized personality, and intelligence as a generalized medium of interchange at the level of the general system of action.

Rationality seen in this perspective, however, is an ideal type of social action in which cognitive components do not stand alone, though they may have primacy, but are combined with all the other primary components of action. This includes the non-rational components which are accessible to study under the heading of the subjective point of view.

The above considerations are very far from being exhaustive of the problems which have been revived for me and in many cases newly defined by my re-reading of Dr. Schütz's manuscript and the interchanges of correspondence between him and myself. I think, however, that I have covered enough of the centrally important points in this letter to give a flavor of the way I look at the problems raised in those documents of more than thirty years ago. I hope I am in a position now to give considerably more sophisticated answers than I did in *The Structure of Social Action* or in my conversations and correspondence with Alfred Schütz at the time when it took place.

I very much appreciate the effort that you, Dr. Natanson, and Mrs. Schütz have undertaken in order to prepare and arrange for the publication of this material.

Sincerely yours,
Talcott Parsons

September 2, 1976

Universität Konstanz
Fachbereich Psychologie und Soziologie
Richard Grathoff

Prof. Dr. Talcott Parsons
Harvard University
Department of Sociology
William James Hall
Cambridge
Mass. 02138
U.S.A.

Dear Professor Parsons:

During the Toronto meeting of the International Sociological Association, exactly two years ago, you were so kind to give me a long letter with your retrospective comments concerning the Schütz-Parsons Correspondence on your book The Structure of Social Action.

The unfortunate delay in preparing those letters and commentaries for publication has been due to the closure of Northwestern University Press. Especially the re-negotiations of Mrs. Schütz were finally successful: our little volume The Schütz-Parsons Correspondence: An Inquiry into the Structure of Social Action has been accepted by Indiana University Press to be published there in Spring 1977.

Also, I am glad to be able to inform you that in the meantime Suhrkamp Verlag in Frankfurt has accepted to publish a German translation of our volume. The manuscript is being prepared by my Konstanz colleague Walter Sprondel and should be out early next year, too.

If you would like me to clarify any final questions, editorial or otherwise, please let me know. Since Sprondel is visiting New York and Boston next month (in behalf of our Konstanz Archive for the Social Sciences), he told me he would be glad to call at your office, if you would like to see him. His New York address would be known by Mrs. Schütz, 25 West 81st Street, New York, SC 4-7273.

I am looking forward to finally being able to send to you the first copy of our volume. I am sure it will contribute considerably to the further development of a unified theory of social action.

I am, with great respect,
sincerely yours,

Richard Grathoff

July 5, 1978

Professor Richard Grathoff
Department of Sociology
University of Toronto
563 Spadina Avenue
Toronto M5S 1A1 Canada

Dear Dr. Grathoff,

I had meant to write you thanking you for sending me the volume of essays in which one of yours was included dealing with the work of Alfred Schütz. In the meantime I have received the copy of your edited English edition of the interchanges I had many years ago with Schütz. In the few days since receiving it, I have in fact been able to read the editorial material, that is the material for which you were responsible, independently of the original documents. This seems to me considerably fuller and more informative than Sprondel's German edition.

I found your essay on Schütz one of the most informative things I have read and I really would like to attempt to come to a better understanding of his work than I have yet been able to reach. I think both essays of yours and your editorial contributions to the edition of the interchanges are very helpful.

I might say, however, that I am still stuck on certain points. I still maintain position on the concept of fact which you will remember Schütz attacks very strongly. Then there is a further item which I mentioned only very briefly in my retrospective statement. I do, however, remember long discussions with Schütz about the problem of the phenomenon of professional practice. As it happened, I was at the time immersed in my own study of medical practice. The issue between us was essentially that of the relation of the dissociation, as Schütz almost maintained it was, between the world of science and that of everyday life. I kept insisting that medical practice, as of that time and even more so today, had to involve a scientifically-trained professional person attempting to communicate constructively with patients who, on the average, were not professionally trained but whose problems of illness were part of their everyday life, in Schütz's sense. My contention was that medical practice simply could not be effective if there were not adequate bridges between these levels of involvement in life concerns. Somehow or other, Schütz and I don't seem to have been able to come to a very clear understanding of what was involved in this type of situation.

Finally, I am greatly pleased that you have plans to follow up on further work on the Schumpeter papers. As it happened, I had a fairly recent work with Smithies[1] about this. He said he had not had any further communication with you but that he would be very glad to facilitate whatever plans you may have to work on them.

[1]Presumably Arthur Smithies, then Professor of Economics at Harvard and an expert on U.S. federal budgetary practices, on Keynesian economics, and on economic development. Although critical of Economy and Society by Parsons and Neil J. Smelser, Smithies admired Parsons' early essays on Marshall and continued to teach them as late as the 1960s. Eds.

I gather that unequivocally he is in the position of trustee of those materials. I personally would be particularly interested in consulting with you whenever this may prove to be appropriate since, though my memories of these occasions are not as clear as they might be, I would be very glad to refresh those memories and to reconsider some of the problems that were involved.

Finally, though I will be a little late, I expect to get a somewhat revised version of my paper for the Gottlieben Conference to Dr. Sprondel before very long.

Sincerely,
Talcott Parsons

October 9, 1978

Universität Bielefeld
Fakultät für Soziologie
Richard Grathoff

Prof. Dr. Talcott Parsons
Harvard University
Department of Sociology
William James Hall
Cambridge, Mass 02138
USA

Dear Professor Parsons,

For a few weeks I have now a letter from you with your very kind remarks about my Schütz essay and the volume with your exchange of letters with Schütz. I had hoped to answer with a more substantial reply: Henderson's conception of fact, your interpretation of this notion, and Schütz' address toward your interpretation form indeed a major point of "revolution". I have spent a few weeks, reading and writing, but I am always returning to a crucial issue, which I believe must be raised at the same time: what is an appropriate understanding of the "empirical" in our field of studies?

I had hoped to finish my answer to you before this new term starts, but today the place is filled with incoming students and I must be occupied for the moment with "business". Hence I am sending my reply with two proposals and a minor request.

First, I hope to finish my answer to you before the end of this year: it will deal critically with the hermeneutical position of "Text-Empirie", which I believe holds also for your notion of the empirical in "The Structure of Social Action".

Secondly, your letter mentioned again the Harvard Seminar on Rationality, Schumpeter's part in it in 39/40, and it's still dormant issues. I wonder, if you would not consider another address to this same issue? I could imagine another "Colloquium on Rationality" – perhaps in 79/80 – a forty year review of that discussion. I am sure that the interest of a German foundation could be found for such a venture.

Along a similar line, I must ask you again for your help. Our proposed work on the Schumpeter papers has found full support by the Thyssen Foundation. We intended to send for an exploratory study a German sociologist, Dr. Peter Zernitz to Harvard. Unfortunately, we got no response from Prof. Smithies: neither by mail nor by phone were we able to get into contact with him. Our request: in order to assess the scope of the papers of Schumpeter, their present condition, and hence get an idea of the funding frame, Dr. Zernitz would simply need an informal letter of invitation to present it to the American Consulate in Frankfurt for visa purposes. Since he is prepared to leave immediately, his stipend being arranged, it is very unfortunate that we could not receive such a note as of this day. Would you be so kind to give another call to Prof. Smithies? Of course, any other letter of invitation (say from the Library Offices) would serve as well.

I am grateful for your attention and interest in this work.

With kind regards
Sincerely Yours
Richard Grathoff

February 28, 1979

Universität Bielefeld
Fakultät für Soziologie
Richard Grathoff

Prof. Dr. Talcott Parsons
Harvard University
Dept. of Sociology
William James Hall
Cambridge, Mass. 02138
USA

Dear Professor Parsons,

Your letter of Jan 31 has arrived some days ago, I have read it with great interest, and I am especially pleased by the prospects of meeting you again during your coming visit to Germany. I very much hope for the chance to seeing you in those coming days.

Thank you very much for the encouraging words concerning my essay on Schütz. I have read those passages myself again during the last days and am looking forward to the prospect of a personal discussion on some of these issues. There is especially one point, on page 396 of my essay, which I remember while writing it as being a more or less implicit assumption concerning your perspective on Schütz and Weber. I am talking there about the early Schützean conception of "Wissenschaftstheorie", which I believe has been monistic, especially in all his formulations in "Sinnhafter Aufbau", and hence very close to your own notion of theory. I have been stating there in the middle of the page 396 that it has been the earlier conviction of Schütz that the mundane social sciences require their foundation in an "verstehende Soziologie". This assumption, which I believe was guiding Schütz in his "Sinnhafter Aufbau", has been – as I formulated there – refuted by Parsons through his own presupposition, that this is precisely what the discovery of the structure of social action has shown. "Wissenschaft könne als monistische Einheit wissenschaftlicher Konstrukte in einer allgemeinen Theorie des Handelns entfaltet werden." I believe this to be the tenor, or at least one of the major aspects of the exchange of letters between you and Schütz in 1940/41. This, however, remains implicit in your own answers, and I would be very interested to know, if my interpretation finds your assent.

There are, of course, plenty of other points which I would like to have a chance to talk to you about. The major issue, your dispute with Schütz about the Henderson concept of fact, remains, as I see it, an unsolved problem for quite a while. For my own preparation, I believe it necessary to read and re-read Pareto on these points, since I believe him to be the major source of Hendersons's interpretation. This is a very serious issue also for myself, and I am even taking some Italian courses this spring, in order to be better prepared to read Pareto in his original language. I am very much moved by your closing statement, that "perhaps the conflicts of opinion are not as serious as I had at one time thought".

I shall definitely try my utmost to meet you during your spring visit to Germany. If your letter indicates to me that your official schedule might leave even some time for a few hours of talk (or a day or two) in Oerlinghausen (my place of residence here in Bielefeld) then I would like to assure you of my most grateful response. Oerlinghausen, as you might know, displays still many remnants of the Max Weber-family, who once owned its textile-mills in this little town. Marianne Weber has been born here, and her "Lebenserinnerungen" contain in their introductory passages quite a few references to this place. Aside of sentimentalities, I should, of course, mention to you, that the Faculty of Sociology in Bielefeld would be most delighted if you also would find the time and energy for some talk or discussion in their round. However, these are obviously two different shoes, and I am always finding it most difficult to choose the footwear even for very good friends. In any case, I would like to assure you that I am going to be prepared to pick you up by car or train if you decide that your visit would be within the scope of your own interests.

I am looking forward to your response. If you do know already more details about your coming visit, which I did not receive from Schluchter yet, this would definitely help me to plan my own time in April and May.

Sincerely Yours
Richard Grathoff

March 27, 1979

Professor Richard Grathoff
Universität Bielefeld
Fakultät für Soziologie
Postfach 8640
4800 Bielefeld 1 Germany

Dear Professor Grathoff,

Thank you for your letter. Before receiving it I had felt that my previous letter to you was somewhat incomplete, and had intended to write you a supplement to it specifically on two topics. These were, first, the one you mention in your letter on the concept of fact and Schütz's objection to my statement in that field. The second was the Schützean emphasis which comes out very strongly in your article on the central importance of the study of "everyday life". I am afraid that just now there is no opportunity to carry out a fully adequate exposition of my views in these two areas. On the concept, of fact, however, let me simply report my impression that Henderson did not derive his statement on the problem primarily from Pareto. I am pretty sure that it antedated his acquaintance with Pareto's work and that it was mainly derived from the Kantian influence to which he was subjected during his student days at Strassbourg where, you will remember, Windelband was a principal teacher of his. This historical account, assuming I am correct about it, however, is intertwined with a number of epistemological issues which I very much hope there will be an opportunity to discuss with you personally.

I have long been intrigued with what has seemed to me to be not only in the writings of Schütz but of some of his ethnomethodologist professors the recurring stress on the importance of the study of everyday life. The thing that has struck me about that stress has been its sharp antithesis to the stress in other quarters on the importance of macro-sociological emphases and studies and the attaining of both a comparative and an evolutionary perspective. Let me merely state a single hunch about the meaning of this "everyday life" stress. It is to the effect that it is another version of what I like to call "*Gemeinschaft* romanticism." There is somehow the feeling that the small-scale – I believe in Schütz's writing the phrase "face-to-face" – recurs frequently. The small-scale face-to-face relationship is of the true "essence" of things social at the human level. This is a conception which is from my point of view decidedly problematical though I do not feel that I can state a dogmatic opinion about it. I would greatly welcome the opportunity to discuss it with you.

One further consideration: I have had two or three interesting meetings here with Dr. Peter Zernitz. I find him a very interesting young man. In my last discussion with him, he mentioned to me that he had been present at the 1964 meeting in Heidelberg which celebrated the centennial of Max Weber's birth. He said he was, I think, a student at the time but he gave me an exceedingly interesting impression of the turbulent political atmosphere which prevailed at that meeting. I will certainly have an opportunity to talk to him at least on one more occasion before I take off on my trip to Europe about a month from now.

I would certainly like very much to sandwich in at least a few hours if not a day on my trip to Germany which is in the very near future. I'm afraid however that I must refer the logistical problem to Professor Schluchter since he has taken responsibility for arranging my schedule from the time I leave Heidelberg which I think will be the 5th of May until I take off for England on the 12th or 13th. Subject to Schluchter's consent and therefore the lack of conflict with other commitments, I would be delighted to have the opportunity to get together with you.

Cordially,
Talcott Parsons

Name Index

H. Staubmann, V. Lidz (eds.), *Rationality in the Social Sciences*,
DOI 10.1007/978-3-319-62377-1

W

Z

FSC
www.fsc.org
MIX
Papier | Fördert
gute Waldnutzung
FSC® C083411

Kolibri 360 GmbH
Ferdinand-Jühlke-Straße 7
99095 Erfurt, Deutschland
produktsicherheit@kolibri360.de